# Global Linkages

# Global Linkages

*Macroeconomic Interdependence and Cooperation in the World Economy*

WARWICK J. MCKIBBIN
JEFFREY D. SACHS

THE BROOKINGS INSTITUTION
*Washington, D.C.*

Copyright © 1991 by

THE BROOKINGS INSTITUTION

1775 Massachusetts Avenue, N.W., Washington, D.C. 20036

Library of Congress Cataloging-in-Publication data:

McKibbin, Warwick J., 1957–
    Global linkages : macroeconomic interdependence and
cooperation in the world economy / Warwick J. McKibbin
and Jeffrey D. Sachs.
        p.    cm
    Includes bibliographical references and index.
    ISBN 0-8157-5600-3 (cloth)—ISBN 0-8157-5601-1
    (pbk.)
    1. Economic policy—Mathematical models.
    2. Economic history—1971– —Mathematical models.
    3. International economic relations—Mathematical
    models.    I. Sachs, Jeffrey    II. Title.
    HD87.M36    1991
    337'.01'5118—dc20                                        91-15301
                                                             CIP


9 8 7 6 5 4 3 2 1

The paper used in this publication meets the minimum
requirements of the American National Standard for
Information Sciences—Permanence of paper for Printed
Library Materials, ANSI Z39.48-1984.

# ⒷTHE BROOKINGS INSTITUTION

The Brookings Institution is an independent organization devoted to nonpartisan research, education, and publication in economics, government, foreign policy, and the social sciences generally. Its principal purposes are to aid in the development of sound public policies and to promote public understanding of issues of national importance.

The Institution was founded on December 8, 1927, to merge the activities of the Institute for Government Research, founded in 1916, the Institute of Economics, founded in 1922, and the Robert Brookings Graduate School of Economics and Government, founded in 1924.

The Board of Trustees is responsible for the general administration of the Institution, while the immediate direction of the policies, program, and staff is vested in the President, assisted by an advisory committee of the officers and staff. The by-laws of the Institution state: "It is the function of the Trustees to make possible the conduct of scientific research, and publication, under the most favorable conditions, and to safeguard the independence of the research staff in the pursuit of their studies and in the publication of the results of such studies. It is not a part of their function to determine, control, or influence the conduct of particular investigations or the conclusions reached."

The President bears final responsibility for the decision to publish a manuscript as a Brookings book. In reaching his judgment on the competence, accuracy, and objectivity of each study, the President is advised by the director of the appropriate research program and weighs the views of a panel of expert outside readers who report to him in confidence on the quality of the work. Publication of a work signifies that it is deemed a competent treatment worthy of public consideration but does not imply endorsement of conclusions or recommendations.

The Institution maintains its position of neutrality on issues of public policy in order to safeguard the intellectual freedom of the staff. Hence interpretations or conclusions in Brookings publications should be understood to be solely those of the authors and should not be attributed to the Institution, to its trustees, officers, or other staff members, or to the organizations that support its research.

# Foreword

MANY OF THE ECONOMIC QUESTIONS currently facing policymakers throughout the world—including the United States—cannot be satisfactorily answered by focusing on a single country. The U.S. trade deficit in recent years is but one example of how today's macroeconomic policy problems require a global framework for analysis. Attempting to use a partial framework can be misleading and may lead to counterproductive policy responses.

In this book Warwick McKibbin and Jeffrey Sachs provide a rigorous analysis of a wide range of current policy issues relevant to the world economy. In addressing these issues, the authors first develop a multicountry simulation model for understanding how policy actions undertaken in one country affect the trade flows and macroeconomic patterns among different countries. They then show that the key macroeconomic features of the 1980s—including the large U.S. trade deficits and Japanese trade surpluses—can be explained by shifts in monetary and fiscal policies in the major economies and by supply shocks due to changes in oil prices. They question the relevance of special explanations—for example, increasingly unfair trade barriers, or heightened Japanese protectionism—to account for the main shifts in trade flows and macroeconomic imbalances. They also question whether direct trade measures—such as quotas on imports from countries running large trade surpluses with the United States—are appropriate responses to international trade imbalances.

Warwick J. McKibbin is a senior fellow in the Brookings Economic Studies program. He is also a visiting scholar at the U.S. Congressional Budget Office, a consultant to the World Bank, and a senior research associate at the Centre for International Economics (Australia). Jeffrey D. Sachs is the Galen L. Stone Professor of International Trade at Harvard University and a research associate of the National Bureau of

Economic Research. He is currently adviser to a number of Latin American and Eastern European governments.

This book, primarily written by McKibbin, is the culmination of a collaborative project undertaken by the two authors. The project was initiated in 1984 while both authors were at Harvard University and the National Bureau of Economic Research. Part of the research was undertaken while they were visiting the Bank of Japan Institute for Monetary and Economic Studies and the Institute for Fiscal and Monetary Policy in the Japanese Ministry of Finance during late 1986. Further work was completed during the following several years while McKibbin was at the Reserve Bank of Australia and then at Brookings and the Congressional Budget Office. The authors would like to express their gratitude to these institutions and to colleagues at each institution for their support of the project.

The authors would also like to thank a number of people who contributed to the ideas and focus of the book and provided helpful comments on various drafts: Henry J. Aaron, Victor Argy, Olivier Blanchard, Barry P. Bosworth, William Branson, Susan Collins, Richard Cooper, Max Corden, Peter Dixon, Barry Eichengreen, Graeme Elliott, Jeffrey Frankel, Hans Genberg, John Hussman, Naoko Ishii, Robert Z. Lawrence, Paul Masson, Ronald McKinnon, Dirk Morris, Alan Powell, Nouriel Roubini, Charles L. Schultze, Eric Siegloff, Mark Sundberg, Heizo Takanaka, Peter Wilcoxen, and John Williamson. Martha Syndott at Harvard provided invaluable help with logistical problems. The authors would especially like to thank Ralph C. Bryant for his support of the project and for many valuable comments and ideas on drafts of the manuscript.

Jim McEuen edited the manuscript, Suzanne Smith and Karan Singh verified it, and Glenn Yamagata provided research assistance in the final stages of its preparation. The index was prepared by Florence Robinson.

Some chapters in this book are based on earlier published work: chapter 6 draws on "Global Adjustments to a Shrinking U.S. Trade Deficit," *Brookings Papers on Economic Activity, 2:1988*, pp. 639–74; chapter 8 draws on "The Economics of International Policy Coordination," *Economic Record*, December 1988, pp. 241–53; and chapter 9 draws on "Implications of Policy Rules for the World Economy," in Bryant and others, *Macroeconomic Policies in an Interdependent World* (Brookings Institution, Centre for Economic Policy Research, and International Monetary Fund, 1989).

The Brookings Institution and the authors are grateful to the following organizations for financial support: the Ford Foundation and National Science Foundation.

The views expressed in this book are solely those of the authors and should not be ascribed to any of the institutions or persons mentioned or to the trustees, officers, or other staff members of the Brookings Institution.

BRUCE K. MAC LAURY
*President*

*May 1991*
*Washington, D.C.*

# Contents

## Appendixes 211

## References 265

## Text Tables

Figures

Appendix Tables

# Global Linkages

# CHAPTER ONE

# Introduction

ONLY RECENTLY have policymakers and politicians in the United States begun to focus on the implications of international macroeconomic interdependence. During most of the postwar period, the United States paid little attention to the international dimension of macroeconomic policymaking—either to the effects of U.S. policies on the rest of the world, or to the effects of foreign policies at home. In large measure, this neglect was a by-product of the dominant position of the United States in the world economy: the United States could afford to go its own way, and other countries would simply have to adjust. As U.S. economic dominance has declined, so has the U.S. insouciance regarding the global macroeconomy. Now the United States carefully scrutinizes the macroeconomic policies of other countries and has also joined in efforts to achieve closer macroeconomic cooperation among the major industrial countries.

## Background to the Study

Heightened interest in the global macroeconomy was spurred most urgently by the emergence of large U.S. trade deficits in the 1980s, which were matched by large surpluses in Germany and Japan. These trade imbalances, shown in figure 1-1, have raised deep worries for U.S. policymakers and public alike. Should the trade deficits at home, and surpluses abroad, be interpreted as signs of American decline, indications of unfair trade practices abroad, the reflection of a boom in the United States that outpaced foreign economic growth, or the result of misguided macroeconomic policies in the United States? On a practical level, do the trade deficits herald a "hard landing" of the U.S. economy, in which foreign creditors pull the plug on the capital inflow into the United States that has been financing the import im-

Figure 1-1. *Trade Balances of the United States, Japan, and Germany, 1978 to 1989*

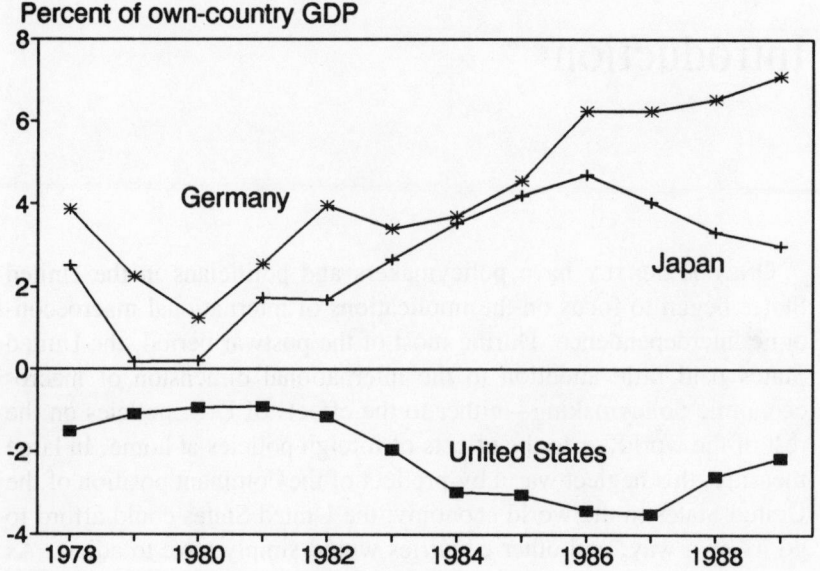

**Percent of own-country GDP**

Source: Organization for Economic Cooperation and Development, *OECD Economic Outlook*, no. 46 (December 1989) (diskette).

balance? If so, what can the United States or other economies do to avoid such a hard landing?

It is perhaps natural, although distressing, that many in the United States were quick to blame other countries, especially Japan, as soon as the large deficits emerged. With little experience in analyzing the forces of international economic interdependence, many Americans easily assumed that ''unfair foreign trade practices'' must be the prime suspect responsible for the large trade deficits. Unfortunately, blaming foreign trade practices does not go far in explaining the United States' predicament. Even if Japanese trading practices are unfair—and in certain sectors of the Japanese economy they probably are—they simply cannot account for the worsening of U.S. bilateral trade deficits with almost all other member countries of the Organization for Economic Cooperation and Development (OECD) in the 1980s, as table 1-1 clearly shows.

A more general macroeconomic phenomenon was at work during the decade. The United States and the other major industrial countries pursued divergent fiscal policies in the 1980s. While U.S. budget

Table 1-1. *Change in U.S. Bilateral Trade Balances with Members of the Organization for Economic Cooperation and Development, 1978–86*

| U.S. bilateral trade balance with | Change (percent of U.S. GDP) |
|---|---|
| Australia | −0.000 |
| Austria | −0.004 |
| Belgium-Luxembourg | −0.060 |
| Canada | −0.135 |
| Denmark | −0.019 |
| Finland | −0.006 |
| France | −0.093 |
| Germany | −0.243 |
| Iceland | 0.020 |
| Ireland | 0.007 |
| Italy | −0.104 |
| Japan | −0.811 |
| Netherlands | −0.089 |
| New Zealand | 0.004 |
| Norway | 0.026 |
| Spain | −0.038 |
| Sweden | −0.054 |
| Switzerland | −0.070 |
| United Kingdom | −0.123 |

Sources: International Monetary Fund, *Direction of Trade Statistics* (Washington, 1989; annual); and OECD, *OECD Economic Outlook*, no. 46 (December 1989) (diskette).

deficits relative to gross national product (GNP) widened during the decade, the budget deficits in Japan and Germany fell (and in Japan actually turned into a surplus). As figure 1-2 suggests, the shifts in trade imbalances among the largest industrial countries are correlated with shifts in fiscal policy; countries with fiscal deficits tend to have current account deficits.

Our own analysis therefore started several years ago with the hypothesis that identifiable macroeconomic changes, rather than shifts in trade practices, could account for the most important global trade imbalances of the past decade. We wanted to examine this general hypothesis with care, using a formal framework in which the global imbalances could be assessed quantitatively as well as qualitatively. As well as asking whether these imbalances could be accounted for by identifiable macroeconomic shifts (not only in fiscal policy, but also in monetary policy, world oil prices, and some other variables), we also wanted to use the framework to examine the policy choices that the industrial countries have for reducing global imbalances.

This book reports on the result of these investigations. To study the issues of global imbalances, we developed a macroeconomic simula-

Figure 1-2. *Fiscal and Current Balances among Industrial Countries, Change from 1978 to 1986*

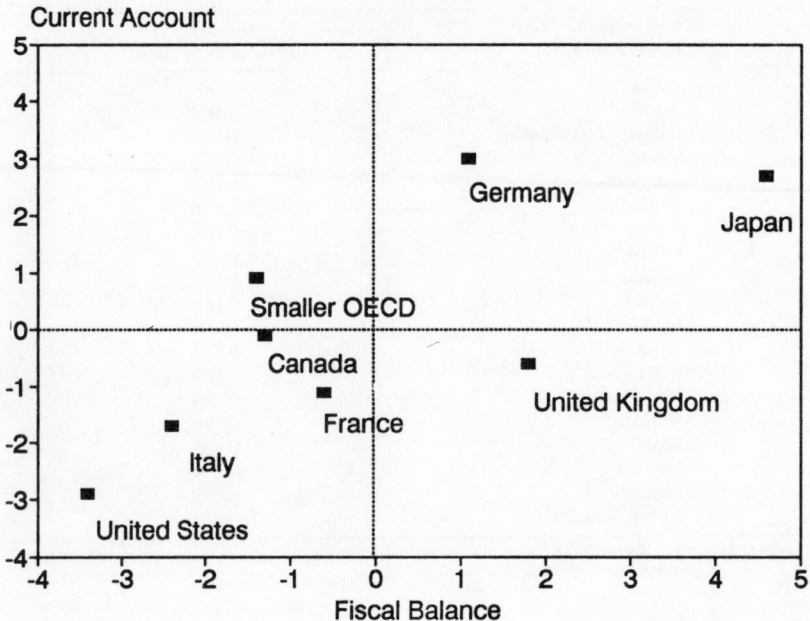

Source: OECD, *OECD Economic Outlook*, no. 46 (December 1989) (diskette); see Tables *R13* and *R20* of the published document.

tion model of the world economy, with a particular focus on the macroeconomic interrelations among the major industrial countries—the United States, Germany, and Japan (the Group of Three).[1] As we stress throughout the study, the model has several strong points not found in previous global macroeconometric models. It is carefully grounded in economic theory. It makes allowances for forward-looking expectations in asset markets and in savings and investment decisions in the economy. And it carefully accounts for the long-run effects of short-run policy changes. All of these features are important in evaluating the effects of macroeconomic policies in the 1980s.

Using the model, we were able to examine the role of macroeconomic policy changes in accounting for the global imbalances. We demonstrate that the major shifts in global imbalances in the 1980s

1. This model is available for use on a personal computer. Information can be obtained by contacting Warwick McKibbin at the Brookings Institution.

can indeed be linked to macroeconomic policy changes. Although we do not claim to present a complete explanation of the global macroeconomic experience during the 1980s, our approach accounts for enough of the changes in a wide range of macroeconomic variables so that we do not need to invoke special explanations—for example, unfair trade barriers or Japanese protectionism—to account for the *main* shifts in trade flows and macroeconomic imbalances. We therefore question whether direct trade policy measures—such as quotas on imports from countries running large trade surpluses with the United States—are appropriate responses to international trade imbalances.[2] Such policies, we show, may have only small effects in reducing external imbalances, but they may have large effects in disrupting the world economy.

It is also clear, however, that much goes on in the world economy that is not captured by the model. Because the model is rather simple in design (without arbitrary lag patterns in the equations that allow standard econometric models to "fit" the data closely), we are not surprised that the model misses many of the year-to-year changes in key variables. Although we fall short of a complete explanation of recent macroeconomic imbalances, our model does allow us to examine other important issues in addition to historical tracking of the data.

First, and most direct, we can use the model to examine alternative policy options for reducing global imbalances. What, for example, would be the effects on the United States and the rest of the world of large cuts in the U.S. budget deficit? Would an elimination of U.S. budget deficits be enough to eliminate U.S. trade deficits? What would be the effects on the rest of the world of U.S. budgetary austerity?

Second, we can use the model to analyze the scope for international policy coordination among the industrial countries. As we stress in the book, there are various ways of looking at this issue. We can ask whether international policy coordination could play a useful role in the immediate historical circumstances. Should the major countries adopt a concerted policy to reduce the global imbalances, or will it be

2. In the Omnibus Trade Act of 1988, the United States has established a procedure, known as "Super 301," under which the president is empowered to respond to discriminatory practices by foreign countries either through direct negotiation or through the imposition of retaliatory tariffs, even in violation of provisions of the General Agreement on Tariffs and Trade (GATT). Discriminatory practices include not only those that violate international agreements such as GATT, but any practice that is deemed to treat unfairly U.S. goods, services, or investment in foreign countries.

enough if each country makes decisions on its own? Should the major countries agree jointly on a shared set of rules for the long-term management of the global economy? Using our model, we are able to evaluate the properties of alternative global macroeconomic rules.

To some extent we are able to answer these questions, and in other cases we merely provide a framework of analysis that we hope will prove useful to future analysts. So that the reader can better understand the areas in which we feel that we have made quantitative progress; those in which we have made conceptual progress, but without substantial quantitative progress; and those in which we think that the policy issues remain on the table, we now turn to a roadmap of our major results.

## Plan and Main Results of the Study

The analysis in the book has four components. Chapters 2 through 4 set forth the basic theory of macroeconomic interdependence and introduces our multicountry simulation model of the world economy. Chapters 5 and 6 apply the theory and the simulation model to the issue of global macroeconomic imbalances, past and prospective. Chapters 7 through 9 use the theoretical framework and the simulation model to study the potential benefits of international macroeconomic coordination. Chapter 10 reviews the major lessons that the analysis suggests for policymakers.

We begin the analysis in chapter 2 with a summary of the theory of economic interdependence among countries and the channels by which macroeconomic policies in one country spill over into another. We focus on the importance of the exchange rate regime, international capital mobility, and wage setting within countries as determinants of how different economies interact. We also introduce intertemporal aspects of macroeconomic policy and the role that expectations can play in affecting the spillovers of macroeconomic policies among countries.

The basic theoretical model of interdependence is the two-country model developed by Robert Mundell (1963) and J. Marcus Fleming (1962). The simple Mundell-Fleming model yields several basic insights that help us to understand the workings of the much more elaborate simulation model of later chapters. As shown by the Mundell-Fleming model, a fiscal expansion under the conditions of floating exchange rates and high capital mobility—the relevant conditions of the 1980s—leads to an expansion of output, a currency appreciation, and a trade deficit. A monetary expansion, in contrast, leads to an expansion of domestic output, a currency depreciation, and an ambiguous and likely small effect on the trade balance.

Thus, the combination of expansionary fiscal policy and contractionary or neutral monetary policy, which we show to be the U.S. policy mix in the first half of the 1980s, produces a force for currency appreciation and overall trade deficit, with the output effect depending on the relative strength of monetary and fiscal policy. A reverse shift toward fiscal contraction and monetary expansion, as in the last half of the 1980s in the United States, would therefore produce a force for currency depreciation and a reduction in the trade deficit (at least relative to the size of the economy). These effects on the United States were further amplified by the fact that U.S. fiscal policy changes in the early 1980s were matched by contrary fiscal policy changes by the United States' leading trading partners, Germany and Japan. The overall effect on the world economy is, of course, the result of the simultaneous application of policies throughout the global economy.

We go on to stress in chapter 2 several features of the simple Mundell-Fleming model that have to be altered in a larger and more realistic model. It is necessary to allow for dynamic effects of policies, such as the long-run effects of trade deficits induced by a fiscal expansion. It is also necessary to allow for price and wage dynamics, because output and exchange rate changes feed back into the economy. And it is necessary to allow for the expectational effects of future policy changes. Anticipations of future policy actions, such as the expectation in the mid-1980s of a *future* reduction of budget deficits, can have an immediate and significant effect on exchange rates and long-term interest rates.

In chapter 3 we use the theoretical insights from chapter 2 to develop a dynamic simulation model of the world economy. As we shall explain, the model—which we call the MSG2 model—has several important attractive features that make it an especially useful tool for analysis. For example, the model deals carefully with both the aggregate demand and supply sides of the major economies; the long-term consequences of debt and capital accumulation; and the role of expectations in the bond, stock, and foreign exchange markets. We describe at some length the derivation of the model, as well as the choice of numerical parameter values. This discussion contains some of the most technical material in the book, and it may be skimmed (or even skipped entirely) by the nonspecialist reader without losing the thread of our analysis.

As we explain, the model is not estimated by econometric methods, as is typical for large-scale macroeconomic models in commercial use. Rather, the model is calibrated by following procedures commonly used by builders of "computable general equilbrium" (or CGE) models. Where certain important elasticities are required, the values of key behavioral parameters are simply "guessed" on the basis of statistical estimates found in published econometric studies. Other parameter values of the model are chosen so that the model replicates the data in the base year (1986).

In chapter 4 we use the model to study the global implications of changes in fiscal and monetary policies in the major economies and regions, supply shocks caused by changes in world oil prices, and changes in the flow of loans to developing countries. The results from our model are compared with the theoretical analysis of the Mundell-Fleming model that we introduced in chapter 2 and with results from other multicountry models. Using the model, we are able to make several quantitative assessments about the effects of macroeconomic policies.

We find that a fiscal expansion in the United States raises output in both the United States and the major foreign economies, appreciates the U.S. exchange rate, and pushes the United States into trade deficit. Initially, U.S. inflation actually falls as the stronger dollar reduces import prices; several years after the fiscal expansion, however, U.S. inflation rises relative to the initial baseline. In contrast to many global econometric models and popular opinion, we find that the increase in foreign output from a fiscal expansion in the United States is quickly reversed after the first year of the policy change. The quick "crowding out" of foreign output occurs through a variety of familiar channels, such as higher world interest rates and rising foreign prices. In addition it occurs through a contraction in foreign aggregate supply as a result of higher factor costs (labor, imported inputs, and higher cost of capital over time). The importance of labor market adjustment for determining the sign of fiscal policy transmission was highlighted in the late 1970s by Argy and Salop (1979) and Sachs (1980). We show that this issue is empirically important, especially when we allow for multifactor inputs (including imported inputs) in the supply side of major economies.

A monetary expansion in the United States also raises output in the short run, but at a much higher inflationary cost than with fiscal policy, because the U.S. dollar depreciates after a monetary expansion. The effects of a monetary expansion on the U.S. trade balance is negligible: the weaker dollar raises export sales, but the stronger output raises import demand. These two effects just about balance.

The negligible effects of U.S. monetary policies on the trade balance point up an important lesson for U.S. policymakers, one that we will return to several times in later chapters. The U.S. trade deficits cannot be reduced measurably (if at all) by a depreciation of the dollar caused by a U.S. monetary expansion. The idea of cutting U.S. interest rates to drive the dollar down, and thereby improve U.S. competitiveness and the trade balance, simply cannot work. The expansionary effects of the monetary ease offset the effects of improved competitiveness. Only *fiscal* policy changes can be relied on to improve the trade balance.

The model also shows the effects of foreign economic policies on the United States. Although the qualitative effects could be guessed by the theory introduced earlier, the quantitative estimates are also important because they help us to make precise the extent to which the U.S. economy is subject to the influences of foreign macroeconomic policy actions. In general, foreign economic policies do have an impact on the United States, but it is a misconception to think that foreign macroeconomic policies have a decisive influence. Put another way, the quantitative results of the model argue strongly that the key to resolving the U.S. trade deficits does not lie with macroeconomic policies abroad (for example, a Japanese fiscal expansion to raise U.S. export sales), but rather with policy actions in the United States.

Starting in chapter 5, we use the model to assess the origins and prospects of the global macroeconomic imbalances of recent years. We show that the model can be used to explain many of the important shifts in the global macroeconomy in the period 1978–89. We suggest that our approach not only explains many of the qualitative features of the period but does reasonably well in explaining the quantitative features as well. Figure 1-3, for example, shows the results of a dynamic simulation of the model starting in 1978. Although it does not capture all the year-to-year changes, the model is successful in explaining the decisive shift in the U.S. trade position. We shall see that the model explains the shifts in the trade deficit mainly as the result of shifts in monetary and fiscal policies in the major industrial countries, combined with the natural dynamics of the model.

Figure 1-3. *Tracking the U.S. Trade Balance*

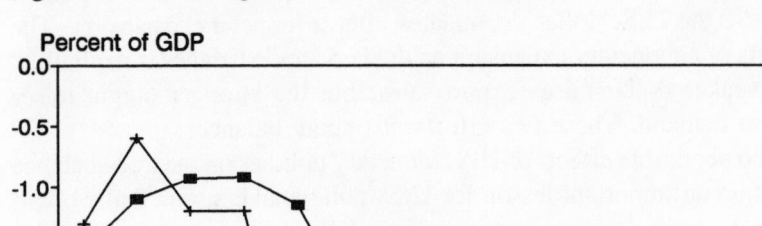

Sources: For actual data, OECD, *OECD Economic Outlook*, no. 46 (December 1989) (diskette); for simulated data, authors' calculations using the MSG2 model (see chapter 5).

As we explain in chapter 5, the tracking approach underlying figure 1-3 is novel and is an important advance over the typical ways of "tracking history." In our model—and presumably in fact—the state of the world economy in any year depends not just on the policies that are followed in that year, but also on the public's *expectations* of the policies that will be followed in the future. Therefore, in attempting to see whether the model can account for year-to-year developments during the period of analysis, we must take into account not only actual changes in policies but also changes in the expectations that were held by the public during each of those years. In this way we show how changes in the world economy result from changes in actual policies as well as from changes in expectations about future policies.

To carry out the historical simulation, we use evidence from the OECD to calibrate the reasonable future expectations of the public about fiscal and monetary policies in each of the major industrial countries in each of the years between 1978 and 1989. For example, on the basis of this methodology, we assume that in 1981 the public expected modest budget deficits in the United States during the entire period 1981–85. By 1982, not only were the forecasts of the current

(1982) deficits much higher, but we assume that the forecasts of all future deficits during 1983–86 had also risen sharply.

The model does not track events precisely, but it seems to track them well enough to justify using it as a basis for judging the likely effects of alternative policies in the future. Therefore, in chapter 6, we use the simulation model to study various policies for reducing the U.S. external deficit. Among the policy options that we examine are changes in fiscal and monetary policies in the United States and abroad, as well as changes in trade policy (represented here by a U.S. tariff on imports from Japan). Of the policies explored, we find that only changes in global fiscal policies—and mainly changes in the U.S. fiscal balance—can have a substantial effect on the U.S. external imbalance. But we also find that even an elimination of the U.S. budget deficit would not entirely eliminate the U.S. trade deficit. To accomplish that objective, there must be an additional rise in U.S. private savings rates or, less desirable, a downward shift in U.S. investment rates.

Our findings for tariff policies are especially important in view of a strong undercurrent in the U.S. view that we must "get tough" with Japan in order to reduce the trade deficit. In this experiment, we assume that the tariff policy is revenue neutral (that is, that tariff revenues are rebated to the public through offsetting tax cuts) in order to keep clear the distinction between trade policy and budget policy.[3] We find that the tariff against Japanese goods does indeed reduce imports from Japan, but that it has several other indirect effects that nullify any overall improvement of the U.S. trade balance. Part of the demand spills over to imports from other countries, and part spills over to increased demand for U.S. goods. The increased domestic demand causes U.S. interest rates to rise, thereby inducing an overall appreciation of the exchange rate that reduces U.S. export competitiveness. In the end, although imports from Japan fall, U.S. exports also fall, and U.S. imports from other parts of the world rise.

The result in our simulation exercise is actually a slight worsening of the overall trade balance. These negative conclusions about the role of trade policy would still hold if the tariff is imposed across the board

3. To the extent that the tariff revenues are earmarked for reducing the budget deficit, the effects in improving the trade balance would be greater than reported, because in this case trade policy would also be contractionary fiscal policy—a measure that we know is effective in reducing the trade deficit.

on all U.S. imports, rather than only on those from Japan. In that case, the appreciation of the dollar and the decline in U.S. export competitiveness could be even greater than for a tariff targeted on Japan.

We also discuss in chapter 6 the evidence for and against the "hard-landing" scenario. We do not dispute the theoretical possibility of a hard landing for the U.S. economy. Indeed, the evidence from the northern hemisphere is clear enough, since Mexico experienced a quintessential hard landing in 1982 when foreign credits suddenly dried up. Rather, we argue against the empirical plausibility of a hard landing during the early 1990s, on the grounds that the international financial conditions of the United States are much superior to those of countries such as Mexico before their hard landings.

This is not to deny that U.S. real growth at the end of 1990 has slowed substantially, but rather we argue that the slowdown is due to a combination of domestic factors and a new international oil shock, rather than to a sudden withdrawal of foreign financing for the U.S. trade deficit. We do not, moreover, rule out that a hard landing could eventually occur if fiscal profligacy in the United States continues long enough to reduce U.S. financial conditions to those of Mexico in 1982.

The third part of the book studies how policymakers in the industrial economies can and should coordinate their actions in view of the interdependence of the industrial economies. Because macroeconomic policies in one industrial country can have important effects on all of the other economies, there is a natural case for coordinating policy decisions. One point of view, expressed with vigor by the Reagan administration in its first term of office, is that, despite the interdependence of the industrial economies, each country should focus its policies on "keeping its own house in order" without needing to coordinate its actions with others. This is not to say that policymakers should be oblivious to policy actions elsewhere, but only that they should take them as given, without the need to negotiate a common package of measures. An alternative point of view, (ironically) championed by the Reagan administration in its second term, is that economic interdependence implies that there are potential gains for all of the countries involved in coordinating their actions.

Our goal is to shed some light on this debate by using the simulation model to evaluate the potential gains from policy coordination. Assuming that the simulation model is "true," how much benefit is there in a coordinated approach to policymaking? If there are potential gains, can the coordinated approach be summarized by a set of policy rules that can be jointly adopted by the major industrial countries?

In chapter 7 we begin our exploration of these questions by introducing the formal game-theoretic study of macroeconomic policy coordination. The game-theoretic approach gives a precise definition of two kinds of policymaking, noncooperative and cooperative. In noncooperative policymaking, the authorities in each country simply do the best they can for their own country (according to a well-defined objective function), taking as given the policy actions abroad. With cooperative policymaking, there is a concerted setting of policy actions by the countries in a kind of treaty arrangement (by which no country is allowed to violate its promise after the common set of policies is set).

In simple settings, the policymakers must be able to do at least as well under cooperative policymaking as under noncooperative policymaking (since they can at least agree on the noncooperative set of policies), and usually they can do better (in the sense that all of the countries are better able to achieve their objectives). In more complex settings, in which governments can commit their actions within a given time period but not in the future, the act of mutual coordination can—at least theoretically—make things *worse* for all of the countries. These cases are examined in chapter 7.

The theoretical ideas set forth in chapter 7 are then applied in chapter 8 by using the multicountry simulation model. In particular, we use special numerical techniques to study the dynamic gains (or losses) to the individual economies from a concerted attempt to coordinate policy actions. This exercise is potentially very useful: although it is plausible that policy coordination could have beneficial effects, it is important to know whether the potential gains, measured empirically, are substantial. We show that there may indeed be gains from policy coordination, although they are almost invariably modest in the examples that we present. We leave these exercises with the feeling that only the surface has been touched with regard to this important topic.

Another way of describing policy coordination is to see it as a system of rules jointly adopted by the participating countries. In the European Community, for example, monetary policy coordination is implemented as a joint decision to keep exchange rates within narrow bands. It now appears that this coordination will be tightened further in the future by monetary union, the actual adoption of a common currency (the ultimate step in fixing exchange rates). The question for the United States, Japan, and the EC (or Germany, as the monetary linchpin of the EC) is whether there are strong reasons to adopt a similar set of rules among themselves—and if so, which rules.

In chapter 9 we use the simulation model to examine several alternative rules that have been proposed to manage the world monetary system. We develop a technique for evaluating a range of alternative rules under various shocks to the world economy. We can identify the "best" rules for a given set of shocks and a given set of objectives, but searching for the optimal global set of rules is like searching for the Holy Grail. There is no single ideal rule, but rather different rules that are best for different shocks. Because the nature of future economic shocks is not knowable today, we cannot choose an optimal rule with confidence.

In general, as is known even from simple models, fixed exchange rates work best when economies are hit by monetary shocks (for example, shifts in the private sector's demand for money) or by global shocks that affect partner countries in similar ways. When there are country-specific shocks, however, there is usually a need for some exchange rate flexibility among the major countries. This suggests that a regime of managed exchange rates, if properly defined, could play a role in stabilizing the international economy, although (as we show) such a system must be carefully designed to avoid policy-induced instabilities.

It might seem convenient to suppose that the statistical pattern of future economic shocks will be like that of past shocks—so that one could pick the rules that would have best managed the kinds of disturbances that have rocked the world economy in the recent past. But even if we could agree precisely on what those past disturbances have been, choosing future rules as if shocks will have the same probabilistic pattern as in the past is not unlike generals constantly preparing to fight a previous war.

There are other reasons that our approach in this section is a start, but only a start, toward a quantitative assessment of international policy coordination. Some of the benefits of close coordination—such as the reduction of transaction costs that will be achieved by Europe's move to a single currency—are not introduced in our macroeconomic model. That close macroeconomic policy coordination might enhance mutual understanding and toleration in other areas of contact between countries (trade, military security, the provision of international public goods) is another source of possible gains to policy coordination that is not accounted for in our framework.

Thus, although our conclusions in the third part of the text are limited, we are still able to shed light on the efficacy of various macroeconomic rules that have been proposed for the world economy. That insight helps us to identify the weakness as well as the potential strengths of these alternative rules, and to discard some rules that are unworkable or are dominated by other rules. Our formal framework provides a methodological starting point for more refined quantitative assessments of international macroeconomic policy coordination.

We conclude this introduction with a word of caution. Although one of our main points is that global macroeconomic imbalances in the 1980s can be interpreted by using a dynamic macroeconometric model of the world economy, we are of course aware of the many issues that are not explained by our approach. We do not, for example, address any of the questions about the slowdown of U.S. productivity growth and the low U.S. private savings rate.

In the same vein, although we very much doubt that Japanese trade or industrial policies can take us far toward understanding the movements in international trade balances in the past ten years—or the prospects for the next ten—we do not wish to imply that the debate over trade and industrial policies is therefore unimportant. Rather, that debate should center on the right issues, such as the effects of alleged Japanese protectionism on the prospects of various U.S. firms and industries, and not on global macroeconomic imbalances, which are signs of other kinds of phenomena. When a U.S. politician points to the trade deficit and complains about Japanese trade practices, the result is not only to distract attention from the real causes of the United States' international financial problems, but also to undermine the possibility for a serious discussion of trade restrictions abroad. We hope that our study not only helps to clarify the evolution of international imbalances, but also helps to redirect the debate on other issues toward more constructive ends.

CHAPTER TWO

# The Theory of Macroeconomic Interdependence

In what ways do macroeconomic policy changes in one country affect the macroeconomic performance of other countries? How, for example, does a U.S. fiscal expansion affect German and Japanese output and inflation? Would a Japanese fiscal expansion have an important effect on the magnitude of the U.S. trade deficit? Our plan is to analyze these questions in two steps. In this chapter, we first study the issue in simple theoretical models. In chapters 3 and 4 we introduce and then experiment with a quantitative simulation model based on the basic theoretical insights of this chapter.

The best theoretical starting point is a two-region model of the world, divided between a "home" and "foreign" country. We adopt as a basic framework the famous Mundell-Fleming model, which has been the workhorse of international economic analysis since its introduction in the early 1960s (Fleming 1962; Mundell 1963; 1968). This model was the first to study macroeconomic interactions in a formal theoretical setting under the realistic assumption of high capital mobility between the countries. Until that time two-country models, which were extremely rudimentary, in general neglected the possibility of international capital movements. In the 1960s many international capital movements were still restricted by extensive capital control regulations that had been in place since the Great Depression and World War II. The extensive liberalization of international capital flows since then has made the Mundell-Fleming assumption of high capital mobility the appropriate starting point for analyzing the macroeconomic interactions of countries.

The two-country Mundell-Fleming model is introduced in the next section to examine the transmission of monetary and fiscal policies under different assumptions about exchange rate flexibility, wage set-

Table 2-1. *A Static Two-Country Model*

| Equation number | Equation[a] |
|---|---|
| (2-1) | $m - p = \phi q - \beta i$ |
| (2-1*) | $m^* - p^* = \phi q^* - \beta i^*$ |
| (2-2) | $q = \delta \lambda - \sigma i + \mu g + \gamma q^* - \upsilon t$ |
| (2-2*) | $q^* = - \delta \lambda - \sigma i^* + \mu g^* + \gamma q - \upsilon t^*$ |
| (2-3) | $p = w + \theta q$ |
| (2-3*) | $p^* = w^* + \theta q^*$ |
| (2-4) | $w = \zeta p^c$ |
| (2-4*) | $w^* = \zeta p^{c*}$ |
| (2-5) | $p^c = \alpha p + (1 - \alpha)(e + p^*)$ |
| (2-5*) | $p^{c*} = \alpha p^* + (1 - \alpha)(-e + p)$ |
| (2-6) | $\lambda = e + p^* - p$ |
| (2-7) | $i = i^*$ |

a. Variables are defined as follows (asterisks indicate foreign-country variables; all variables except $i$, the level of the interest rate, are in logarithmic form):
$m$ = nominal money balances
$p$ = price level
$w$ = nominal wage
$q$ = real output
$i$ = level of interest rate
$e$ = exchange rate defined as the price in domestic currency of a unit of foreign currency
$\lambda$ = real exchange rate
$p^c$ = consumer price
$g$ = real government expenditure
$t$ = real taxes.

ting, and capital mobility.[1] The model is deliberately kept simple: it focuses only on *short-run* effects of policy changes and ignores several long-run issues. The simplicity is useful in obtaining some clear results and is excusable in that we examine many important complexities when we introduce the simulation model. In the following section we consider some dynamic aspects of macroeconomic interdependence, although we put off a detailed treatment of macroeconomic adjustments until the next chapter. In the final section of this chapter we introduce the consequence of supply shocks into the basic model.

## Short-run Macroeconomic Interdependence

To understand the key mechanisms by which macroeconomic policy changes are transmitted to other countries, we consider the basic two-country Mundell-Fleming model given in equations 2-1 through 2-7 in table 2-1. The two symmetric economies are the home country and

1. We focus on policy transmission in a two-country world. See Argy, McKibbin, and Siegloff (1989) for a similar approach in a three-country world where one country is small relative to the other two.

the foreign country. The goal is to use the model to find policy multipliers of the sort $dX/dY$; that is, the change in variable $X$ as a function of a given change in a policy variable $Y$ ($Y$ might be fiscal spending, $G$, the money supply, $M$, and so forth). When the variable $X$ and the policy variable $Y$ correspond to the same country, we refer to own-country multipliers; when $X$ and $Y$ correspond to different countries, we refer to cross-country multipliers, or international transmission effects.

The reader interested in the formal analysis can find a description of the model in this section. Readers interested only in the results of the analysis can skip directly to the subsection entitled "Monetary Policy Transmission."

In the formal model, it is assumed that each country produces one good that is an imperfect substitute for the other country's good. Both goods are tradable, in that they are used in the country of origin and are exported to the other country. Because the countries are symmetric, each equation for the home country has an identical counterpart in the foreign country (indicated by an asterisk appended to the equation number in table 2-1). The model ignores the role of expectations of inflation and exchange rate changes (technically, individuals are assumed to have static expectations; that is, the expectation of no changes in prices or the exchange rate). Therefore, there is no attempt to distinguish between real and nominal interest rates and no attempt to allow for the expectation of future changes in the exchange rate.

Equation 2-1 is a standard LM curve expressing money demand in each country as a function of real output and the interest rate. The IS curve is given in equation 2-2, with aggregate demand written in semireduced form as a function of the (logarithm of the) real exchange rate, $\lambda$, the interest rate, government spending, foreign demand, and the level of taxation.[2] The real exchange rate is defined in equation 2-6 as the relative price of foreign goods to domestic goods, $EP^*/P$. Note that $E$ is defined as units of domestic currency per unit of foreign currency (that is, $E$ is the price of a unit of foreign exchange in terms of domestic money). A rise in $E$ is a depreciation of the home currency, and a fall is an appreciation. In log-levels, we write the real exchange rate as $\lambda = p^* + e - p$. When the real exchange rate depreciates ($\lambda$ rises), foreign goods become more expensive relative to the domestic

2. In this section we focus on a change in government spending rather than on changes in tax policy. Taxation will be discussed at greater length in the section on "Intertemporal Linkage."

good. A real exchange rate depreciation thereby causes a shift in world demand away from foreign goods and toward home goods, thereby boosting aggregate demand at home.

In what follows, we must be extremely clear about the terms used to define exchange rate changes. We will always describe the exchange rate from the point of view of the home country. Thus, when we say that the home currency appreciates (or the exchange rate falls), we are always talking about the price of a unit of the foreign currency in terms of the domestic currency.

In equation 2-3 we assume that the domestic price is a markup over factor costs (wages, in this case), where the markup is a function of demand in the economy. This equation is consistent with firms' equating the marginal product of labor with the real wage. In equation 2-4, nominal wages in turn are assumed to be either fixed ($\zeta = 0$)[3] or are indexed to the price of the domestic agents' consumption bundle, which is defined in equation 2-5 as a weighted average of the price of domestically produced goods and the price of imports. Finally, the interest parity condition is given in equation 2-7. Capital is assumed to be *perfectly mobile* internationally (that is, there are no capital controls), and home and foreign bonds are taken to be perfect substitutes. Because we assume static expectations (so that the exchange rate is expected to remain unchanged), the joint assumption of perfect capital mobility and perfect asset substitutability results in the condition that $i = i^*$.[4]

Although full capital mobility is assumed to be the norm, we also want to consider the case in which capital is immobile across borders because of capital controls. This condition still applies for some countries, although by the end of the 1980s almost all industrial countries (and all the main ones) had substantially eliminated capital controls. In the case of immobile capital, the interest parity condition is no longer relevant and is replaced by a condition that the trade balance

---

3. In this model, wages change only because of indexation clauses. Thus, the case of fixed nominal wages is the same as the case of zero indexation ($\zeta = 0$). Note that when we solve for this case, we also assume that prices are fixed ($\theta = 0$).

4. The general condition for perfect capital mobility and perfect asset substitutability is that the interest rate differential is equal to the expected rate of depreciation:

$$i_t - i^*_t = e_{t+1} - e_t.$$

With static expectations, the expected rate of depreciation is zero, so that the nominal interest rate at home, $i$, must equal the nominal interest rate abroad, $i^*$.

is zero.[5] This condition determines the exchange rate. Interest rates are then determined independently in each country in the separate money markets.

The basic model ignores the role of wealth and intertemporal aspects of interdependence. These considerations will be introduced later in this chapter, and especially in subsequent chapters with reference to the simulation model. We will not examine the consequence of imperfect asset substitutability; the reader is referred to Oudiz and Sachs (1985) and to Branson and Henderson (1985) for discussions of this issue.

The nature of policy transmission depends on the institutional context. Consider, for example, the effect of a home (U.S.) monetary expansion on the rest of the world. If nominal wages are assumed to be fully fixed, this effect is positive under fixed exchange rates and negative under flexible exchange rates. Under flexible rates, the negative transmission effect becomes positive if the foreign country has a high degree of wage indexation![6] Clearly, the institutional setting matters greatly.

We are therefore interested in the consequences—for the international transmission of policies—of alternative assumptions about the exchange rate regime, the wage regime, and the degree of capital mobility, as follows.

—For exchange rates, a floating exchange rate; a fixed exchange rate with the home country having the responsibility for pegging the rate; and a fixed exchange rate with the foreign country having the responsibility for pegging the rate.

—For wage setting, fixed wages in both economies; fixed wage in the home country with full indexation to consumer prices in the foreign country; and full indexation to consumer prices in the home country and fixed wage in the foreign country.

5. Technically, with complete capital immobility the condition is that the current account balance is zero (residents can neither accumulate nor decumulate foreign assets), but in this simple static framework we are not distinguishing between the trade account and the current account.

6. In addition to the wage assumption, other assumptions are crucial to determining the sign of the transmission of shocks among countries. For example, alternative assumptions about how expectations of exchange rates influence capital flows can also reverse the standard results. This issue, however, is not pursued further here.

Table 2-2. *Transmission of Policy under Perfect and Zero Capital Mobility*[a]

| Exchange rate and wage regime | Monetary policy | | | | | Fiscal policy | | | | |
|---|---|---|---|---|---|---|---|---|---|---|
| | $q$ | $p^c$ | $\lambda$ | $q^*$ | $p^{c*}$ | $q$ | $p^c$ | $\lambda$ | $q^*$ | $p^{c*}$ |
| | *Perfect capital mobility* | | | | | | | | | |
| *Floating exchange rate* | | | | | | | | | | |
| Fixed wages | + | + | + | − | − | + | − | − | + | + |
| Foreign indexation | + | + | + | + | − | + | ± | ± | ± | + |
| Home indexation | 0 | 1 | 0 | 0 | 0 | + | ± | − | + | + |
| *Fixed exchange rate (home peg)* | | | | | | | | | | |
| Fixed wages | 0 | 0 | 0 | 0 | 0 | + | 0 | 0 | + | 0 |
| Foreign indexation | 0 | 0 | 0 | 0 | 0 | + | + | + | + | + |
| Home indexation | 0 | 0 | 0 | 0 | 0 | + | + | − | + | + |
| *Fixed exchange rate (foreign peg)* | | | | | | | | | | |
| Fixed wages | + | 0 | 0 | + | 0 | + | 0 | 0 | ± | 0 |
| Foreign indexation | + | + | + | + | + | + | ± | ± | ± | ± |
| Home indexation | + | − | + | + | + | + | + | − | ± | + |
| | *Zero capital mobility* | | | | | | | | | | |
| *Floating exchange rate* | | | | | | | | | | |
| Fixed wages | + | + | + | 0 | − | + | + | + | 0 | − |
| Foreign indexation | + | + | + | 0 | − | + | + | + | 0 | − |
| Home indexation | + | + | + | 0 | − | + | + | + | 0 | − |
| *Fixed exchange rate (home peg)* | | | | | | | | | | |
| Fixed wages | + | 0 | 0 | + | 0 | + | 0 | 0 | + | 0 |
| Foreign indexation | + | + | + | + | + | + | + | + | + | + |
| Home indexation | + | + | − | + | + | + | + | − | + | + |
| *Fixed exchange rate (foreign peg)* | | | | | | | | | | |
| Fixed wages | + | 0 | 0 | + | 0 | + | 0 | 0 | + | 0 |
| Foreign indexation | + | + | + | + | + | + | + | + | + | + |
| Home indexation | + | + | − | + | + | + | + | − | + | + |

a. All signs assume $\gamma < 1$.

—For capital mobility, perfect capital mobility and zero capital mobility.

A summary of the key results under the alternative combination of regimes in the static model is given in table 2-2. Several points should be highlighted before considering the results in detail. First, in determining the sign of changes in the variables, we assume that $0 < \gamma < 1$. When we consider the case of sticky wages, we also assume sticky prices; therefore both $\zeta = 0$ and $\theta = 0$ in this case.

We will initially focus on the standard Mundell-Fleming model, which assumes *complete capital mobility* (again assuming that home and foreign bonds are perfect substitutes), *flexible exchange rates*, and *sticky wages and prices*. We will then consider changes in the underlying assumptions. The initial discussion will maintain the assumption of perfect capital mobility. At the end we will briefly discuss the implications of relaxing this assumption. Although we focus on extreme cases, some idea of the outcomes for the intermediate cases can be gained by combining the results in the different parts of the tables.

### Monetary Policy Transmission (Domestic Money Expansion)

We have noted that the impact of monetary policy on the home country and the foreign country is very sensitive to the alternative assumptions we consider. To understand why transmission changes under each regime, consider the standard Mundell-Fleming model, which has floating exchange rates, sticky prices, and perfectly mobile capital.

FLOATING EXCHANGE RATES. In this model a rise in the stock of home money lowers home interest rates and stimulates domestic demand. The falling interest rates lead to an incipient capital outflow that depreciates the nominal value of the home currency and, with sticky prices, also causes a depreciation of the real value (that is, reduces the relative price of home goods). This depreciation increases net exports. The result is higher home output, higher home consumer prices (because of higher import prices caused by the home currency depreciation), and a real depreciation of the home currency. Note that the effects on the trade balance are ambiguous. Stronger domestic demand will tend to raise imports and worsen the trade balance. The real depreciation of the home currency will tend to raise exports and lower imports, which improves the trade balance.

Consider now the effects in the foreign country. Foreign output actually *falls* because both foreign and home residents substitute away from foreign goods to home goods in response to the change in relative prices. The result is that monetary policy is beggar-thy-neighbor: a monetary expansion in the home country reduces foreign output. At the same time, the depreciation of the home currency lowers the price of home goods in the foreign market, which lowers the foreign consumer price index.

Now consider the impact of assumptions about wage setting on this standard Mundell-Fleming result.[7] In the case of home indexation ($w = p^c$), the price consequences of the monetary expansion increase, and the output consequences are reduced. In the extreme case we consider, with full home indexation, the output consequences in both economies disappear. As the home currency depreciates, both home wages and home prices (through the pass-through of wage increases) rise. Therefore the real exchange rate does not change, and there is no substitution of demand away from foreign goods toward home goods. Real money balances do not change despite the change in nominal money balances (since prices rise by the same proportion), and therefore interest rates do not change, which implies no reduction in home real demand. The result is monetary neutrality.

In the case that domestic nominal wages are fixed but foreign nominal wages are indexed, we get very different results (both from the standard model and from the case of domestic indexation). After the domestic monetary expansion, the home currency depreciates and interest rates fall (as in the initial version of the model). But now, as the foreign currency appreciates, foreign wages and prices fall, which diminishes the real depreciation of the home currency and reduces the foreign country's loss of competitiveness. The foreign country still experiences lower world interest rates—which stimulates demand— but without the loss in demand for its goods in foreign markets due to the loss in competitiveness. The result of the home monetary expansion is therefore an output *gain* for both the foreign country and the home country, although the home country's output gain is smaller. The foreign country still experiences a fall in consumer prices because of the appreciation of its currency and because of lower home goods prices.

Thus, the domestic monetary expansion always causes a depreciation of the home currency and a rise in home output (except in the extreme case of full domestic indexation). It causes a fall in foreign output if foreign nominal wages are rigid, but a rise in foreign output if foreign nominal wages are indexed.

FIXED EXCHANGE RATES. The flexibility of the exchange rate and the transmission of monetary policy through changes in relative prices are important to the story outlined above. Pegging the exchange rate changes the transmission mechanism. In discussing a fixed exchange

---

7. This result was highlighted by Sachs (1980) and Argy and Salop (1979).

rate it is important to specify which country is responsible for maintaining the peg: once a country pegs the exchange rate, it no longer has an independent monetary policy.

We first consider the case in which the country undertaking a monetary expansion pegs the exchange rate and, second, the case in which the foreign country pegs the exchange rate.[8] The first point to note from the top half of table 2-2 is that an attempt to expand the domestic money supply under a fixed exchange rate (and domestic responsibility for pegging) has *no effect*. As domestic credit expands, the fall in domestic interest rates leads to an incipient capital outflow that induces an incipient depreciation of the home currency. The home country must sell foreign exchange to maintain the exchange rate, and in the process it reverses the initial expansion in the money supply. The outflow of foreign reserves reduces the reserve component of the domestic money stock by exactly the amount of the domestic credit expansion.

In the case in which the foreign country is responsible for fixing the exchange rate, the monetary expansion in the home country will lead to a monetary expansion in the foreign country that is necessary to hold the exchange rate fixed. The result is a global monetary expansion. In the Mundell-Fleming world of sticky prices, this raises output both at home and abroad and reduces global interest rates. In contrast to the case of flexible exchange rates, the money supply increase is now positively transmitted. If nominal wages are fixed, there will also be no effect on prices because all prices are assumed to be a fixed markup over wages. Once we allow for price and wage adjustment through a combination of variable markup of prices over wages and nominal wage indexation, we see that both foreign and home prices will rise as a result of the global monetary expansion. The output effects of the expansion are therefore reduced in both countries.

### Fiscal Policy Transmission

The consequences of fiscal policy are more complex. For the purposes of initial exposition in the top half of table 2-2, we have greatly

8. Other alternatives include a more symmetric regime whereby one country pegs the exchange rate and the other country targets a world stock of money. This is the McKinnon (1984) proposal for global monetary policy and is discussed in detail in chapter 9.

simplified the model to ignore the intertemporal issues associated with accumulation of government debt. We have also assumed perfect asset substitutability, which does away with any effect of changes in the stock of government debt on the risk premiums that investors require. The analysis here focuses solely on the standard short-run demand effects of changes in government expenditure financed by issuing government debt. Changes in taxes in this simple model can be viewed similarly to the change in government spending with the assumption that $\theta < \mu$; that is, the propensity to consume out of after-tax income is assumed to be less than unity.

FLOATING EXCHANGE RATES. In the standard Mundell-Fleming model with sticky prices, floating exchange rates, and high capital mobility, we see from the top part of table 2-2 that a fiscal expansion (a rise in government spending) in the home country raises home output. The key difference between a fiscal expansion and a monetary expansion emerges from the effects that the two policy expansions have on interest rates. The monetary expansion lowers interest rates, whereas the bond-financed fiscal expansion raises interest rates. The rise in interest rates leads to a capital inflow that appreciates the home currency and raises world interest rates. The appreciation of the real value of the currency shifts demand toward foreign goods, thereby raising demand abroad. Even aside from the exchange rate change, the higher level of domestic demand also directly raises the demand for foreign goods. The result is that fiscal policy is positively transmitted: higher fiscal spending at home raises output abroad. There is an offsetting effect of higher interest rates, but in the standard Mundell-Fleming model this effect is necessarily outweighed by the expansionary effects.[9]

Note that the domestic fiscal expansion has a negative effect on the price level because the appreciation of the home currency lowers the price of foreign goods in the home market. This result has an important

---

9. The reason is rather subtle. Consider what happens in the foreign money market. World interest rates rise after the fiscal expansion, tending to reduce the demand for foreign money balances. But real money balances abroad are unchanged by the home fiscal expansion (both $m^*$ and $p^*$ remain fixed). Therefore, unless foreign output also rises, there will be an excess supply of foreign money (demand for $m^* - p^*$ will fall, but the quantity will remain unchanged). With an excess supply of foreign money, there will be a tendency for $e$ to fall (for the home currency to appreciate). In fact, $e$ will fall enough to ensure that demand for foreign goods rises enough so that the excess supply of foreign money is eliminated by an expansion of foreign output (which leads to a rise in demand for $m^* - p^*$).

implication: on impact, and per unit of output expansion achieved, fiscal policy is less inflationary than monetary policy. Whereas monetary policy causes a currency depreciation, which feeds through into higher import prices, fiscal expansion does the opposite. It is also important to point out that the fiscal expansion unambiguously worsens the trade balance of the home country. For the monetary expansion the real depreciation of the home currency tends to improve the trade balance; in the case of the fiscal expansion the real appreciation of the home currency worsens the trade balance, reinforcing the effect of stronger domestic demands.

Once we allow wages to adjust to price level changes, we again find that the transmission of fiscal policy can be affected in important ways. With foreign indexation, the home fiscal expansion no longer necessarily raises foreign output. In this case the nominal appreciation of the home currency raises foreign wages and prices, and this reduces the extent of the improvement in foreign competitiveness. The negative effect of higher world interest rates, together with a smaller improvement in foreign competitiveness (or even worsening of), can be sufficient to offset the positive spillovers from higher demand in the home economy. Therefore foreign output can fall. Note also that home prices can rise if foreign prices rise by more than the home currency appreciates, so that import prices in the domestic currency can actually rise rather than fall.

FIXED EXCHANGE RATES. If the home country fixes the exchange rate, a change in home fiscal policy also implies a change in monetary policy. As we saw above, a home fiscal expansion tends to appreciate the home currency. To offset the incipient appreciation requires a monetary expansion in the home country. The output effects are clear because the monetary policy expansion will reinforce the expansionary effects of the fiscal expansion. With prices and the nominal exchange rate fixed, the real exchange rate and consumer prices in both countries cannot change. With indexation and variable prices in either the foreign country or the home country, a fiscal expansion with the home country pegging the exchange rate now unambiguously raises output and prices both at home and abroad. Fiscal policy is therefore positively transmitted. In the case of foreign indexation, the rise in output raises foreign prices and depreciates the real value of the home currency (that is, home competitiveness is improved as $\lambda$ rises). The opposite occurs with home indexation, which raises home prices and therefore causes the real exchange rate $\lambda$ to fall rather than to rise.

The results are less clear when the fiscal expansion is undertaken by the country *not* responsible for pegging the exchange rate. From the top part of table 2-2, we see that when the home country expands and the foreign country pegs the exchange rate, a monetary expansion in the home country results in a foreign monetary expansion, whereas a home fiscal expansion results in a foreign monetary contraction. Now home output still rises in response to the home fiscal expansion, but foreign output may rise or fall because of the foreign monetary contraction. A similar ambiguity occurs in the response of prices once they are allowed to adjust to the demand pressure.

Under a given exchange rate regime, the move to indexation reduces the real effects on output (both home and foreign) of a given fiscal policy change.

### Importance of Capital Mobility

The results so far have concentrated on the Mundell-Fleming model, which assumes perfect capital mobility and asset substitutability. In the bottom half of table 2-2 we reexamine the model under the opposite assumption of no capital flows between the two economies. This approach corresponds to the working assumption in the pre-1960s literature (see especially Meade 1951). Under the case of floating exchange rates, we assume that the trade balance is always equal to zero. The exchange rate adjusts to maintain trade balance. Under the case of a fixed exchange rate, we assume that the domestic interest rate adjusts to clear the money market at the given exchange rate and that the trade balance is matched by an equivalent gain or loss in international reserves.[10]

Several interesting results are apparent from the second part of table 2-2. When capital flows are prohibited, a floating exchange rate perfectly insulates the economy from foreign shocks. Because the trade

---

10. Technically speaking, as noted before the change in reserves would be equal to the current account balance, not the trade balance. In the simple static models in this chapter, the distinction is not operationally important. Note the reason that the reserve change is equal to the current account. Under a regime of zero capital mobility, exporters sell their foreign exchange back to the central bank, thereby leading to a gain in reserves; importers purchase their foreign exchange from the central bank, thereby leading to a fall in reserves. The central bank also earns interest on its stock of foreign exchange reserves. Adding up these pieces, we see that the change in reserves is equal to the net trade flow plus the interest earnings on the stock of foreign exchange reserves. That is, the change of reserves is equal to the current account balance.

account is always in balance, any changes in policy in one country have no effects on the trade balance. The exchange rate change does feed into import prices, but in the model this has no effects on home demand. We assume that the price of domestic goods enters the calculation of real money balances. Monetary policy and fiscal policy both raise home output and prices and lower foreign consumer prices, but with no effect on foreign output under either wage assumption.

Fixing the exchange rate has several interesting implications. First we must be careful to specify how the exchange rate is fixed. The standard assumption (for example, Marston 1985) is that in the short run the monetary authority accumulates or decumulates reserves if the trade balance moves into surplus or into deficit. Over time this change in reserves feeds into the money supply, and this tends to reduce the money supply and to reequilibrate the trade account. This implies that a domestic credit expansion can have short-lived real effects, although the adjustment to reserves tends to offset it over time. The results for fixed exchange rates in the second part of table 2-2 are clear, given our discussion of adjustment under floating exchange rates and zero capital mobility. With fixed prices and a fixed exchange rate, domestic output rises for both monetary and fiscal expansions. By assumption, consumer prices and the real exchange rate cannot change. The trade balance would deteriorate for both policy changes, and this would mean a positive spillover to the foreign economy. Over time, the fall in foreign reserves would reduce the domestic money supply, which would contract domestic demand and leave both fiscal and monetary policy ineffective in the long run.

### Intertemporal Linkage

The basic Mundell-Fleming model outlined above does not account for some potentially important factors. It ignores many intertemporal considerations, such as dynamic adjustments in prices, capital stocks, and financial wealth, as well as the role of expectations. In a world of rational expectations, expectations of future policy changes can have an important impact on current private behavior.

A vast literature has expanded on the Mundell-Fleming framework to include dynamics and expectations. In later chapters we build such features into the empirical simulation model, but in the process make the model too complicated to solve analytically. In this section we will highlight some of the key implications for our static analysis of alternative intertemporal issues.

### Adding Dynamics

Once time and dynamics are incorporated in the model, a distinction needs to be drawn between the short-run impact of policy and the long-run consequences. Fiscal deficits lead to the accumulation of government debt; investment leads to accumulation of the capital stock; and trade deficits lead to accumulation of foreign debt. As these asset stocks change, so too do asset prices and private consumption and investment behavior. Some of the effects of incorporating the accumulation or decumulation of physical and financial assets have been surveyed by Branson and Henderson (1985). Here, we introduce one major aspect introduced by dynamic considerations: the long-term budget constraints imposed on public sector borrowing and international borrowing.

The change in real government debt outstanding (denoted by $B$, for bonds) is equal to the excess of real government spending on goods and services $(G)$ over real tax revenue $(T)$, plus the real cost of servicing outstanding government debt. Let $B_t$ be the debt at the beginning of period $t$. Then, the change in $B_t$ may be written as:

$$(2\text{-}8) \qquad B_{t+1} - B_t = G_t + r_{t-1} B_t - T_t.$$

Here, $r_{t-1}$ is the real interest rate, approximately equal to the nominal interest rate paid between periods $t-1$ and $t$ on debt held at the end of period $t-1$ minus the inflation rate between periods $t-1$ and $t$:

$$(2\text{-}9) \qquad (1 + r_{t-1}) = (1 + i_{t-1}) (P_{t-1}/P_t).$$

In any particular period, when interest on the debt falls due the government may choose to borrow the funds that it needs to meet the interest bill. But in the long run, the government must be able to service its debts out of its own revenues rather than out of further borrowing. Otherwise, the debt would grow explosively fast—at the rate of real interest—with $B_{t+1} = (1 + r_{t-1}) B_t$. Eventually, wary creditors would stop lending. If we rule out the case of an endless explosion of debt, we can derive a basic intertemporal budget constraint on the government. If the real interest rate is assumed to be constant (only for the purpose of simplifying the presentation), we may derive the following:

$$(2\text{-}10) \qquad B_t = \sum_{\tau=t}^{\infty} (1 + r)^{-(\tau-t)} (T_\tau - G_\tau).$$

This equation says that if the government has a stock of debt $B_t$, which has been inherited from the budget deficits in the past up until time $t$, it must run future surpluses on the *primary budget*, which is the budget balance excluding interest payments on the debt. More specifically, the present value of future primary surpluses must sum to the initial stock of debt. Equation 2-10 has an intuitive meaning. In the long run, a government services its debts by running primary surpluses. The government does not have to run primary surpluses each period, but it must implement a budget policy such that the present value of the primary budget surpluses and deficits equals the initial stock of debt that must be serviced, $B_t$. Thus, a government that starts out with an initial heavy debt burden $B_t$ will have to run larger primary surpluses in the future than a government with a smaller initial debt burden.

There is nothing to guarantee that a government will plan to satisfy the intertemporal budget constraint. A government may try to borrow endlessly without attention to the need to satisfy the long-term budget constraint. But eventually creditors will restrict their lending and demand that the government begin to service its debt out of its own resources, rather than out of continued loans. At that point the government will be forced to raise taxes, to lower spending, or to carry out some combination of the two. When we specify fiscal policy choices in later chapters, we will *impose* the long-run budget constraint, in the sense that our alternative policy choices will explicitly take into account that any accumulation of debt must eventually be serviced through future primary budget surpluses.

A similar dynamic equation holds for the change in the net foreign asset position of an economy:

$$(2\text{-}11) \qquad A_{t+1} - A_t = M_t - X_t + r A_t.$$

In equation 2-11, $A$ is defined as real net foreign debt; that is, net claims of foreigners abroad on home residents, deflated by the home price deflator. It is assumed that these claims earn the home rate of interest. From this equation it can be seen that a rise in imports relative to exports will increase the rate at which foreign debt is being accumulated.

As with the government's budget constraint, the country as a whole faces a budget constraint imposed by the rest of the world (more precisely, because countries do not operate as a monolithic unit, we should note that the country's budget constraint can be derived by adding up the intertemporal budget constraints facing the separate agents in the economy). As with the budget, a nation as a whole will not be allowed—in the long run—to service its international debts simply by borrowing the money needed to make the international service payments. Specifically, the country's international creditors will not allow the net international debt to grow forever at the real interest rate. It can be proved, in the same way that the government's long-run budget constraint was established, that the residents of a country face the following long-term budget constraint:

$$(2\text{-}12) \qquad A_t = \sum_{\tau=t}^{\infty} (1 + r)^{-(\tau-t)} (X_\tau - M_\tau).$$

According to this equation, a country must service its net international debt by running trade surpluses (in goods and services) in the future, with the present discounted value of trade surpluses equal to the initial net indebtedness. A country that begins period $t$ with a large initial net debt $A_t$ must run large trade surpluses in the future (of course, not necessarily every period). Thus, since the United States has accumulated a large net international debt in the course of the 1980s according to the official data,[11] the United States will have to run larger trade surpluses in the future.

As with the budget deficit, it is not automatic that the economy will adjust smoothly to comply with the intertemporal budget constraint in equation 2-12. Residents of the country (especially in the public sector) may try to borrow heavily from the rest of the world, until the point that the foreign lending stops abruptly and thereby pushes the country suddenly from a trade deficit to a trade surplus. But if the accumulation of foreign debt reflects a low level of private savings, there is more of an automatic adjustment mechanism. As national wealth declines because

11. According to the 1990 *Economic Report of the President* (p. 409), the position of the United States at the end of 1988 was a net debt of $532.5 billion. There are some analysts, however, that believe that this number overstates the U.S. net debt by undervaluing key U.S. assets abroad. Nonetheless, it is clear that the U.S. net international investment position ($A_t$) fell sharply in the course of the 1980s.

of growing foreign debt, households will cut back on their consumption, thereby causing a fall in imports $M$ and a rise in exports $X$.

To capture wealth effects, we may introduce the household sector's financial wealth into the IS curve. In general, private financial wealth will include holdings of government bonds ($B$), plus holdings of equity, minus net private debt to the rest of the world ($A$).[12] We will ignore equity wealth until the next chapter and write household financial wealth as $B - A$. The IS curve becomes

$$(2.2') \quad q = \delta\lambda - \sigma i + \mu g + \gamma q^* + \Phi (B_t - A_t) - \upsilon t.$$

Suppose now that private saving starts out low, so that aggregate demand is high and the country is running a trade deficit. Over time, $A$ would rise, thereby causing overall aggregate demand to decline and eventually shifting the economy from a trade deficit to trade surplus. If the economy is dynamically stable (a feature of the model that we will verify numerically), then the adjustment of the trade balance will be such as to guarantee that the long-run budget constraint in equation 2-12 is satisfied.

In the simulation model, wealth will be introduced more carefully. First, we must include equity holdings. Second, we must allow for the fact that government bonds are not net wealth, to the extent that households discount the future tax payments that must be levied in order to service the government debt. In some extreme cases, noted later, government debt is not counted at all as household wealth. More generally, a portion of $B$ should properly be considered as net wealth, after subtracting the discounted value of future tax payments when calculating the household's overall wealth position.

### Incorporating Rational Expectations

A further extension of the basic Mundell-Fleming model is to assume that expectations are forward-looking, so that expectations concerning future variables have an effect on current behavior. Dornsbusch (1976), for example, extended the basic Mundell-Fleming model by allowing

12. In the simulation model, we will take into account the fact that both the government and private sector may have foreign assets and liabilities. Here, for purposes of exposition we are assuming that all government debt is held domestically and that all international assets and liabilities belong to the private sector. Equity wealth will be taken into account in the next chapter.

for forward-looking behavior with respect to exchange rate changes and analyzed the implications for monetary policy. Sachs and Wyplosz (1985) took essentially the same framework and analyzed the implications for fiscal policy. Many of the key extensions in this area that focus on forward-looking asset prices were surveyed by Obstfeld and Stockman (1985).

To illustrate the implications of forward-looking expectations, let us replace the assumption of static expectations in the interest parity condition (equation 2-7) by rational expectations:

$$(2\text{-}13) \qquad i_t = i_t^* + {}_te_{t+1} - e_t,$$

where the $t$ subscript preceding $e_{t+1}$ represents the expectation of $e_{t+1}$ that is held at time $t$ (${}_te_{t+1}$ is therefore the one-period-ahead forecast of the exchange rate). Equation 2-13 is the condition, known as uncovered interest arbitrage, that the interest differential is equal to the expected change in the exchange rate.

Now, by suitable addition and subtraction, let us rewrite equation 2-13 in terms of *real* interest rates and the real exchange rate:

$$(2\text{-}14) \quad i_t - ({}_tp_{t+1} - p_t) = [i_t^* - ({}_tp_{t+1}^* - p_t^*)]$$
$$+ [({}_te_{t+1} + {}_tp_{t+1}^* - {}_tp_{t+1}) - (e_t + p_t^* - p_t)].$$

According to our definitions of real interest rates and real exchange rates, we can therefore write $r_t = r^*_t + ({}_t\lambda_{t+1} - \lambda_t)$. If we rearrange this expression, we can write the current real exchange rate in terms of the future real exchange rate plus the real interest rate differential:

$$(2\text{-}15) \qquad \lambda_t = {}_t\lambda_{t+1} + (r_t^* - r_t).$$

Now, this substitution can be repeated for $T$ periods, where $T$ is a large number, until we can express the current exchange rate as equal to the sum of expected future interest differentials until period $T$, plus the *long-run* real exchange rate (defined as the exchange rate expected at period $t + T$):

$$(2\text{-}16) \qquad \lambda_t = \sum_{i=0}^{T} {}_t(r_{t+i}^* - r_{t+i}) + {}_t\lambda_{t+T}.$$

With rational expectations and risk-neutral investors, the $T$-period real interest rate at time $t$ will equal the average of the expected short-term real interest rate during the time interval between period $t$ and period $t + T$:

$$r_L = (1/T) \sum_{i=0}^{T} {}_t r_{t+i} \text{ and } r_L^* = (1/T) \sum_{i=0}^{T} {}_t r_{t+i}^*.$$

Thus, equation 2-16 can finally be written as:

(2-17)                    $\lambda_t = T^* (r_L^* - r_L) + {}_t\lambda_{t+T}.$

Equation 2-17 will be very important in the analysis. It says that, with rational expectations, the real exchange rate today must equal the "long-run" real exchange rate ($T$ periods from now) plus a multiple $T$ times the long-run real interest rate differential. When foreign interest rates are higher than domestic interest rates, the real value of the home currency today is depreciated relative to its long-run value ($\lambda_t$ is high relative to $\lambda_{t+T}$); when domestic real interest rates exceed foreign real interest rates, the real value of the home currency is appreciated relative to its long-run value. In this way, policies that affect the long-term real interest rate also have a powerful effect on the real exchange rate. As an example, the combination of expansionary fiscal policy and contractionary monetary policy in the United States in the early 1980s raised U.S. real interest rates sharply, thereby causing a real appreciation of the dollar in relation to the currencies of other industrial countries.

There is an alternative derivation of the exchange rate that is also instructive. Start again with equation 2-13 and substitute for the nominal interest rates using the money demand equations 2-1 and 2-1*. The result is

(2-18)          $e_t = {}_t e_{t+1} + (1/\beta) [\phi(q_t^* - q_t)$
$+ (p_t^* - p_t) - (m_t^* - m_t)].$

We can also rewrite the conditions for equilibrium in the goods market in the home and foreign economies given in equations 2-2 and 2-2*, assuming $\gamma = 0$ for simplicity, to find

(2-19)    $q_t^* - q_t = - 2\delta(e_t + p_t^* - p_t) + \mu(g_t^* - g_t).$

Now, suppose that purchasing power parity also holds ($e = p - p^*$). This causes the real exchange rate to drop out of the exchange rate equation 2-17. The output differential is now only a function of the differential in fiscal spending. In addition, the price differential can be replaced by the exchange rate. Equation 2-17 becomes

$$(2\text{-}20) \quad e_t = [1/(1 + \beta)] [\beta e_{t+1} - \phi\mu (g_t - g_t^*) + (m_t - m_t^*)].$$

This equation explains $e_t$ as a function of $_t e_{t+1}$ and differences in fiscal and monetary policy. Because $e_{t+1}$ can similarly be written in terms of $_{t+1} e_{t+2}$, and so forth, we can recursively substitute for future exchange rates until we find

$$(2\text{-}21) \quad e_t = [1/(1+\beta)] \sum_{i=0}^{\infty} [\beta/(1+\beta)]^i [\phi\mu(g_{t+i}^* - g_{t+i})$$
$$- (m_{t+i}^* - m_{t+i})].$$

From equation 2-21 it can be seen that a current or *future* change in the money supply or fiscal policy will have an effect on the nominal exchange rate today. If it is suddenly expected that $m$ will rise in five periods, then the home currency will depreciate today, by an amount $[\beta/(1+\beta)]^5$ times the change in $m$. With rational expectations, expected changes in future policies affect today's exchange rate, although the effect is smaller the farther off in the future the anticipated change in policy is thought to be.

### Other Intertemporal Extensions

Other important extensions assuming forward-looking behavior can be incorporated into private demand decisions. One example is the inclusion of human wealth as well as financial wealth into private consumption decisions. Human wealth is the present value of future after-tax labor income. Aspects of this relationship have been incorporated into the standard two-country framework by Frenkel and Razin (1988). Another area where expectations can enter into private demand decisions is through investment. In the dynamic simulation model, we shall specify investment demand to depend on Tobin's $q$, which is the ratio of the equity value of a unit of capital to the replacement cost of the unit of capital. The equity value, in turn, depends on the discounted value of expected profits and in this way links investment with expectations of future changes in the economy.

The extension of the Mundell-Fleming framework to include forward-looking consumption behavior can lead to results for the effect of fiscal policy that are dramatically different from those obtained with the simple model. In terms of the framework above, we now add human wealth together with nonhuman wealth in the demand equation. Total wealth becomes

$$(2\text{-}22) \qquad\qquad Z = B + H - A,$$

where

$$(2\text{-}23) \qquad H_t = \sum_{\tau=t}^{\infty} [1/(1 + r_h)^{(\tau - t)}] [Q_\tau - T_\tau].$$

The variable $r_h$ is the real interest rate at which households discount future after-tax labor income (it is assumed to be constant in equation 2-23 but will be allowed to vary in the simulation model). This rate may differ from the real interest rate of government securities for reasons of risk or the finite lifetimes of households.[13] In the simulation model, we will impose the condition that $r_h > r$.

Recalling the government's intertemporal budget constraint in equation 2-10, we have

$$(2\text{-}24) \qquad B_{t-1} = \sum_{\tau=t}^{\infty} [1/(1 + r)^{(\tau - t)}] [T_\tau - G_\tau].$$

The impact of a change in government policy now depends on how the consumer discounts the future stream of after-tax income. If $r_h$ is always equal to $r$ (a case we do *not* consider to be empirically relevant), then we can substitute the government's budget constraint in equation 2-23 to write human wealth as

$$(2\text{-}25) \qquad H_t = \sum_{\tau=t}^{\infty} [1/(1 + r)^{(\tau - t)}] [Q_\tau - G_\tau] - B_t.$$

Using the relationship that wealth $Z_t$ is equal to $B_t + H_t - A_t$, we now have

13. See Blanchard (1985) for a theoretical analysis of how the finite lifetimes of individuals affect the appropriate discount rate of human capital.

$$(2\text{-}26) \qquad Z_t = \sum_{\tau=t}^{\infty} [1/(1 + r)^{(\tau - t)}] [Q_\tau - G_\tau] - A_t.$$

Note that changes in bonds no longer lead to changes in overall aggregate wealth. Note also that the household's wealth is affected by the discounted value of future government spending, and not by taxes per se. This is the strong —and unrealistic—result known as Ricardian equivalence: that government bonds are not net wealth, and that the timing of (lump-sum) taxes does not affect household wealth and, therefore, household consumption patterns.[14]

One implication of Ricardian equivalence is that a permanent rise in government spending, even if financed by bonds rather than by taxes, may result in an equal fall in consumption because the agent internalizes the government's budget constraint. When $G$ goes up, $C$ falls by the same amount, thereby canceling the expansionary demand effect. In our view, this is more of a theoretical curiosity than a practical result.

If $r_h$ is greater than $r$, which we assume in the simulation model, then these strong results no longer hold. In that case, household wealth is affected by the timing of taxes, not just the discounted value of government spending. It is expansionary in general to push taxes off into the future, even if the discounted value of taxation remains unchanged (using the discount rate $r$). Thus, budget deficits are expansionary.

In addition, government bonds become net wealth. Suppose that bonds $B$ are serviced by a stream of tax revenue $T'$ such that

$$B_t = \sum_{\tau=t}^{\infty} [1/(1+r)^{(\tau-t)}] T'.$$

These taxes reduce household wealth by the amount

$$D_t = \sum_{\tau=t}^{\infty} [1/(1+r^h)^{(\tau-t)}] T'.$$

Because $r_h > r$, $B_t$ is greater than $D_t$. Therefore the positive wealth

14. This result is due to Barro (1974). See also Bernheim (1987) for a discussion of the many reasons why this result may break down.

effect of higher holdings of government bonds outweighs the negative effect of the future tax stream necessary to service those bonds.

These intertemporal extensions to include consumption and investment demand emerge naturally in fully specified models based on a representative agent's maximizing an intertemporal utility or cost function, subject to intertemporal budget constraints and production technologies. This is the approach taken in chapter 3 when we present the simulation model. The reader is also referred to Frenkel and Razin (1988) for a detailed analysis using this framework.

## The Supply Side

Except for a consideration of the implications of wage indexation, the analysis so far has concentrated entirely on the demand side of the basic model. An alternative approach to transmission of shocks has emerged from the "real business cycle" approach, which has focused wholly on the supply side (for example, the papers in Barro 1989; Dellas 1986; and Tesar 1990). It seems to us that both supply and demand factors should be considered in attempts to understand the international transmission of economic shocks and policy changes. In developing the role of the supply side, we will follow the approach taken by Bruno and Sachs (1985), which introduced both demand and supply shocks into the Mundell-Fleming framework. We will draw on their approach to highlight how the supply side affects the transmission mechanism already outlined.

Assume that each economy produces its good using three factors of production: capital $(K)$, labor $(L)$, and an intermediate input $(N)$. The intermediate input is assumed to be imported from a third region. The production technology can be described by a production function of the form $Q = Q [V (K, L), N]$, where $Q$ is gross output of the economy and $V$ is the value added by domestic factors of production. The representative firm in each economy is assumed to choose quantities of the three factors to maximize profits, for a given stock of capital $K$ inherited from past investment decisions.

In solving the profit-maximizing problem of the representative firm, it can be shown that the firm sets the marginal product of each variable factor of production $(L$ and $N)$ equal to its price relative to the price of final output. These profit-maximizing conditions define the demand function for each factor. It can be shown (see Bruno and Sachs 1985, chapters 3 and 5) that the result is an aggregate supply schedule of the form

(2-27) $$q^s = -a(w - p) - b(p^n - p) + k,$$

where the coefficients $a$ and $b$ are functions of the elasticities of substitution between $N$ and $V$ and between $K$ and $L$, as well as the shares of each factor in production.

In this framework, a rise in the price of the intermediate good $N$ will lower output and reduce the marginal products of capital and labor. With flexible real wages, the result will be a fall in real wages (and in the profitability of the existing capital stock). With sticky real wages—prevented from falling by unions or contracts—unemployment would be the result. In addition, for a given cost of capital there would be a tendency for investment to fall after the rise in the relative price of $N$. Note that equation 2-27 can also be written as a *price equation*, to replace equation 2-3 in our original expository model:

(2-28) $$p = [a/(a + b)]w + [b/(a + b)]p^N$$
$$+ [1/(a + b)] (q - k).$$

Now, a rise in imported input prices, $p^N$, pushes up the domestic price level.

As well as including the intermediate good in the supply side, we may also want to include it as a component of aggregate demand. If the country is a net importer of $N$, a rise in the price of $N$ will tend to lower domestic demand. Unless a rise in demand from abroad by the producers on $N$ compensates for the lower domestic demand, it is likely that aggregate demand will fall after the price of $N$ increases. Thus, if $N$ is oil (the most relevant case for the 1970s and 1980s), a rise in $p^N$ tends to lower aggregate demand in the oil-importing countries, and that demand has not been fully compensated by the rise in demand from the oil exporters.

The results for a supply shock in this amended model are given in table 2-3. A supply shock, such as a rise in the price of the intermediate good, will shift the aggregate supply curve back and would probably reduce aggregate demand. The result would be unambiguously lower output in the home and foreign economies and ambiguous effects on home and foreign prices. The ambiguities depend on the effect of the shock on demand. With sticky wages, unemployment would rise, although with flexible wages unemployment need not change. With

Table 2-3. *Results for a Supply Shock in the Static Model*

| Exchange rate and wage regime | Rise in intermediate good's price | | | | |
|---|---|---|---|---|---|
| | $q$ | $p^c$ | $\lambda$ | $q^*$ | $p^{c*}$ |
| *Floating exchange rate* | | | | | |
| Fixed wages | − | ± | 0 | − | ± |
| Foreign indexation | + | + | + | 0 | − |
| Home indexation | − | ± | ± | − | ± |
| *Fixed exchange rate (home peg)* | | | | | |
| Fixed wages | − | ± | 0 | − | ± |
| *Fixed exchange rate (foreign peg)* | | | | | |
| Fixed wages | − | ± | 0 | − | ± |

identical economies, there would be no effect on the exchange rate between the home and foreign economies.

## Summary

If we try to include in a single model all of the features we have discussed in this chapter, the algebra would quickly become intractable. This is especially the case if we attempt a careful integration of dynamics and expectations in the model, since the problems of calculating solutions to dynamic models with forward-looking variables is great. This does not mean that the complexities should be ignored. Rather, our strategy is to resort to a numerical simulation analysis in order to solve the model incorporating all of the important features.

It is also clear that the theoretical ambiguities that arise from modifying the basic model will be compounded. We are able to derive clean, unambiguous results only for the simplest framework, with fixed prices and wages and static expectations. Once we add the complications, the theoretical predictions become less clear. This difficulty implies that we must assign some quantitative estimates to key structural parameters if we are to draw inferences that are useful for macroeconomic policy. It is worth highlighting, nonetheless, that the short-run multipliers that we found from the basic, static Mundell-Fleming model (given wage-setting and exchange rate regimes) are remarkably robust to the inclusion of dynamics, expectations, and aggregate supply considerations. The intuition provided by this basic model is therefore very useful, even for understanding the complete simulation model developed in later chapters.

# CHAPTER THREE

# A Dynamic General Equilibrium Model of the World Economy

AS WE HAVE SEEN, the Mundell-Fleming model can be used with a variety of extensions to highlight many of the important channels whereby macroeconomic policies are transmitted between countries. But the exposition in chapter 2 showed that even a simple model quickly becomes difficult to manipulate when stock accumulation and forward-looking expectations are incorporated. It was also clear that the scale and sign of the international transmission of shocks require empirical magnitudes to resolve ambiguities. To pursue the issues further, it seems inevitable to use an empirical model of the world economy. In this chapter we develop in detail a dynamic general equilibrium macroeconomic model that incorporates the key features highlighted in the preceding chapter.[1]

Several features distinguish this model from other empirical global models.

—Both the demand and supply side of the major economies are explicitly modeled.
—Demand equations are based on a combination of intertemporal optimizing behavior and liquidity constrained behavior.
—Major flows such as physical investment, fiscal deficits, and current account imbalances cumulate into stocks of capital, government debt, and net external debt, which in turn change the composition and level of global wealth over time.
—Wealth adjustment determines stock equilibrium in the long run but also feeds back into short-run economic conditions through forward-looking share markets, bond markets, and foreign exchange markets.

1. The model presented here has become known as the McKibbin-Sachs Global model. The current version is called MSG2.

—These national asset markets are linked globally through the high international mobility of capital.

In this chapter we focus on developing the model for application in later chapters. The first section gives a relatively nontechnical outline of the approach we follow in developing the model and a quick summary of the model itself. A more detailed description of the model is provided in the subsequent section. Issues of model calibration and solution are discussed in a following section. A full listing of the model equations and parameters is contained in appendix A to the book. The technical sections of this chapter can be overlooked by the nonspecialist without losing the flow of the analysis.

## History, Methodology, and Overview

The MSG model has been developed in two distinct stages. The first version was a multiregion model based on the theoretical Mundell-Fleming model of chapter 2, with sticky prices. This was essentially a standard Keynesian model with the additional assumption of rational expectations in the asset markets. It formed the basis of the work in Sachs and McKibbin (1985); McKibbin and Sachs (1986a); McKibbin and Sachs (1986b); Ishii, McKibbin, and Sachs (1985); Sachs (1986a); and the Brookings model comparison reported in Bryant and others (1988).

The new model developed in this chapter, which we call MSG2, is based more firmly on microeconomic foundations. It relies heavily on the assumption that economic agents maximize intertemporal objective functions. This idea is very similar to that underlying the class of models known as computable general equilibrium (CGE) models,[2] except that the concepts of time and dynamics are of fundamental importance in the MSG2 model. The various rigidities that are apparent in macroeconomic data are taken into account by allowing for deviations from the fully optimizing behavior. As with any modeling project that purports to describe reality, some trade-offs between theoretical rigor and empirical regularities are inevitable.

The MSG2 model can be described as a dynamic general equilibrium

2. Such models are the basis of the work by Dixon and others (1982), Whalley (1985), and Deardorff and Stern (1986).

model of a multiregion world economy. In this book the countries and regions modeled are the United States, Japan, Germany, the rest of the European Monetary System (denoted REMS),[3] the rest of the Organization for Economic Cooperation and Development economies (denoted ROECD),[4] non-oil developing countries (denoted LDCs),[5] and oil-exporting countries (as for the organization of Petroleum Exporting Countries, denoted OPEC).[6] The model is of moderate size (about three dozen behavioral equations for each industrial region). It is distinctive relative to most other global models in that it solves for a full intertemporal equilibrium in which agents have rational expectations of future variables. In theoretical conception, therefore, the model is close in design to the intertemporal dynamic models of fiscal policy developed in Lipton and Sachs (1983) and Frenkel and Razin (1988). Like the present model, those studies examined fiscal policy in an intertemporal perfect-foresight environment, with considerable attention given to intertemporal optimization and intertemporal budget constraints. Frenkel and Razin are noteworthy for having derived analytical results from their model, rather than relying on simulations as in the current project.

The model has a mix of Keynesian and classical properties by virtue of a maintained assumption of slow adjustment of nominal wages in the labor markets of the United States, Germany, the REMS, and the ROECD (Japan is treated somewhat differently, as described below). Both the German and REMS regions are also assumed to experience long periods of "hysteresis" when unemployment emerges.

We typically solve the model in a linearized form, to facilitate policy optimization exercises with the model and to use linear-quadratic dynamic game theory and dynamic programming solution techniques.[7] We have experimented with the full nonlinear model and have found that the properties of the full, nonlinear model correspond closely to

3. The REMS bloc of countries comprises Belgium, Denmark, France, Ireland, Italy, Luxembourg, and the Netherlands.

4. The ROECD group of countries comprises Australia, Austria, Canada, Finland, Iceland, Norway, Spain, Sweden, Switzerland, the United Kingdom, and New Zealand.

5. The aggregate "non-oil developing countries" is based on the grouping in IMF, *Direction of Trade Statistics* (1989) (annual).

6. As for LDCs, we use the definition provided in the 1989 issue of IMF, *Direction of Trade Statistics* (annual).

7. In general, quantity variables are linearized around their levels relative to potential gross domestic product (GDP), whereas price variables are linearized in logarithmic form.

those of the linearized version, particularly over the initial years of any shocks. The global stability of the linearized model can be readily confirmed by an analysis of the model's eigenvalues.

In fitting the model to macroeconomic data, we adopt a mix of standard CGE calibration techniques and econometric time-series estimates. In CGE models, the parameters of production and consumption decisions are determined by assuming a particular functional form for utility functions and production functions and by assuming that ex post data from an expenditure-share matrix or an input-output table represent an equilibrium of the model. For example, if utility is assumed to be a Cobb-Douglas nesting of the consumption of different goods, then the parameters of the utility function—and, therefore, the demand functions for different goods—are given by the expenditure shares found in actual historical data. The demand function for each good in the system will have price and income elasticities of unity. In most cases the data will determine the parameters of the model, although in some cases additional econometric analysis is required. Issues involved in calibrating the model will be discussed further below.

The model has several attractive features that warrant emphasis in this overview. First, all stock-flow relations are carefully observed. Budget deficits cumulate into stocks of public debt; current account deficits cumulate into net foreign investment positions; and physical investment cumulates into the capital stock. Underlying growth of Harrod-neutral productivity plus growth in the labor force is assumed to be 3 percent for each region. Given the long-run properties of the model, the world economy settles down to the 3 percent steady-state growth path after any set of initial disturbances.

A second attractive feature is that the asset markets are efficient in the sense that asset prices are determined by a combination of intertemporal arbitrage conditions and rational expectations. By virtue of the rational expectations assumption and the partially forward-looking behavior of households and firms, the model can be used to examine the effects of anticipated future policy changes, such as the sequence of future budget deficit cuts called for by the Gramm-Rudman legislation in the United States. Indeed, one of the technical difficulties of using the MSG2 model is that every simulation requires that the "entire" future sequence of anticipated policies be specified. In practice, forty-year paths of policy variables, or endogenous policy rules, must be specified.

A third attractive feature of the model is the specification of the supply side. There are several noteworthy points here. First, factor input decisions are based in part on intertemporal profit maximization by firms. Labor and intermediate inputs are selected to maximize short-run profits, given a stock of capital that is fixed within each period. The capital stock is adjusted according to a "Tobin's $q$" model of investment, derived along the lines in Hayashi (1979). Tobin's $q$ is the shadow value of capital and evolves according to a rational expectations forecast of future after-tax profitability.

Another point of interest regarding the supply side is the specification of the wage-price dynamics in each of the industrial regions. Extensive macroeconomic research has demonstrated important differences in the wage-price processes in the United States, Europe, and Japan, and these differences are incorporated in the model. In particular, the United States and the ROECD (including Canada and Australia) are characterized by nominal wage rigidities arising from long-term nominal wage contracts. In Japan, in contrast, nominal wages are assumed to be renegotiated on an annual, synchronized cycle, with nominal wages selected for the following year to clear the labor market on average. In the ROECD, nominal wages are assumed to be more forward-looking than in the United States, although real wages adjust slowly to clear the labor market. In Germany and the REMS, we assume a degree of hysteresis: if unemployment rises, it remains above the market-clearing level for a substantial period.

## The Model

The complete listing of equations for the MSG2 model is presented in appendix A to the book. In this section the theoretical basis of these equations is outlined.[8]

Each of the regions in the model produces a good that is an imperfect substitute in the production and spending decisions of the other regions. Each industrial region is assumed to produce one final good that is used for investment and consumption purposes in that region and in all of the other regions. The LDC and OPEC regions each produce one good that is a primary input in the production processes of the

8. Note that the parameter notation used in this chapter does not correspond to the notation used in chapter 2.

industrial regions. Demands for the output of the LDC and OPEC regions are therefore derived demands for the production inputs.

In this book only the five industrial country regions are fully modeled with an internal macroeconomic structure. In the LDC and OPEC regions, only the foreign trade and external financial aspects are modeled. Note that in referring to variables of the various regions, we will use the following notation: United States $(U)$, Japan $(J)$, Germany $(G)$, REMS $(E)$, ROECD $(R)$, OPEC $(O)$, and LDCs $(L)$.

To understand the model, it is best to consider one block of the model, that for the United States, and to indicate where necessary any differences in the modeling of the other OECD regions. Within each economy the decisions of households, firms, and governments are modeled.[9]

### Households

Households are assumed to consume a basket of goods in every period; the basket is made up of domestic goods (both public and private) and imported goods from each of the industrial regions. Households receive income to purchase the goods by providing labor services for production and receiving a return from holding financial assets.

Aggregate consumption $(C)$ is nested in the following way:

$$C = C\{C^d, C^m\}$$
$$C^m = C^m\{C_J^U, C_G^U, C_E^U, C_R^U\},$$

where $C^d$ is consumption of the domestic good, $C^m$ is consumption of the imported bundle, and $C_i^U$ is consumption by the United States of goods produced in country $i$ $(i = J, G, E, R)$. Note that in the model listing in appendix A, the superscript for the home country is dropped for convenience.

The decision on how consumption expenditure is allocated among the various goods across time is based on a representative consumer who maximizes an intertemporal utility function of the form[10]

---

9. The reader is referred to Turnovsky (1982) for an excellent discussion of designing a consistent macroeconomic model.

10. For notational convenience we will present all derivations assuming perfect foresight.

$$\int_{t}^{\infty} [U(C_s) + V(G_s)] \, e^{-(\theta - n)(s - t)} \, ds,$$

subject to the wealth constraint

(3-1)     $dF/ds = (r_s - n) (F_s - M_s/P_s)$

$+ W_s L_s (1 - \tau_1)/P_s - P^c {}_s C_s/P_s$

(3-2)     $F_s = M_s/P_s + B_s + q_s K_s$

$+ A_s + VOIL_s + VPE_s.$

Utility in any period is written as an additively separable function of consumption of the private good ($C$) and the public good ($G$). In discounting the future stream of per capita consumption, the rate of time preference ($\theta$) adjusted by the real growth rate ($n$) is used. The wealth accumulation equation given in equation 3-2 assumes that the change in real financial asset holdings ($dF/ds$) consists of a flow return on initial assets ($[r - n] F$), plus real after-tax labor income, less real expenditure on consumption. Financial assets are defined as real money balances ($M/P$), government bonds in the hands of the public ($B$), equity wealth ($qK$), and net foreign asset holdings ($A$). In the definition of financial wealth we also include the value of claims to domestic oil reserves ($VOIL$) and the present value of net profit arising from the pricing behavior of domestic firms in foreign markets ($VPE$).[11] Note that $P$ is the price of the domestic good and $P^c$ is the price of the bundle of consumption goods ($p^c = P^c/P$). Note also that bonds are included as part of financial wealth, but, as the solution given below will show, this does not imply that bonds are part of total wealth.

Setting up the Hamiltonian for this problem, assuming $U(C) = \log C$, and solving gives the familiar first-order conditions:

(3-3)     $p^c {}_t \mu_t = 1/C_t$

(3-4)     $d\mu_t/dt = (\theta - r_t)\mu_t,$

where $\mu$ is the shadow value of consumption. Solving these conditions gives

(3-5)     $dp^c C/dt = (r_t - \theta) \, p^c {}_t C_t.$

11. The treatment of oil is discussed in the next subsection. For treatment of the pass-through

Equation 3-5 implies that if $r = \theta$, per capital real consumption is constant in the steady state.

The budget constraint given in equation 3-1 can be integrated and written as

$$(3\text{-}6) \qquad \int_t^\infty p^c \, {}_sC_s \, e^{-(Rs-n)(s-t)} \, ds = H_t + F_t,$$

where $H_t$ is real human wealth in period $t$ and is defined as

$$(3\text{-}7) \qquad \int_t^\infty W_sL_s \, (1 - \tau_1)/P_s \, e^{-(Rs-n)(s-t)} \, ds = H_t.$$

Real human wealth is the present discounted value of the entire future stream of real, after-tax labor income, where

$$R_s = 1/(s-t) \int_t^s r_v dv$$

and $r_i$ is the period - $i$ short-term real interest rate.

From the first-order condition given in equation 3-5, we find[12]

$$(3\text{-}8) \qquad \int_0^\infty p^c \, {}_tC_t e^{-(Rt-n)s} dt = p^c \, {}_0C_0/(\theta - n).$$

This can be substituted into 3-6 to give

$$(3\text{-}9) \qquad C_t = (\theta - n) \{F_t + H_t\}/p_t^c.$$

Rewriting the human wealth condition gives

$$(3\text{-}10) \qquad dH_t/dt = (r_t - n)H_t - w_tL_t(1 - \tau_1).$$

This solution for aggregate consumption is a familiar life-cycle model where, by the assumption of logarithmic utility, we find that aggregate consumption is a linear function of real wealth, which comprises financial wealth and human wealth.

---

of exchange rate changes into prices by firms operating in foreign markets, see the subsection entitled "Effect of Exchange Rates on Import Prices," below.

12. We obtain equation 3-8 by imposing on equation 3-5 the transversality condition

$$\lim_{t \to \infty} P_t^c C_t \, e^{-(Rt-n)t} = 0.$$

By assuming that aggregate consumption is a CES (constant elasticity of substitution) nesting of domestic and foreign goods, we find equations for expenditure on each good as a function of aggregate expenditure:

(3-11) $\qquad C^d = [\beta_2^{\sigma_1}(P^c/P)^{\sigma_1}]C \qquad \sigma_1 = 1/(1 - \beta_3)$

(3-12) $\qquad C^m = [(1 - \beta_2)^{\sigma_1}(P^c/P^m)^{\sigma_1}]C,$

where

$$P^c C = P^m C^m + PC^d$$
$$P^{c(1 - \sigma_1)} = \beta_2^{\sigma_1} P^{(1 - \sigma_1)} + (1 - \beta_2)^{\sigma_1} P^{m(1 - \sigma_1)}.$$

and $\sigma_1$ is the elasticity of substitution between domestic and imported goods in the consumption bundle. Similarly, if the lower-level nesting of imported goods is assumed to be a CES function, we find similar demand functions for each imported good. Note that, with $\sigma_1 = 1$, this becomes the familiar linear expenditure system.

There is a large body of empirical evidence (see, for example, Hayashi 1982 and Campbell and Mankiw 1987) that suggests that aggregate consumption is determined partially along life-cycle lines, with considerable intertemporal consumption smoothing, and partially along simpler Keynesian lines (perhaps because of liquidity-constrained households). Thus, we specify that consumption spending is a fixed proportion of current net-of-tax income (with no consumption smoothing of the labor income flow), as in standard Keynesian models, and a fixed proportion of wealth, as in standard life-cycle models with infinitely-lived individuals. Thus the aggregate consumption equation takes the following form (note that $\theta = \beta_1$):

(3-13) $\quad C = \beta_6 (\theta - n) (F + H) P/P^c + (1 - \beta_6) (Y - T).$

We also introduce an additional term into the equation for human wealth. This is a risk premium that drives a wedge between the rate at which private individuals can borrow in the capital markets and the rate at which governments borrow.

These modifications to capture empirical regularities in aggregate consumption are assumed not to change the lower-level demand functions. Note that in this model we assume that $r > n$, which introduces another source of saddle-point stability into the model. This assumption is necessary if human wealth is to be positive in the steady state.[13]

### Firms

The cornerstone of aggregate supply in the model is a representative firm that maximizes its value by producing a single output $Q$ at price $P$, subject to a two-input production function. All variables are written in terms of efficiency labor units. Potential long-run growth in the model is assumed to be 3 percent and unchanging over time. Thus, aggregate production is given as

$$(3\text{-}14) \qquad\qquad Q = Q(V, N).$$

Gross output, $Q$, is produced with value added, $V$, and with primary inputs, $N$. In turn, $V$ is produced with capital $K$ and labor $L$, whereas $N$ is produced with imports from the LDCs ($N_L$) and energy, which consists of imports from OPEC ($N_O$) and domestic oil production ($N_P$):

$$(3\text{-}15) \qquad\qquad V = V(K, L)$$
$$(3\text{-}16) \qquad\qquad N = N(N_o, N_L, N_P).$$

We assume that domestic oil resources and imports of OPEC oil are perfect substitutes. Total oil demand as an intermediate input is assumed to be divided between the two sources on the basis of historical shares. As noted above, we also assume that households hold claims to domestic oil resources.

The capital stock changes according to the rate of fixed capital formation $J$ and the rate of geometric depreciation $\delta$:

$$(3\text{-}17) \qquad\qquad dK/dt = J_t - (\delta + n)K_t.$$

Note that $n$ appears in equation 3-17 because $K$ is in efficiency labor units rather than in levels. Fixed capital formation $J$ is itself a composite good, produced with a Cobb-Douglas technology that has as inputs the domestic goods from the United States and the final goods of Germany, REMS, Japan, and the ROECD. The price of $J$ is simply a weighted sum of the prices of the home goods $P$ ($P^U$ for the United

---

13. Steady-state human wealth is $WL(1 - \tau_1)/(r - n)$.

States) and the dollar import prices ($E^i P^i$; $i = J, G, E, R$) of goods from the other OECD regions:

(3-18) $\quad J = \Pi_i \, (Q^i)^{\beta_{18i}} \qquad i = \{U, J, G, E, R\}, \quad \Sigma_i \beta_{18i} = 1$

(3-19) $\qquad P^J = \Pi_i \, (E^i P^i)^{\beta_{18i}} \qquad i = \{U, J, G, E \, R\}.$

Following the cost of adjustment models of Lucas (1967) and Treadway (1969), we assume that the investment process is subject to rising marginal costs of installation, with total real investment expenditures $I$ equal to the value of direct purchases of investment $P^J * J/P$, plus the unit costs of installation. These unit costs, in turn, are assumed to be a linear function of the rate of investment $J/K$, so that adjustment costs are $P^J * J \, [(\phi_o/2) \, (J/K)]/P$. Total investment expenditure is therefore

(3-20) $\qquad\qquad I = [P^J + P^J \, (\phi_o/2)(J/K)] \, J/P.$

The goal of the firm is to choose inputs of $L$, $N$, and $J$ to maximize intertemporal after-tax profits. The firm faces a stochastic problem, a point that is ignored in the derivation of the firm's behavior (in other words, the firm is assumed to believe its estimates of future variable with subjective certainty). The firm's deterministic problem, formally stated, is

$$\int_t^\infty \{(1-\tau_2)\,[Q_s - (W_s/P_s)L_s - (P_s^N/P_s)N_s] - (P_s^J/P_s)I_s\} \; e^{-(R_s - n)s} \; ds,$$

subject to equations 3-14 through 3-20.

Solving the firm's problem, we find the set of conditions expressed in equations 3-21 through 3-24:

(3-21) $\qquad\quad Q_L = w \qquad = W/P$

(3-22) $\qquad\quad Q_N = p^n \qquad = P^n/P$

(3-23) $\qquad\qquad \lambda = p^J \, (1 + \phi_o J/K), \text{ where } \qquad p^J = P^J/P$

(3-24) $\quad d\lambda_s/ds = (r + \delta)\lambda_s \quad - (1-\tau_2) \, Q_K$
$$\qquad\qquad\qquad - 0.5 p^J \phi_o (J/K)^2,$$

where $\lambda$ is the shadow value of investment.

There are three key points to be noted from these solutions. First, inputs of $L$ and $N$ are hired to the point at which the marginal pro-

ductivities of these factors equal their factor prices. This relation yields
the equations for the derived demand for $L$ and $N$ given in equations
3-21 and 3-22.

The second point in seen by interpreting equation 3-24, which can
be integrated to find

$$(3\text{-}25) \qquad \lambda_t = \int_t^\infty [(1 - \tau_2) Q_{Ks} + \Phi_K] \, e^{-(R_s+\delta)s} \, ds.$$

Here $Q_K$ is the marginal product of capital in the production function,
and $\Phi_K$ ($= 0.5p^I {}_s\phi_o[J_s/K_s]^2$) is the marginal product of capital in
reducing adjustment costs in investment. Therefore $\lambda$ is the increment
to the value of the firm from a unit increase in investment. It has an
interpretation similar to that of Tobin's $q$. If we assume that $q = p^I\lambda/P$, we can rewrite equation 3-23 as

$$(3\text{-}26) \qquad\qquad J = [(q-1)/\phi_o]K.$$

The third point is that gross fixed capital formation can be written
in terms of Tobin's "marginal" $q$ as in equation 3-26.

In the specific application in the MSG2 model, the gross output
production function is taken to be a two-level Cobb-Douglas function
in $V$ and $N$, where $V$ is a Cobb-Douglas function of $L$ and $K$ and $N$ is
a Cobb-Douglas function of oil and non-oil primary inputs. Oil is then
a Cobb-Douglas function of domestic production and imports from
OPEC. Following the results in Hayashi (1979), we have also modified
the investment function derived in equation 3-26, for empirical realism,
by writing $J$ as a function not only of $q$ but also of the level of flow
capital income at time $t$. One argument for the inclusion of current
profits is that it captures the existence of firms that are unable to borrow
and lend, as assumed in the theoretical derivation, and therefore invest
out of retained earnings. The modified investment equation is of the
form

$$(3\text{-}26') \quad J_t = \beta_{16} [(q-1)/\phi_o] K + (1-\beta_{16}) [Q - (W/P)L - (P^N/P)N].$$

The supply side of the U.S. block of the model is completed with
the wage equation. Wages are specified following a modified Taylor
(1980) overlapping contract model. The nominal wage change is a
function of past consumer price changes ($\pi^c_{t-1}$), rationally expected
future price changes ($\pi^c_t$), and the level of unemployment in the econ-

omy (labor demand, $L$, relative to full employment, $L^f$), according to a standard Phillips curve mechanism:

$$(3\text{-}27) \qquad d \log W/dt = \beta_{22}\pi_t^c + (1 - \beta_{22}) \pi_{t-1}^c$$
$$+ 0.2^* \log (L/L^f),$$

where $L^f$ represents the inelastically supplied full-employment stock of labor. The parameter $\beta_{22}$ in equation 3-27 determines how much weight is given to backward-looking versus forward-looking price expectations.

As already noted, we allow for differences in the wage dynamics of the different regions. Wage behavior in the United States and the ROECD is characterized by equation 3-27. In Japan, we specify that wages are set one period ahead at their expected market-clearing levels. Thus, let $(_tW_{t+1})^f$ be the wage expected to clear the labor market at time $t + 1$, in the sense that $_tL_{t+1} = L^f$:

$$(3\text{-}28) \qquad W_{t+1}^J = (_tW_{t+1}^J)^f.$$

Following Blanchard and Summers (1986) and Sachs (1986b), we build "hysteresis" into the labor markets in Germany and the REMS. For each of these regions we modify the wage equation in the following way:

$$(3\text{-}29) \quad d \log W/dt = \beta_{22}\pi_t^c + (1-\beta_{22})\pi_{t-1}^c + 0.1(L/L^* - 1)$$

$$(3\text{-}30) \qquad L^* = L^f + 0.2(L^*_{t-1} - L^f) + 0.7(L_{t-1} - L^f).$$

In equation 3-29, wages respond to the difference between labor demand and the short-run natural rate ($L^*$). The short-run natural rate adjusts slowly to the long-run natural rate, and it can deviate from the full employment level for a substantial period.

### Government

We assume that the government in each country divides spending $G$ among final goods in the same proportion as does the private sector, so that

$$(3\text{-}31) \qquad G_i^U/G^U = C_i^U/C^U \qquad i = J, G, E, R.$$

The government finances this spending through company taxes and personal income taxes and by issuing government debt. The government budget constraint can be written as[14]

(3-32) $$dB/dt = DEF = G - T + (r-n)B.$$

Assuming a transversality condition that debt has value,

$$\lim_{s \to \infty} B_s e^{-(Rs-n)} = 0,$$

equation 3-32 can be integrated and written as

$$B_t = \int_t^\infty (T_s - G_s)e^{-(Rs-n)(s-t)}ds.$$

The current level of debt to GDP is the present value of future primary budget surpluses. With an outstanding stock of debt, if a government runs a budget deficit today it must run a budget surplus at some point in the future; otherwise, the debt will have no value.

In simulating fiscal policy we make several assumptions. The government can choose policy either exogenously or on the basis of dynamic optimization of some objective function. In the case of an exogenous change in fiscal policy, it is important that tax and spending policies be consistent with the intertemporal budget constraint of the public sector. In particular, as already mentioned, starting from any initial stock of public debt, the discounted value of current and future taxes must equal the discounted value of government spending plus the initial value of outstanding public debt.

If the tax schedule were not subsequently altered, the stock of public debt would eventually rise without bound, at an explosive geometric rate. To prevent this, we assume that labor income taxes are increased each year by enough to cover the increasing interest costs on the rising stock of public debt. Letting $B_0$ be the stock of debt before expansion, the tax rule is therefore

(3-33) $$T_t = T_o + \tau_1 [(W/P)L] + \tau_2 [Q - (W/P)L - (P_N/P)N] + T_s.$$

Here, $\tau_1$ is the average tax rate on labor income; $\tau_2$ is the average tax rate (corporate and personal) on capital income; $T_s$ is a shift term in

14. Note that we have explicitly taken the change in the stock of money out of the government budget constraint. This implies that fiscal changes are funded by changes in debt or taxes. All changes in the stock of money occur through open market operations by the central bank.

the tax schedule that rises along with the increase in interest payments on the public debt, $r_tB_t - r_0B_0$; and $T_o$ is an exogenous tax shift parameter. It is assumed that $T_s$ falls entirely on labor income (this assumption is made for convenience only, and will be modified in a later version of the model).

### Financial Markets

It is a common dilemma in general equilibrium models to explain why agents desire to hold money balances. A demand for money can be derived only if money gives direct utility, if money is a factor of production, or through a constraint that money must be used in transactions. In the MSG2 model, money is given a role by assuming that it is a factor of production. It is a factor of production not because firms require money balances in day-to-day operations, but because the final produced good cannot be consumed by agents until it is purchased with money. Using this interpretation, we can modify the producer's decision by adding a first-order condition similar to that for the other variable factors; the derived demand for money will be a function of output and the relative price of money. By specifying a CES technology in purchasing goods, we impose a unitary income elasticity, but an interest elasticity proportional to the elasticity of substitution between money and the final good. The empirical literature on money demand can be used to determine the interest elasticity and, therefore, an implied elasticity of substitution.

Asset markets are assumed to be perfectly integrated across the OECD regions. In the model calibrated on 1986 data, which is the basis of the empirical calculations in this book, we assume that capital controls in the REMS are not effective. Expected returns on loans denominated in the currencies of the various regions are equalized period to period, according to the following interest arbitrage relation:

$$(3\text{-}34) \qquad i_t^i = i_t^j + ({}_tE_{jt+1}^i - E_{jt}^i)/E_{jt}^i,$$

where $E_{jt}$ is the exchange rate between currencies of countries $i$ and $j$.

Thus, we do not allow for risk premiums on the assets of alternative currencies. We choose the assumption of perfect capital mobility and zero risk premiums in light of the failure of the empirical literature on exchange rates to demonstrate the existence of stable risk premiums among international currencies. In the simulations of the model, this is equivalent to assuming that the risk premiums are independent of the shocks imposed on the model and the adjustment of any endogenous variables in the model.

### Balance of Payments and the LDCs and OPEC

Any trade imbalances are financed by flows of assets among countries. To determine net asset positions, we make several simplifying assumptions. All new OPEC loans to each region are assumed to be in historical proportions. Similarly, new loans to the LDCs are also fixed in historical proportions. All other net capital flows are restricted to be consistent by imposing the constraint that current account balances and trade account balances sum to zero for the world as a whole. For the United States, Japan, Germany, ROECD, and OPEC, the current account is determined under the assumption that domestic agents have free, unrationed access to international borrowing and lending at the international interest rate. It is assumed for simplicity that all international borrowing and lending takes place in dollar-demonstrated assets. For the LDCs, in contrast, the scale of borrowing is set exogenously under the assumption that the amount of loans available to the LDCs is rationed by considerations of country risk. Note that the rate of interest on these loans does not have a risk premium built into it. For example, loans from the United States and OPEC are made in U.S. dollars at the interest rate on U.S. government debt.

For the goods of OPEC and the LDCs that feed into the production processes of the industrial regions, there is a single uniform world price of goods that applies in all markets at all times (that is, the law of one price holds). Letting $P^O$ be the dollar price of OPEC goods, we assume that $P^O$ is a variable markup over a basket of OECD goods, so that

$$(3\text{-}35) \quad P^O = P^O(P^U, E_U^J P^J, E_U^G P^G, E_U^E P^E, E_U^R P^R)\, h(X^O)$$
$$h' > 0.$$

Note that $E_U^i$ is in dollars per unit of currency $i$. The function $P^O$ $(.\,,.\,,.\,,.)$ is linear homogeneous and increasing in the prices of the OECD goods. The function $h(X^O)$ makes the OPEC markup an increasing function of the total demand for OPEC exports $X^O$ to the other regions. An analogous equation governs the price of LDC commodities. The local currency price of OPEC goods in a non-U.S. region $j$ is then given by $P_j^O = E_j^U P^O$, according to the law of one price. A similar equation applies for the LDC commodity export.

### Effect of Exchange Rates on Import Prices

Recent studies such as those by Baldwin and Krugman (1987) and Mann (1987) have pointed to the existence of a significant lag in the pass-through of exchange rate changes into import prices in the U.S. economy. The appreciation of the U.S. dollar during 1981–85 did not bring about an instantaneous and equivalent fall in import prices, and the recent depreciation of the U.S. dollar has not been associated with a commensurate rise in import prices. To capture part of this effect, we assume a lag in the exchange rate effect on imports of the following form:

$$(3\text{-}36) \qquad e_t^{i*} = e_{t-1}^{i*} + \beta_{23}\,(e_t^i - e_{t-1}^i) + (1 - \beta_{23})$$
$$\times\,(e_{t-1}^{*i} - e_{t-2}^{*i}) + 0.05\,(e_{t-1}^i - e_{t-1}^{*i}),$$

where $e_t^{*i}$ is the logarithm of the exchange rate that enters the pricing and demand equations in each country. This formulation assumes that each foreign firm prices the same way in a particular country but (possibly) differently in different countries. For example, both Japanese and German firms selling goods in the U.S. market allow the same proportional flow-on of exchange rate changes in pricing in the U.S. market. This behavior is consistent with various arguments about imperfect competition in international trade (see Dornbusch 1987 or Krugman 1986). The profits and losses of the firms involved in exporting are translated into the valuation of the firm in the original economies and therefore also into the wealth calculations for each economy.

### Model Closure

The model is completed by assuming market-clearing conditions. Prices in the United States (and the other OECD regions) are fully flexible within each period, so that demand for U.S. output (domestic demand plus export demand) equals output supply. Short-term nominal interest rates adjust to clear the money market.

## Calibration and Model Solution

Before we can use the model developed above for numerical simulation, we need to provide values for the parameters (calibration),
and we need a method for solving models in which expectations are
forward looking.

### Calibration

There are two issues that need to be dealt with in calibrating this
model for use in empirical simulations: first, to choose specific empirical values for the behavioral parameters; second, to choose a cross-
section of data at some time around which to linearize the model for
game-theoretic applications. The data and parameters must be internally consistent with the model specification. In finding parameters
for the model, we use a mix of techniques from the CGE literature as
well as time-series evidence.

In most CGE models, both the data and the model parameters are
manipulated to replicate an equilibrium of the model. In a dynamic
model such as the MSG2 model, a corresponding procedure would be
to choose a steady state of the model around which to calibrate. In
principle, this is reasonable for a theoretical model because we could
assume that we start at a steady state, since we are not concerned with
recreating any actual year of data (see McKibbin 1986). To replicate
an actual data set is more problematic because we are trying to keep
within the bounds consistent with this data set. For example, a positive
stock of outstanding debt for a country in the steady state should be
associated with a trade balance surplus, since the stock of debt needs
to be serviced in the steady state. Yet during a period of adjustment
away from the steady state, positive debt is usually associated with a
trade account deficit during the early stages of debt accumulation. It
is important to ensure that the data replicate the trade position as well
as the initial debt position, and this is not always possible by assuming
steady-state relationships.

Our technique is to choose a set of behavioral parameters that fall
within the range found in the many empirical studies of time-series
relations (for example, factor shares and elasticities of substitution).
Given this set of parameters and data for macro aggregates (for example, output and consumption expenditure), which are based on data
for 1986, we can use steady-state relations in the model to generate

other data (for example, human wealth). A summary of the key features of this procedure follows. The notation used is that found in appendix A (the actual values of parameters are also listed in appendix A, and a full listing of data sources is given in appendix D).

For behavioral parameters, we assume the same price and income elasticities in each industrial economy. The exception is the treatment of labor markets, as discussed above.

The real sector is calibrated using steady-state and first-order conditions where possible. We want to use as much actual data as possible to maximize the relevance of the model, especially since we linearize the model for the dynamic game applications. Some steady-state conditions, however, cannot be used, as already mentioned. For example, the actual asset stocks for 1986 and actual trade flows in 1986 are not consistent with being in the steady state; a positive holding of net foreign debt should be associated with a trade balance surplus. That we cannot assume that the historical data represent a steady state of the model is unavoidable. The point around which the model is linearized should be interpreted as a point on the stable adjustment path toward the steady state.

For any equation in which adjustment occurs according to some share formulation, we assume that the shares are those prevailing in 1986. For example, the use of Japanese goods in U.S. investment is assumed to be equal to the 1986 ratio of Japanese goods in total U.S. consumption. In addition, the share of total LDC expenditure on each industrial country's good is assumed to equal that share in 1986. Any change in total LDC expenditure is then proportionately allocated among the goods from the different regions.

We also need data for trade flows and asset stocks around which to linearize the model. The 1986-based data that we use for the matrix of bilateral trade flows is given in table 3-1. The assumptions on asset holdings are given in table 3-2. Because of the assumption that assets are perfect substitutes, only net debt positions are required for asset holdings. The data on asset stocks by country are poor. We combine data from different sources and make approximating assumptions as required. Details of the procedures are given in appendix D to the book.

We select the long-run potential growth rates ($n$) of each region at 3 percent annually and the steady-state value for the real interest rate ($r_0$) at 5 percent. We also assume that the rate of time preference is equal to the real rate of interest. The choice of equal rates of time

Table 3-1. *1986 Trade as a Percentage of Importing Country GDP*

| | Exporter | | | | | | |
|---|---|---|---|---|---|---|---|
| Importer[a] | United States | Japan | Germany | REMS | ROECD | LDCs | OPEC |
| United States | . . . | 2.009 | 0.620 | 0.756 | 2.452 | 2.285 | 0.474 |
| Japan | 1.437 | . . . | 0.214 | 0.277 | 0.937 | 1.764 | 1.302 |
| Germany | 1.287 | 1.218 | . . . | 8.890 | 4.927 | 3.268 | 0.669 |
| REMS | 1.725 | 0.769 | 5.662 | . . . | 4.889 | 2.977 | 1.391 |
| ROECD | 4.120 | 1.431 | 3.605 | 9.727 | . . . | 2.292 | 0.526 |
| LDCs[b] | 1.495 | 1.355 | 0.792 | 1.297 | 1.215 | . . . | 0.526 |
| OPEC[b] | 0.249 | 0.281 | 0.197 | 0.408 | 0.373 | 0.426 | . . . |

Sources: Authors' calculations from International Monetary Fund, *Direction of Trade Statistics*, as of July 1987 monthly publication. Note that each bilateral flow is an average of reported imports of A from B and exports from B to A.

a. REMS, rest of the European Monetary System countries (see note 3 to text); ROECD, rest of Organization for Economic Cooperation and Development (see note 4); LDCs, non-oil developing countries (see note 5); OPEC, oil-exporting countries (see note 6).

b. Percent of U.S. GDP.

Table 3-2. *1986 Portfolio Matrix*
Ratio of net asset holdings to U.S. GDP

| | Claim held by | | | | | | |
|---|---|---|---|---|---|---|---|
| Claim on | United States | Japan | Germany | REMS | ROECD | LDCs | OPEC |
| United States | 30.00 | 1.20 | 1.20 | 4.90 | 0.10 | 0 | 4.30 |
| Japan | 0 | 12.13 | 0 | 0 | 0 | 0 | 0.60 |
| (**) | 0 | 25.80 | 0 | 0 | 0 | 0 | 1.28 |
| Germany | 0 | 0 | 4.83 | 0 | 0 | 0 | 0.60 |
| (**) | 0 | 0 | 22.60 | 0 | 0 | 0 | 2.81 |
| REMS | 0 | 0 | 0 | 13.46 | 0 | 0 | 0.60 |
| (**) | 0 | 0 | 0 | 35.00 | 0 | 0 | 1.56 |
| ROECD | 0 | 0 | 0 | 0 | 11.68 | 0 | 0.60 |
| (**) | 0 | 0 | 0 | 0 | 25.00 | 0 | 1.28 |
| LDCs | 7.60 | 2.70 | 2.60 | 2.80 | 3.50 | 0 | 1.70 |
| OPEC | 0 | 0 | 0 | 0 | 0 | 0 | 0 |

Sources: Authors' calculations from IMF, *World Economic Outlook* (Washington, April 1988); World Bank, *World Debt Tables* (1988); *Economic Report of the President, (1988)*; Chouraqi, Jones, and Montador (1986); Japanese Ministry of Finance; and Mattione (1985).

(**) percent of own-country GDP.

preference for the residents of each country is dictated by the problem that in infinite-horizon multicountry models, one country would dominate the world eventually.[15] All initial prices are normalized at 1 (= 0 in logarithms).

To ensure that all equations are consistent, we modify some of the data used to calibrate the model. Given the bilateral trade flows, we have data on trade balances. Given values for $Y$, $C$, and $G$ from the

15. Alternative assumptions can be made, such as allowing for unrelated agents in the model as in McKibbin (1986), but this is somewhat artificial.

national accounts of individual countries, we can (by the goods-market-clearing identity) generate data for investment:

$$I = Q - C - G - TB.$$

Given assumed values for $K$ and $\beta_{15}$ (the cost of adjusting capital), we can use the net investment equation

$$I = J(1 + 0.5\beta_{15}J/K),$$

to generate a value for $J$. We choose the positive-valued solution. The next step is to find a value for $q$, the shadow value of capital. We can use the equation for gross capital formation to find $q$:

$$q = 1 + (J/K)\beta_{15}.$$

This result can be substituted into the equation for the evolution of $q$, assuming that $q$ is unchanging, to find the steady-state marginal product of capital:

$$dq/dK = [(r + \beta_{14})q - p^I(\beta_{15}/2)(J_t/K_t)^2] / (1 - \tau_2).$$

We know that the share of capital in production is a function of the marginal product of capital, the capital stock, and output. Given the share of capital, the capital stock, and output, we can derive the share of labor. The real wage is normalized at unity, and therefore we use the first-order condition for labor demand to obtain labor measured in efficiency units. Given $Y$, $K$, $L$, factor shares, and assumptions about factor substitutability, we can derive an implied value for the constant $(\beta_{10})$ in the production function.

To calibrate the household sector of the model, we use similar techniques of appealing to first-order conditions and steady-state relations. The steady-state human wealth equation is:

$$H = WL(1 - \tau_1)/(r - n).$$

We can now generate a series for human wealth that, when combined with assumptions of initial asset holdings, gives a series for total wealth.

The assumptions about substitutability between consumption of different goods and initial shares of the goods in the utility function are based on empirical estimates of price elasticities. Consider equation 3-11 above, which can be rewritten in the form of percentage change:

$$c^d = c + \sigma_1 (p^c - p + \log \beta_2),$$

where

$$p = \log P$$
$$c = \log C.$$

Now $dc^d/dp$ is the price elasticity of the demand for the domestic good ($\epsilon_{cp}$), and we find that $\epsilon_{cp} = -\sigma_1$.

In the case of the CES function, there is a unique relation between the price elasticity and the elasticity of substitution in consumption. Taking the ratio of equations 3-11 and 3-12, it can be shown that

$$c^d/c^m = \{\beta_2 P^m/[(1 - \beta_2)P]\}_1^{\sigma}.$$

In solving for $\beta_2$, it can be shown that

$$\beta_2 = (C^{ds_1})/(C^{ms_1} + C^{ds_1}) \qquad s_1 = 1/\sigma_1.$$

We can now use these to find the shares ($\beta_2$) and elasticity of substitution ($\sigma_1$), given price elasticities and initial consumption levels. Alternatively, we can use any empirical evidence on the elasticity of substitution and expenditure shares to find the implied price elasticities.

### Model Solution

Solving a model such as the MSG2 model, which assumes rational expectations in different markets, is not a straightforward exercise. Forward-looking variables such as asset prices, consumption, and investment decisions are conditioned on the entire future path of all variables in the model. We are presented with a two-point, boundary-value problem; values for inherited variables (state variables) are known, and the expected paths of exogenous variables are assumed to be known. But for forward-looking variables we can only assume some terminal conditions. Various techniques are available for solving these models, such as the "multiple shooting" algorithm outlined by Lipton and others (1982) and the technique for nonlinear models given by Fair and Taylor (1983). An analytical solution is provided by Blanchard and Kahn (1980) for linear models. We use a technique that we will call the MSG technique. We will introduce it here only briefly; the reader is referred to appendix C of the book for more details and a comparison of this technique with other techniques.

The MSG technique is based on a backward-recursion algorithm used for solving dynamic games. An advantage of this technique is that we can solve for dynamic game equilibria, as well as for the standard rational expectation equilibria, with minimal computational cost.

The model is first linearized. This is done because we use the model for dynamic games that require linearity for a unique solution.[16] Once the model is linearized, we express it in minimal state-space representation. Because the model has been linearized, we know from the Blanchard-Kahn technique that we can express the jumping (or expectation) variables as a function of the known state variables in any period and the future path of exogenous variables. The goal of the technique is to find this rule numerically. In the algorithm used, we first assume a terminal period ($T$) in which we impose stationarity conditions on the expected variables in the model. The model is then solved in period $T - 1$, conditional both on the initial conditions in period $T - 1$ and on the terminal solution we have imposed for period $T$. The period of solution is then moved back to period $T - 2$, and the model is solved—again conditional on the path for expected variables we found for the period $T - 1$ solution and on the imposed terminal solution. Each period we find a rule linking jumping variables to state variables and exogenous variables that is, in general, time dependent. We continue moving backward and solving forward until the rule converges to a time-invariant rule. The form of the rule itself is independent of the shock or the initial conditions.

By compressing the entire future of the economy into a rule of this form, we have transformed the model into a standard difference equation model. For any shock, the rule we have found will give the value of the jumping variables. The model can then be simply solved forward. The extension of this technique to dynamic games is discussed in appendix C.

Each time the model is changed, the search for saddle-point stable rules for the jumping variables need only be performed once. After the rule is found, any shock to exogenous variables or initial conditions can be simply solved as with any standard difference equation model.

---

16. An earlier nonlinear version of the model was solved using the Fair-Taylor technique, and the nonlinear model was found to have properties quite similar to those of the linear model. Given the potential saving in computing time and computing constraints, we continue to use the linear model.

## Summary

The model developed in this chapter will play a key role in subsequent chapters. Although there appears to be a substantial amount of complication introduced in the model, the model's firm basis in economic theory makes the results from the model used in the following chapters relatively easy to understand.

# CHAPTER FOUR

# International Transmission of Shocks and Policy Changes

WE ATTEMPT in this chapter to place some empirical magnitudes on the size of the policy spillovers among countries by using the multi-country model developed in chapter 3. We are able to explore both the long-run and short-run consequences of a given shock, explicitly incorporating expectations of the nature of the shock. For the long-run response we have an analytical solution to the model, and for the short-run properties we use the numerical simulation technique outlined in chapter 3.

We consider the domestic and cross-border consequences of four kinds of shocks: actual and anticipated changes in monetary policy in each region; actual and anticipated changes in fiscal policy in each region; an exogenous increase in the price of oil-exporting countries' (OPEC) oil; and an exogenous cutback in lending to the non-oil developing countries (LDCs).

In some of the results the direct effects familiar from other macroeconometric models are offset or reversed by changes in market participants' expectations of the future path of the world economy, especially in cases of changes in policy that are announced in advance, such as the Gramm-Rudman deficit reduction package in the United States. The shocks we examine are implemented assuming that asset market participants fully understand the shock, forming rational expectations of future shocks and understanding the way in which the global economy works. This is obviously an extreme assumption, but it gives a benchmark for comparison of the results obtained from the traditional approach of assuming slowly changing expectations. The traditional approach used in many large-scale macroeconometric models leads to small movements in asset prices in response to changes in the economy and is unable to account for the large changes in asset prices experienced during the 1980s. Our approach highlights the fundamental importance of expectations formation in determining many macroeconomic outcomes.

To aid in digesting the vast amount of material generated by the combination of a large range of variables and shocks, we will present graphical results for several key variables. A full set of tabular results can be found in appendix B.

## Fiscal Policy Transmission

When a change in fiscal policy is implemented, it is important that tax and spending policies in any country be consistent with the inter-temporal budget constraint facing each government. The actual policy change is a permanent increase in the level of government expenditure, with taxes rising only because of endogenous changes in tax receipts as the result of changes in economic activity. Over time, taxes on labor income are also assumed to rise to cover the increasing interest burden of a rising stock of public debt. The overall fiscal deficit remains permanently higher, although the primary fiscal deficit (defined as spending net of interest payments minus total taxes) eventually turns to a surplus to prevent the explosive growth of government debt.

In this section we examine the effects of fiscal expansions in the major regions, focusing on the United States, Japan, and Germany. We examine two alternative fiscal expansions. The first is a permanent increase of 1 percent of GDP in the level of government expenditure. The second is an announced gradual expansion of fiscal spending equal to 1 percent of GDP in the first year, 2 percent of GDP in the second year, and then (permanently) 3 percent of GDP from the third year onward. The announced policy is assumed to be perfectly credible to the private sector.

### Long Run

For each change in fiscal policy we examine, the long-run results will be qualitatively the same. Recall that we implement the fiscal expansion so that a permanent deficit emerges. The long-run ratio of the level of government debt to GDP is equal to the long-run ratio of the deficit to GDP divided by the gap between the real interest rate and the real growth rate. In our example—with a permanent increase in the deficit by 1 percent of GDP, an initial real interest rate of 5 percent, and a real growth rate of 3 percent—this would imply a long-run increase in the ratio of debt to GDP of 50.0 percent. But our assumption that taxes adjust to cover interest servicing implies that the long-run ratio of debt to GDP only rises by 33.3 percent (for example, 1/0.03).

Consumption in this model is affected by the path of taxes in part because of short-run liquidity constraints, but also because in the model consumers discount future income at a higher rate than the real interest rate. This implies that, for a given rise in government spending, steady-state consumption will not fall by as much as the rise in government spending. With excess demand in the long run, real interest rates rise, partially crowding out private spending. Lower investment expenditure results in a lower capital stock, which is consistent with the higher marginal product of capital. Although the lower capital stock implies a lower level of output, the real growth rate of output returns to 3 percent.

The assumption of perfect asset substitutability and the large size of the U.S. economy imply that world interest rates will also rise in response to a U.S. fiscal expansion. This implies that, in the long run, the transmission of the fiscal expansion will be negative with respect to foreign output. In addition to the buildup of domestic government debt, there will be an accumulation of foreign debt. To service this foreign debt, the long-run trade position must move toward surplus, and this implies a relatively depreciated real home currency in the long run.

*Short-run Dynamics*

For the short-run dynamics the distinction between the anticipated and unanticipated permanent fiscal expansion is important. The two types of shocks will be examined in turn.

PERMANENT FISCAL EXPANSION. Consider the short-run simulation results for an unanticipated U.S. fiscal expansion defined as a permanent rise in the level of government spending by 1 percent of GDP. The detailed short-run simulation results for this fiscal expansion can be found in table B-1 in appendix B and are summarized in figure 4-1. We use the same scaling conventions as discussed in appendix B. Output and the trade and current account balances are measured as deviations from a baseline that is expressed as a proportion of baseline potential GDP in the home country. Inflation (defined in terms of the

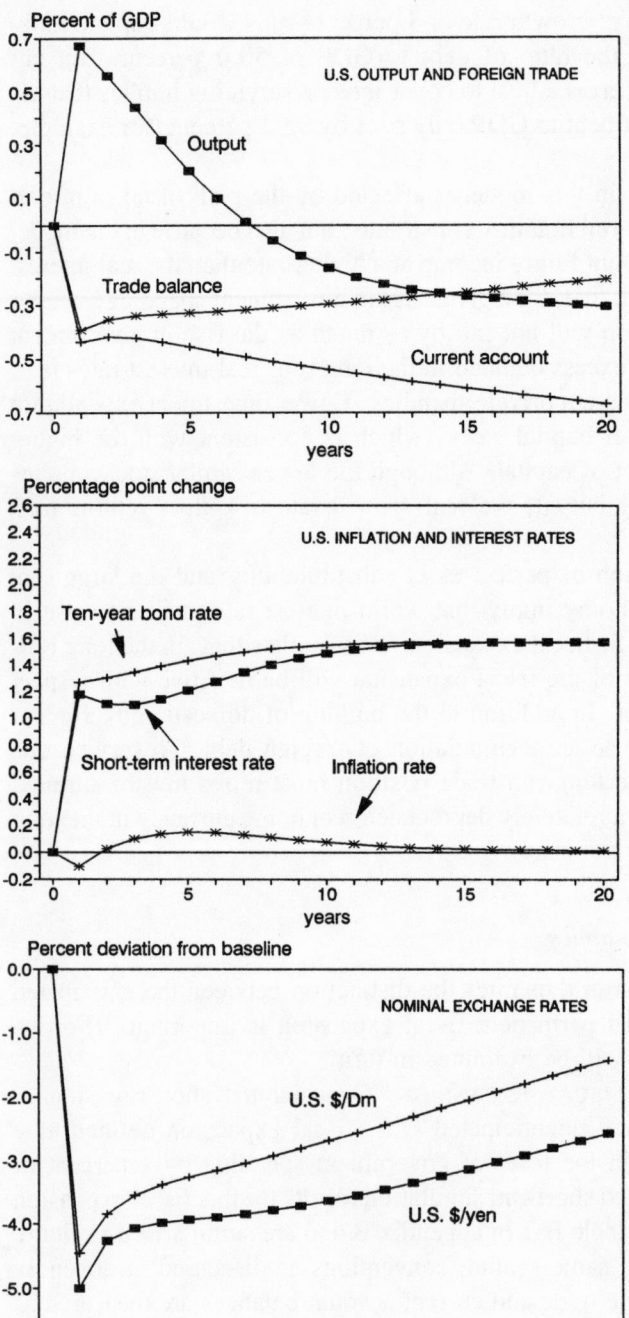

Figure 4-1.
*Permanent U.S.
Fiscal Expansion of
1 Percent of GDP*

a. For details on the scaling notation in this and subsequent figures in the chapter, see appendix B.

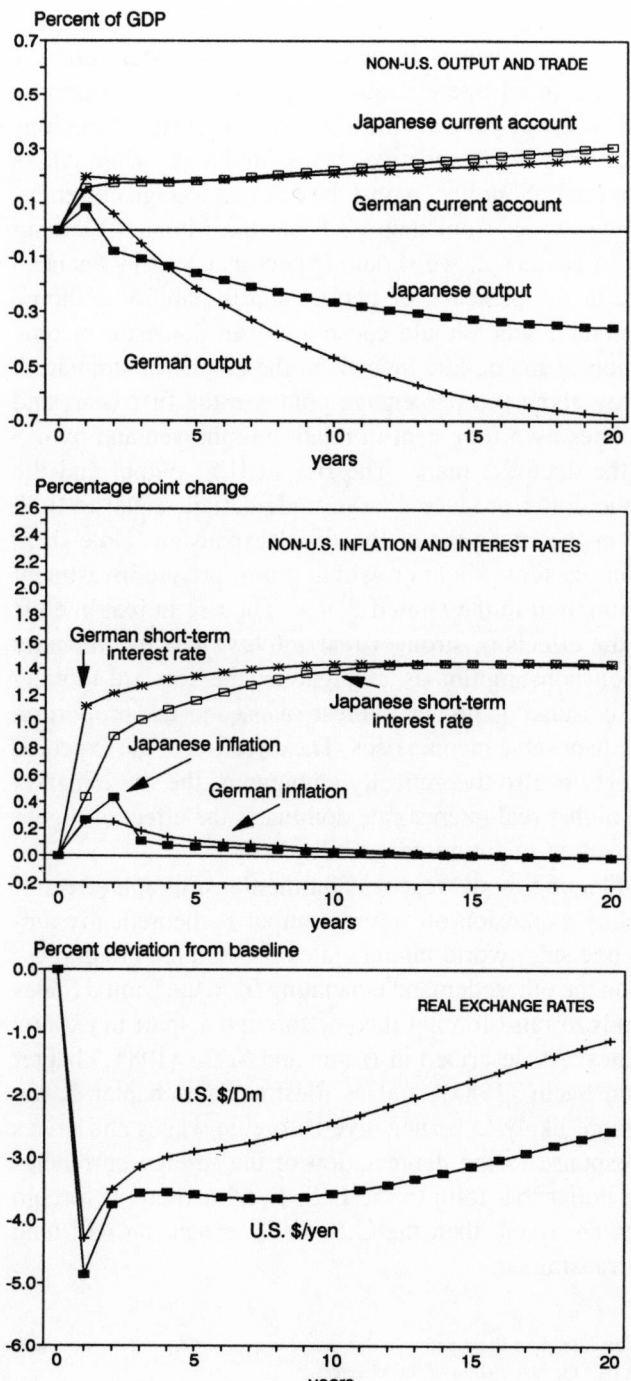

consumer price index) and interest rates (both one-year and ten-year bonds) are expressed as changes in percentage points; therefore a 1 percentage point rise in an interest rate is equal to 100 basis points. Nominal and real exchange rates are measured as percentage deviations from the baseline. Note that a negative change in the exchange rate is an appreciation of the U.S. dollar against the relevant foreign currency.

What should we expect from theory? From the Mundell-Fleming model presented in chapter 2, we should expect that a bond-financed fiscal expansion, in the presence of perfect substitutability of home and foreign financial assets, should cause a rise in domestic income and an appreciation of the dollar. Indeed, in the empirical simulation U.S. GDP rises by about 0.6 percentage points in the first year, and the dollar appreciates by 5.0 percent in relation to the yen and by 4.5 percent against the deutsche mark. The rise in U.S. output and the appreciation of the dollar produce a large trade deficit, equal to 0.39 percent of GDP in the first year of the fiscal expansion. Note from table B-1 that there is some slight crowding out of private investment and private consumption in the United States. The rise in real interest rates dominates the effects of stronger real activity. The theoretically expected effect on consumption is ambiguous: the forward-looking component falls because of higher interest rates, and the proportion driven by current disposable income rises. The direction of the expected effect on investment is also theoretically ambiguous: the share market falls because the higher real interest rate dominates the effect of higher output on the valuation of future profitability.

The Mundell-Fleming model teaches that the transmission effect of a U.S. fiscal policy expansion on foreign output is theoretically ambiguous. On the one side, world interest rates rise and tend to depress foreign income; on the other, demand emanating from the United States increases and tends to raise foreign income through a spurt in exports to the United States. As described in Bruno and Sachs (1985, chapter 6) and Oudiz and Sachs (1984), and as illustrated in chapter 2, the transmission is more likely to be negative if foreign wages and prices rise rapidly in response to the depreciation of the foreign currencies in relation to the dollar that follows the U.S. fiscal action.[1] If foreign wages and prices are fixed, then the U.S. fiscal expansion will tend to be positively transmitted.

1. The negative transmission of fiscal policy in this model is quite different from the results of other major models (see the last section of this chapter).

As can be seen from figure 4-1, the effect of the permanent fiscal expansion is initially positive transmission to Germany and Japan. Very quickly, however, the transmission becomes negative because of wage adjustment and rising real interest rates. Wages adjust slowly in Europe but very quickly in Japan. As is evident from the figure, the negative effects on foreign consumption and investment from higher interest rates start to dominate the expansionary effects of greater exports to the United States as early as the second year for Japan and the third year for Germany.

Wages play a part in determining the sign of the transmission of fiscal policy, but the role of imported inputs in the supply functions of countries also contributes to the explanation of the negative transmission of fiscal policy in this model. As the currencies of foreign economies depreciate, the real price of imported intermediate inputs rises in these economies, and aggregate supply contracts. The theoretical discussion of the role of wage adjustment applies equally to any of the factors of production. The more important imported intermediate inputs are in the production process of a country, the more likely a U.S. fiscal expansion will reduce the output of that country because currency depreciation raises the cost of those inputs. This channel is similar to the one argued by Fitoussi and Phelps (1986), who focused on the effects of a fiscal expansion on the global cost of capital. In the MSG2 model, the effects of a fiscal policy on the cost of capital show up only on the supply side over time.

Inflation is increased throughout the world after the U.S. fiscal expansion. Most of the inflationary effect abroad arises because the foreign currencies depreciate against the dollar.

Tables B-2, B-3, B-4, and B-5 of appendix B show the effects of permanent fiscal expansions in Japan, Germany, the REMS, and the ROECD, respectively.[2] In figures 4-2 and 4-3, we present the results for Japan and Germany, respectively. The Japanese and German fiscal expansions have negligible effects on U.S. GDP because these economies are considerably smaller than that of the United States. A bond-financed Japanese fiscal expansion of 1 percent of GDP is seen to appreciate the yen by about 6.7 percent and to worsen the Japanese trade balance by about 0.84 percent of Japanese GDP. Overall, the U.S. bargaining strategy of pressuring a Japanese fiscal expansion

2. Abbreviations for regions are as defined in chapter 3 (notes 3–6).

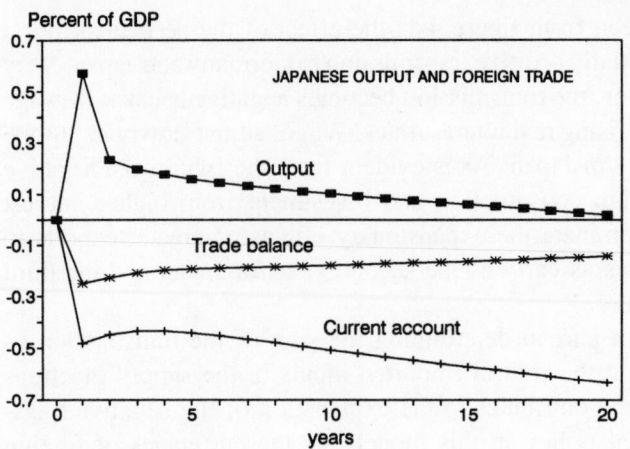

Figure 4-2.
*Permanent Japanese
Fiscal Expansion of
1 Percent of GDP*

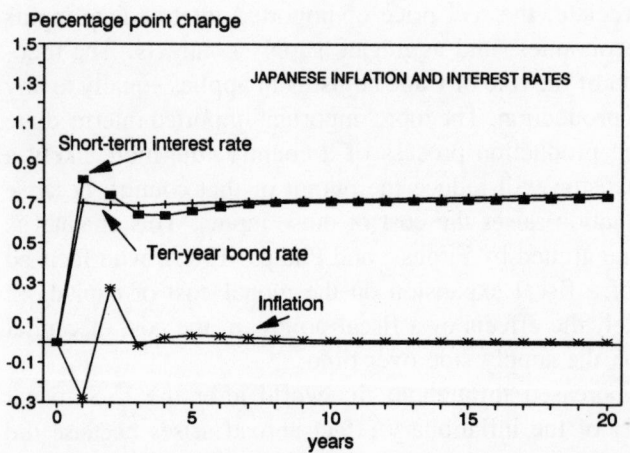

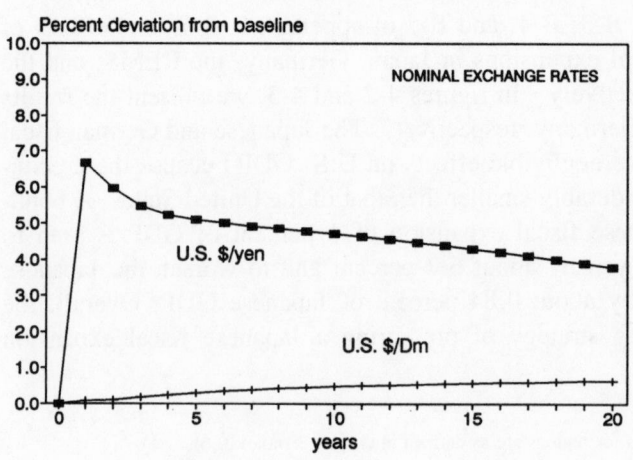

Percent of GDP

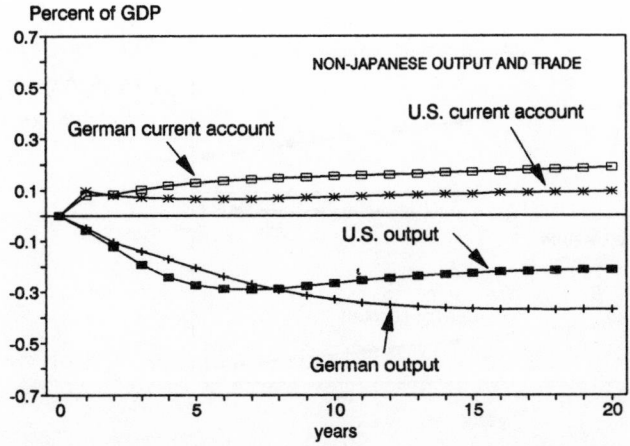

Percentage point change

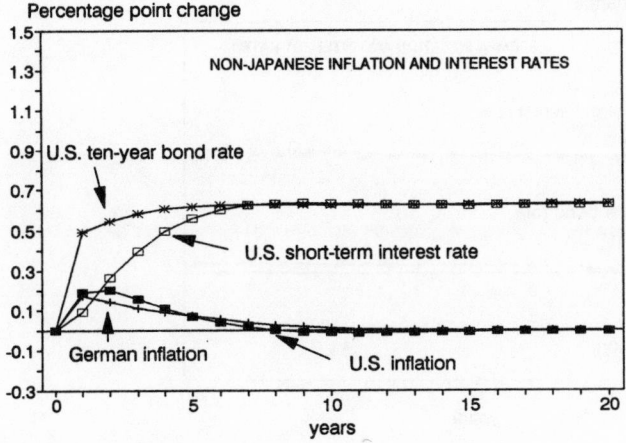

Percent deviation from baseline

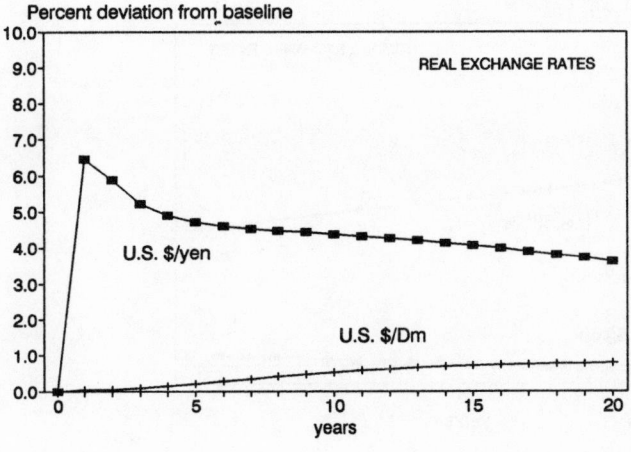

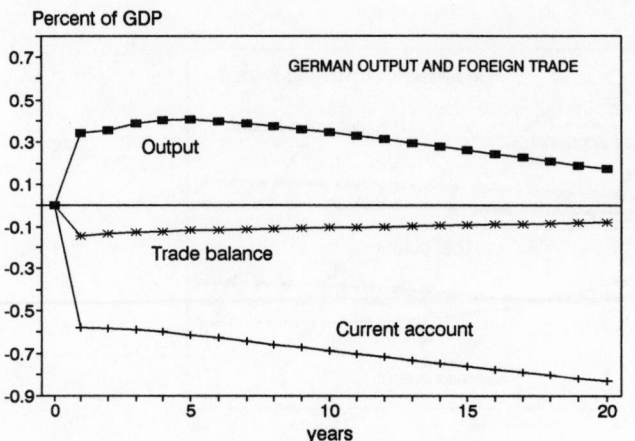

Figure 4-3.
*Permanent German
Fiscal Expansion of
1 Percent of GDP*

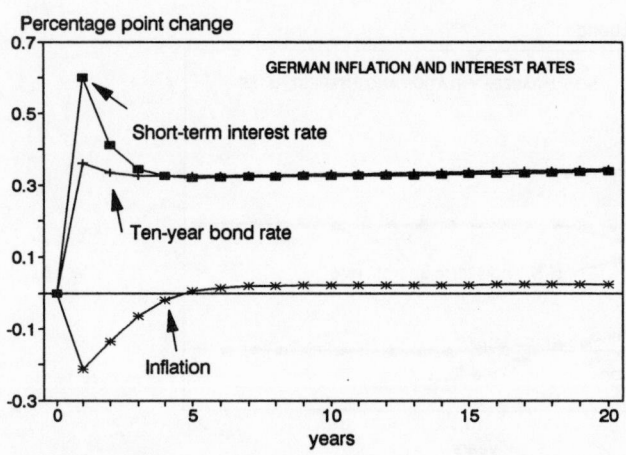

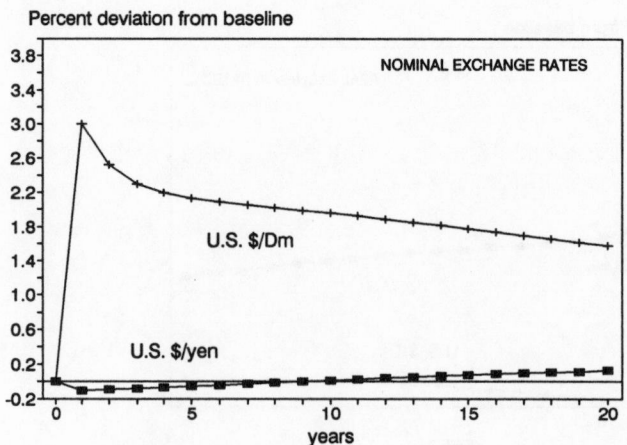

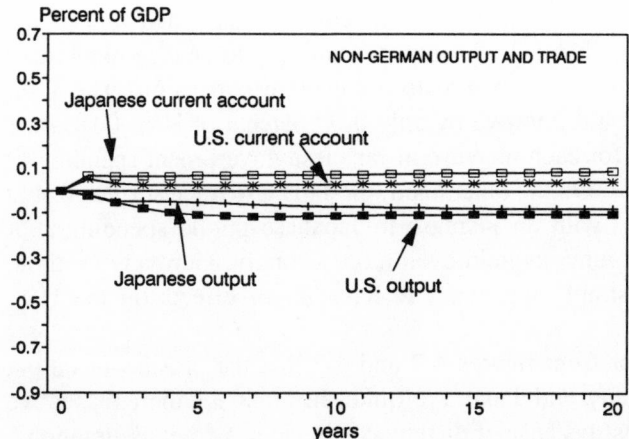

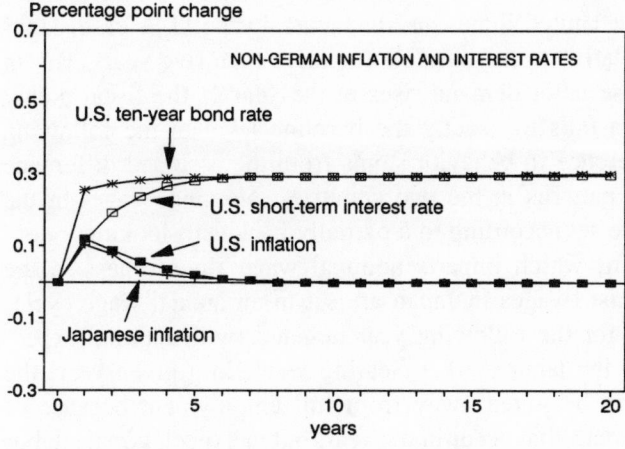

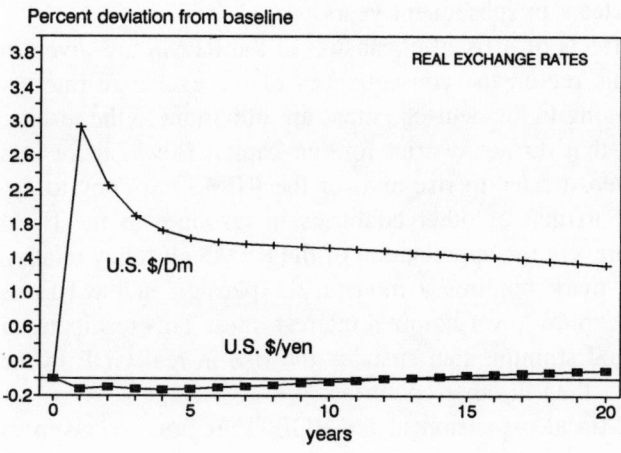

during the latter part of the 1980s can be seen to have had very mixed merit. On the one hand, U.S. output is unlikely to change much, and could even decline in response to a Japanese expansion. The U.S. trade balance would improve by only 0.09 percent of U.S. GDP (less than $4 billion) for each increase in Japanese government spending of 1 percent of GDP. On the other hand, the Japanese trade surplus would fall substantially with an increase in Japanese public spending. For Germany, these remarks hold even more strongly. Germany (without the REMS) is simply too small to have major effects on the U.S. economy.

It is also clear from figures 4-2 and 4-3 that the profiles of output paths for Germany and Japan are quite different for their respective fiscal expansions, because of differences in labor market assumptions. Compare in tables B-1 and B-2 the employment effects of a fiscal expansion in the United States and in Japan. In the U.S. case, labor demand rises relative to the baseline for more than five years. But in the Japanese case labor demand rises in the year of the fiscal policy change and then falls to exactly the baseline level in the following years. The difference in behavior stems from the assumed difference in wage-setting patterns in the two countries. Nominal wages in the United States are set according to a partially backward-looking index-ation mechanism, which imparts nominal wage sluggishness in the model. In contrast, wages in Japan are set in an annual wage cycle, with the wages for the following year targeted (with rational expec-tations) to meet the labor-market-clearing level. In a given year, the labor market can be jolted away from full employment because of unanticipated shocks that occur in the year, but in expectation the labor market always clears in subsequent years.

The output effects of a fiscal expansion in the REMS are given in table B-4. In this region the consequences of the exchange rate as-sumption of pegging to the deutsche mark are important to the results. As in countries that do not restrict foreign capital flows, there is a tendency for interest rates to rise and for the REMS currency to ap-preciate relative to that of other countries in response to the fiscal expansion. To prevent the appreciation of the REMS currency relative to the deutsche mark requires a monetary expansion in the REMS region in an attempt to lower nominal interest rates. This results in an additional demand stimulus that sustains the rise in real GDP in the REMS for longer than in other countries.

Results for a fiscal expansion in the ROECD region are given in table B-5. The demand stimulus within the ROECD region is smaller than that found for the equivalent policy change in the region relative to the United States, primarily because of the openness of the ROECD region relative to the United States. The crowding out of real GDP through a deterioration in net exports is larger than for the equivalent policy in the United States. In addition, the positive stimulus to real GDP in other regions, especially Germany and REMS, indicates the larger trade flows between the ROECD region and these other European economies.

GRADUAL FISCAL EXPANSION. Table B-6 and figure 4-4 show the results for an announced, gradual increase in fiscal expenditure in the United States. The experiment is a three-year rise in fiscal expenditure: 1 percent of GDP in the first year, 2 percent of GDP in the second year, and 3 percent of GDP from the third year onward. Since this simulation involves an anticipated sequence of future deficit increases in the United States, the forward-looking properties of the asset markets in the MSG model are important in the analysis. Given the linearity of the model, reversing the signs of the results gives a fair interpretation of a credible Gramm-Rudman deficit-reduction package.

The announcement of a sequence of rising fiscal deficits leads to a rise in long-term interest rates and a fall in short-term interest rates. The U.S. dollar appreciates against the other major currencies, causing U.S. exports to fall. Most of the appreciation occurs in the first year because of the forward-looking nature of the asset markets, although there is further appreciation in the second and third years. The increase in long-term interest rates leads to a fall in domestic demand that, together with the fall in exports, lowers GDP in the first year. As the spending increases take effect over time, GDP rises until the fourth year, when conventional crowding out begins to take hold.

The expansionary fiscal change in the United States is negatively transmitted to each region through large rises in long-term real interest rates throughout the world, which dominate the short-run stimulus of higher U.S. demand.

In terms of the Gramm-Rudman deficit-reduction package, a sequence of announced cuts in expenditures would raise output currently, mainly by reducing long-term real interest rates and depreciating the dollar upon announcement of the policy. Later on, as the fiscal deficits are actually cut, the negative demand effects on the economy from the fiscal contraction would show up in reduced output and employment.

Table B-7 of appendix B contains results for the effect of an equiv-

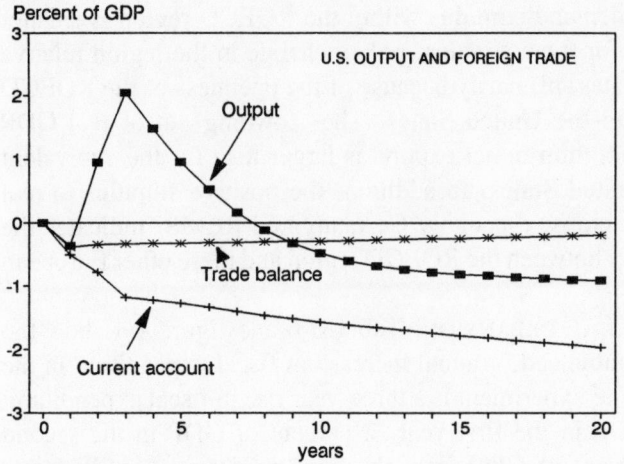

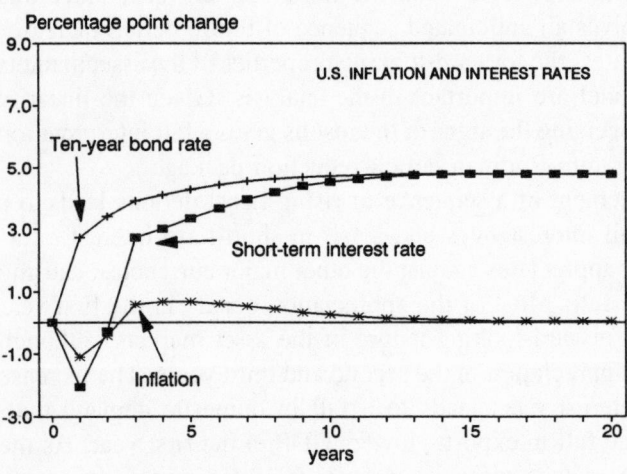

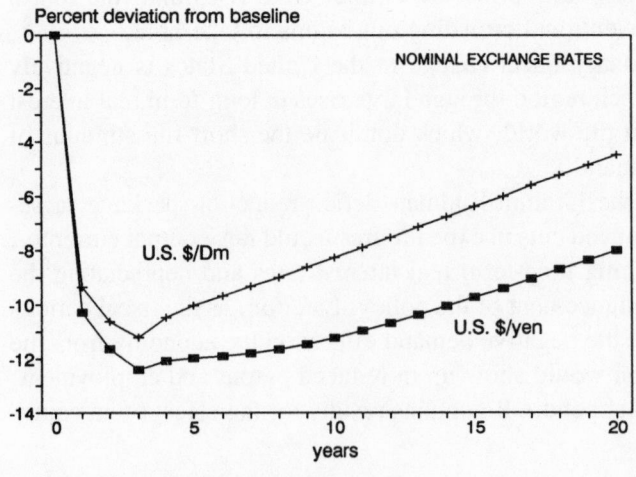

Figure 4-4.
*Anticipated Gradual
U.S. Fiscal
Expansion of 1, 2,
and 3 Percent of
GDP over Three
Years*

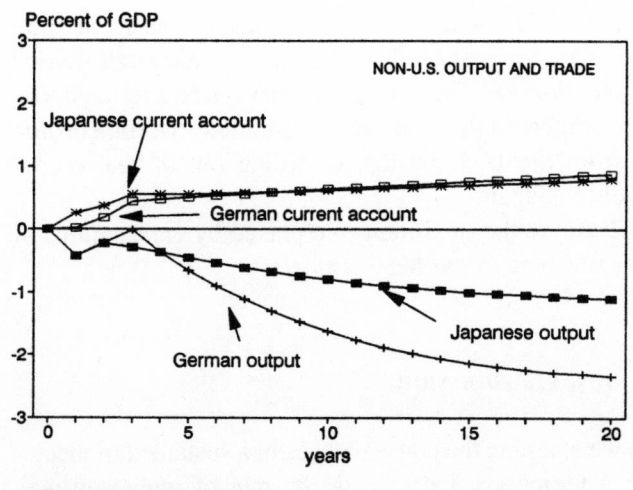

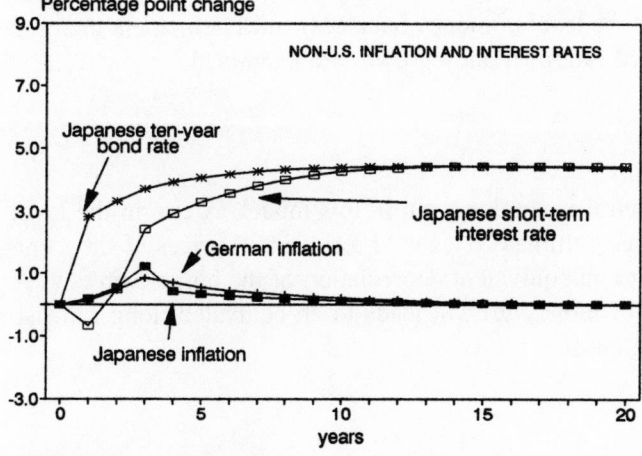

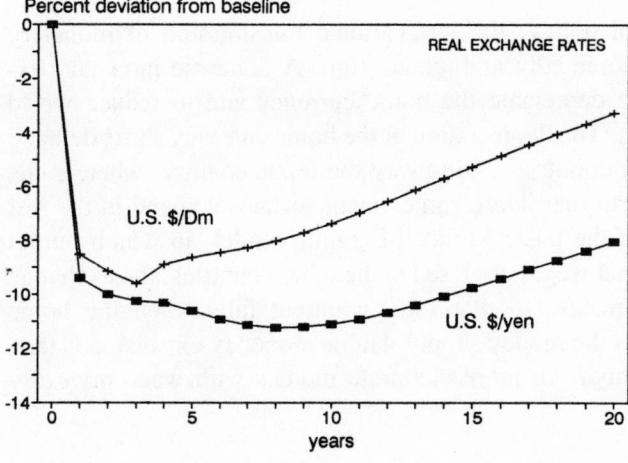

alent anticipated, gradual fiscal expansion in Japan. The results are qualitatively similar to those of the U.S. simulation, although several points are worth mentioning. The yen appreciates relative to the dollar by a massive 12.4 percent in the first year. In addition, the time profile of GDP differs from the U.S. results; crowding out of real output occurs immediately in Japan.

These results illustrate the important role played by expectations of anticipated policy changes in the MSG model.

## Monetary Policy Transmission

In this section we examine the consequences of a sustained monetary expansion. Both a temporary increase in the rate of money growth (that is, a rise in the level of money balances) and a permanent increase in the anticipated rate of money growth are examined.

### Long Run

Money is neutral in the long run in this model. A rise in the level of money balances ultimately leads to a rise in all prices of the same magnitude and to an equivalent depreciation of the home currency. A rise in the rate of money growth leads to an equivalent long-run rise in the rate of inflation.

### Short Run

As with fiscal policy, the international transmission of monetary policy has a theoretically ambiguous sign. A domestic monetary expansion tends to depreciate the home currency and to reduce world real interest rates. The depreciation of the home currency shifts demand away from other countries and toward the home country, whereas the reduction in world real interest rates tends to raise demand in the rest of the world. In the basic Mundell-Fleming model, in which output prices and nominal wages are fixed in the other countries, the exchange rate effect dominates, so that foreign output falls when the home country increases the money supply. Home monetary expansion is then beggar-thy-neighbor. In more elaborate models with wage price dynamics, either the exchange rate channel or the interest rate channel might dominate.

Monetary policy is also ambiguous with respect to the effect on the domestic trade and current account balances. Higher domestic money supply improves international competitiveness by depreciating the home currency. If the standard Marshall-Lerner conditions are assumed to hold (as they do in the MSG2 model), this effect tends to improve the trade balance and current account. But the fall in interest rates and the increase in domestic demand tend to raise investment demand and to lower savings, thereby worsening the trade and current account balances. Because the expenditure-switching and income-absorption effects work in opposite directions, the overall effect is ambiguous.

Finally, note the magnitude of the effect of a monetary expansion on the nominal exchange rate. It is well known from the Dornbusch (1976) model that the home currency will depreciate upon a permanent, once-and-for-all increase in the money supply, but that the size of the depreciation on impact many exceed ("overshoot") or fall below ("undershoot") the long-run change in the nominal rate, which just equals the proportionate change in the money stock. If the effect of the exchange rate on domestic demand is large (through the effect on the trade balance), and if the effect of domestic demand on money demand is large (through the income elasticity of demand for money), and if the home currency depreciation causes a rapid rise in domestic prices, then it can be shown that home nominal interest rates will tend to rise after the money expansion, and that the home exchange rate will tend to undershoot its long-run change. But if one or all of these three channels are weak, then domestic nominal interest rates will tend to fall after the money expansion, and the exchange rate will tend to overshoot its long-run change.

Let us now examine these effects in the MSG2 model. As seen in figure 4-5 (and table B-8 of appendix B), a sustained (permanent) 1 percent rise in U.S. money balances raises U.S. output by 0.42 percent in the first year and causes the dollar to depreciate by 1.5 percent, overshooting its long-run level of 1 percent. Previous studies using an earlier version of the MSG model found almost no overshooting. The reason for the current result is the assumption that import prices in the United States do not adjust fully to exchange rate changes in the short run. This finding is in line with the empirical results of Baldwin and Krugman (1987) and Mann (1987). U.S. inflation increases by one-

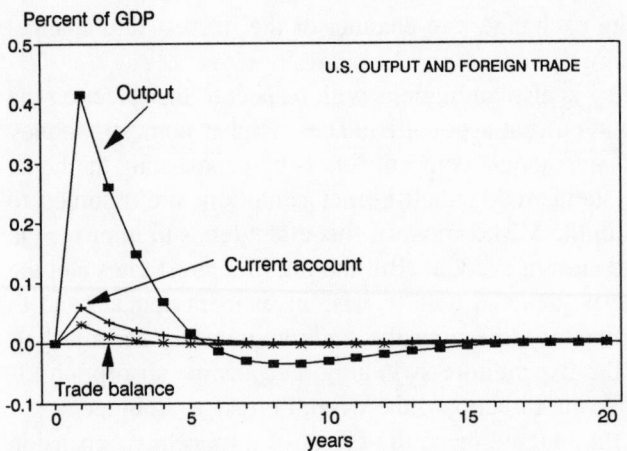

Figure 4-5.
*Permanent 1 Percent
Rise in U.S. Money
Balances*

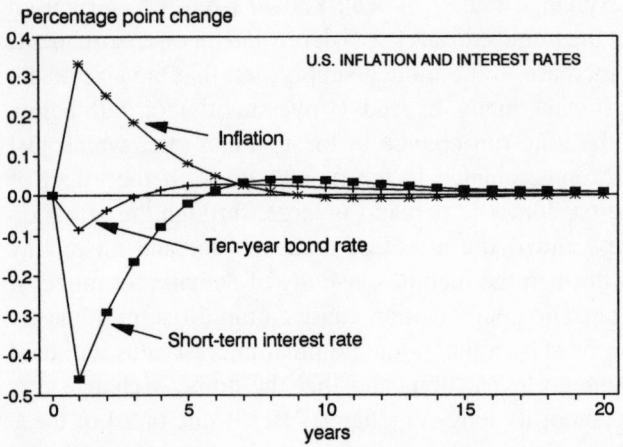

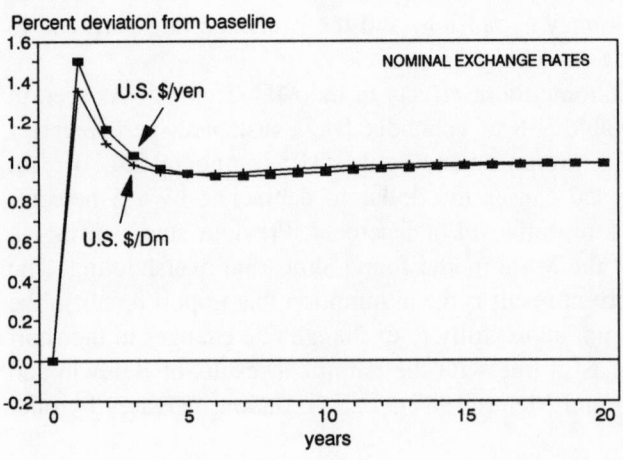

Percent of GDP

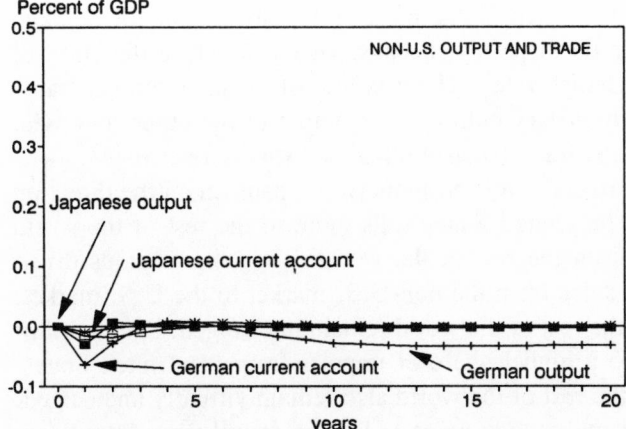

Percentage point change

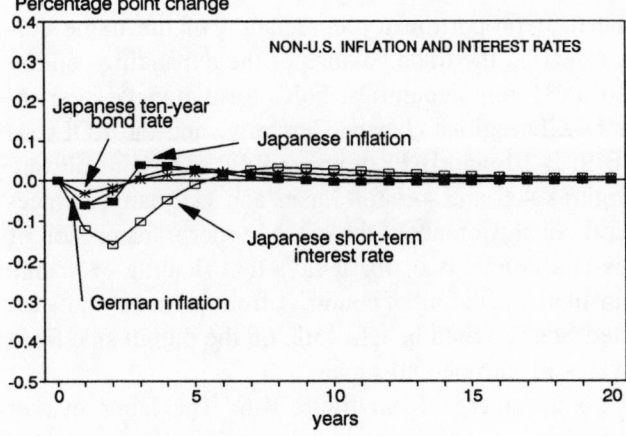

Percent deviation from baseline

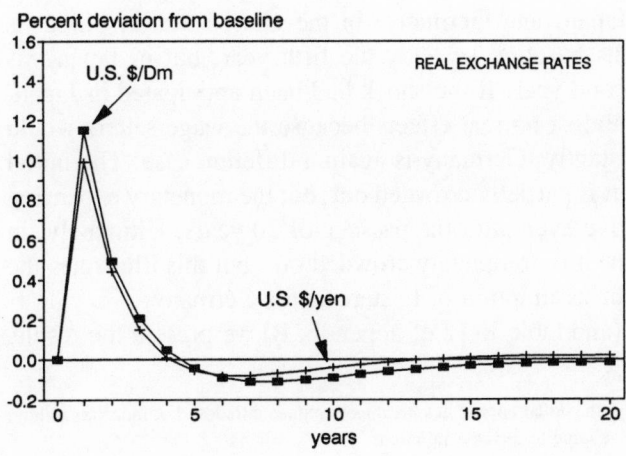

third of a percent, which is far more inflation per unit of demand stimulus than for fiscal policy, because of the opposite direction of effect on the exchange rate.[3] There is almost no international transmission of U.S. monetary policy to the output of the other countries. Moreover, the U.S. trade balance remains virtually unchanged.

Consider the effects of a U.S. monetary expansion on the direction of trade flows. The United States sells more to the rest of the world and buys more from the rest of the world. The other regions divert their own export sales from the non-U.S. market to the U.S. market. Total imports in the rest of the world remain unchanged, but they shift in composition to a higher share of imports from the United States. Total exports in the rest of the world also remain virtually unchanged, but they shift to supply the growing U.S. market and away from third, non-U.S. markets.

The same pattern of proportionate depreciation of the home currency, with little effect on the trade balance of the expanding country or on the output of the foreign countries, holds for a monetary expansion in the other OECD regions (Japan, Germany, and the ROECD) shown in tables B-9, B-10, and B-11 of appendix B. These results are summarized in figures 4-6 and 4-7 for Japan and Germany, respectively. This general conclusion about the cross-border transmission of monetary policies is a crucial one, for it says that floating exchange rates effectively insulate the output of countries from monetary policies abroad. The United States would benefit little on the output side from cuts in discount rates in Europe and Japan.

Several other points emerge from figure 4-6. The labor market assumptions again drive the differences in output responses in the United States, Japan, and Germany. In the United States, output is almost back to its baseline level by the fifth year, but in Japan this occurs in the second year. If the shock had been anticipated in Japan, there would be almost no real effects because the wage setters would have adjusted instantly. Germany is again a different case. The initial stimulus to output is partially crowded out, but the monetary expansion remains stimulative even after the passage of 20 years. Ultimately, in the very long run, it is completely crowded out, but this illustrates the importance of our assumption of hysteresis for Germany.

In figure 4-8 (and table B-12 of appendix B) we present the results

---

3. For fiscal policy, the dollar appreciates, tending to reduce inflation. For monetary policy, the dollar depreciates, tending to increase inflation.

for a permanent 1 percent increase in the rate of money growth in the United States. The assumption of sticky nominal wages and partially backward-looking behavior by wage setters in the United States is illustrated here. Output remains high for a longer period. Nominal interest rates rise rather than fall because of the expected inflation built into short-term (one-year) and long-term (ten-year) rates. The dollar depreciates by 3.1 percent in the first year and settles down to a long-run depreciation of 1 percent a year, which is consistent with the widening of the inflation differential between the United States and the rest of the world.

Transmission of this policy change to other countries is also small in this case. Japanese inflation and German inflation initially fall because of the appreciation of their respective currencies. Nominal interest rates also initially fall in Germany and Japan, but they rise in the United States. Again the interest differential is consistent with the persistent depreciation of the home currency. Note that there is a net improvement in the currency account (although very small) from this policy that is more than the short-run trade improvement. This result can be explained by the facts that U.S. foreign debt is denominated in dollars and that the policy shock was unanticipated. The United States experiences a sustained valuation gain during the period that the home currency is relatively depreciated in real terms, but the importance of this effect depends very much on the initial ratio of external debt to GDP.

We present results for an increase in the rate of money growth in Japan in table B-13 of appendix B. The importance of the Japanese wage equation is illustrated here. The policy has real effects in the first year but is quickly offset in subsequent years because of the flexible Japanese labor market.

## OPEC Oil Price Rise

This section presents results for the effects of a permanent 100 percent rise in OPEC oil prices.

### Long Run

The long-run effects of a permanent rise in OPEC oil prices (in real and nominal terms) are determined primarily by the supply side of the

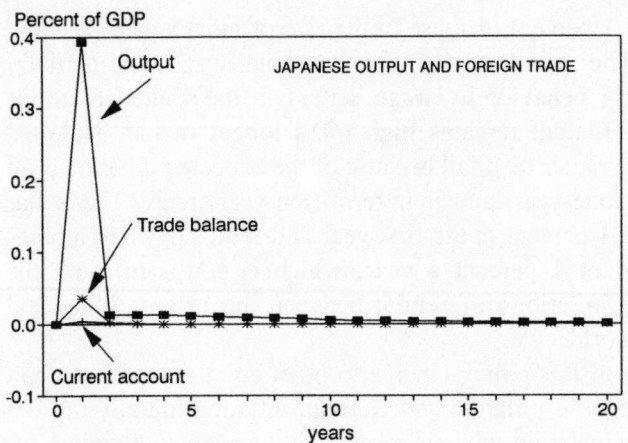

Figure 4-6.
*Permanent 1 Percen*
*Rise in Japanese*
*Money Balances*

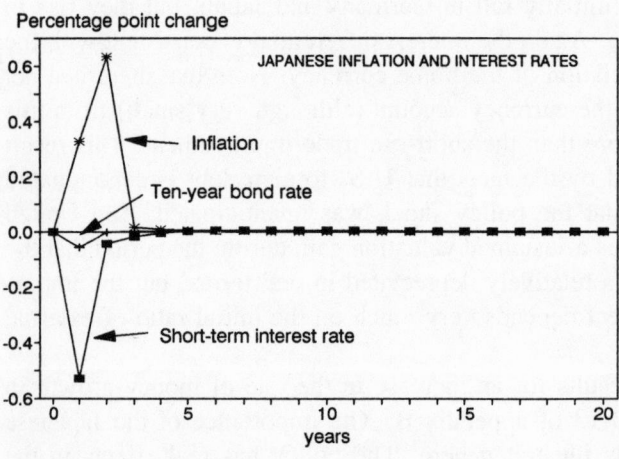

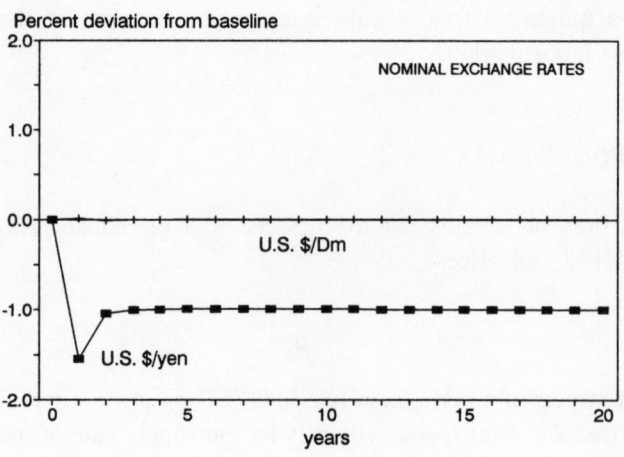

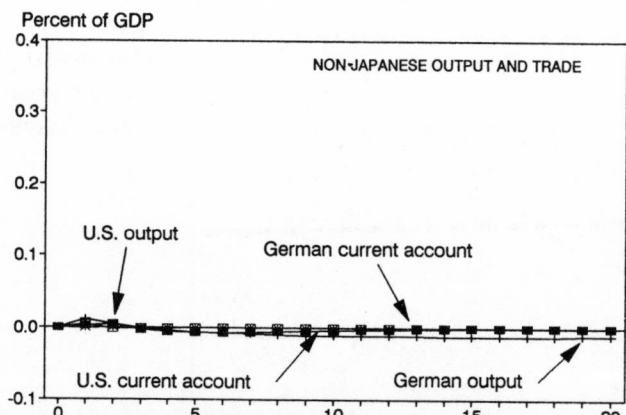

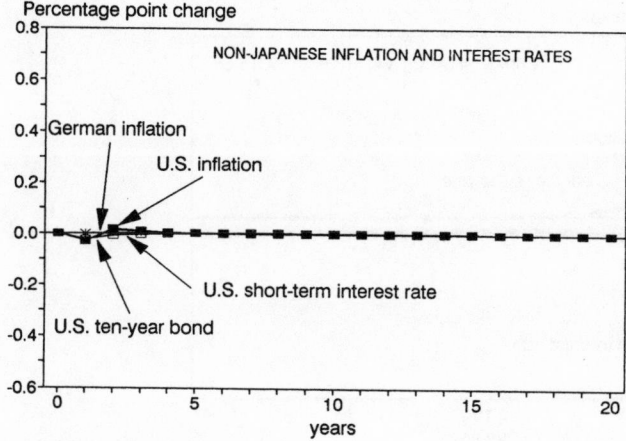

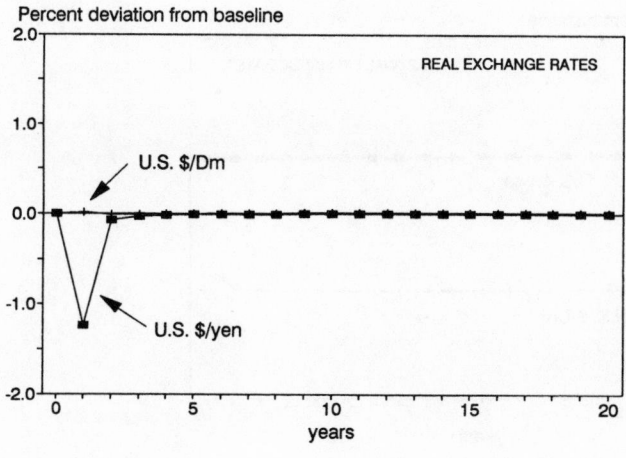

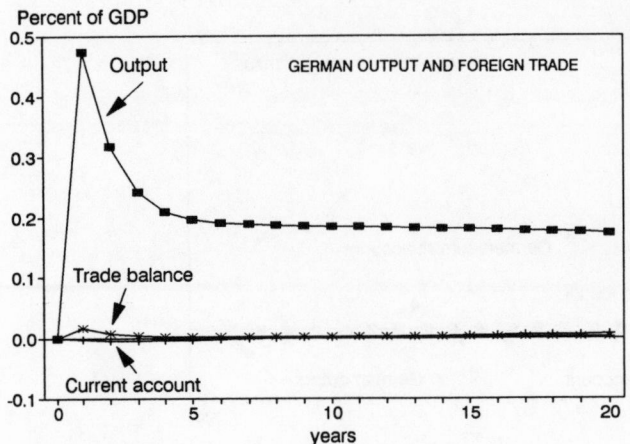

Figure 4-7.
*Permanent 1 Percent
Rise in German
Money Balances*

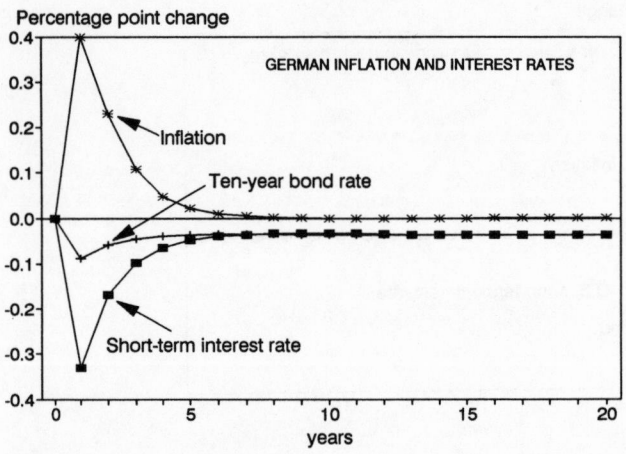

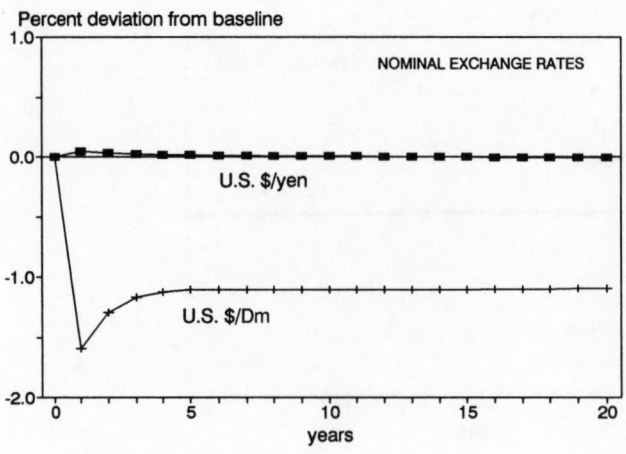

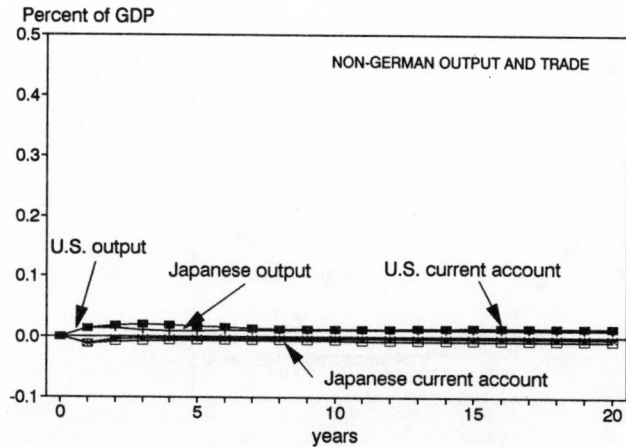

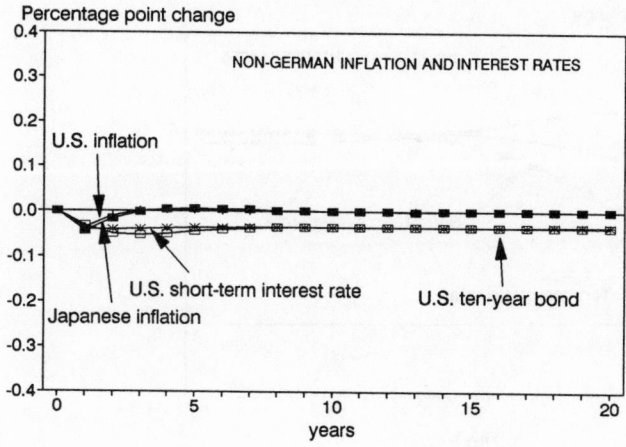

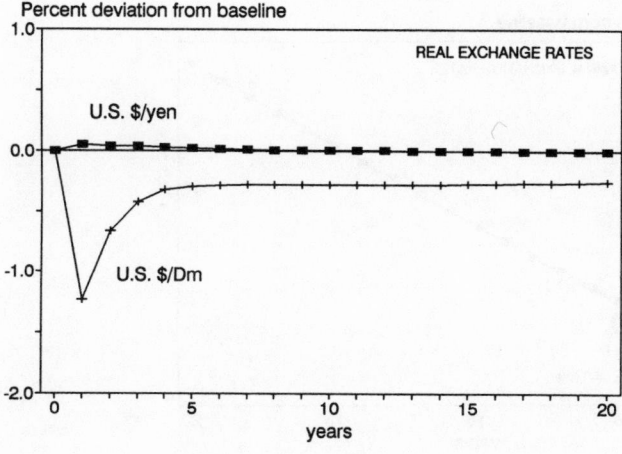

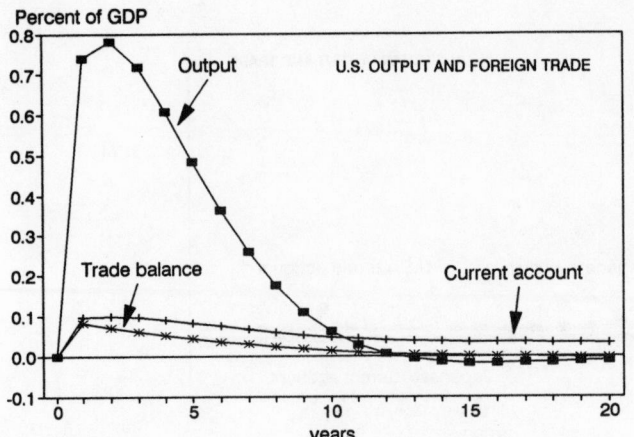

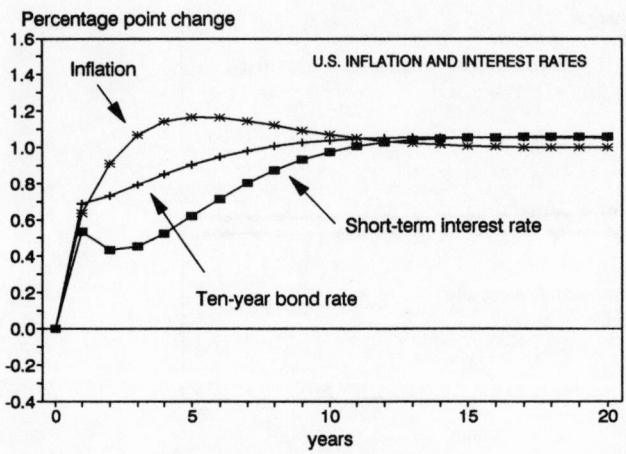

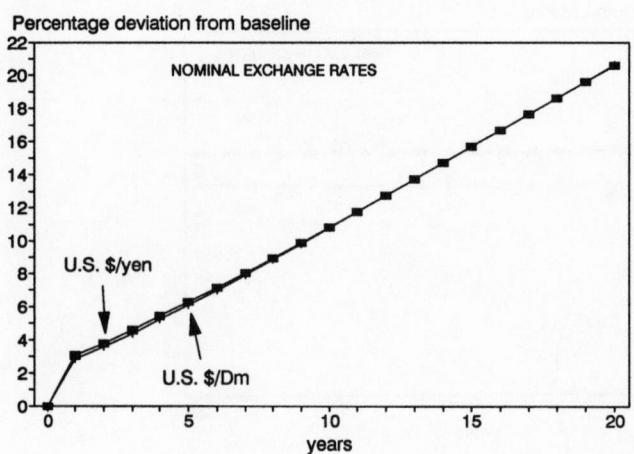

Figure 4-8.
*Permanent 1 Percen⟨*
*Rise in U.S. Money*
*Growth*

Percent of GDP

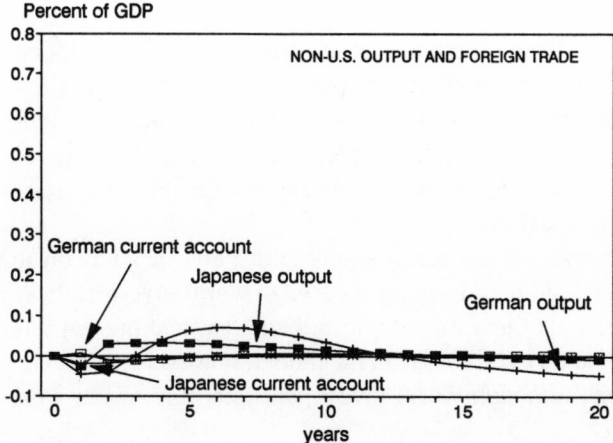

Percentage point change

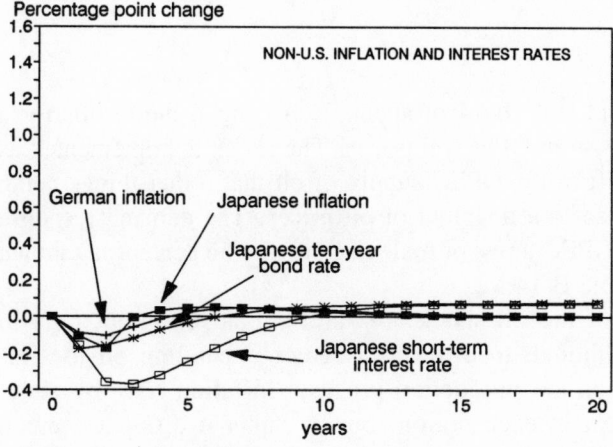

Percent deviation from baseline

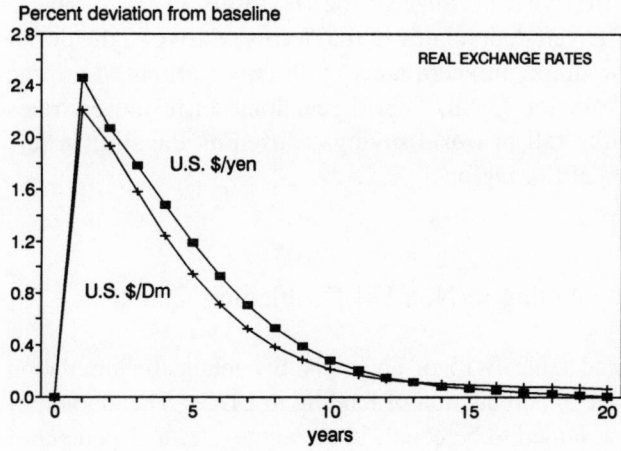

model (see Sachs 1982). The rise in the relative price of oil leads to
a substitution away from oil toward labor, capital, and other imported
inputs in all the industrial regions. Output is permanently lower in all
regions, even though the growth rates in all regions ultimately return
to 3 percent. As shown in chapter 2 and in Bruno and Sachs (1985,
chapter 3), the capital stock must fall because of the constant-returns
technology we have assumed.

The effect on real interest rates is ambiguous and depends on the
impact of the shock on world saving relative to world investment. We
argued in chapter 2 that investment will fall and that real interest rates
will consequently tend to be lower. In the model, however, real interest
rates rise because, although world investment falls, the fall in world
saving is greater.

*Short Run*

Figure 4-9 and table B-14 of appendix B contain the results for a
permanent increase in OPEC oil prices. The shock is implemented as
a permanent shift in the OPEC supply of oil that, other things being
equal, would lead to a doubling of oil prices. The demand response
is such that the OPEC terms of trade rise only by 66 percent, as shown
at the end of table B-14.

The effects of the oil shock are stagflationary. Output falls in
each region, although to differing degrees depending on the importance of oil in the production process. Inflation rises by about
the same amount in each region, but in Japan it dissipates much
faster after the first year because of the flexibility of the Japanese
labor market. The yen depreciates in real terms relative to the dollar
and the deutsche mark, in accordance with expectations of a large
terms of trade loss for Japan. World real long-term interest rates
rise because of the fall in world savings caused by the shift in real
resources to the OPEC region.

## Cessation of Lending to Non-Oil Developing Countries

Figure 4-10 and table B-15 of appendix B contain the simulation
results of an exogenous reduction of lending to LDCs. The amount of
the reduction is assumed to be equal, in the aggregate, to 1 percent of

U.S. GDP and is allocated among lending countries on the basis of their share of lending in the 1986 base year.

The result is a trade balance surplus (or smaller deficit) relative to the baseline in the LDCs, which is matched by a worsening of the trade balances of the industrial countries. The exogenous reduction in lending by the industrial economies leads to an excess of world savings, and world real interest rates are reduced sufficiently to equilibrate world savings and investment. Output initially falls in the industrial economies because of the fall in LDC demand for industrial country goods, but the fall in output is subsequently offset by the increase in domestic demand in each country resulting from the fall in real interest rates.

The properties of the model in response to the change in fiscal and monetary policies in the different regions and exogenous shocks to oil prices and LDC lending give some indication of the likely performance of the model in tracking the world economy during the 1980s. It has been shown that relative asset prices can fluctuate substantially, especially when there are shifts in expectation about future policy paths.

## Summary and Comparison with Other Models

In this section we summarize the own-effects and cross-country spillovers of policy changes in the different regions. The results from the MSG2 model are also compared with those from several other multicountry macroeconometric models.

Table 4-1 shows the sign of the own-country and cross-country multipliers for U.S. monetary and fiscal policy in the first year of the shock. The same multipliers are presented in table 4-2 for the fifth year of the shock and in table 4-3 for the long run.

Table 4-1 shows that, in the MSG2 model, both U.S. fiscal and monetary expansions are expansionary for domestic output. Foreign output initially rises after a fiscal expansion but falls after a monetary expansion. In contrast, U.S. inflation rises after a monetary expansion and falls after a fiscal expansion, primarily because of the pass-through of exchange rate changes into the consumption bundle in the United States. For the same reason, foreign inflation falls after a domestic monetary shock and rises after a domestic fiscal expansion. From table 4-2 it can be seen that after five years the only change in sign from the initial impact is for the inflationary consequences of the fiscal expansion. The short-run effect of the appreciation of the home cur-

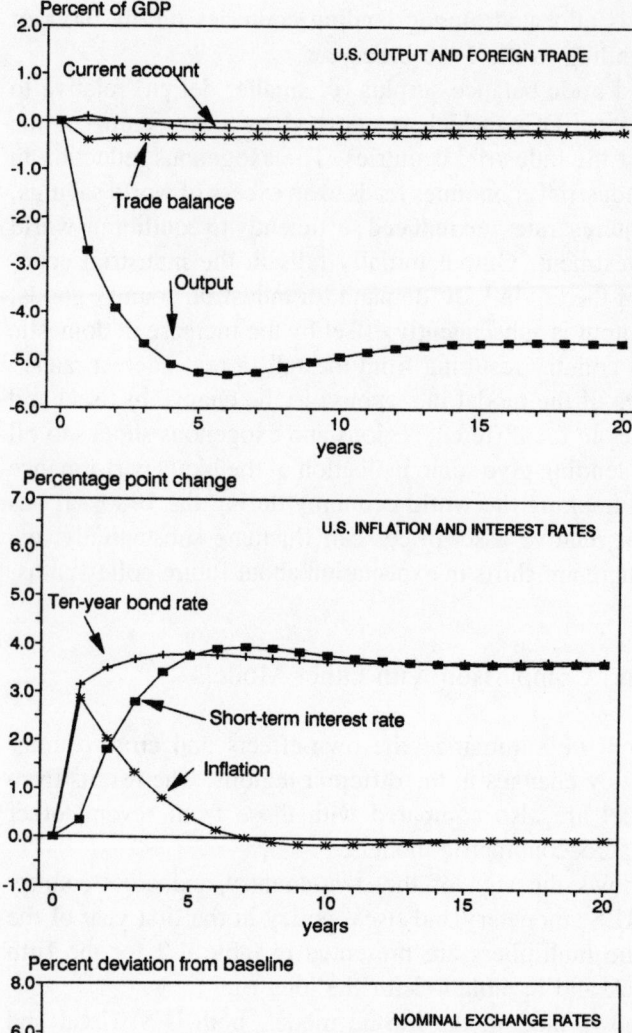

Figure 4-9.
*Permanent 100
Percent Rise in
OPEC Oil Prices*

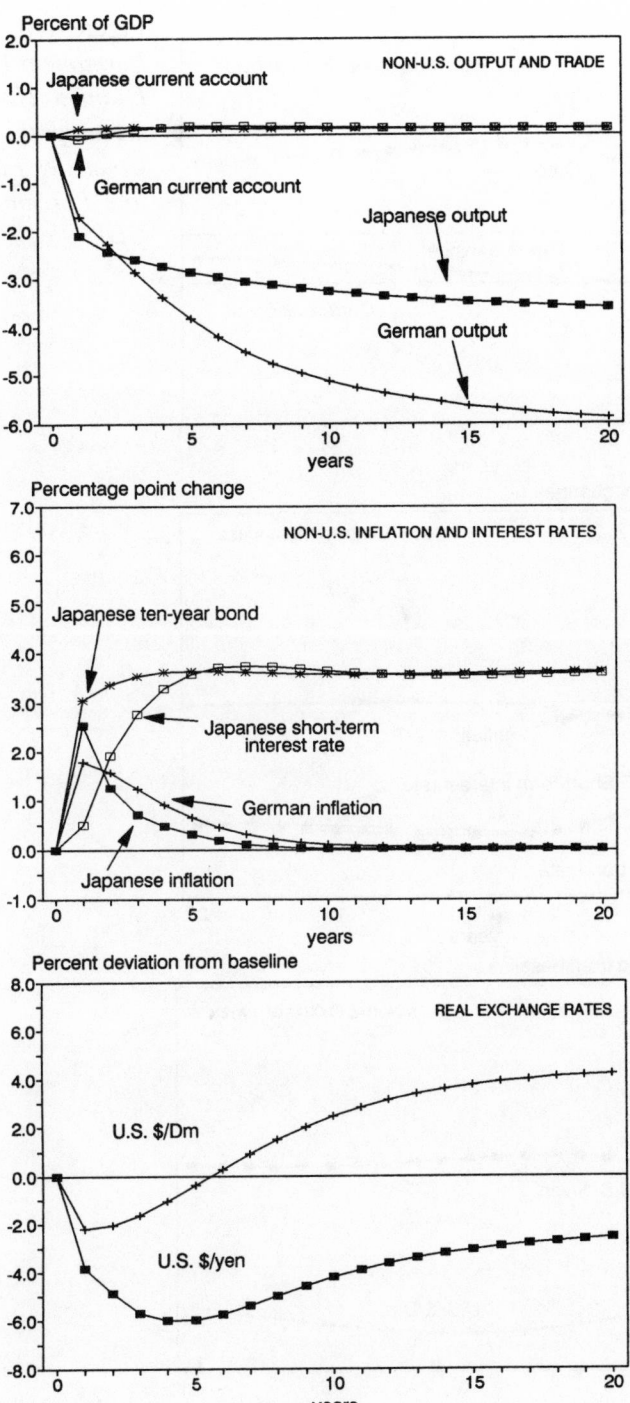

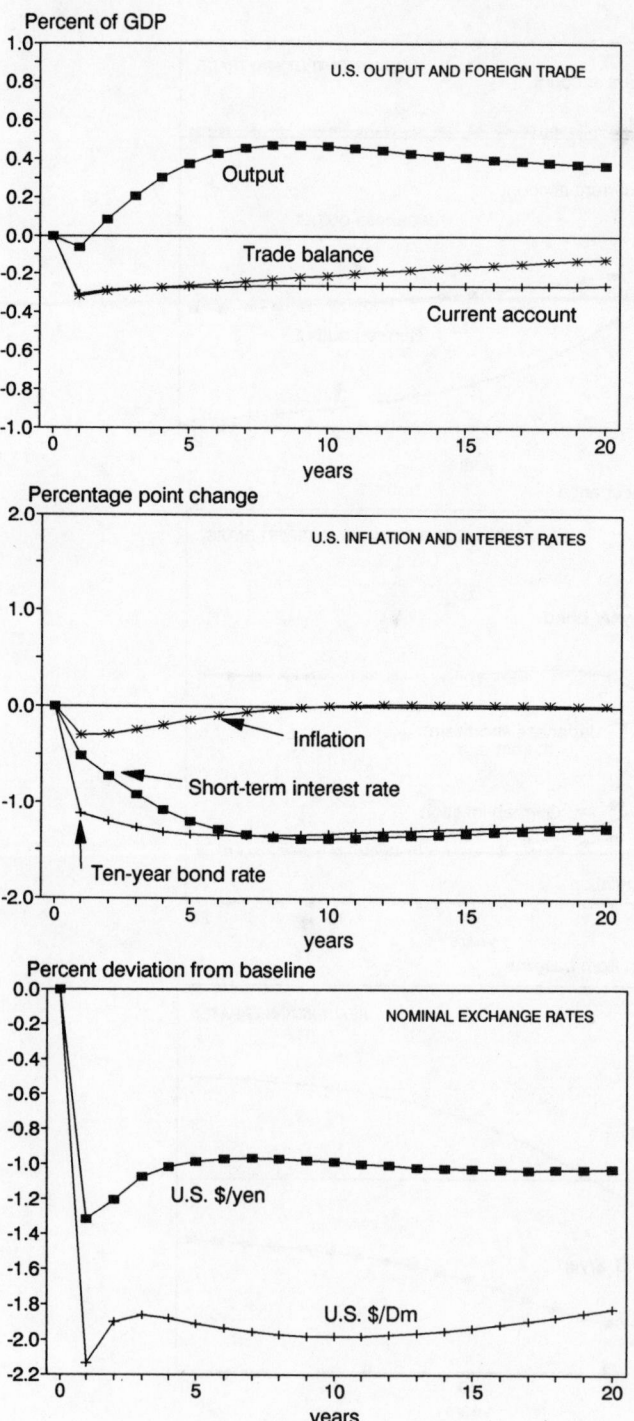

Figure 4-10.
*Permanent Fall in
Loans to Non-Oil
Developing
Countries Equivalent
to 1 Percent of U.S.
GDP*

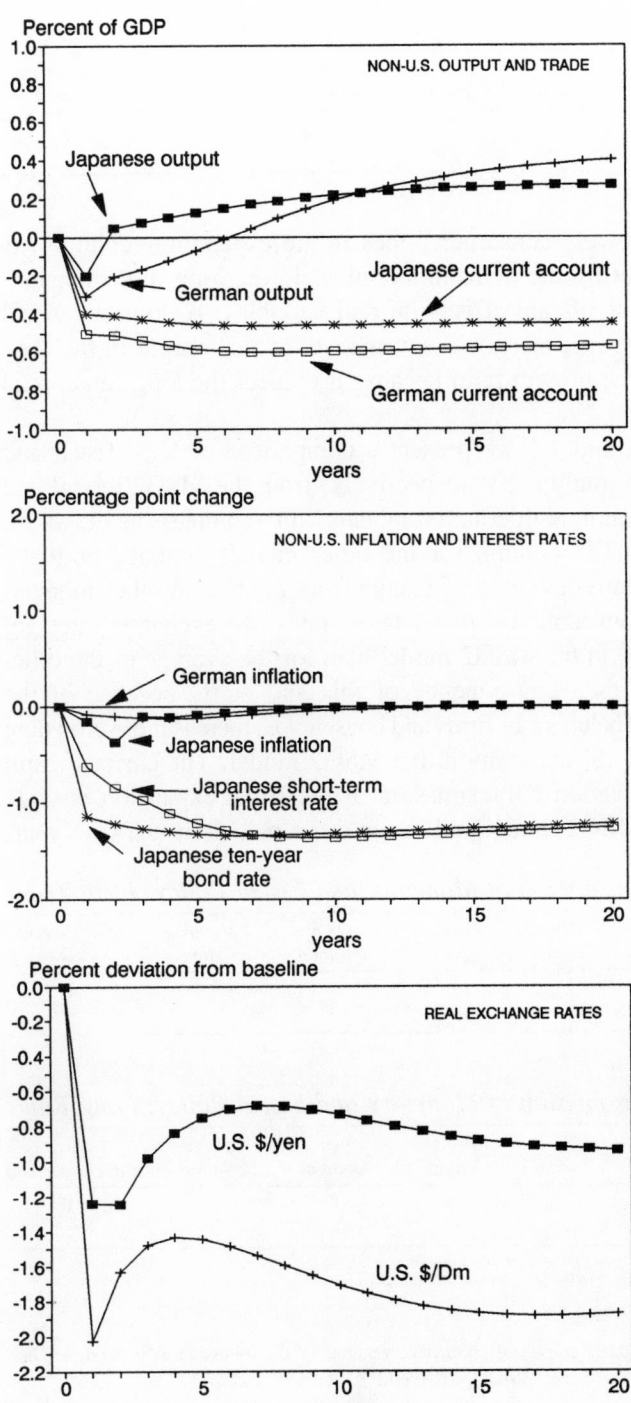

Table 4-1. *Transmission of Monetary and Fiscal Policy: First Year*

| Policy | Own output | Foreign output | Own inflation | Foreign inflation | Own current account |
|---|---|---|---|---|---|
| Monetary expansion | + | − | + | − | + |
| Fiscal expansion | + | + − [a] | − | + | − |

a. Negative for Japanese and German policies but positive for U.S. policy.

rency, which lowers consumer prices in the expanding economy, is more than offset by the demand stimulus. In the long run, monetary policy has no significant effects on real variables. A domestic fiscal expansion, however, leads to a lower level of real output in the long run (but the same growth rate) because it reduces the long-run capital stock.

In tables 4-4 and 4-5 we present a comparison of U.S. fiscal and monetary policy multipliers, respectively, from the MSG2 model and twelve other major multicountry models (this comparison draws on Bryant 1989).[4] The column for the other models contains both the mean and standard deviation of results from the twelve other models.

It is clear from table 4-4 that interest rates and exchange rates are more responsive in the MSG2 model than for the average of the other models. Partly as a consequence of this and partly because of the forward-looking behavior of firms and households, there is more crowding out within the U.S. economy in the MSG2 model. The curious result is that the international transmission of the fiscal expansion is quite similar in the MSG2 model and in the other models in the first year.

Table 4-2. *Transmission of Monetary and Fiscal Policy: Fifth Year*

| Policy | Own output | Foreign output | Own inflation | Foreign inflation | Own current account |
|---|---|---|---|---|---|
| Monetary expansion | + | − | + | − | + |
| Fiscal expansion | + | − | + | + | − |

Table 4-3. *Transmission of Monetary and Fiscal Policy: Long Run*

| Policy | Own output | Foreign output | Own inflation | Foreign inflation | Own current account |
|---|---|---|---|---|---|
| Monetary expansion | 0 | 0 | 0(+)[a] | 0 | 0 |
| Fiscal expansion | − | − | 0 | 0 | −[b] |

a. For increase in rate of money growth, the sign is positive.
b. Trade balance is positive even though current account is negative.

4. The twelve models consist of alternative versions of the following eight models: DRI, EEC, INTERMOD, MCM, MINIMOD, MULTIMOD, OECD, and TAYLOR.

Table 4-4. *Comparison of U.S. Fiscal Policy Multipliers with Other Models*

| Model region and variable | Year 1 | | | Year 5 | | |
| | | Other models[a] | | | Other models[a] | |
| | MSG2 | Mean | Standard deviation | MSG2 | Mean | Standard deviation |
|---|---|---|---|---|---|---|
| *United States* | | | | | | |
| GNP | 0.56 | 1.40 | 0.31 | 0.06 | 0.64 | 0.35 |
| Inflation | −0.11 | 0.15 | 0.14 | 0.15 | 0.64 | n.a. |
| Short-term interest rate | 1.17 | 0.68 | 0.33 | 1.21 | 1.48 | 0.81 |
| Long-term interest rate | 1.31 | 0.37 | 0.22 | 1.37 | 1.06 | 0.68 |
| Exchange rate[b] | −4.99 | −1.86 | 2.00 | −3.92 | −1.94 | 2.01 |
| Current account | −0.45 | −0.24 | 0.10 | −0.47 | −0.44 | 0.21 |
| *Japan* | | | | | | |
| GNP | 0.18 | 0.39 | 0.15 | −0.05 | 0.69 | 0.61 |
| Inflation | 0.27 | 0.11 | 0.14 | 0.07 | 0.34 | n.a. |
| Short-term interest rate | 0.44 | 0.16 | 0.42 | 1.24 | 0.54 | 0.22 |
| *Germany* | | | | | | |
| GNP | 0.21 | 0.22 | 0.11 | −0.14 | 0.36 | 0.29 |
| Inflation | 0.26 | 0.16 | 0.13 | 0.12 | 0.34 | n.a. |
| Short-term interest rate | 0.56 | 0.25 | 0.23 | 1.10 | 0.60 | 0.26 |
| *ROECD[c]* | | | | | | |
| GNP | 0.17 | 0.24 | 0.09 | −0.15 | 0.44 | 0.26 |
| Inflation | 0.24 | 0.14 | 0.12 | 0.10 | 0.37 | n.a. |
| Short-term interest rate | 0.50 | 0.16 | 0.12 | 1.09 | 0.59 | 0.27 |

n.a. Not available.

a. Twelve models consisting of alternative versions of the following models: DRI, EEC, INTERMOD, MCM, MINIMOD, MULTIMOD, OECD, and TAYLOR. For further details, see results of the Brookings model comparison project reported in Bryant and other (1989).

b. For the MSG2 model, US $/¥ rate; for other models, weighted average exchange rate. A negative value is an appreciation of the U.S. dollar.

c. ROECD is rest of the Organization for Economic Cooperation and Development, as defined in the text (chapter 3, note 4).

The crowding out of the initially positive stimulus is more rapid in MSG2, as shown by the negative transmission by the fifth year, whereas the other models are still showing higher foreign output. The explanation for this result has already been outlined above.

In table 4-5 we compare the multipliers in the MSG2 model and other models for U.S. monetary policy. In this case the MSG2 model has a larger output response than the average of the other models (although within 1 standard deviation). The stimulus is crowded out much faster in the MSG2 model and is almost dissipated by the fifth year.

This comparison illustrates that, for monetary policy changes, the MSG2 model produces short-run results that are similar to those from many of the other major multicountry models. Where there does seem to be a difference is in the domestic effects and foreign transmission

Table 4-5. *Comparison of U.S. Monetary Policy Multipliers with Other Models*

| | Year 1 | | | Year 5 | | |
|---|---|---|---|---|---|---|
| | | Other models[a] | | | Other models[a] | |
| Model region and variable | MSG2 | Mean | Standard deviation | MSG2 | Mean | Standard deviation |
| *United States* | | | | | | |
| GNP | 0.42 | 0.27 | 0.16 | 0.02 | 0.14 | 0.12 |
| Inflation | 0.33 | 0.09 | 0.08 | 0.08 | 0.11 | n.a. |
| Short-term interest rate | −0.46 | −0.80 | 0.59 | −0.02 | −0.12 | 0.16 |
| Long-term interest rate | −0.07 | −0.24 | 0.21 | 0.00 | −0.09 | 0.11 |
| Exchange rate | 1.50 | 1.47 | 1.05 | 0.93 | 1.06 | 0.49 |
| Current account | 0.05 | −0.04 | 0.05 | 0.00 | 0.02 | 0.05 |
| *Japan* | | | | | | |
| GNP | −0.05 | −0.08 | 0.15 | 0.00 | −0.10 | 0.16 |
| Inflation | −0.06 | −0.03 | 0.04 | 0.03 | −0.00 | n.a. |
| Short-term interest rate | −0.12 | −0.06 | 0.13 | −0.01 | −0.04 | 0.04 |
| *Germany* | | | | | | |
| GNP | −0.08 | 0.03 | 0.05 | 0.01 | −0.05 | 0.12 |
| Inflation | −0.06 | −0.06 | 0.08 | 0.03 | −0.10 | n.a. |
| Short-term interest rate | −0.20 | −0.03 | 0.18 | −0.02 | −0.10 | 0.19 |
| *ROECD* | | | | | | |
| GNP | −0.06 | −0.02 | 0.06 | 0.01 | −0.04 | 0.10 |
| Inflation | −0.09 | −0.06 | 0.06 | 0.03 | 0.01 | n.a. |
| Short-term interest rate | −0.17 | −0.07 | 0.08 | −0.03 | −0.07 | 0.09 |

n.a. Not available.
a. See table 4-4, note a.

of fiscal policy. This is not surprising, given the use of forward-looking behavior, the imposition of intertemporal budget constraints, and the explicit treatment of imported intermediate inputs on the supply side in the MSG2 model. Our approach illustrates that these issues are important for understanding the international transmission of fiscal policy. In addition, the greater variability of asset prices in the MSG2 model relative to the other models seems more in accord with the experience of the 1980s. We explore this issue in detail in chapter 5.

CHAPTER FIVE

# Explaining the World Economy in the 1980s

BETWEEN 1979 AND 1985 the U.S. dollar appreciated by over 40 percent in real terms relative to other major currencies. Then the dollar depreciated by close to 50 percent relative to the same currencies between 1985 and 1988. The U.S. current account deficit rose from approximate balance in 1979 to 3.6 percent of GNP in 1986, while over the same period the current account surpluses of Japan and Germany each grew from close to balance to 4.4 percent of own GNP. Many causes have been alleged for these wild swings in the world economy, including divergent fiscal policies, divergent monetary policies, trade frictions, capital flight to the U.S. "safe haven," cessation of lending to developing countries, and shifts in productivity among countries.

The purpose of this chapter is to quantify the importance of changes in monetary and fiscal policies in the major industrial countries, of OPEC oil price shocks, and of the developing country debt crisis in explaining the evolution of the world economy during the 1980s. Using the model developed in earlier chapters, we find that these macroeconomic shocks go a long way toward explaining the characteristic macroeconomic features of the 1980s.

We first examine the behavior of key macroeconomic variables for the major regions of the world economy during the 1980s. The novel approach used in undertaking the tracking exercise is then discussed and the results of the exercise are presented.

We show that the changes in macroeconomic policies and oil price shocks can account for a large part of the swings in exchange rates and, roughly, for the global current account imbalances and outcomes for major variables in each region. These results suggest that our simulation framework is useful for understanding important interdependencies in the world economy.

Table 5-1. *Real Bilateral Exchange Rates in Relation to the U.S. Dollar*

| Country | 1978 | 1979 | 1980 | 1981 | 1982 | 1983 | 1984 | 1985 | 1986 | 1987 | 1988 | 1989 |
|---|---|---|---|---|---|---|---|---|---|---|---|---|
| *Average during calendar year* | | | | | | | | | | | | |
| United States | 1.000 | 1.000 | 1.000 | 1.000 | 1.000 | 1.000 | 1.000 | 1.000 | 1.000 | 1.000 | 1.000 | 1.000 |
| Japan | 1.000 | 0.903 | 0.832 | 0.802 | 0.681 | 0.692 | 0.676 | 0.665 | 0.934 | 1.048 | 1.150 | 1.043 |
| Germany | 1.000 | 1.046 | 1.014 | 0.774 | 0.707 | 0.669 | 0.590 | 0.569 | 0.772 | 0.920 | 0.926 | 0.850 |
| Canada | 1.000 | 0.983 | 0.999 | 0.984 | 0.978 | 0.989 | 0.936 | 0.884 | 0.867 | 0.920 | 0.998 | 1.044 |
| France | 1.000 | 1.072 | 1.102 | 0.873 | 0.759 | 0.691 | 0.623 | 0.625 | 0.827 | 0.949 | 0.956 | 0.885 |
| United Kingdom | 1.000 | 1.163 | 1.397 | 1.234 | 1.078 | 0.947 | 0.843 | 0.837 | 0.957 | 1.087 | 1.218 | 1.149 |
| Percentage change from 1978 | | | | | | | | | | | | |
| Japan | ... | −9.7 | −16.8 | −19.8 | −31.9 | −30.8 | −32.4 | −33.5 | −6.6 | 4.8 | 15.0 | 4.3 |
| Germany | ... | 4.6 | 1.4 | −22.6 | −29.3 | −33.1 | −41.0 | −43.1 | −22.8 | −8.0 | −7.4 | −15.0 |
| Canada | ... | −1.7 | −0.1 | −1.6 | −2.2 | −1.1 | −6.4 | −11.6 | −13.3 | −8.0 | −0.2 | 4.4 |
| France | ... | 7.2 | 10.2 | −12.7 | −24.1 | −30.9 | −37.7 | −37.5 | −17.3 | −5.1 | −4.4 | −11.5 |
| United Kingdom | ... | 16.3 | 39.7 | 23.4 | 7.8 | −5.3 | −15.7 | −16.3 | −4.3 | 8.7 | 21.8 | 14.9 |
| *End of calendar year* | | | | | | | | | | | | |
| United States | 1.000 | 1.000 | 1.000 | 1.000 | 1.000 | 1.000 | 1.000 | 1.000 | 1.000 | 1.000 | 1.000 | 1.000 |
| Japan | 1.000 | 0.768 | 0.864 | 0.749 | 0.672 | 0.660 | 0.596 | 0.734 | 0.919 | 1.143 | 1.091 | 0.934 |
| Germany | 1.000 | 1.009 | 0.857 | 0.706 | 0.658 | 0.570 | 0.485 | 0.616 | 0.785 | 0.953 | 0.831 | 0.858 |
| Canada | 1.000 | 1.026 | 1.017 | 1.035 | 1.020 | 1.018 | 0.954 | 0.899 | 0.908 | 0.976 | 1.071 | 1.111 |
| France | 1.000 | 1.052 | 0.957 | 0.763 | 0.685 | 0.583 | 0.526 | 0.685 | 0.822 | 0.991 | 0.871 | 0.905 |
| United Kingdom | 1.000 | 1.150 | 1.351 | 1.097 | 0.939 | 0.856 | 0.689 | 0.882 | 0.908 | 1.172 | 1.169 | 1.063 |
| Percentage change from 1978 | | | | | | | | | | | | |
| Japan | ... | −23.2 | −13.6 | −25.1 | −32.8 | −34.0 | −40.4 | −26.6 | −8.1 | 14.3 | 9.1 | −6.6 |
| Germany | ... | 0.9 | −14.3 | −29.4 | −34.2 | −43.0 | −51.5 | −38.4 | −21.5 | −4.7 | −16.9 | −14.2 |
| Canada | ... | 2.6 | 1.7 | 3.5 | 2.0 | 1.8 | −4.6 | −10.1 | −9.2 | −2.4 | 7.1 | 11.1 |
| France | ... | 5.2 | −4.3 | −23.7 | −31.5 | −41.7 | −47.4 | −31.5 | −17.8 | −0.9 | −12.9 | −9.5 |
| United Kingdom | ... | 15.0 | 35.1 | 9.7 | −6.1 | −14.4 | −31.1 | −11.8 | −9.2 | 17.2 | 16.9 | 6.3 |

Sources: Authors' calculations from OECD, *Economic Outlook,* no. 47 (June 1990) (diskette); IMF, *International Financial Statistics* (1990 annual). Relative prices are defined in terms of final half-year GDP deflators.

## The World Economy, 1978–89

Table 5-1 shows the swings in real exchange rates from 1978 through 1989. The exchange rate data in the top part of the table are an annual average of daily rates for the year in question and thus understate some of the important swings within years. To supplement these data, we also present end of period real exchange rates in the bottom part of table 5-1.

The general trend in the data is quite clear. The U.S. dollar appreciated from mid-1980 to early 1985 against all major currencies. Since 1985 the dollar has depreciated against all major currencies. Despite the general trend, there are some interesting differences among currencies. The dollar appreciated against the yen almost continually from 1979 to 1982. It then stabilized (on an annual average basis and relative to the earlier swings) from 1982 to late 1984 before depreciating substantially from 1985 to 1988. The deutsche mark, in contrast, appreciated relative to the dollar during 1979 and 1980 before a substantial depreciation from mid-1980. This depreciation continued to 1985. The deutsche mark then followed the yen in appreciating against the dollar from 1986 to 1988.

Table 5-2 shows the shift in current account balances over the recent decade. The U.S. economy moved from approximate balance during 1978 and 1979 to a large deficit in 1986. Correspondingly, Japan and Germany moved further into surplus over this period. Since 1986 the U.S. current account deficit has fallen while the Japanese current account surplus has also declined. The German current account surplus has been maintained, with the corresponding deficit emerging in the rest of Europe and in Canada. The balances of the other major countries changed little. The overall current account balance of the member countries of the Organization for Economic Cooperation and Development (OECD) has remained virtually unchanged.

The dynamics of adjustment of the current account are worth examining closely. The U.S. current account balance began deteriorating in 1982, and the deterioration accelerated during 1983. Japan, in contrast, began moving toward surplus from 1981, whereas the German surplus did not get significantly larger until 1984.

Table 5-3 gives an indication of the change in fiscal policies in each of the major regions.[1] The measure used in the table is the general

---

1. The appropriate measure of fiscal stance would be an inflation-adjusted structural fiscal

Table 5-2. *Current Accounts of Major Regions, 1978–89*
Percent of GDP

| Year | United States | Japan | Germany[a] | EC | Canada | Smaller OECD[b] | LDCs[c] | OPEC[c] | Total OECD |
|------|------|------|------|------|------|------|------|------|------|
| 1978 | −0.7 | 1.7 | 1.4 | −0.5 | −2.0 | −0.4 | −8.1 | −3.3 | 0.2 |
| 1979 | 0.0 | −0.9 | −0.7 | 0.5 | −1.7 | −1.4 | 1.2 | 19.2 | −0.4 |
| 1980 | 0.1 | −1.0 | −1.7 | 0.4 | −0.4 | −2.8 | 3.7 | 25.2 | −0.9 |
| 1981 | 0.3 | 0.4 | −0.5 | −0.2 | −1.7 | −1.7 | −6.3 | 8.3 | −0.3 |
| 1982 | −0.2 | 0.6 | 0.8 | −1.4 | 0.8 | −1.2 | −11.1 | −5.1 | −0.3 |
| 1983 | −1.2 | 1.8 | 0.8 | −0.6 | 0.8 | −0.2 | −8.8 | −6.5 | −0.2 |
| 1984 | −2.6 | 2.8 | 1.6 | −1.2 | 0.6 | 0.9 | −4.0 | −0.6 | −0.7 |
| 1985 | −3.0 | 3.7 | 2.6 | −1.9 | −0.4 | 0.7 | −3.3 | 1.2 | −0.7 |
| 1986 | −3.6 | 4.4 | 4.4 | −3.0 | −2.1 | 0.5 | −6.5 | −18.6 | −0.3 |
| 1987 | −3.5 | 3.6 | 4.0 | −3.2 | −1.7 | 0.1 | 0.3 | −1.9 | −0.4 |
| 1988 | −2.6 | 2.8 | 4.0 | −3.7 | −1.7 | 0.2 | −1.5 | 10.5 | −0.4 |
| 1989 | −2.0 | 2.0 | 4.4 | −4.4 | −3.0 | −0.4 | −1.5 | −2.0 | −0.6 |
| Change 1978–79 to 1986 | −3.3 | 4.0 | 4.1 | −3.0 | −0.2 | 1.4 | 3.1 | −26.6 | −0.2 |
| 1978–79 to 1989 | −1.7 | 1.6 | 4.1 | −4.4 | −1.1 | 0.5 | 2.0 | 10.0 | −0.5 |

Sources: OECD, *Economic Outlook*, no. 47 (June 1990), table R21; and IMF, *World Economic Outlook*, May 1990 and April 1986, table A35.
a. European Community excluding Germany. Authors' calculations.
b. Australia, Austria, Belgium, Finland, Greece, Netherlands, Norway, Portugal, Spain, Sweden, Switzerland.
c. Expressed as percentage of exports.

government fiscal position as defined by the OECD. It therefore includes the positions of all levels of government. From this table it can be seen that the U.S. fiscal deficit increased in two distinct stages: the first in 1980 and 1981, and the second (and more dramatic) from 1982 to 1986. The first increase was due primarily to a slowing U.S. economy, whereas the second increase was due to a change in the stance of fiscal policy and a recession. These developments are discussed in more detail below, where the fiscal policy announcements are examined.

In contrast, the Japanese fiscal deficit fell continually, from a deficit of 5.5 percent of GNP in 1978 to a surplus of 2.7 percent of GNP by 1989. Germany, however, experienced an increasing deficit until 1981 that peaked at 3.7 percent of GNP. The German deficit then declined, from 1982 onward, to a surplus of 0.2 percent of GNP in 1989.

deficit. We present the actual deficit because this is the relevant concept for the tracking exercise. In a full model simulation, the inflation and cyclical adjustment is implicitly accounted for within the model.

Table 5-3. *General Government Financial Balances of Major Countries, 1978–89*
Percent of GDP

| Year | United States | Japan | Germany | Canada | France | United Kingdom | Smaller OECD countries | Total OECD |
|------|------|------|------|------|------|------|------|------|
| 1978 | 0.0 | −5.5 | −2.4 | −3.1 | −2.1 | −4.4 | −2.3 | −2.7 |
| 1979 | 0.5 | −4.7 | −2.6 | −2.0 | −0.8 | −3.3 | −2.7 | −2.3 |
| 1980 | −1.3 | −4.4 | −2.9 | −2.8 | 0.0 | −3.4 | −2.9 | −2.8 |
| 1981 | −1.0 | −3.8 | −3.7 | −1.5 | −1.9 | −2.6 | −4.3 | −3.0 |
| 1982 | −3.5 | −3.6 | −3.3 | −5.9 | −2.8 | −2.4 | −4.8 | −4.2 |
| 1983 | −3.8 | −3.7 | −2.5 | −6.9 | −3.1 | −3.3 | −5.1 | −4.3 |
| 1984 | −2.8 | −2.1 | −1.9 | −6.5 · | −2.8 | −3.9 | −4.3 | −3.5 |
| 1985 | −3.3 | −0.8 | −1.1 | −6.8 | −2.9 | −2.7 | −4.1 | −3.3 |
| 1986 | −3.4 | −0.9 | −1.3 | −5.5 | −2.7 | −2.4 | −3.7 | −3.2 |
| 1987 | −2.4 | 0.7 | −1.8 | −4.4 | −1.9 | −1.2 | −2.5 | −2.3 |
| 1988 | −2.0 | 2.1 | −2.1 | −2.6 | −1.8 | 1.1 | −2.0 | −1.6 |
| 1989 | −2.0 | 2.7 | 0.2 | −3.4 | −1.4 | 1.3 | −1.7 | −1.2 |
| Change 1978–79 to 1986 | −3.7 | 4.2 | 1.2 | −3.0 | −1.3 | 1.5 | −1.2 | −0.7 |
| 1978–79 to 1989 | −2.3 | 7.8 | 2.7 | −0.9 | −0.1 | 5.2 | 0.8 | 1.3 |

Source: OECD, *Economic Outlook*, no. 47 (June 1990), tables R14 and 6.

Table 5-4 gives an overall summary of the main macroeconomic features we are attempting to explain. The table contains results for the United States, Japan, and Germany for output, inflation, short-term nominal interest rates, trade balances, current account balances, fiscal deficits, and real exchange rates (on a bilateral basis with the United States) for the period 1978 through 1989. The general trends in the data are clear from this table: slowing world inflation from 1980 until 1987; a rise in world interest rates to 1981 and subsequent decline until 1987; growing U.S. trade deficit and Japanese and German trade surpluses until 1986; a large real appreciation then depreciation of the dollar and divergent real growth relative to trend, with the United States contracting until 1983 and then growing strongly, Germany consistently growing below trend, and Japan maintaining close to trend growth on average.

The data presented above are actual realizations of economic variables. When undertaking the tracking exercise in a forward-looking model such as the MSG2 model, we also need to make assumptions about the paths of future variables that households and firms expect. Because we maintain the working hypothesis of rational expectations,

Table 5-4. *Macroeconomic Experience of the United States, Japan, and Germany, 1978–89*
Percent

| Country and variable | 1978 | 1979 | 1980 | 1981 | 1982 | 1983 | 1984 | 1985 | 1986 | 1987 | 1988 | 1989 |
|---|---|---|---|---|---|---|---|---|---|---|---|---|
| **United States** | | | | | | | | | | | | |
| GNP growth | 5.3 | 2.5 | -0.2 | 1.9 | -2.5 | 3.6 | 6.8 | 3.4 | 2.7 | 3.7 | 4.4 | 3.0 |
| Output gap (trend = 2.5) | -0.0 | -0.0 | -2.7 | -3.3 | -8.3 | -7.2 | -3.0 | -2.1 | -1.9 | -0.7 | 1.2 | 1.7 |
| Inflation | 7.6 | 11.3 | 13.5 | 10.3 | 6.1 | 3.2 | 4.3 | 3.5 | 1.9 | 3.7 | 4.1 | 4.8 |
| Long-term interest rate | 8.7 | 9.6 | 11.9 | 14.2 | 13.8 | 12.0 | 12.7 | 11.4 | 9.0 | 8.4 | 8.8 | 8.5 |
| Short-term interest rate | 7.2 | 10.1 | 11.4 | 14.0 | 10.6 | 8.6 | 9.5 | 7.5 | 6.0 | 5.8 | 6.7 | 8.1 |
| Trade balance[a] | -1.5 | -1.1 | -0.9 | -0.9 | -1.2 | -2.0 | -3.0 | -3.0 | -3.4 | -3.5 | -2.6 | -2.2 |
| Current account[a] | -0.7 | 0.0 | 0.1 | 0.2 | -0.3 | -1.4 | -2.8 | -3.0 | -3.6 | -3.5 | -2.6 | -2.0 |
| Fiscal deficit[a] | 0.0 | 0.5 | -1.3 | -1.0 | -3.5 | -3.8 | -2.8 | -3.3 | -3.4 | -2.4 | -2.0 | -2.0 |
| **Japan** | | | | | | | | | | | | |
| GNP growth | 5.2 | 5.3 | 4.3 | 3.7 | 3.1 | 3.2 | 5.1 | 4.8 | 2.6 | 4.6 | 5.7 | 4.9 |
| Output gap (trend = 4.2) | -1.1 | -0.0 | 0.1 | -0.5 | -1.6 | -2.5 | -1.7 | -1.0 | -2.7 | -2.4 | -0.9 | -0.4 |
| Inflation | 3.8 | 3.6 | 8.0 | 4.9 | 2.7 | 1.9 | 2.2 | 2.1 | 0.4 | -0.2 | 0.1 | 1.7 |
| Long-term interest rate | 6.6 | 7.7 | 8.9 | 8.4 | 8.3 | 7.8 | 7.3 | 6.5 | 5.2 | 5.0 | 4.8 | 5.3 |
| Short-term interest rate | 4.4 | 5.9 | 10.9 | 7.4 | 7.0 | 6.7 | 6.5 | 6.6 | 5.1 | 4.2 | 4.5 | 5.4 |
| Trade balance[a] | 2.5 | 0.2 | 0.2 | 1.7 | 1.7 | 2.7 | 3.5 | 4.2 | 4.7 | 4.0 | 3.3 | 3.0 |
| Current account[a] | 1.7 | -0.9 | -1.0 | 0.4 | 0.6 | 1.8 | 2.8 | 3.7 | 4.4 | 3.6 | 2.8 | 2.0 |
| Fiscal deficit[a] | -5.5 | -4.7 | -4.4 | -3.8 | -3.6 | -3.7 | -2.1 | -0.8 | -0.9 | 0.7 | 2.1 | 2.7 |
| Real exchange rate[b] | 0.0 | -9.7 | -16.8 | -19.7 | -31.9 | -30.8 | -32.4 | -33.5 | -6.6 | 4.9 | 15.0 | 4.1 |
| Nominal exchange rate[b] | 0.0 | -4.7 | -8.0 | -5.4 | -17.5 | -12.9 | -12.8 | -12.9 | 21.8 | 36.8 | 48.8 | 41.7 |
| **Germany** | | | | | | | | | | | | |
| GNP growth | 3.3 | 4.0 | 1.5 | 0.0 | -1.0 | 1.9 | 3.3 | 1.9 | 2.3 | 1.7 | 3.6 | 4.3 |
| Output gap (trend = 2.5) | -1.3 | 0.1 | -0.9 | 3.4 | -6.9 | -7.5 | -6.7 | -7.2 | -7.4 | -8.2 | -7.1 | -5.6 |
| Inflation | 2.7 | 4.1 | 5.5 | 6.3 | 5.3 | 3.3 | 2.4 | 2.2 | -0.2 | 0.2 | 1.2 | 3.1 |
| Long-term interest rate | 6.1 | 7.6 | 8.4 | 10.1 | 8.9 | 8.1 | 8.0 | 7.0 | 6.2 | 6.2 | 6.5 | 7.0 |
| Short-term interest rate | 3.7 | 6.7 | 9.5 | 12.1 | 8.9 | 5.8 | 6.0 | 5.4 | 4.6 | 4.0 | 4.3 | 7.1 |
| Trade balance[a] | 3.9 | 2.2 | 1.2 | 2.5 | 4.0 | 3.4 | 3.7 | 4.6 | 6.2 | 6.3 | 6.5 | 7.2 |
| Current account[a] | 1.4 | -0.7 | -1.7 | -0.5 | 0.8 | 0.8 | 1.6 | 2.6 | 4.4 | 4.0 | 4.0 | 4.4 |
| Fiscal deficit[a] | -2.4 | -2.6 | -2.9 | -3.7 | -3.3 | -2.5 | -1.9 | -1.1 | -1.3 | -1.8 | -2.1 | 0.2 |
| Real exchange rate[b] | 0.0 | 4.6 | 1.4 | -22.6 | -29.3 | -33.1 | -41.0 | -43.1 | -22.8 | -8.0 | -7.4 | -15.5 |
| Nominal exchange rate[b] | 0.0 | 9.1 | 9.9 | -11.8 | -19.0 | -24.0 | -34.7 | -37.7 | -7.6 | 11.0 | 13.4 | 6.0 |

Sources: OECD, *Economic Outlook*, no. 47 (June 1990), tables R1, R14, 5, 8, 13, R20. Data for consumer prices are from table R11 in OECD, *Economic Outlook*, no. 46 (June 1989).
a. Percent of GDP.
b. Percentage change from 1978.

this implies that only expected paths of future exogenous variables are required.[2] The problem of dealing with expected variables is dealt with by using the following procedure. There are various sources of information on fiscal deficits, such as the Congressional Budget Office and administration forecasts for the United States or the OECD forecasts for a broader range of countries. The OECD forecasts are the most convenient to use, because of both coverage and availability. The procedure followed here is to use the two-year forecasts for fiscal deficits contained in the OECD's *Economic Outlook*. Past the two-year period, we assume that agents expected the deficit to be unchanged as a percentage of GNP from the last forecast (except where noted for the Gramm-Rudman simulation). We can also use OECD forecasts of oil prices and current account developments in developing countries. This leaves monetary policy assumptions, which are discussed in detail below.

Table 5-5 contains the budget deficit forecasts for the United States, Japan, and Germany given by the OECD since 1979. This table is constructed by using the December *Economic Outlook* for each year. The first column of the table gives the year in which the forecast was published. For each country there are two columns of forecast data. The first of these gives the expected fiscal outcomes for the year of the forecast and for the following year. The second column gives the actual outcome for the year in which the forecast was published. For example, in 1980 the OECD forecast for the U.S. deficit was 1 percent of GNP in 1980 and 0.6 percent of GNP in 1981. The actual outcome for 1980 was a deficit of 1.3 percent of GNP; from the 1981 OECD forecast, the actual U.S. deficit in 1981 was 1.0 percent of GNP.

It can be seen that the rise in the U.S. deficit in 1980 was a little larger than forecast in 1979. The deficit in 1982 was a large surprise from the vantage point of 1981: the forecast was 1.3 percent of GNP, and the outcome was 3.5 percent of GNP. The actual outcomes from 1983 to 1986 were less expansionary than forecast in each year.

For Japan, the gradual decline in deficits was forecast one year ahead, although the forecast deficit tended to be smaller than the outcome between 1980 and 1983 and larger than the outcome between 1984 and 1987. Japanese deficits fell slightly more slowly than forecast in the earlier period and fell faster than forecast in the later period.

---

2. In the MSG2 model the exogenous variables are money stocks and government spending in each region, OPEC oil supply, and lending to non-oil developing countries (LDCs).

Table 5-5. *Forecasts of General Government Budget Balances in the United States, Japan, and Germany*
Percent of GDP

| Date of forecast | Year | United States | | Japan | | Germany | |
|---|---|---|---|---|---|---|---|
| | | Expected | Actual | Expected | Actual | Expected | Actual |
| 1979 | 1979 | 0.4 | 0.6 | −4.9 | −4.8 | −3.1 | −2.7 |
| | 1980 | −0.8 | ... | −4.7 | ... | −3.0 | ... |
| 1980 | 1980 | −1.0 | −1.3 | −4.5 | −4.4 | −3.3 | −2.9 |
| | 1981 | −0.6 | ... | −3.7 | ... | −3.5 | ... |
| 1981 | 1981 | −0.7 | −1.0 | −3.6 | −3.8 | −4.4 | −3.7 |
| | 1982 | −1.3 | ... | −2.0 | ... | −4.0 | ... |
| 1982 | 1982 | −3.7 | −3.5 | −3.3 | −3.6 | −4.1 | −3.3 |
| | 1983 | −4.4 | ... | −2.3 | ... | −4.1 | ... |
| 1983 | 1983 | −3.8 | −3.8 | −3.4 | −3.7 | −3.1 | −2.5 |
| | 1984 | −3.7 | ... | −2.5 | ... | −2.1 | ... |
| 1984 | 1984 | −3.2 | −2.8 | −2.2 | −2.1 | −1.7 | −1.9 |
| | 1985 | −3.6 | ... | −0.8 | ... | −0.9 | ... |
| 1985 | 1985 | −3.9 | −3.3 | −1.7 | −0.8 | −1.2 | −1.1 |
| | 1986 | −3.7 | ... | −1.1 | ... | −0.9 | ... |
| 1986 | 1986 | −3.4 | −3.4 | −1.5 | −1.1 | −1.0 | −1.3 |
| | 1987 | −2.3 | ... | −1.4 | ... | −0.9 | ... |
| 1987 | 1987 | −2.4 | −2.3 | −1.2 | −0.3 | −1.7 | −1.7 |
| | 1988 | −2.4 | ... | −1.1 | ... | −2.3 | ... |
| 1988 | 1988 | −1.7 | −1.7 | −0.2 | −0.2 | −2.0 | −2.0 |
| | 1989 | −1.5 | ... | −0.2 | ... | −1.2 | ... |

Source: Each forecast is from the indicated year of OECD, *Economic Outlook*, published in December. The actual values used are from OECD, *Economic Outlook*, no. 45 (December 1988), p. 26.

The opposite pattern emerges for Germany. From 1980 to 1984, the projected deficit was well above the actual outcome. For example, in 1981 the deficit for 1982 was forecast to be 4 percent of GNP, and the actual outcome was 3.3 percent. Similarly, in 1982 the deficit for 1983 was forecast to be 4.1 percent of GNP, whereas the actual outcome for 1983 was 2.5 percent of GNP.

Table 5-6 gives a very rough guide to the general setting of policy as discussed in the OECD *Economic Outlook* of the relevant year. This table is obviously subjective, but it does give some guidance for interpreting the policy stance at the time as well as expected policy changes. For example, in 1980 there was discussion of fiscal cuts in Japan as well as discussion of possible U.S. tax cuts beginning in

Table 5-6. *Summary of OECD Description of Policy Stance in the United States, Japan, and Germany, 1979–87*

| Year | Country | Monetary policy | Fiscal policy |
|------|---------|-----------------|---------------|
| 1979 | United States | Tight | Stable |
|      | Germany | Tight | Spending cuts |
|      | Japan | Stable | Spending cuts |
| 1980 | United States | Tight | Tax cuts possible in 1981 |
|      | Germany | Easing | Stable |
|      | Japan | Easing | Spending cuts |
| 1981 | United States | Very tight | Tax cuts announced to be implemented August 1981, July 1982, and July 1983 |
|      | Germany | Very tight | Spending cuts |
|      | Japan | Very tight | Spending cuts |
| 1982 | United States | Eased | Loose |
|      | Germany | Eased | Spending cuts |
|      | Japan | Tight | Spending cuts |
| 1983 | United States | Stable | Concern over large deficit |
|      | Germany | Stable | Spending cuts |
|      | Japan | Stable | Spending cuts |
| 1984 | United States | Stable | Loose |
|      | Germany | Stable | Spending cuts |
|      | Japan | Stable | Spending cuts |
| 1985 | United States | Loose | Gramm-Rudman legislation adopted August 1985 |
|      | Germany | Tight | Tax cuts announced for January 1986 |
|      | Japan | Tight | Spending cuts |
| 1986 | United States | Loose | Deficit improves |
|      | Germany | Tight | Stable |
|      | Japan | Tight | Stable |
| 1987 | United States | Stable | Gramm-Rudman legislation reinforced |
|      | Germany | Stable | Tax cuts announced |
|      | Japan | Stable | Spending expansion |

Source: OECD, *Economic Outlook* (various years).

1981. Monetary policy was described as easing in Japan and Germany, but the United States was following a tight monetary policy (however interpreted). The discussion of policy stance and the direction of fiscal forecasts give some guidance for the assumed expectations used in the tracking exercise described in the next section.

## Tracking Procedure

The main shocks we are going to examine in the tracking exercise are changes in OPEC oil prices, lending to LDCs, and fiscal and monetary policies in the major OECD countries. As the results in chapter 4 show, it is very important to specify the expected future path of shocks and policy changes.

In an earlier study (McKibbin and others 1989) we showed that the model was capable of explaining the average experience of the early 1980s. In this chapter we follow a new iterative procedure that focuses on year-by-year changes in key variables. For each period, we assume an exogenous path for OPEC oil prices and the current account of developing countries, and we generate expectations of future fiscal policy that are based primarily on OECD fiscal forecasts. These assumptions tie down the long-term real rate of interest. The level of money balances and the expected future growth of money in each country are then geared toward approximately reaching the realized output gap that occurred in each year and toward attempting to reach observed short-term and long-term nominal interest rates (working partly on inflationary expectations). By targeting money on the term structure of interest rates, we are implicitly adjusting the stock of money for velocity shocks during the period and therefore do not report the results for the money stock, focusing instead on short-term and long-term interest rates. Given the output result and the cyclical fiscal deficit that accompanies it, we then adjust the exogenous fiscal instruments until we reach the actual and expected deficits as well as the term structure. This iterative procedure takes some time to converge. When major fiscal policy announcements have been made, these are taken into account.

## Tracking Results

Table 5-7 shows the path for the economy generated by the model for 1979 through 1991. Starting in 1979, and given the assumed expectations about future policies, the model is solved forward to 2019. The model is then solved starting in 1980, inheriting the results from the 1979 simulation and taking into account any new information from policy announcements and actual realizations of policy variables. This procedure is then repeated until 1988. When interpreting the results in table 5-7, note that the numbers shown are levels of variables. The model is not solved in levels, however, but is solved as deviations from some level. Each new shock implies cumulative deviations from the underlying baseline. To express the results as levels of variables, we add the cumulative deviations of variables to their levels in 1978. Implicitly this assumes that, had all nominal variables in each country remained at their 1978 growth rates, the model would have generated a path for the real economies that would have remained unchanged. This is not strictly the outcome of simulating the model in levels, since inherited dynamics from 1978 would in principle have some effect on the path for the following decade. We argue that the size of shocks are such that they dwarf the inherited dynamics.

To read table 5-7, remember that the output gap is the cumulative deviation of GDP from potential output. To convert these data to an actual growth rate for output, the change in output gap should be added to the trend growth rate for each economy (for the United States one could use, say, 2.5 percent). For example, a move in the cumulative deviation from −8.2 percent in 1984 to −6.4 percent in 1985 is a rate of growth of output over this period of 4.3 percent [= −(−8.2 + 6.4) + 2.5]. In this case the output gap narrows because the U.S. economy grew faster than trend. The other quantities are expressed as a percentage of GNP for real variables. The real exchange rate is the percentage change from the 1978 value.

The shocks that we impose on the model are shown in table 5-8: fiscal deficits, OPEC oil prices, and the *change* in lending to LDCs. As we have already mentioned, the monetary policy stance was solved by an iterative technique whereby the term structure of nominal interest rates was targeted given the fiscal stance and other exogenous shocks. The term structure is reported in table 5-7.

Perhaps the surprising feature of table 5-7 is how well the model tracks the global economic features outlined in the first section of the chapter. Note that all arbitrage conditions hold ex ante, but only hold ex post if there are no surprises in the world economy. In every year, however, there are policy surprises, some of them quite large.

The path of the world economy generated by the model in the

Table 5-7. *Tracking Results for Model Regions, 1979–91*
Percent levels of variables

| Region | 1979 | 1980 | 1981 | 1982 | 1983 | 1984 | 1985 | 1986 | 1987 | 1988 | 1989 | 1990 | 1991 |
|---|---|---|---|---|---|---|---|---|---|---|---|---|---|
| **United States** | | | | | | | | | | | | | |
| Output gap | -0.3 | -1.9 | -3.5 | -9.0 | -9.1 | -8.2 | -6.4 | -0.5 | .0 | 0.3 | 0.6 | 0.4 | 0.1 |
| Inflation | 9.0 | 10.8 | 11.7 | 6.6 | 4.7 | 2.9 | 2.8 | 4.2 | 5.6 | 6.4 | 7.3 | 7.9 | 8.3 |
| Long-term interest rate | 10.2 | 13.2 | 14.3 | 12.4 | 11.1 | 9.6 | 8.6 | 8.6 | 9.4 | 9.5 | 9.7 | 10.0 | 10.2 |
| Short-term interest rate | 9.3 | 12.9 | 12.5 | 10.3 | 10.2 | 9.7 | 7.0 | 9.5 | 6.9 | 5.4 | 5.5 | 6.0 | 6.7 |
| Trade balance[a] | -0.6 | -1.2 | -1.2 | -3.0 | -3.6 | -3.8 | -3.9 | -3.3 | -3.1 | -3.0 | -2.8 | -2.7 | -2.6 |
| Budget deficit[a] | -1.7 | -0.3 | 0.2 | 2.8 | 3.5 | 3.7 | 3.5 | 2.5 | 2.1 | 1.7 | 1.6 | 1.7 | 1.8 |
| **Japan** | | | | | | | | | | | | | |
| Output gap | -1.1 | -1.1 | -4.0 | -2.4 | -1.8 | -1.1 | -1.0 | -0.8 | -1.8 | -0.6 | -0.8 | -0.9 | -1.0 |
| Inflation | 4.9 | 7.2 | 5.9 | 3.0 | 3.0 | 1.2 | 1.5 | -1.2 | -3.6 | -0.8 | 2.2 | 2.7 | 3.5 |
| Long-term interest rate | 7.5 | 9.5 | 9.8 | 9.3 | 7.4 | 5.8 | 4.7 | 3.7 | 6.3 | 6.5 | 6.8 | 7.2 | 7.6 |
| Short-term interest rate | 7.9 | 11.9 | 8.7 | 7.0 | 6.3 | 5.4 | 3.1 | 3.2 | 5.5 | 2.9 | 3.0 | 3.8 | 6.1 |
| Trade balance[a] | 1.1 | 2.3 | 2.7 | 3.4 | 3.0 | 3.2 | 3.6 | 2.6 | 2.0 | 2.0 | 1.9 | 1.8 | 1.6 |
| Budget decficit[a] | 4.3 | 4.2 | 3.8 | 3.5 | 3.3 | 2.3 | 1.4 | 1.2 | 1.8 | 1.8 | 2.1 | 2.5 | 2.8 |
| Real exchange rate[b] | -0.1 | -14.0 | -14.6 | -37.8 | -39.1 | -41.9 | -43.5 | -25.7 | -18.8 | -20.2 | -18.3 | -16.6 | -14.7 |
| **Germany** | | | | | | | | | | | | | |
| Output gap | -0.7 | -1.9 | -2.7 | -2.7 | -3.1 | -4.9 | -6.5 | -5.9 | -7.1 | -6.2 | -5.1 | -4.2 | -3.9 |
| Inflation | 3.9 | 5.1 | 5.6 | 6.5 | 6.6 | 5.0 | 3.1 | 1.2 | 0.1 | 0.8 | 1.8 | 2.7 | 3.1 |
| Long-term interest rate | 8.1 | 10.3 | 11.4 | 11.4 | 9.9 | 8.1 | 6.6 | 5.5 | 6.7 | 6.7 | 6.8 | 7.0 | 7.1 |

| | | | | | | | | | | | | | |
|---|---|---|---|---|---|---|---|---|---|---|---|---|---|
| Short-term interest rate | 7.4 | 8.9 | 8.7 | 9.7 | 10.4 | 9.5 | 6.8 | 7.3 | 5.6 | 3.6 | 3.3 | 4.2 | 4.7 |
| Trade balance[a] | 2.3 | 2.4 | 2.4 | 4.0 | 4.4 | 5.2 | 4.3 | 3.3 | 3.1 | 3.2 | 3.2 | 3.1 | 3.3 |
| Budget deficit[a] | 2.8 | 3.3 | 3.5 | 2.6 | 1.9 | 0.5 | 1.0 | 1.2 | 1.6 | 1.7 | 1.7 | 1.8 | 1.7 |
| Real exchange rate[b] | -1.0 | -4.8 | -4.6 | -30.4 | -33.9 | -34.8 | -27.6 | -13.9 | -10.4 | -11.8 | -12.8 | -13.2 | -13.9 |
| *REMS* | | | | | | | | | | | | | |
| Output gap | 0.1 | -1.4 | -2.6 | -0.6 | -0.9 | -1.8 | -4.6 | -4.1 | -4.9 | -3.9 | -2.9 | -2.1 | -1.5 |
| Inflation | 5.7 | 7.1 | 7.6 | 9.1 | 8.9 | 7.2 | 4.1 | 1.6 | 1.0 | 2.0 | 3.0 | 3.9 | 4.5 |
| Short-term interest rate | 8.6 | 10.1 | 9.5 | 9.9 | 11.3 | 4.3 | 3.0 | 5.1 | 11.3 | 10.1 | 8.8 | 7.5 | 5.3 |
| Trade balance[a] | 1.6 | 1.3 | 1.4 | 0.6 | 0.3 | 0.5 | 0.9 | 0.9 | 1.0 | 1.3 | 1.5 | 1.6 | 1.6 |
| Budget deficit[a] | 4.0 | 4.5 | 4.9 | 6.6 | 5.4 | 4.8 | 4.7 | 4.5 | 4.8 | 4.4 | 4.1 | 3.9 | 3.7 |
| Real exchange rate[b] | -0.7 | -3.8 | -3.0 | -27.3 | -29.7 | -29.9 | -23.4 | -11.0 | -8.2 | -10.2 | -11.5 | -12.2 | -13.1 |
| *ROECD* | | | | | | | | | | | | | |
| Output gap | -0.8 | -2.2 | -4.2 | -4.8 | -5.0 | -5.9 | -6.9 | -5.0 | -4.1 | -3.0 | -2.1 | -1.5 | -1.3 |
| Inflation | 7.6 | 10.1 | 10.0 | 11.0 | 11.1 | 9.0 | 7.1 | 4.6 | 4.7 | 5.1 | 6.0 | 6.7 | 7.2 |
| Long-term interest rate | 7.7 | 9.8 | 11.0 | 11.9 | 10.5 | 8.8 | 7.1 | 5.8 | 6.5 | 6.5 | 6.6 | 6.7 | 6.8 |
| Short-term interest rate | 6.2 | 7.0 | 7.6 | 9.9 | 10.9 | 11.3 | 8.1 | 7.5 | 5.0 | 3.5 | 3.1 | 3.5 | 4.1 |
| Trade balance[a] | -2.0 | -1.4 | -1.9 | 1.0 | 0.4 | -0.1 | -0.5 | -1.1 | -1.4 | -1.5 | -1.4 | -1.2 | -1.2 |
| Budget deficit[a] | 3.1 | 3.6 | 4.2 | 3.0 | 2.8 | 2.6 | 2.5 | 2.1 | 2.2 | 1.9 | 1.6 | 1.4 | 1.4 |
| Real exchange rate[b] | -0.2 | -4.7 | -1.6 | -27.8 | -29.2 | -27.6 | -22.5 | -11.8 | -10.3 | -11.5 | -12.8 | -13.4 | -13.8 |

Source: Authors' calculations. Abbreviations are as defined in chapter 3 (notes 3 and 4).
a. Percent of GDP.
b. Percentage change from 1978.

Table 5-8. *Exogenous Policy Changes and Shocks:*
*Five-Year Expectations*
Percent level of variables

| Year of forecast and | Year | | | | |
|---|---|---|---|---|---|
| policy or shock | 1 | 2 | 3 | 4 | 5 |
| *1979* | *1979* | *1980* | *1981* | *1982* | *1983* |
| U.S. budget deficit[a] | −1.7 | −1.7 | −1.7 | −1.6 | −1.6 |
| Japanese budget deficit[a] | 4.5 | 4.5 | 4.5 | 4.5 | 4.6 |
| German budget deficit[a] | 3.8 | 3.8 | 3.7 | 3.7 | 3.7 |
| OPEC oil prices[b] | 26.7 | 28.5 | 30.5 | 32.5 | 34.5 |
| Loans to LDCs[c] | 0.0 | 0.0 | 0.0 | 0.0 | 0.0 |
| *1980* | *1980* | *1981* | *1982* | *1983* | *1984* |
| U.S. budget deficit[a] | −0.3 | −0.1 | 0.1 | 0.2 | 0.3 |
| Japanese budget deficit[a] | 4.4 | 4.0 | 3.5 | 3.1 | 3.1 |
| German budget deficit[a] | 3.3 | 3.3 | 3.4 | 3.5 | 3.6 |
| OPEC oil prices[b] | 67.1 | 71.1 | 74.4 | 77.3 | 80.7 |
| Loans to LDCs[c] | 0.0 | 0.0 | 0.0 | 0.0 | 0.0 |
| *1981* | *1981* | *1982* | *1983* | *1984* | *1985* |
| U.S. budget deficit[a] | 0.3 | 0.5 | 0.7 | 0.8 | 0.9 |
| Japanese budget deficit[a] | 4.0 | 3.8 | 3.8 | 3.8 | 3.9 |
| German budget deficit[a] | 3.5 | 3.7 | 3.8 | 3.9 | 4.0 |
| OPEC oil prices[b] | 91.9 | 95.9 | 99.9 | 103.5 | 107.0 |
| Loans to LDCs[c] | 0.0 | 0.0 | 0.0 | 0.0 | 0.0 |
| *1982* | *1982* | *1983* | *1984* | *1985* | *1986* |
| U.S. budget deficit[a] | 2.8 | 3.5 | 3.9 | 4.1 | 4.3 |
| Japanese budget deficit[a] | 3.7 | 3.8 | 3.9 | 3.9 | 4.0 |
| German budget deficit[a] | 2.6 | 2.6 | 2.6 | 2.9 | 3.1 |
| OPEC oil prices[b] | 72.4 | 72.7 | 70.6 | 68.1 | 65.7 |
| Loans to LDCs[c] | 0.0 | 0.0 | 0.0 | 0.0 | 0.0 |
| *1983* | *1983* | *1984* | *1985* | *1986* | *1987* |
| U.S. budget deficit[a] | 3.5 | 3.9 | 4.2 | 4.4 | 4.3 |
| Japanese budget deficit[a] | 3.5 | 3.7 | 3.7 | 3.7 | 3.7 |
| German budget deficit[a] | 1.9 | 1.9 | 1.9 | 2.1 | 2.2 |
| OPEC oil prices[b] | 67.5 | 66.4 | 63.7 | 61.3 | 59.2 |
| Loans to LDCs[c] | −1.0 | −1.0 | −1.0 | −1.0 | −1.0 |
| *1984* | *1984* | *1985* | *1986* | *1987* | *1988* |
| U.S. budget deficit[a] | 3.7 | 3.9 | 4.0 | 3.9 | 3.7 |
| Japanese budget deficit[a] | 2.5 | 2.7 | 2.7 | 2.7 | 2.7 |
| German budget deficit[a] | 0.5 | 0.9 | 1.0 | 1.1 | 1.2 |
| OPEC oil prices[b] | 49.3 | 47.3 | 44.5 | 42.2 | 39.6 |
| Loans to LDCs[c] | 1.0 | 1.0 | 1.0 | 1.0 | 1.0 |
| *1985* | *1985* | *1986* | *1987* | *1988* | *1989* |
| U.S. budget deficit[a] | 3.5 | 3.7 | 3.6 | 3.5 | 3.4 |
| Japanese budget deficit[a] | 1.6 | 1.8 | 1.7 | 1.7 | 1.7 |
| German budget deficit[a] | 1.0 | 1.2 | 1.3 | 1.3 | 1.3 |
| OPEC oil prices[b] | 41.1 | 38.7 | 36.3 | 33.7 | 31.1 |
| Loans to LDCs[c] | −1.0 | −1.0 | −1.0 | −1.0 | −1.0 |
| *1986* | *1986* | *1987* | *1988* | *1989* | *1990* |
| U.S. budget deficit[a] | 2.5 | 2.0 | 1.6 | 1.6 | 1.6 |
| Japanese budget deficit[a] | 1.4 | 1.5 | 1.7 | 2.0 | 2.3 |
| German budget deficit[a] | 1.2 | 1.3 | 1.2 | 1.1 | 0.9 |
| OPEC oil prices[b] | 7.9 | 6.6 | 5.9 | 5.7 | 6.2 |
| Loans to LDCs[c] | −1.0 | −1.0 | −1.0 | −1.0 | −1.0 |

Table 5-8 *(continued)*

| Year of forecast and policy or shock | Year | | | | |
|---|---|---|---|---|---|
| | 1 | 2 | 3 | 4 | 5 |
| 1987 | 1987 | 1988 | 1989 | 1990 | 1991 |
| U.S. budget deficit[a] | 2.1 | 1.7 | 1.6 | 1.7 | 1.8 |
| Japanese budget deficit[a] | 1.9 | 2.0 | 2.3 | 2.7 | 3.0 |
| German budget deficit[a] | 1.6 | 1.7 | 1.7 | 1.8 | 1.7 |
| OPEC oil prices[b] | 8.6 | 7.0 | 6.9 | 7.6 | 8.4 |
| Loans to LDCs[c] | − 1.0 | − 1.0 | − 1.0 | − 1.0 | − 1.0 |

Source: Authors' calculations.
a. As percent of real GDP.
b. Percentage change from 1978.
c. Percent of U.S. GDP, deviation from 1978.

early years is dominated by the rise in OPEC prices from 1979 through 1981. In 1981 and 1982 the world economy is dominated by a global monetary contraction that is particularly severe in the United States. The 1982 recession also reflects an expected fiscal expansion in the United States[3] as well as the expected Japanese fiscal contraction. Recall the simulation properties of the model noted in chapter 4: in the first year of an announced fiscal expansion, output actually falls because interest rates rise before the impact of the future spending increase feeds through to the economy. This, together with the monetary contraction, explains the 1982 recession as well as the strong U.S. dollar. Both tight monetary policy and expected expansionary fiscal policy cause an appreciation of the real value of the dollar because they raise the real interest rate. Long-term nominal interest rates have a tendency to rise because of the rise in long-term real interest rates caused by the expected fiscal expansion. This is offset by the lower expected inflation rate from the monetary tightness. The fiscal stimulus in the U.S. economy begins to flow into output by 1984, when real growth is close to 3.4 percent. This is less than the actual outcome of nearly 7 percent; in the model, the strong growth also spills over into 1985, where the average growth over 1984 and 1985 is approximately equal to that experienced. By 1983 the contractionary German fiscal policy adds further to the dollar's appreciation relative to the deutsche mark.

Up to 1985, the model tracks quite well in terms of broad trends

3. For a similar argument see Branson and others (1986).

in the data.[4] From 1985 the performance of the model is not as good. It is not clear if this is due to accumulating errors from the earlier six years or if some factors not present in the model become important.

For 1985, it is assumed that a shift in expectations about global monetary policy occurs. Both actual and expected U.S. monetary policy become more expansionary, whereas actual and expected German and Japanese monetary policy tighten. This causes a large real and nominal depreciation of the dollar relative to the deutsche mark and yen in 1985, 1986, and 1987. In the model, by 1985 the real appreciation of the dollar relative to the yen is 10 percent more than was experienced. The fall in the dollar relative to both the yen and the deutsche mark during 1986 and 1987 is close to what was experienced, although the level of the yen-dollar rate settles at about 10 percent to 15 percent higher than what was actually experienced during 1988. The model's result for the exchange value of the dollar relative to the deutsche mark is much closer to the actual experience. In addition, the predicted German and Japanese trade imbalances improve by more than what was experienced over this period. The tracking of the U.S. trade balance is quite good, suggesting that the behavior of the ROECD, REMS, LDC, or OPEC regions may be causing the excessive improvement of the Japanese and German trade imbalances. There is also a built-in expectation of Japanese fiscal expansion from 1987 that partially explains the turnaround of the Japanese trade balance in the model.

Global inflation begins to rise gradually from 1986, although the largest rise occurs in the United States. The rise in inflation in the United States is less than the monetary expansion would predict because of the fall in OPEC oil prices in 1986. In Japan, from 1987 there is a steady rise in inflation, reflecting the strong rise in demand. U.S. inflation by 1988 is 6.4 percent annually, which is above the level experienced.[5]

The results from 1988 onward illustrate that the depreciation of the dollar induced by monetary policy only goes part of the way toward reducing the U.S. trade imbalance. The fundamental reason is that, as

4. Note that in this study the increases in the U.S. fiscal deficit from 1982 to 1985 are assumed to be permanent. Morris (1988) has attempted to track the real exchange rate for the period to 1985 in a small empirical IS/LM model, assuming that fiscal deficits from 1982 were perceived to be temporary and that, each year, the continuing U.S. fiscal deficit was a surprise.

5. The inflation path produced by the model is much closer to the actual outcomes for the implicit deflator for consumer expenditures published in OECD, *Economic Outlook* (June 1990), table R11.

shown in chapter 4 for policy multipliers, a monetary expansion depreciates the exchange rate and tends to raise exports, but it also stimulates demand and raises imports, with very little net improvement in the overall trade balance. Any improvement in the U.S. trade balance reflects the partial fiscal adjustment in the United States. The net effect is the prospect of very little adjustment of U.S. trade imbalances up to 1991, given the lack of further U.S. fiscal adjustment assumed in the simulation. It should also be pointed out that the markets for equity shares in the model do not experience the scale of the surge of 1986 and 1987 nor the subsequent crash.

The results for the U.S. economy are summarized graphically in figure 5-1. This figure plots the actual outcomes from table 5-4 in comparison with the model outcomes from table 5-7. As discussed above, the model does well in capturing broad trends in the data, although several turning points are missed by a year.

Several caveats should be made about the results from 1988 to 1991. First, the results from 1988 onward inherit a good deal of inertia from any errors from earlier periods, since we do not adjust the model for errors accumulated from 1979. These accumulated errors, after a decade, could potentially be quite large. Our intention in this exercise was to put as much burden as possible on the model to explain history without adjusting for errors. Second, the forecasts assume that there are no significant changes in policy from 1987 on. This assumption is made only for convenience because, as shown in McKibbin and Sachs (1986a), governments are likely to have incentives to change policy, especially if they continue to target the trade imbalances with monetary policy alone or if the commodity price surge feeds into inflation, as the OPEC price shock did in 1979–80. A tightening of monetary policy in one major economy has a tendency to lead to excessive global tightening because of the international linkage among countries, which is commonly ignored by policymakers. The extent of the monetary contraction in 1981–82 in the United States surprised many observers because the rest of the world echoed the U.S. policy change, and this made the global consequences quite severe.

## Summary

This chapter has shown that the MSG2 model performs reasonably well in tracking broad macroeconomic trends in the world economy

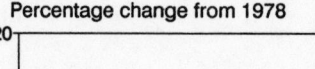

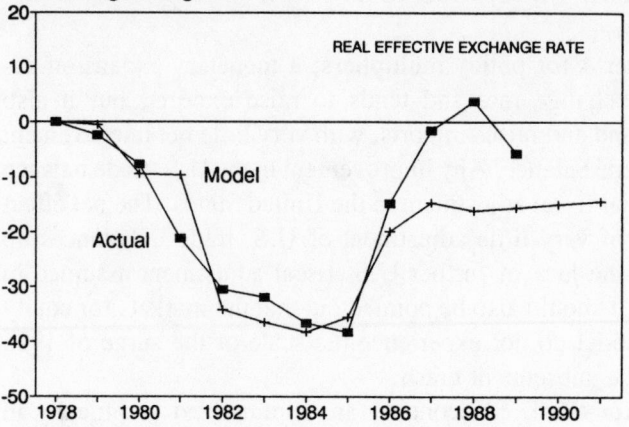

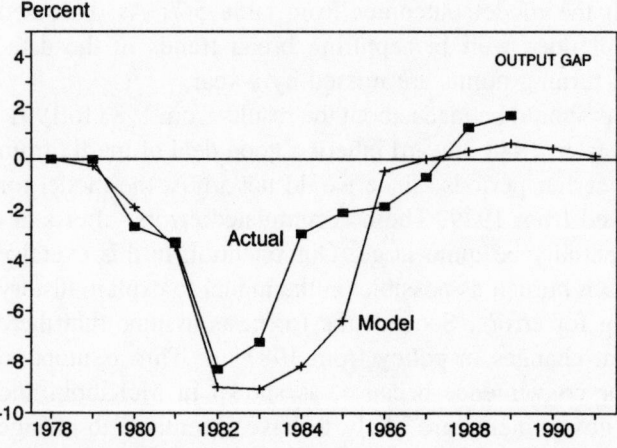

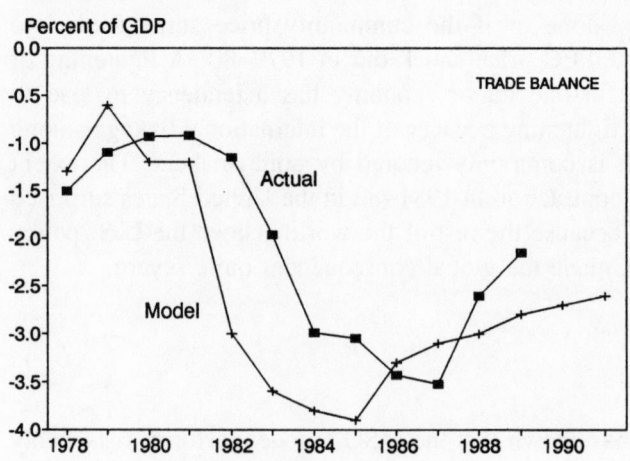

Figure 5-1. *Actual versus Simulated Outcomes for the U.S. Economy, 1978–91*

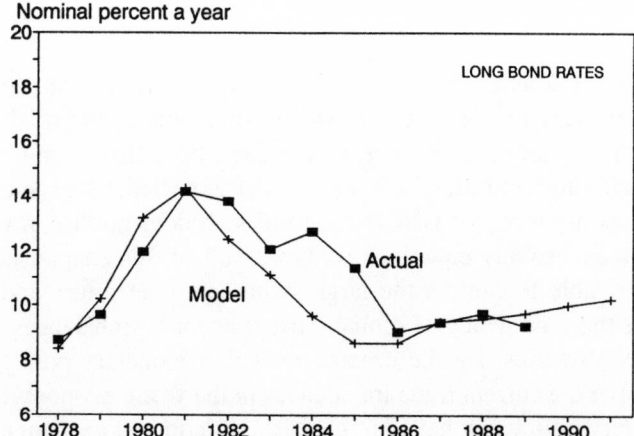

Nominal percent a year

LONG BOND RATES

Actual

Model

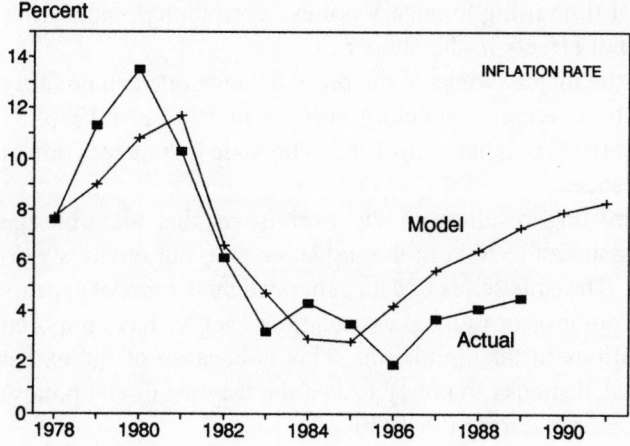

Percent

INFLATION RATE

Model

Actual

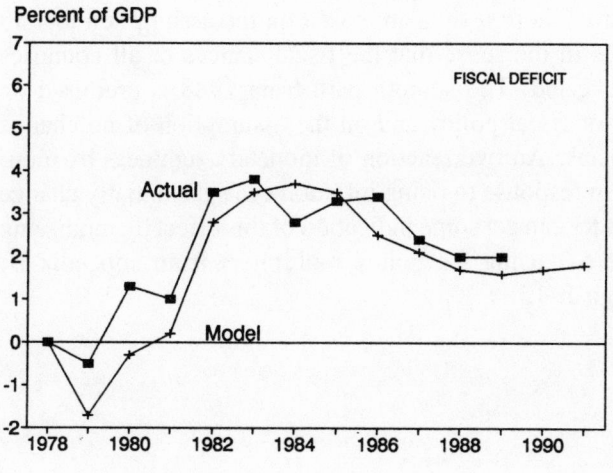

Percent of GDP

FISCAL DEFICIT

Actual

Model

during the 1980s, although it fails to pick up the surge and subsequent crash in share markets in 1987. It does so by using shocks to OPEC prices (which are assumed to be permanent each time they occur), lending to developing countries, and actual and expected fiscal and monetary policies in the major OECD economies. It does not use any artificial adjustments to any equations. A key result of this chapter is that the model is able to capture the large swings in asset prices and can account for the emergence of global current account imbalances.

These results also illustrate the crucial point that monetary policy alone cannot solve the current trade imbalances in the world economy, although monetary policy can have large effects on nominal exchange rates. In the MSG2 model, it is not possible to target a trade balance for any length of time using monetary policy, even though money has very strong output effects in the short run.

We find that the major swings in the real exchange rate can be fairly well explained by divergent monetary policies in 1982 and 1986–87 and by divergent fiscal policies from 1982. The trade imbalances reflect the fiscal imbalances.

Another interesting result from the exercise is that all arbitrage conditions are assumed to hold in the model ex ante but obviously do not hold ex post. The time series of data generated by the model appears to violate the hypothesis of rational expectations, yet we have imposed rational expectations in the simulation. This is because of the extent of the unanticipated shocks to policy (given the way we model policy) in the world economy during the 1980s.

Several notes of caution should be repeated as regards the forecast from 1988 onward. These results are based on the assumption that all policies are stable in the sense that the fiscal stances of all countries are eventually reversed. The smooth path from 1988 is premised on this assumption for fiscal policy and on the assumption of no change in monetary policies. An overreaction of monetary tightness by monetary authorities in response to rising inflation can substantially change this path. The reader can get some indication of this effect by modifying the path in table 5-7 using the policy multipliers from appendix B, tables B-1 through B-15.

CHAPTER SIX

# Alternative Policies to Correct
# Global Trade Imbalances

PUBLIC OPINION makes the fundamental mistake of viewing trade imbalances as a reflection of trade policies and trade distortions, rather than as a reflection of saving and investment behavior usually unrelated to trade policies. Although there may be instances in which a change in trade policies can affect the trade balance (through indirect effects on saving and investment behavior), we have suggested in chapter 5 that the growing trade or current account imbalances in the industrial countries since the early 1980s have very little to do with changes in trade policies in this period.

As ample research has stressed, and as we have shown in chapter 5, two macroeconomic developments adequately account for the bulk of the current account imbalances. The first is the prevalence of divergent fiscal policies in the OECD, primarily the growth of U.S. fiscal deficits and the reduction of fiscal deficits in Germany and Japan at a time when there was liberalization of international capital flows in several countries, especially Japan in the early 1980s. The second is the cutoff in lending to the debtor developing countries, which caused greater trade deficits in the rest of the world.

Since 1985, when the U.S. administration began to encourage the depreciation of the dollar to reduce the U.S. trade imbalance, there has been considerable discussion of the need for international policy coordination to bring about a "soft landing" for the world economy. Two kinds of recessionary risks have been widely discussed. The first risk is that the United States will do little about its budget deficit, so that foreigners will be called on to provide significant financing for many years to come. If foreigners become reluctant to lend, it is argued, then U.S. interest rates could soar, causing the dollar to collapse and pushing the United States into a recessionary balance of payments crisis.

The second recessionary risk starts from an almost opposite premise: that the United States would cut its budget deficit sharply, without a compensatory fiscal expansion abroad, and thereby throw the world into an aggregate demand slump. Since 1985, U.S. Treasury officials strongly have urged more expansionary fiscal policies in Germany and Japan to avoid this outcome, and influential independent economists have concurred with this advice.

This chapter examines the prospects for reducing the U.S. trade imbalance and the plausibility of the hard-landing scenarios. We first use the model developed in chapter 3 to generate a baseline for the world economy from 1986 to 1993 under the assumption of "no policy change" from 1989. The model does not generate a "hard landing," and so we examine the risks around our baseline. We then examine the implications of a set of possible macroeconomic policy options— specifically, five possible solutions to the U.S. trade imbalance:

—The United States cuts its fiscal deficit gradually beginning in 1990 to achieve approximate balance by 1994; U.S. monetary policy targets employment;

—the same as the first solution, with the addition that Japan and Germany adjust monetary policy to target inflation;

—the same as the first solution, with the addition that Japan and Germany gradually expand fiscal policy and use monetary policy to target inflation;

—a policy of driving down the dollar; or

—a 30 percent rise in U.S tariffs against Japanese goods.

We show that it is possible for the large U.S. current account deficit to be partially reduced by a U.S. fiscal contraction without that change in policy causing a major slowdown in the world economy. We also show that attempts to depreciate the dollar can only be successful in reducing the trade imbalances if the depreciation is the result of actual or credible fiscal actions. A policy in the United States of raising bilateral tariffs against Japanese goods is shown to improve the U.S.-Japan bilateral trade balance, as proponents of tariff policy argue, but this policy is also shown to worsen the total U.S. trade balance through general equilibrium changes in relative prices and incomes.

## A Model-Generated Scenario for 1986–93

This section is divided into two parts. The first subsection contains discussion of the technique for generating a historical simulation by using a general equilibrium model that contains rational expectations.

The second subsection contains a detailed examination of the baseline scenario. The nontechnical reader can bypass the first technical subsection and move directly to the second subsection without any loss in continuity.

## The Technique

The solution of the model that we generated in chapter 5 from 1979 to 1992 ignored the inherited dynamics at the beginning of the simulation and concentrated on cumulating shocks and adding these to an assumed steady state in 1978. The technique we use to generate the base path in this chapter differs from that used in chapter 5 in that we actually solve the model in levels from 1986, inheriting the implied dynamics in the data between 1985 and 1986. The technique we use is an intertemporal version of the standard technique followed in computable general equilibrium (CGE) models. It is standard in CGE modeling to generate the base year of the data base as an equilibrium of the CGE model; this is part of the calibration process of the model. In our case this procedure is more difficult: the solution for the base year of 1986 is conditional on assumptions about the future paths of all exogenous variables in the model. For example, to calculate investment in 1986 we need to calculate Tobin's $q$, which depends on the expected future path of firms' profitability.

The way we resolve this problem is to add sufficient constants to equations in the model such that, when we solve the model for 1986, all variables in 1986 are exactly equal to their actual (or assumed) values in the 1986 data base. From 1987, without any revisions to expectations, the path of variables will be determined by the inherited dynamics from 1985 and by the paths of exogenous variables from 1987. If the state variables are not changing from 1985 to 1986 and if exogenous variables are constant as a share of GDP from 1986 onward, this technique generates a solution for 1987 that is identical to 1986 except for the levels of nominal variables, which would be changing given the inflation rate in the model implied by the rate of money growth. In effect, 1986 would be a steady-state solution of the model in this case. By introducing initial dynamics, we begin the simulation by assuming that the data do not represent a steady state of the model but are on the unique stable path toward a steady state.

We calculate one constant for each jumping variable in the model. In the case of Tobin's $q$ and human wealth, we add constants to the investment and consumption equations respectively for each country. In effect, for these jumping variables we are normalizing the solution value for 1986 to be equal to the data base values of the jumping variables. For real exchange rates, wherever they appear in the model *except in the arbitrage equations,* we replace the model solution by the model solution plus a normalizing constant. We wish to impose the condition that expected inflation in 1986 equals our assumed value, so that simulated real and nominal interest rates match the data base; hence we add a constant to the wage equation that effectively changes the gap between current employment and full employment in that equation.

In total, we need to solve for eighteen constants, each of which is conditional on the model, the future paths of all variables, and the values of each constant. The exact solution to this problem is not developed further here. Suffice it to say that the solution involved an iterative process that includes numerically calculating partial derivatives of all variables in the model with respect to small changes in each constant and then solving a set of simultaneous equations, linking constants to actual and simulated values of all variables.

### The Model-Generated Soft Landing

Table 6-1 presents the levels of a range of variables from 1986 through 1991. This table is generated by commencing the baseline simulation in 1986 (the year of model calibration), solving the model out to 2026 (given expected future paths for policy in each country), and calculating constants to force the model to replicate 1986. The model is then solved from 1987, inheriting the simulation from 1986 and changing expected policy paths in a similar way to the iterative technique presented in chapter 5. We then solve from 1988 onward with the same adjustments. We assume that there are no revisions to expectations about monetary and fiscal policies after 1988. In other words, no new information for 1989 or 1990—such as developments in Eastern and Western Europe and the Middle East—is included in the baseline.

To read table 6-1, note that all quantity variables are expressed as a percentage of GDP. Exchange rates are shown as percentage changes from the levels prevailing in 1986.

These results show a world economy that grows quickly in 1987 because of expansionary monetary policy, particularly in the United

Table 6-1. *Model Baseline, from 1986–92*
Percent levels of variables

| Model region and variable | 1986 | 1987 | 1988 | 1989 | 1990 | 1991 | 1992 |
|---|---|---|---|---|---|---|---|
| *United States* | | | | | | | |
| Output gap | −3.00 | −0.55 | −0.65 | −0.82 | −1.14 | −1.47 | −1.77 |
| Trade balance[a] | −3.64 | −2.91 | −2.96 | −3.01 | −3.00 | −2.97 | −2.91 |
| Trade balance [b] | −151.77 | −121.23 | −123.53 | −129.02 | −132.65 | −135.06 | −136.61 |
| Budget deficit[a] | 3.50 | 2.10 | 1.96 | 2.03 | 2.13 | 2.23 | 2.33 |
| Inflation | 2.00 | 4.71 | 4.87 | 5.23 | 5.33 | 5.37 | 5.37 |
| Short-term interest rate | 7.00 | 7.89 | 7.12 | 7.04 | 7.03 | 7.09 | 7.17 |
| *Japan* | | | | | | | |
| Output gap | −2.00 | −1.64 | −1.11 | −1.83 | −1.80 | −1.78 | −1.76 |
| Trade balance[a] | 4.84 | 2.96 | 3.31 | 3.18 | 3.20 | 3.20 | 3.20 |
| Trade balance[b] | 94.77 | 57.97 | 64.84 | 64.19 | 66.50 | 68.49 | 70.49 |
| Budget deficit[a] | 0.90 | 1.63 | 1.47 | 1.67 | 1.66 | 1.65 | 1.64 |
| Inflation | 0.50 | −0.28 | −0.02 | 2.08 | 1.27 | 1.42 | 1.51 |
| Short-term interest rate | 4.50 | 5.36 | 3.64 | 3.67 | 3.38 | 3.31 | 3.37 |
| Real exchange rate[c] | 0.00 | 20.43 | 16.50 | 16.99 | 16.32 | 16.03 | 15.95 |
| *Germany* | | | | | | | |
| Output gap | −10.00 | −9.90 | −8.98 | −8.55 | −8.11 | −7.70 | −7.33 |
| Trade balance[a] | 6.22 | 4.91 | 4.27 | 4.38 | 4.42 | 4.43 | 4.42 |
| Trade balance[b] | 55.35 | 43.68 | 38.04 | 0.11 | 41.74 | 43.10 | 44.31 |
| Budget deficit[a] | 1.10 | 1.51 | 2.18 | 2.05 | 1.91 | 1.78 | 1.67 |
| Inflation | −0.00 | −0.34 | −0.27 | 0.09 | 0.33 | 0.50 | 0.60 |
| Short-term interest rate | 4.00 | 4.24 | 4.09 | 3.20 | 2.75 | 2.52 | 2.40 |
| Real exchange rate[c] | 0.00 | 13.30 | 12.24 | 10.16 | 8.98 | 8.36 | 8.15 |
| *REMS*[d] | | | | | | | |
| Output gap | −10.00 | −10.85 | −10.81 | −10.28 | −9.96 | −9.75 | −9.60 |
| Trade balance[a] | −1.09 | −1.89 | −1.54 | −1.26 | −1.08 | −0.97 | −0.89 |
| Trade balance[b] | −17.54 | −30.25 | −24.64 | −20.73 | −18.44 | −16.99 | −16.02 |
| Budget deficit[a] | 4.00 | 4.16 | 4.18 | 4.04 | 3.95 | 3.88 | 3.83 |
| Inflation | −0.00 | −0.71 | −0.77 | −0.05 | 0.34 | 0.56 | 0.69 |
| Short-term interest rate | 4.00 | 4.24 | 4.09 | 3.20 | 2.75 | 2.52 | 2.40 |
| Real exchange rate[c] | 0.00 | 13.00 | 11.22 | 8.90 | 7.70 | 7.16 | 7.05 |
| *ROECD*[d] | | | | | | | |
| Output gap | −6.00 | −5.92 | −6.14 | −5.94 | −5.66 | −5.39 | −5.18 |
| Trade balance[a] | 0.18 | −0.57 | −0.54 | −0.69 | −0.83 | −0.98 | −1.15 |
| Trade balance[b] | 3.58 | −11.09 | −10.43 | −13.83 | −17.11 | −20.84 | −25.26 |
| Budget deficit[a] | 4.00 | 3.96 | 4.03 | 3.96 | 3.87 | 3.79 | 3.72 |
| Inflation | 4.00 | 3.81 | 3.37 | 3.37 | 3.47 | 3.58 | 3.65 |
| Short-term interest rate | 8.00 | 8.10 | 6.70 | 6.01 | 5.61 | 5.38 | 5.24 |
| Real exchange rate[c] | −0.00 | 11.71 | 10.36 | 9.00 | 8.17 | 7.82 | 7.86 |

a. Percent of real GDP.

b. Billions of U.S. dollars in constant 1986 prices.

c. Percentage change from level prevailing in 1986. Positive value represents appreciation of currency in relation to U.S. dollar.

d. Abbreviations here and in subsequent tables in the chapter are as defined in chapter 3 (notes 3–6).

States. The output gap in the United States falls to 0.55 percent in 1989 from 3 percent in 1986, implying a real growth rate of about 5.4 percent in 1987. The growth rate then levels out at 2.9 percent in 1988 and drops below 3 percent nearing 1993, a result of rising real interest rates. The U.S. fiscal deficit is assumed to remain at about 2.3 percent of GDP over the horizon of the simulation, resulting in little improvement in the U.S. trade deficit. Inflation continues to rise throughout the period. The real value of the dollar depreciates sharply in 1987, by 20.43 percent relative to the yen and 13.30 percent relative to the deutsche mark. The outcome for the U.S.-Japanese bilateral real exchange rate in 1988 is a 16.5 percent depreciation of the dollar relative to 1986, but this constitutes a 4 percent appreciation relative to 1987.

The Japanese economy slows down from 1988, owing primarily to rising real world interest rates and a slowing U.S. economy. Germany grows consistently above trend from 1988 onward, gradually reducing its large initial output gap.

This baseline from 1986 differs from that from 1979 given in chapter 5. The main reason for this difference is that the cumulation of errors in the simulation of chapter 5 is possibly large by 1986. In this chapter we are using actual data as initial conditions for 1986. We have also included constants in a number of equations, and this will affect short-term dynamics in the current baseline from 1986 but not the steady state to which the model is converging in both cases.

## The Possibility of a Hard Landing

The baseline scenario produced from the model is very much a soft landing, but with little improvement in the U.S. trade balance. Policies to reduce the trade deficit are considered in the next section. Here we will briefly assess the risks to the baseline we have generated.

### The Case of a Hard Landing

One theme of the school predicting a hard landing for the U.S. economy is that if the U.S. fiscal authorities do not close the budget deficit sufficiently to balance the external deficit, the external creditors of the United States will close the external deficit themselves by reducing the inflow of foreign capital.[1] Such a cutoff in lending would likely be disorderly, would cause a large jump in interest rates and a sharp fall in the dollar, and would thereby provoke a recession in the United States combined with a jump in inflation following the collapse of the dollar. Many commentators during 1987 and 1988 viewed the steep depreciation of the dollar that had already occurred as the first manifestation of the feared hard landing. Although a theoretical possibility of that kind existed, a quantitative assessment of the risks shows that such fears were exaggerated, at least for the short run.

The theoretical case is straightforward. A current account deficit depends on the availability of foreign financing. With a net capital inflow of zero, no external current account deficit is possible. In the event that foreign creditors were to stop lending to U.S. residents completely, U.S. residents can continue to run current account deficits only so long as they run down accumulated gross assets—assets held abroad and official foreign exchange reserves. Eventually, as the gross stock of assets is reduced, the current account must come into balance and even move into surplus if an amortization of foreign liabilities is required by foreign creditors (and if there is no default on these liabilities).

If it is assumed that the budget deficit remains large, the cutoff in foreign lending could lead to a sharp increase in domestic interest rates, until the private net financial position (private saving less private investment) were to rise sufficiently, through lower investment spending and higher saving, to finance the budget deficit entirely out of surplus private domestic funds. The cutoff in foreign funds thereby would convert the effects of the budget deficit from one of external crowding out (deterioration of the current account deficit) to the traditional closed-economy case of internal crowding out of investment.

At the moment that the foreign inflow were to cease, there would be a steep drop in demand for domestic goods and a sharp real dollar depreciation, in the sense both of a reduction in the price of domestic goods relative to foreign goods and of a reduction in the price of nontradable goods relative to tradable goods. It is likely that the collapse in internal demand caused by the rise in domestic interest rates would lead to unemployment. Workers laid off by the declining nontradable sector would be unlikely to be absorbed instantly into export- and import-competing sectors.[2] Part of the adjustment mechanism of

1. This risk has been stressed, for example, by Marris (1985) and Feldstein (1987).

2. There are several reasons that the adjustment process is likely to result in a transitional period of (perhaps high) unemployment. The sudden drop in internal demand requires a real-

the sudden balancing of the current account, therefore, is likely to be a steep drop in domestic output and a rise in unemployment.

The case of Mexico in 1982–83 is a classic example of a hard landing (but almost any Latin American country in the 1980s would serve the purpose of illustration). During 1979–82, the Mexican government ran enormous budget deficits that reached 14 percent of GDP in 1981, on the eve of the crisis.[3] These fiscal deficits contributed to large current account deficits of more than 5 percent of GDP in 1981. Through the combination of a steep rise in world interest rates, weakening oil prices, and growing skepticism about Mexican financial management, private foreign investment shifted remarkably, from a net capital inflow of medium- and long-term funds of $11.5 billion in 1981 to $6.1 billion in 1982 and only $2.7 billion in 1983. Mexico tried to roll over existing debts in the spring of 1982 but found itself unable to attract the desired loans. It announced in the summer of 1982 that it would therefore be unable to meets its principal obligations in the short run. That announcement in turn provoked a virtually instantaneous and complete withdrawal of new credits.

The cutoff in lending had the expected effects. The Mexican current account moved from a deficit of $6.2 billion in 1982 to a surplus of $5.3 billion in 1983. The currency collapsed, inflation accelerated sharply, and Mexican GNP declined 5 percent in real terms in 1983.

The plausibility of a hard landing for the United States is often argued on the basis of three assertions. First, the U.S. fiscal and external positions are serious enough to generate profound external concern and reticence to lend. Second, even if the budget deficit is not large relative to U.S. GNP, the foreign financing required ($150 billion a year in 1989) is large relative to the rest of the world. Third, the sharp fall of the dollar since its peak in 1985 reflects a dwindling of the foreign appetite for dollar-denominated assets. All three assertions are dubious.

Analogies between the United States and Latin America are misleading. The U.S. situation, for example, differs significantly from

---

location of resources from nontradable production to tradable production. This resource reallocation requires a fairly sharp drop in real wages to induce firms in the tradable sector to hire the labor laid off by the nontradable sector. If there is any form of real wage resistance (or nominal wage rigidity combined with a monetary authority that resists internal inflation), the result will be a rise in unemployment.

3. The data and descriptions for Mexico are based on Buffie (1989).

that of Mexico in 1981. The Mexican current account deficit was more than 5 percent of GNP, compared with a U.S. current account deficit during 1988 of about 3 percent of GNP. More important, the Mexican terms of trade were deteriorating sharply as a result of the fall of oil prices in 1982, thereby causing a sharp deterioration of the trade balance and the budget deficit. The Mexican ratio of net debt to GNP was on the order of 50 percent of GNP, compared with the U.S. net foreign investment position at the end of 1987 of around 8 percent of GNP.

Perhaps most important of all, the net indebtedness of the Mexican public sector was increasing rapidly. The public sector deficit in 1981 was on the order of 14 percent of GNP, and the inflation-adjusted deficit was on the order of 11 percent of GNP, a magnitude that was leading to an explosion of the ratio of public sector debt to public sector revenue. Given the prevailing policy path of 1981–82, it was evident that the Mexican public sector could experience profound financial distress.

In the United States, in contrast, the net indebtedness of the public sector had approximately stabilized by the end of 1989 as a percentage of GNP and as a percentage of annual government revenues, even on a projection of continuing budget deficits of about $150 billion a year at least until 1995. According to the Congressional Budget Office as of January 1990, the federal debt held by the public reached 42.5 percent of GNP in 1989 and was projected to reach 41.5 percent of GNP in 1993 under budget policy as of January 1990. The reason for the projected stability in the ratio should be clear. With nominal GNP projected to grow about 6.5 percent a year, the nominal debt itself could grow at the same rate without an increase in the ratio of debt to GNP. Because the federal debt was 42.5 percent of GNP in 1989, it could grow each year by approximately 2.8 percent of GNP (6.5 × 0.425), or about $145 billion in 1989, without an increase in the ratio of debt to GNP. Since the deficit after 1990 is projected to be somewhat less than 2.8 percent of GNP, the projected ratio of debt to GNP begins to fall very slightly after 1990 (Congressional Budget Office 1990, table 11.1, p. 33). A similar path for the ratio of government debt to GDP is generated by the model simulation shown in table 6-1.

Thus, the burden of the external indebtedness of the United States, and of the public debt, seemed to be under broad control in early 1990 compared with the explosive situation in Mexico and many other Latin American countries in 1982. But the argument is some-

Table 6-2. *U.S. Budget and Current Account Deficits Relative to Foreign Saving and Income, 1987*
Billions of dollars unless otherwise noted

| Item | Gross national saving | Gross domestic product |
|------|----------------------|------------------------|
| Japan | 774 | 2,375 |
| European Community | 822 | 3,928 |
| Total | 1,596 | 6,303 |
| U.S. budget deficit (percent of total) | 9.5 | 2.4 |
| U.S. current account (percent of total) | 9.6 | 2.4 |

Source: OECD, *National Accounts.* Yen figures were converted to dollars using average annual exchange rate as reported in International Monetary Fund, *International Financial Statistics* (1987).

times made that, even if the external and internal deficits are manageable relative to U.S. GNP, the amounts of foreign financing implied by the current situation are nonetheless too large from the point of view of the world economy. Will the world continue to lend the United States $150 billion a year without demanding a sharp increase in interest rates?

Skeptics point out that the implied capital flows are far larger, relative to the size of the world economy, than anything experienced in the past thirty years. But the historical record is not all that helpful on this point. Until the 1980s, capital controls were sufficiently extensive to bar a sustained capital transfer among the industrial countries. Effective controls were in place in Japan, the United Kingdom, France, Italy, and most of the smaller European countries. By 1987, most controls had been eliminated. Moreover, in 1989 the European Community committed itself to complete internal capital market liberalization by 1992, which, when combined with free international capital mobility in the largest European countries, will effectively integrate the entire European Community in the world pool of savings.

Table 6-2 shows the 1987 U.S. budget and current account deficits as a percentage of a conservatively estimated pool of foreign saving and income that ignores OPEC savers and includes only Japan and the European Community. In flow terms, the 1987 U.S. external deficit was 9.6 percent of the combined annual saving of Japan and the European Community. Although financing the U.S. budget deficit and external deficit is not necessarily a desirable use of world savings, it would seem to be at least a feasible one.

*The Decline in the Dollar as Further Evidence*
*for a Hard Landing?*

The view presented above is optimistic about the ability of the United States to finance its external deficits. An important competing view holds that the decline of the dollar in recent years is itself grounds for pessimism. Martin Feldstein (1987), among others, contends that the decline of the dollar is the result of foreigners' increasing reluctance to hold dollar-denominated claims, which has consequently reduced the private capital inflows into the United States, causing a sharply falling dollar. In this interpretation, sharply rising interest rates will be needed to encourage the requisite flows of capital from abroad, unless the U.S. budget deficit is decisively cut. Without a sudden hard landing, as in Mexico, there will at least be a progressive reduction in domestic demand through an escalation of real interest rates.

To examine this argument, let us begin with the simple theoretical model of exchange rate determination set out in chapter 2, which also underpins the results from the MSG2 model (see also Sachs 1985 and Hooper and Mann 1989). In chapter 2 we showed that the real exchange rate in period $t$ could be written as a function of the real exchange rate in period $T$ plus the sum of expected future interest differentials up to period $T$. Assume that period $T$ is sufficiently far in the future so that the real exchange rate is expected to be back to equilibrium. Suppose further that the expected equilibrium level of $\lambda$ is a constant, $\lambda^c$. For example, as Krugman (1989) has recently argued on both theoretical and empirical grounds, the real exchange rate might return in the long run to a given rate based on purchasing power parity considerations. Then, equation 2-17 in chapter 2 can be written as

$$(6\text{-}1) \qquad \lambda_t = \lambda^c + T({}_t r^*_n - {}_t r_n).$$

Now suppose that a divergent macroeconomic policy mix between the United States and the rest of the world leads to a rise in the real interest rate differential of, say, 6 percentage points (as was the experience between 1978 and 1984), and say that $n$ is six years. Then, equation 6-1 would predict that the 6 percentage point rise in the real interest differential in favor of the United States would cause a real dollar appreciation of 36 percent.

This view of determinants of exchange rates therefore stresses the importance of long-term real interest rate differentials and uses the

Figure 6-1. *The Dollar and the Real Interest Differential, 1978–88*[a]

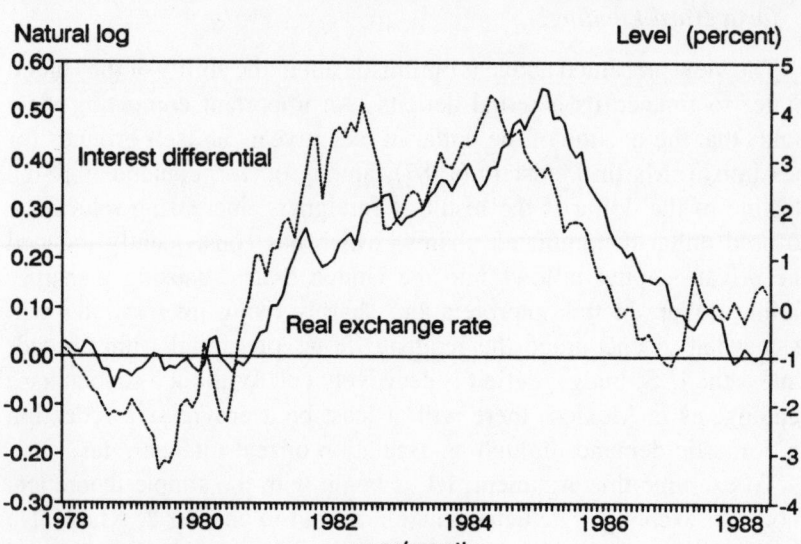

Source: Update of Hooper and Mann (1989).

a. Real interest rates are calculated as the long-term rate minus the consumer price index inflation rate of that month over the same month of the previous year. Differential measured between the United States and a weighted average of other countries, as listed in note 6 to this chapter.

working hypothesis of long-term constancy of the real exchange rate. In turn, it is macroeconomic policies (for example, the expansionary U.S. fiscal policy combined with the contractionary Japanese fiscal policy) that contribute to the shifting interest rate differential. This simple model does reasonably well in accounting for the overall movement of the dollar in the past decade, as shown in figure 6-1.[4]

The figure shows the real interest rate differential between the United States and a weighted average of other countries, together with the movement in the logarithm of the real exchange rate of the dollar in relation to those other currencies.[5] (The figure uses $-\lambda = -(e + p^* - p)$ on the left-hand exchange rate axis, so that a rise in the index signifies a real appreciation of the dollar.) The real interest rate for

4. The figure updates a diagram in Hooper and Mann (1989).

5. The index is a weighted average of eight major countries for which up-to-date data are available. The weights are determined by the share of the countries in total trade (exports minus imports) of the group in 1980. The countries and weights are: Austria, 0.029; Canada, 0.091;

each country is calculated simply as the long-term rate minus the consumer price index inflation rate of that month over the same month in the previous year. The scaling of the diagram is such that each 1 percentage point in the interest rate differential corresponds to a 6.6 percent movement in the real exchange rate ($T = 6.6$).[6] The rise in the dollar between 1980 and early 1985 corresponds to a sharp increase in the real interest rate differential in favor of the United States, whereas the fall of the dollar corresponds to an elimination of the interest rate differential between 1985 and 1988.

The Feldstein-Marris contention that the fall of the dollar signifies a growing risk attached to U.S. dollar-denominated securities can be readily incorporated in the model just described. Instead of assuming perfect asset substitutability, assume that a time-varying risk premium is necessary to induce foreigners to hold assets denominated in U.S. dollars. Denote the risk premium per period by $d$, where an increase in $d$ represents an increase in the relative return on dollar assets required by investors to hold dollars in their portfolios. The interest arbitrage equation, equation 2-15, becomes

$$(6\text{-}2) \qquad {}_t(\lambda_{t+1}) = \lambda_t + (r_t - r_t^* - d_t).$$

Summing over $T$ years as before, and denoting the average of the risk premiums between year $t$ and $t+T$ as $d_{Tt}$, yields

$$(6\text{-}3) \qquad \lambda_t = \lambda^c - T({}_tr_t - {}_tr_T^* - d_{Tt}).$$

Now, a rise in the risk premium requires either an incremental real depreciation of the dollar or a rise in the interest rate differential, or (probably) both.

The argument that the dollar fell from 1985 to 1988 because of a rising $d_{Tt}$ can be checked by asking whether the dollar has fallen more than would be implied by a falling interest rate differential. Indeed,

---

France, 0.163; Germany, 0.254; Italy, 0.123; Japan, 0.089; Netherlands, 0.098; United Kingdom, 0.154.

6. This coefficient is based on the following regression, for monthly data from January 1978 through June 1988:

$$\log (P/EP^*) = \underset{(22.55)}{-0.1688} + \underset{(19.83)}{0.066^* (r - r^*)}$$

$R^2 - 0.76$; Durbin-Watson $= 0.24$.

if the United States were in a true hard landing, the interest rate differential actually should have been rising while the dollar was falling. We can see from figure 6-1 that this was not the case. At least through June 1988, there was little evidence that a rising risk premium on the dollar was an important factor in the decline of the dollar. We also see this in the tracking exercise in chapter 5, in which we captured the broad trends of the rise and fall in the dollar without appealing to changes in risk premiums.

## Global Macroeconomic Repercussions of Alternative Policies to Shrink the U.S. Trade Deficit

A common refrain of U.S. policymakers and many economists is that the declining dollar and shrinking U.S. trade deficit impose contractionary forces on the rest of the world economy. If the declining dollar reduces U.S. demand for imports and raises U.S. exports, the argument goes, domestic demand abroad will tend to decline, since foreigners will lose part of the U.S. market and at the same time devote more of their demand to less expensive U.S. products. Therefore, policy abroad—and particularly fiscal policy abroad—should become more expansionary to counteract the deflationary impulses coming from the United States.

This argument is certainly not correct as a general proposition, and even the sign of the effect of U.S. policies on output abroad is difficult to predict, for reasons outlined below. Fitoussi and Phelps (1986), for example, have argued that the U.S. fiscal expansion was a major contractionary force in Europe and that a U.S. fiscal contraction would be an expansionary policy for Europe. The arguments that follow, based on a different approach from that taken by Fitoussi and Phelps, also suggest that as the United States reduces its budget deficit, a sufficient action abroad to maintain demand would be mildly expansionary monetary policy. Indeed, it may actually turn out that the U.S. fiscal contraction is expansionary in its effect on foreign economies, even with an unchanged path of the foreign money supply.

The effects of a falling dollar on growth in the rest of the world depend on the source of the dollar decline. If the dollar moved randomly without any link to economic fundamentals, then perhaps it would be possible to speak about the effects of an ''exogenous'' change in the exchange rate. As it is, we believe that many movements of the dollar are linked to shifts in macroeconomic policy.[7] Most of the rise in the dollar, at least until early 1984, followed the jump in U.S. real interest rates, which in turn resulted from the policy mix of loose fiscal and tight monetary policy. The decline in the dollar since 1985 is in turn tied to the partial reversal of that policy mix and the expectation of a further reduction of the deficit as a proportion of GNP, which has in turn lowered U.S. real interest rates relative to interest rates abroad.

The shifts in fiscal policy expectations, and in actual fiscal policy after 1985, are well known and are developed in detail in chapter 5. The federal government budget deficit fell from a peak of 5.4 percent of GNP in 1985 to 3.2 percent in 1988, 2.9 percent in 1989, and a projected 2.5 percent in 1990 (Congressional Budget Office 1990, pp. 33, 123). The decline to date, which is projected to continue under current legislation to a level of about 2.1 percent of GNP in 1993, should by itself account for an improvement in the current account balance of about $0.4 \times (5.4 - 2.5) = 1.16$ percent of GNP, or roughly $65 billion in 1990.

It is less appreciated that at the same time that the fiscal shift began, the Board of Governors of the Federal Reserve System began a sustained monetary expansion, in support of the policy of driving down the dollar. Table 6-3 shows the year to year rates of growth of reserve money and M1 on a quarterly basis from 1984 through 1987 (the period during which the dollar depreciated). There is a clear shift toward easier monetary policy at the beginning of 1985, at the same time that the interest rate differential started to narrow. The high money growth continued until early 1987, when it began to slow. In response to this money growth, the economy expanded faster than the underlying steady-state growth rate, resulting in a fall in the unemployment rate between 1985 and 1988 of about 1.5 percentage points. In the tracking exercise in chapter 5 the loosening of monetary policy is important in explaining part of the large fall in the dollar and the subsequent strength of the U.S. economy.

Given this preview, we now focus on the five policy options to further reduce the U.S. trade deficit that we mentioned at the beginning of the chapter.

---

7. Although we acknowledge the body of empirical work, such as Meese and Rogoff (1983), that indicates that exchange rates deviate from fundamentals, we believe the empirical work to date does not adequately deal with expectations about future fiscal and monetary policies.

Table 6-3. *Money Growth Rates in the United States, First Quarter of 1984 through Second Quarter of 1987*
Percent

| Year and quarter | Reserve money | M1 |
|---|---|---|
| 1984:1 | 4.0 | 8.4 |
| 1984:2 | 6.7 | 7.5 |
| 1984:3 | 6.0 | 6.2 |
| 1984:4 | 6.3 | 5.9 |
| 1985:1 | 8.5 | 6.7 |
| 1985:2 | 8.4 | 8.3 |
| 1985:3 | 8.9 | 11.3 |
| 1985:4 | 9.9 | 12.4 |
| 1986:1 | 9.6 | 11.8 |
| 1986:2 | 9.5 | 13.1 |
| 1986:3 | 10.5 | 13.4 |
| 1986:4 | 14.9 | 16.5 |
| 1987:1 | 11.6 | 15.5 |
| 1987:2 | 8.7 | 11.8 |

Source: Authors' calculations using IMF, *International Financial Statistics*, and updates from OECD, *Economic Outlook*. Growth rates are quarter relative to same quarter of the previous year. Reserve money is defined by the IMF as the sum of currency in circulation, bank reserves, and demand deposits of the private sector with the monetary authorities.

## U.S. Fiscal Contraction

The first policy option is a gradual U.S. fiscal contraction sufficient almost to balance the budget in 1994, together with monetary policy adjusted to target employment.[8] This package consists of a 0.5 percent cumulative cut in government expenditures from 1990 until 1994, when government expenditure is assumed to be 2.5 percent below baseline. The cut is assumed to remain at 2.5 percent of GDP forever. The results are presented in table 6-4.

The change in fiscal policy leads to a real dollar depreciation against the yen of 4.7 percent on impact, rising to a real depreciation of 8.6 percent by the third year. This depreciation results from the fall in U.S. interest rates relative to foreign interest rates on impact of the policy change.

The simulation also shows the likely trade balance effects of a sustained application of budget cuts, both on the United States and on the rest of the world. According to the simulation results, the five-year program of budget cutting reduces the real U.S. trade deficit

8. The targeting of monetary policy is set using a feedback rule for money. The technique is developed fully in chapter 8.

Table 6-4. *Announced Gradual U.S. Fiscal Contraction with U.S.*
*Monetary Policy Stabilizing Employment*
Deviation from baseline

| Model region and variable | 1990 | 1991 | 1992 | 1993 | 1994 |
|---|---|---|---|---|---|
| *United States* | | | | | |
| GDP[a] | −0.12 | −0.13 | −0.12 | −0.10 | −0.06 |
| Private consumption[a] | −0.16 | −0.16 | −0.12 | −0.03 | 0.15 |
| Private investment[a] | 0.06 | 0.20 | 0.36 | 0.52 | 0.66 |
| Trade balance[a] | 0.33 | 0.50 | 0.65 | 0.79 | 0.91 |
| Budget deficit[a] | −0.44 | −0.91 | −1.39 | −1.88 | −2.38 |
| Inflation[b] | 0.34 | 0.71 | 0.98 | 1.19 | 1.28 |
| Nominal long-term interest rate[b] | −1.91 | −2.35 | −2.81 | −3.25 | −3.63 |
| *Japan* | | | | | |
| GDP[a] | 0.27 | 0.01 | 0.02 | 0.05 | 0.09 |
| Trade balance[a] | −0.47 | −0.66 | −0.76 | −0.83 | −0.81 |
| Inflation[b] | −0.01 | −0.09 | −0.58 | −0.72 | −0.89 |
| Nominal long-term interest rate[b] | −2.26 | −2.50 | −2.72 | −2.90 | −3.02 |
| Exchange rate (US$/yen)[c] | 4.78 | 7.71 | 10.76 | 14.00 | 16.95 |
| Real exchange rate[c] | 4.65 | 6.97 | 8.60 | 10.05 | 10.93 |
| *Germany* | | | | | |
| GDP[a] | 0.36 | 0.20 | 0.14 | 0.13 | 0.03 |
| Trade balance[a] | −0.46 | −0.61 | −0.71 | −0.77 | −0.71 |
| Inflation[b] | 0.05 | −0.19 | −0.41 | −0.59 | −0.82 |
| Nominal long-term interest rate[b] | −2.15 | −2.40 | −2.63 | −2.83 | −2.97 |
| Exchange rate (US$/DM)[c] | 4.39 | 7.09 | 9.95 | 12.86 | 15.38 |
| Real exchange rate[c] | 4.33 | 6.29 | 7.90 | 9.16 | 9.66 |
| *REMS* | | | | | |
| GDP[a] | 0.39 | 0.21 | 0.12 | 0.07 | −0.13 |
| Trade balance[a] | −0.60 | −0.74 | −0.84 | −0.86 | −0.68 |
| Inflation[b] | 0.01 | −0.22 | −0.45 | −0.64 | −0.89 |
| *ROECD* | | | | | |
| GDP[a] | 0.42 | 0.21 | 0.11 | 0.07 | 0.01 |
| Trade balance[a] | −0.32 | −0.51 | −0.65 | −0.76 | −0.81 |
| Real exchange rate | 3.47 | 5.47 | 7.02 | 8.19 | 8.67 |
| *LDCs* | | | | | |
| Trade balance[d] | 0.43 | 0.37 | 0.25 | 0.04 | −0.50 |
| Terms of trade[c] | 3.28 | 4.63 | 5.68 | 6.48 | 6.60 |
| *OPEC* | | | | | |
| Trade balance[d] | −0.21 | −0.13 | −0.04 | 0.09 | 0.4 |
| Terms of trade[c] | 2.93 | 4.53 | 5.88 | 7.09 | 8.07 |

a. As percent of real GDP.
b. Absolute deviation.
c. Percentage deviation.
d. As percent of U.S. GDP.

relative to baseline by about 0.65 percent of GNP by the third year, and by 0.9 percent of GNP by the fifth year. The 2.5 percentage point phased reduction in fiscal deficits (from a level of some 2.4 percent of GNP in calendar year 1989) does not come close to eliminating the trade deficit, which starts at 2.2 percent of GNP in the baseline in 1989.

By the fifth year, the reduction in the U.S. trade deficit by 0.9 percent of GNP is accommodated by a shrinkage in the Japanese surplus equal to 0.8 percent of Japanese GNP, and by a shrinkage in the German surplus on the order of 0.7 percent of German GNP.

The demand effects of such a policy mix on the rest of the world can also be examined. The surprising feature of these simulations, one that is contrary to much conventional wisdom, is that the shift in the U.S. policy mix toward fiscal contraction and monetary expansion imparts an expansionary boost to foreign economies, on the scale necessary to offset the inevitable negative drag on the growth of these economies as the U.S. trade deficit is eliminated.

To understand the reason for the positive transmission effects, it is helpful to turn to the standard Mundell-Fleming model developed in chapter 2. The direction of international transmission of monetary and fiscal policy in the basic theoretical model is ambiguous. In a U.S. fiscal contraction, for example, the cut in the U.S. budget deficit leads to a dollar depreciation, a fall in U.S. output, and a reduction in world interest rates. The first two effects have a contractionary effect on economies other than the United States, as U.S. demand for exports from these economies falls; the third "crowding-in" effect (the decline in world interest rates) has, other things being equal, an expansionary effect by raising consumption and investment in these other economies. The net effect is therefore ambiguous, even though many commentators (and most other empirical models) presume that a U.S. fiscal contraction must slow growth abroad.

The overall sign of transmission depends on the reaction of prices of foreign factors of production, particularly wages, to the appreciation of foreign currencies against the dollar after the U.S. fiscal contraction. If foreign nominal wage growth slows down as foreign currencies appreciate, then it is more likely that the foreign economies will expand in reaction to the U.S. fiscal contraction. But if the foreign nominal wage is perfectly rigid, then simple theory demonstrates that the foreign economy must contract in response to contractionary U.S. fiscal policy.

The conventional wisdom is based on the simple model of fixed nominal wages and lack of any supply side in many empirical models. The MSG2 simulation model, in contrast, explicitly captures supply-side factors and assumes a fairly high response of the nominal wage changes to consumer price changes in Europe and Japan. This implies indirectly a high response of wages to exchange rate changes.

The theoretical ambiguity of the sign of international transmission is also true for monetary policy. A U.S. monetary expansion put in place alongside a contractionary fiscal policy has three effects: a dollar depreciation, a rise in U.S. output, and a fall in world interest rates. The first "expenditure-switching" effect tends to reduce foreign aggregate demand by shifting overall demand from foreign goods to U.S. goods. The second and third effects tend to raise foreign demand. Once again, the overall effect depends on the foreign nominal wage response to the exchange rate appreciation of the foreign currency that is caused by the U.S monetary expansion. With nominal wage rigidity abroad, the U.S monetary expansion must cause a decline in foreign output. With high nominal wage flexibility, the U.S. monetary expansion will cause a rise in foreign output.

These simulation results undermine the presumption that a shift in the U.S. policy mix toward fiscal contraction and easier money will reduce foreign aggregate demand. The presumption is especially weakened in view of the substantial evidence of a rather close relationship between nominal wage change and consumer price changes in Europe and Japan. The simulation results cannot, of course, prove the case one way or another. The sign and size of the transmissions effects from the United States to the rest of the world must remain uncertain.

The skepticism that the simulations generate about the conventional view, however, seems more realistic than the continual "surprise" expressed between 1987 and 1989 about the vigorous growth in the European and Japanese economies despite the depreciating dollar. As predicted by the simulation model, Japan experienced a domestic demand boom during 1987 and 1988 that more than compensated for the negative growth effects of the declining real trade surplus. Similarly, in 1988 Germany experienced 3.5 percent to 4.0 percent annual growth for the first time in many years, based on domestic-led investment demand. Many forecasters had predicted German growth in 1988 of 2 percent or under. It is notable that German unemployment continued to rise throughout 1982–84, when the deutsche mark was weak and exports to the United States were booming, and began to fall only after 1985, with the advent of dollar depreciation and deutsche mark appreciation.

## U.S. Fiscal Adjustment with Foreign Monetary Policy Response

It is likely that any change in U.S. fiscal policy will meet with a policy response in the rest of the world. In this section we endogenize the policy reactions of Japan and Germany using the technique for calculating policy rules described in detail in chapter 9. We first assume that both Germany and Japan adjust monetary policies to keep inflation at the level experienced in 1989. These results are given in table 6-5.

When Japanese and German monetary policy is assumed to adjust to stabilize inflation relative to the level before the change in U.S. policy, we find that both Japan and Germany initially tighten monetary policy but then loosen over time. The result is slightly faster real growth and less own-currency appreciation associated with monetary ease in both Japan and Germany. There is very little effect on the change in trade balances.

## U.S., Japanese, and German Fiscal Adjustment with Monetary Policy Response

In table 6-6 we present results for the gradual U.S. fiscal contraction combined with gradual Japanese and German fiscal expansions of 0.5 percent of own GDP, cumulatively, from 1990 to 1992 when government expenditure in these economies is 1.5 percent of own GNP above baseline. The United States is assumed to adjust monetary policy to maintain U.S. employment growth, whereas Japan and Germany adjust monetary policy to target inflation. As before, all fiscal policy changes are assumed to be announced in advance and to be fully credible.

The result of including a substantial Japanese and German fiscal expansion in the package of policy changes further improves the U.S. trade deficit, but by a relatively modest additional 0.25 percent of GDP by 1992. In contrast, the German and Japanese trade balances deteriorate by a further 1.2 percent and 1.1 percent of own GDP, respectively, by 1992. World interest rates decline by less than when the

Table 6-5. *Announced Gradual U.S. Fiscal Contraction with U.S.,*
*Japanese, and German Monetary Policy Response*
Deviation from baseline

| Model region and variable | 1990 | 1991 | 1992 | 1993 | 1994 |
|---|---|---|---|---|---|
| *United States* | | | | | |
| GDP[a] | −0.11 | −0.12 | −0.10 | −0.07 | −0.02 |
| Private consumption[a] | −0.16 | −0.15 | −0.10 | −0.00 | 0.19 |
| Private investment[a] | 0.07 | 0.22 | 0.38 | 0.55 | 0.69 |
| Trade balance[a] | 0.32 | 0.48 | 0.63 | 0.76 | 0.89 |
| Budget deficit[a] | −0.44 | −0.91 | −1.40 | −1.89 | −2.39 |
| Inflation[b] | 0.34 | 0.68 | 0.93 | 1.11 | 1.18 |
| Nominal long-term interest rate[b] | −1.96 | −2.42 | −2.88 | −3.32 | −3.68 |
| *Japan* | | | | | |
| GDP[a] | 0.28 | 0.01 | 0.03 | 0.05 | 0.09 |
| Trade balance[a] | −0.48 | −0.67 | −0.76 | −0.82 | −0.78 |
| Nominal long-term interest rate[b] | −2.13 | −2.37 | −2.64 | −2.88 | −3.05 |
| Exchange rate (US$/yen)[c] | 4.70 | 7.52 | 9.81 | 12.12 | 14.12 |
| Real exchange rate[c] | 4.58 | 6.91 | 8.41 | 9.72 | 10.64 |
| *Germany* | | | | | |
| GDP[a] | 0.31 | 0.35 | 0.48 | 0.64 | 0.72 |
| Trade balance[a] | −0.51 | −0.60 | −0.66 | −0.69 | −0.52 |
| Nominal long-term interest rate[b] | −1.96 | −2.25 | −2.54 | −2.80 | −3.03 |
| Exchange rate (US$/DM)[c] | 4.57 | 6.56 | 8.58 | 10.53 | 11.66 |
| Real exchange rate[c] | 4.47 | 5.91 | 7.11 | 8.04 | 8.03 |
| *REMS* | | | | | |
| GDP[a] | 0.32 | 0.36 | 0.45 | 0.54 | 0.55 |
| Trade balance[a] | −0.64 | −0.72 | −0.76 | −0.76 | −0.50 |
| Inflation[b] | −0.06 | −0.01 | −0.01 | −0.03 | −0.02 |
| *ROECD* | | | | | |
| GDP[a] | 0.48 | 0.22 | 0.12 | 0.09 | 0.03 |
| Trade balance[a] | −0.31 | −0.54 | −0.70 | −0.81 | −0.86 |
| Inflation[b] | 0.25 | −0.16 | −0.45 | −0.68 | −0.93 |
| Real exchange rate[c] | 3.39 | 5.33 | 6.77 | 7.84 | 8.19 |
| *LDCs* | | | | | |
| Trade balance[d] | 0.48 | 0.41 | 0.27 | 0.03 | −0.58 |
| Terms of trade[c] | 3.30 | 4.48 | 5.38 | 6.04 | 6.00 |
| *OPEC* | | | | | |
| Trade balance[d] | −0.22 | −0.14 | −0.04 | 0.10 | 0.43 |
| Terms of trade[c] | 2.90 | 4.33 | 5.53 | 6.61 | 7.50 |

a. As percent of real GDP.
b. Absolute deviation.
c. Percentage deviation.
d. As percent of U.S. GDP.

Table 6-6. *Announced Gradual U.S. Fiscal Contraction and Gradual German and Japanese Fiscal Expansion with U.S., Japanese, and German Monetary Policy Response*
Deviation from baseline

| Model region and variable | 1990 | 1991 | 1992 | 1993 | 1994 |
|---|---|---|---|---|---|
| *United States* | | | | | |
| GDP[a] | −0.18 | −0.21 | −0.21 | −0.18 | −0.14 |
| Private consumption[a] | −0.30 | −0.40 | −0.46 | −0.39 | −0.21 |
| Private investment[a] | −0.10 | −0.02 | 0.09 | 0.24 | 0.37 |
| Trade balance[a] | 0.48 | 0.69 | 0.85 | 0.98 | 1.10 |
| Budget deficit[a] | −0.40 | −0.85 | −1.32 | −1.80 | −2.30 |
| Inflation[b] | 0.51 | 1.11 | 1.62 | 1.88 | 2.00 |
| Nominal long-term interest rate[b] | −0.30 | −0.60 | −0.97 | −1.37 | −1.72 |
| *Japan* | | | | | |
| GDP[a] | 0.60 | 0.02 | 0.01 | −0.01 | −0.01 |
| Trade balance[a] | −0.81 | −1.39 | −1.88 | −1.84 | −1.75 |
| Budget deficit[a] | 0.24 | 0.88 | 1.33 | 1.33 | 1.32 |
| Nominal long-term interest rate[b] | −1.36 | −1.25 | −1.25 | −1.51 | −1.67 |
| Exchange rate (US$/yen)[c] | 8.20 | 14.43 | 19.79 | 21.95 | 24.37 |
| Real exchange rate[c] | 8.07 | 13.55 | 17.61 | 18.05 | 18.56 |
| *Germany* | | | | | |
| GDP[a] | 0.37 | 0.53 | 0.78 | 0.86 | 0.90 |
| Trade balance[a] | −0.74 | −1.21 | −1.75 | −1.73 | −1.53 |
| Budget deficit[a] | 0.34 | 0.77 | 1.17 | 1.13 | 1.12 |
| Nominal long-term interest rate[b] | −1.12 | −1.12 | −1.35 | −1.59 | −1.80 |
| Exchange rate (US$/DM)[c] | 6.26 | 9.61 | 13.34 | 15.84 | 17.72 |
| Real exchange rate[c] | 6.09 | 8.62 | 11.02 | 11.77 | 11.71 |
| *REMS* | | | | | |
| GDP[a] | −0.04 | −0.14 | −0.14 | 0.11 | 0.11 |
| Trade balance[a] | −0.50 | −0.60 | −0.73 | −0.65 | −0.38 |
| *ROECD* | | | | | |
| GDP[a] | 0.28 | 0.16 | 0.06 | −0.14 | −0.26 |
| Trade balance[a] | −0.21 | −0.33 | −0.47 | −0.66 | −0.74 |
| Real exchange rate[c] | 4.65 | 6.68 | 8.58 | 9.96 | 10.43 |
| *LDCs* | | | | | |
| Trade balance[d] | 0.23 | 0.30 | 0.48 | 0.26 | −0.33 |
| Terms of trade[c] | 4.62 | 6.73 | 8.55 | 9.04 | 8.95 |
| *OPEC* | | | | | |
| Trade balance[d] | −0.11 | −0.07 | −0.06 | 0.04 | 0.35 |
| Terms of trade[c] | 4.69 | 6.92 | 8.72 | 9.56 | 10.36 |

a. As percent of real GDP.
b. Absolute deviation.
c. Percentage deviation.
d. As percent of U.S. GDP.

U.S. action was considered alone, which reduces the positive transmission of U.S. fiscal adjustment to economies other than Japan and Germany, such as the REMS and ROECD groups.

## A Policy of Forcing Down the Dollar

The second half of the 1980s witnessed a great deal of public debate about the need to force a depreciation of the U.S. dollar to correct the U.S. trade imbalance. It should be clear by this stage of the book that, other things being equal, a fall in the dollar will improve the trade balance, but that in a general equilibrium setting the exchange rate is an endogenous variable that can be changed only in conjunction with changes in other economic variables. For example, we see that, in the MSG2 model, a monetary expansion will depreciate the dollar but will also stimulate demand and, consequently, lead to an ambiguous effect on the balance of payments. In contrast, a fiscal contraction will depreciate the dollar and reduce demand, both of which act to improve the trade balance.

In figure 6-2 we plot several alternative policies to "bring down the dollar" in nominal terms by 15 percent relative to baseline after three years. We also plot the associated outcomes for the U.S. trade balance, output, and inflation. It can be seen from these results that, per unit of exchange rate depreciation, monetary policy is more inflationary and results in stronger output growth than fiscal policy. Yet only the fiscal adjustment leads to any permanent improvement in the trade balance.

These results highlight the point that we have made throughout this book: it matters how the dollar is brought down. The movement in the currency by itself should not be treated as an exogenous event.

## A U.S. Tariff against Japanese Imports

In table 6-7 we present results for a final hypothesized policy: a bilateral tariff imposed by the United States against imports from Ja-

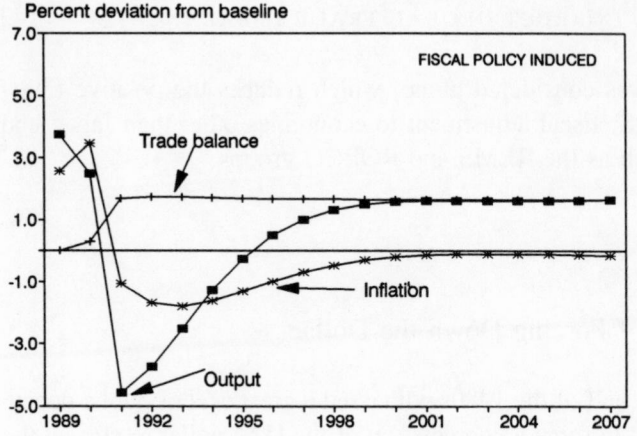

Figure 6-2.
*Alternative Policies to Bring Down the Dollar*[a]

Percent deviation from baseline

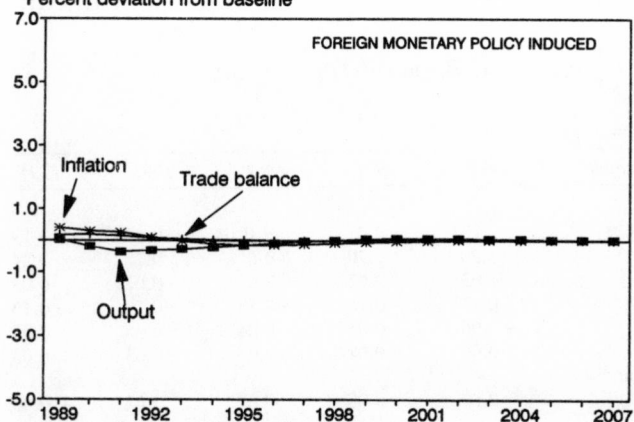

Percent deviation from baseline

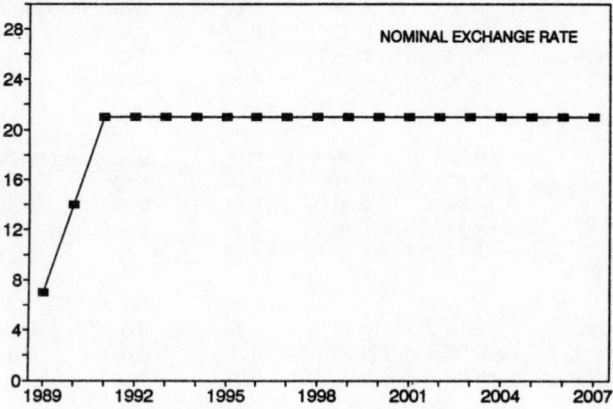

a. Inflation is deviation from baseline in percentage points; output is percent deviation from baseline; trade balance is deviation from baseline as a percent of baseline GDP.

Table 6-7. *Ten Percent U.S. Bilateral Tariff against*
*Japanese Goods*
Deviation from baseline

| Model region and variable | 1990 | 1991 | 1992 | 1993 | 1994 |
|---|---|---|---|---|---|
| **United States** | | | | | |
| GDP[a] | 0.29 | 0.21 | 0.19 | 0.18 | 0.19 |
| Private consumption[a] | 0.20 | 0.20 | 0.21 | 0.22 | 0.24 |
| Private investment[a] | 0.03 | 0.02 | 0.02 | 0.02 | 0.03 |
| Trade balance[a] | −0.17 | −0.16 | −0.16 | −0.16 | −0.16 |
| Budget deficit[a] | −0.06 | −0.05 | −0.04 | −0.05 | −0.05 |
| Inflation[b] | 0.06 | −0.02 | −0.03 | −0.03 | −0.03 |
| Nominal long-term interest rate[b] | 0.09 | 0.08 | 0.07 | 0.07 | 0.06 |
| **Japan** | | | | | |
| GDP[a] | −0.13 | 0.01 | 0.01 | 0.02 | 0.01 |
| Trade balance[a] | 0.10 | 0.04 | 0.00 | −0.01 | −0.01 |
| Inflation[b] | 0.28 | 0.05 | 0.07 | 0.03 | 0.01 |
| Exchange rate (US$/yen)[c] | −5.77 | −5.28 | −5.08 | −5.05 | −5.09 |
| Real exchange rate[c] | −5.56 | −5.06 | −4.78 | −4.70 | −4.71 |
| **German** | | | | | |
| GDP[a] | 0.05 | 0.08 | 0.08 | 0.07 | 0.06 |
| Trade balance[a] | 0.07 | 0.07 | 0.06 | 0.05 | 0.05 |
| Inflation[b] | −0.04 | 0.00 | 0.01 | −0.00 | −0.01 |
| Exchange rate (US$/DM)[c] | −1.50 | −1.38 | −1.34 | −1.35 | −1.36 |
| Real exchange rate[c] | −1.42 | −1.33 | −1.28 | −1.25 | −1.25 |
| **REMS** | | | | | |
| GDP[a] | 0.10 | 0.12 | 0.10 | 0.09 | 0.08 |
| Trade balance[a] | 0.08 | 0.07 | 0.06 | 0.05 | 0.05 |
| Inflation[b] | −0.01 | 0.02 | 0.01 | 0.00 | −0.00 |
| **ROECD** | | | | | |
| GDP[a] | 0.05 | 0.07 | 0.06 | 0.04 | 0.04 |
| Trade balance[a] | 0.07 | 0.06 | 0.04 | 0.03 | 0.03 |
| Inflation[b] | −0.02 | 0.01 | 0.01 | 0.00 | −0.01 |
| Exchange rate (US$/roe)[c] | −1.48 | −1.33 | −1.28 | −1.27 | −1.28 |
| Real exchange rate[c] | −1.41 | −1.28 | −1.20 | −1.17 | −1.16 |
| **LDCs** | | | | | |
| Trade balance[d] | 0.00 | 0.01 | 0.02 | 0.01 | 0.01 |
| Terms of trade[c] | −1.74 | −1.59 | −1.53 | −1.52 | −.153 |
| **OPEC** | | | | | |
| Trade balance[d] | −0.07 | −0.06 | −0.04 | −0.02 | −0.01 |
| Terms of trade[c] | −1.96 | −1.80 | −1.72 | −1.69 | −1.69 |

a. As percent of real GDP.
b. Absolute deviation.
c. Percentage deviation.
d. As percent of U.S. GDP.

pan.[9] We find an intriguing result, that the overall U.S. trade balance actually deteriorates as a result of the tariff. This emerges from two sources. First, U.S. residents substitute away from Japanese goods toward other imported goods and toward U.S. goods. This tends to appreciate the U.S. dollar relative to the yen directly, as well as to cause domestic interest rates to rise in response to the extra demand pressure, which further appreciates the dollar relative to the yen and other currencies. The result is a real dollar appreciation of 5.6 percent relative to the yen and of 1.4 percent relative to the deutsche mark. The substitution toward foreign consumption and investment goods tends to worsen the trade balance. In addition, the stronger domestic demand and increase in domestic production lead to a rise in the demand for imported intermediate goods from OPEC and the LDC regions that further worsens the U.S. trade balance.

## Summary

This chapter has used the MSG2 model to generate a "soft landing" for the world economy from 1986 through 1992 under the assumption of very little U.S. fiscal adjustment over the period. Simulations of the model for a substantial U.S. fiscal adjustment from 1990 suggest that the cutback in U.S. fiscal spending would not necessarily lead to a global slowdown in activity, although this depends on the credibility of the package and the response of U.S. and foreign monetary authorities.

Balancing the U.S. current account would not follow from merely balancing the U.S. fiscal deficit, but the improvement would be substantial. Adjusting fiscal policies in Japan and Germany would also improve the U.S. trade balance, but only slightly relative to the size of the foreign fiscal expansions. Monetary policies have very little

9. The results in this table differ somewhat from those reported in Ishii, McKibbin, and Sachs (1985) because of two key changes in the model since that paper was written. The first is the more detailed supply side of the latest model, which includes imported intermediate inputs. The second is the assumption of slow pass-through of exchange rate changes into import prices, especially by foreign firms in the U.S. market. In the earlier study we found that the tariff increase caused an appreciation of the U.S. dollar as U.S. residents substituted away from Japanese goods to other foreign goods as well as to domestic goods. The result was a small rise in U.S. GDP, an improvement in the bilateral U.S.-Japan trade balance, but very little improvement in the overall trade balance.

effects on the real trade balance. A bilateral U.S. tariff against Japan, although improving the bilateral trade balance between Japan and the United States, worsens the overall U.S. trade balance. The least satisfactory way to reduce the U.S. trade deficit is through bilateral tariffs, which may indeed have the opposite effect.

This ranking of policies is determined by the effect on the U.S. trade balance rather than by the ultimate desirability of the policies. For example, we believe that preservation of tight fiscal policies in the European and Japanese economies is desirable in a world of insufficient overall saving, and with a particular scarcity of capital for the developing world. One alternative to a direct fiscal expansion in Europe and Japan would be to increase the recycling of money to the cash-constrained debtor countries.

CHAPTER SEVEN

# The Theory of Macroeconomic Policy Coordination

IN EARLIER CHAPTERS we examined the transmission of policies and shocks among countries under the assumption that policies are set exogenously by policymakers. Although this is a useful analytical assumption for highlighting the major channels of transmission, in practice foreign policymakers can be expected to react to shocks of the type we examined. As we shall see, the reaction of policymakers can have important implications for the transmission of shocks among countries.

In the remainder of the book we build on the earlier chapters by allowing for policy adjustment in response to shocks. Once we begin to consider how policymakers endogenously respond to shocks, the issue naturally arises whether policymakers in different countries may gain from coordinating their policy responses rather than adjusting policies in isolation. We approach this particular aspect of policy interdependence by assuming that policymakers act strategically in setting macroeconomic policy to reach a set of domestically oriented goals. Once we frame policymaking this way, it is natural to adopt a game-theoretic framework to understand the interaction of policymakers across countries.

We first attempt to reveal the intuition behind the key results from the expanding theoretical literature on macroeconomic policy coordination by considering two classic examples of inefficient equilibria in a game between two players. We then survey results from the existing theoretical literature, distinguishing between static and dynamic games. In the second section of the chapter we apply the game-theoretic approach to the two-country Mundell-Fleming model of chapter 2. We first analyze a static game between two countries. Dynamics are then introduced, and the problem of time-consistency in policy formulation is discussed. The entire analysis is set in a world of complete information. In the final section of the chapter we consider the impact of uncertainty on the results from the theoretical models.

The second section is necessarily technical; the nonspecialist can skip over it without losing the flow of the analysis.

## Overview of Existing Theoretical Approaches

The early work of Meade (1951) pointed to the problem of policy conflicts among countries. Cooper (1968) further developed the major themes of coordination given this policy interdependence. Since the mid 1970s, there has been a surge in rigorous technical analyses of the problem of coordinating macroeconomic policies. Two distinct approaches have been followed. The first examines the international transmission of economic disturbances and draws conclusions about policy conflicts.[1] The second has been more technical in applying techniques of game theory to address the issues of policy coordination. The latter approach is usually credited to the pioneering work of Hamada (1974), who built on the classic Tinbergen instruments-and-targets approach to policy used in Niehans (1968) and Cooper (1969) to analyze strategic monetary interdependence under a fixed exchange rate regime. The latter approach, using a game-theoretical framework, will be the focus of this chapter. The empirical implications of using these techniques in the empirical model are explored in chapter 8.

### The Intuition behind Game-theoretic Approaches

The game-theoretic approach to modeling policy conflicts among countries can be understood by considering a few simple examples.

THE PRISONER'S DILEMMA. Suppose two countries are faced with an inflation shock and can choose between following a tight monetary policy or a loose monetary policy. Suppose also that the outcomes of the shock and policy response can be measured by a summary value, such as Okun's Misery Index.[2] We have two policy responses by each country and therefore four combinations of outcomes. These can be conveniently summarized in a payoff matrix:

---

1. See Mussa (1979), Bryant (1980), and Marston (1985) for comprehensive discussions of the transmission of economic disturbances under alternative exchange rate regimes.

2. That is, the sum of inflation and the rate of unemployment. See Okun (1965).

Country 2

|  |  | Loose money | Tight money |
|---|---|---|---|
| Country 1 | *Loose money* | −8, −8   (A) | −10, −7 (B) |
|  | *Tight money* | −7, −10 (C) | −9, −9 (D) |

In the payoff matrix, the two columns refer to the policy moves by country 2 and the two rows to the policy moves of country 1. Each cell in the matrix contains two payoffs: the first for country 1, and the second for country 2. In the first cell (A), if both country 1 and country 2 follow loose monetary policy, the loss to country 1 is −8, and the loss to country 2 is −8.

We have not specified the model of the economy that implicitly lies behind the effects of the shock, the policy responses, and the outcomes contained in the payoff matrix. The issue of whether the example of a Prisoner's Dilemma is applicable to standard economic models will be explored later.

We now can use game-theoretic concepts to determine the equilibrium of the game we have set up. One solution concept is the Nash-Cournot equilibrium. The basis of this solution is to assume that each player will choose the strategy that maximizes its own payoff (or minimizes its loss), with the move of the other player taken as given. Using this criterion, we see that if country 2 follows a loose monetary policy, country 1 can minimize its loss by following a tight monetary policy because in this case it will lose 7. If country 1 followed a loose monetary policy, it would lose 8. Similarly, we can see that if country 2 follows a tight monetary policy, country 1 will also follow a tight monetary policy. This implies that country 1 will always follow a tight monetary policy, whatever policy country 2 pursues. By symmetry, we see that country 2 will pursue the same strategy. The Nash-Cournot equilibrium is therefore unique in this case and is shown in cell D, with a loss of 9 to both countries.

Now it is clear that a Pareto-improving outcome exists in the payoff matrix. If both countries follow loose monetary policy (cell A), they are both better off than the Nash-Cournot equilibrium. When countries act in their individual self-interests, there is an efficiency loss in this world. Without any binding commitments (either explicit or implicit through some reputational device), the outcome in cell A cannot be maintained because each country has an incentive to tighten policy—and be better off—if the other country abides by the agreement. If instead of allowing each player to choose policy we allow a central player to minimize the weighted average of the two players' losses, then we can see that the equilibrium will be cell A. In the remainder of the book we define the noncooperative equilibrium outcome as the Nash-Cournot equilibrium and the cooperative equilibrium as the case in which a central authority maximizes a weighted average of the payoffs.

BATTLE OF THE SEXES. We can construct another payoff matrix to illustrate other equilibria that may be relevant for the interaction among countries. The following figure contains a payoff matrix for an example known as the "battle of the sexes":

|  | | *Country 2* | |
|---|---|---|---|
|  | | *Loose money* | *Tight money* |
| *Country 1* | *Loose money* | $-8, -9$  (A) | $-20, -20$  (B) |
|  | *Tight money* | $-20, -20$  (C) | $-9, -9$  (D) |

In this case it can be seen that there is no unique Nash-Cournot equilibrium. If country 1 moves first, then cell A will be the outcome; if country 2 moves first, then cell D will be the outcome. It is quite possible that an equilibrium can emerge whereby both countries set policies that threaten the other country with a bad outcome in an attempt to shift the equilibrium in the threatening country's favor. For example, country 1 may follow loose monetary policy, knowing that if its policy is credible to country 2, then country 2 will also follow loose monetary policy to avoid the severe global loss from divergent policies. If both countries pursue this same game of "chicken," the outcome could be a very bad equilibrium.

The examples given above obviously are contrived. In principle, the Nash-Cournot equilibrium need not be inefficient. It is useful, however, to explore the nature of the payoff matrix in theoretical models. In many theoretical two-country models, an inefficient equilibrium is indeed possible. The nature of these equilibria are examined below. Once the possibility of inefficient equilibria is established theoretically, it is interesting to place some empirical magnitudes on the loss associated with the inefficiency from the lack of cooperation. In chapter 8 we apply the technique developed in this chapter to place some empirical magnitudes on the elements in the payoff matrix and to determine the source of gains to cooperation.

## Overview of Results from Studies Using Static Games

The Hamada (1974) study and numerous subsequent papers under both fixed and flexible exchange rate regimes used techniques from static game theory.[3] In these models, the inefficiency of policy depends on several factors, including the way in which policy is transmitted between countries, whether fiscal or monetary policy (or both) are the strategic instruments, and the targets of policymakers. In models of fixed exchange rates, the strategy centers on manipulation of reserves. For instance, Hamada (1974) showed that, under a fixed exchange rate regime, the desire by each country to accumulate reserves can lead to overcontractionary monetary policies in an attempt to generate balance of payments surpluses. Similarly, Eichengreen (1985) found that, under a fixed exchange rate system based on the gold standard, non-cooperative manipulation of central bank discount rates tended to be overcontractionary as policymakers attempted to accumulate gold.

In the models assuming a flexible exchange rate regime, the policy conflict is focused on the exchange rate. In such a regime, Canzoneri and Gray (1985) showed that, when monetary policy is negatively transmitted between countries and policymakers care about output and long-run inflation, the Nash-Cournot equilibrium is overexpansionary because policymakers attempt to export short-run unemployment.[4] In contrast, Oudiz and Sachs (1984) pointed out that, in the case of negative transmission of monetary policy, the Nash-Cournot equilibrium can be overcontractionary if policymakers care about short-run inflation because they attempt to appreciate the exchange rate and to export inflation. Assuming that both monetary and fiscal policy instruments are available, McKibbin and Sachs (1986a) showed that, in response to an inflationary shock, each country follows a policy mix of fiscal expansion and monetary contraction in an attempt to export inflation and to offset the recessionary effect on output. Canzoneri and Henderson (1986) considered the difference between symmetric and asymmetric shocks. They showed that, although the Nash-Cournot equilibrium is overcontractionary for symmetric or global shocks, it

3. Studies of strategic interactions using static game theory include those by Hamada (1976, 1979), Eichengreen (1985), Corden (1985), Canzoneri and Gray (1985), Canzoneri and Henderson (1986), and Roubini (1986a).

4. The Nash-Cournot equilibrium is based on the assumption that each policymaker does the best he can, taking as given the behavior of the other policymaker.

can be overcontractionary for one country and overexpansionary for the other country in the case of asymmetric shocks.

In summary, the literature using static game theory has found that the Nash-Cournot equilibrium can be overexpansionary or overcontractionary relative to the cooperative equilibrium. The outcome depends on the transmission of policies, the type of shocks, and the objectives of policymakers. The main conclusion is that the Nash-Cournot equilibrium will in general be suboptimal and, therefore, that there are gains to coordinating macroeconomic policies.

## Results from Studies Using Dynamic Games

Recently, the focus of research has shifted to the intertemporal aspects of economic interdependence. With this shift has come a move toward using dynamic game theory to analyze the coordination issue. The collection of papers in the volume by Buiter and Marston (1985)— especially the papers by Oudiz and Sachs (1985), Currie and Levine (1985), and Miller and Salmon (1985)—provides comprehensive analyses of the problems that emerge in dynamic games.[5] In these papers it is shown that the issue of time consistency discussed in Kydland and Prescott (1977) can be important.[6] In general, in models with forward-looking agents the optimal control policy that is chosen in period $t$ to be followed in the future will no longer be the desired policy if reoptimization is undertaken in period $t + 1$. The suboptimality occurs because private agents have precommitted their actions in period $t$ on the basis of the announced policy to be followed in the future. Given these precommitted actions, the policymaker will have an incentive to change policy. A time-consistent policy can be defined as a policy that is optimal, taking as given that the policy will be followed in the future.[7]

The introduction of intertemporal considerations and dynamic games

5. McKibbin (1986) and van der Ploeg (1987a) extended these studies by using an optimizing model of individual behavior to derive the objective function of the policymakers. The intuition from the cited studies of dynamic games still follows.

6. For a survey of this problem, see Persson (1988) and McKibbin (1988).

7. The time-consistent policy satisfies Bellman's principle of optimality: "An optimal path has the property that whatever the initial conditions and control values over some initial period, the control over the remaining period must be optimal for the remaining problem, with the state resulting from the early decisions considered as an initial condition." See Kamien and Schwartz (1983), p. 238.

can also lead to cases in which cooperation is not always beneficial. One example is when time consistency is imposed on the policymakers. This point was first demonstrated by Rogoff (1983), who examined, for both closed and open economies, the case in which a monetary authority and a wage-setting body act strategically. The key to this result is that the wage setter moves first in selecting a nominal wage, and the policymaker then decides on policy. The policymaker has the incentive to announce a low expected price level to commit the wage setter to a low nominal wage. Once the wage setter has chosen the wage, the policymaker then has the incentive to expand monetary policy to achieve short-term gains in output. In the closed economy, the time-consistent equilibrium is inflationary because the forward-looking wage setter seeks a higher wage in anticipation of the policymaker's incentive to inflate away the real wage for output gains. In an open economy, the threat of a depreciating exchange rate imposes additional discipline on the policymaker's actions. Cooperation between policymakers in a two-country world removes the exchange rate constraint, and both policymakers go for global inflation. The result is higher inflation and lower output than under noncooperation.

To illustrate this point and the general issues that arise in the formal analyses of coordination under flexible exchange rates found in the literature, the remainder of this chapter will adopt the two-country Mundell-Fleming model used in chapter 2.

## Illustration of a Static Game

It is convenient to reproduce the equations for the home country from the Mundell-Fleming model in chapter 2, with a few simplifications. We will assume that $\gamma = \upsilon = \mu = 0$ and focus primarily on monetary policy for illustration:

(7-1) $$m - p = \phi q - \beta i$$

(7-2) $$q = \delta(e + p^* - p) - \sigma i$$

(7-3) $$p^c = \alpha p + (1 - \alpha)(p^* + e)$$

(7-4) $$i = i^*,$$

where variables are as defined in chapter 2. Recall that foreign variables are denoted by an asterisk.

Prices in each country are normalized as $p = p^* = p_0 > 0$, and the assumption of sticky prices implies that $dp = dp^* = 0$. Note that $p_0$ can be considered as an initial shock to prices.

As done in chapter 2, the model can be solved to determine the transmission of policies between countries. It is useful to be explicit about the form of the solution. Solving gives

$$(7\text{-}5) \qquad q = \Omega_1 m - \Omega_2 m^* - (\Omega_1 - \Omega_2)p_0$$

$$(7\text{-}6) \qquad q^* = \Omega_1 m^* - \Omega_2 m - (\Omega_1 - \Omega_2)p_0$$

$$(7\text{-}7) \qquad e = (m - m^*)/2\delta\phi$$

$$(7\text{-}8) \qquad p^c = p_0 + \gamma (m - m^*),$$

where

$$\gamma = (1 - \alpha)/2\delta\phi$$

$$\Omega_1 = \frac{2\sigma\phi + \beta}{\phi(2\sigma\phi + 2\beta)}$$

$$\Omega_2 = \frac{\beta}{\phi(2\sigma\phi + 2\beta)}.$$

As we showed in chapter 2 and as can be seen from equations 7-5 and 7-6, in this model a monetary expansion in the home country raises output in the home country and reduces foreign output. The policy is negatively transmitted to the foreign country because it causes a real depreciation of the home currency that reduces foreign competitiveness. It also raises domestic consumer prices and lowers foreign consumer prices through the exchange rate depreciation. It will be seen below that the sign and nature of this transmission is crucial for determining the differences between coordinated and uncoordinated policy.

Now consider the implications of introducing optimizing policy-makers in each country. Assume that policymakers care if output and consumer prices deviate from their desired levels (which are normalized to zero). More specifically, policymakers in both countries choose monetary policy ($m$) to minimize a loss function of the form

(7-9) $$U = q^2 + \mu \, (p^c)^2,$$

where $\mu$ is the relative weight attached to consumer prices relative to output. Note that including the level of consumer prices in the loss function is equivalent to including the rate of inflation because the model is static.

It is clear that by using a standard Mundell-Fleming, sticky-price model we have constrained any policy effects on inflation to operate through the exchange rate. This constraint sharpens the focus of the policy conflict between countries, although it does mean that the results must be interpreted in the context of the model used. It is also the case that, in more complicated models with market-clearing prices, the exchange rate effect on inflation is still a very important channel for conflict between countries. The assumed loss function is also crucial for the results. We use this loss function here because it is the standard form used in the literature and because it simplifies the analytical solutions. The whole question of specifying a government objective function is a complex one, yet the particular assumptions embodied in the objective function are fundamental to the analysis. Recent work by Alesina (1987) and Persson and Svensson (1988) suggests that, in economies with multiple political parties with different constituencies, the objective function may change over time. All these issues are ignored in the remainder of this chapter but are important areas for future research.

First, we examine a noncooperative equilibrium. Assume that policymakers in each country choose monetary policy to minimize the objective function specified in equation 7-9, taking as given the policy rules of the other policymaker. This is the Nash-Cournot equilibrium.[8]

Since the countries are assumed to be symmetric, it is convenient to consider the problem from the perspective of the home country. As is standard in optimization problems, the policymaker should adjust policy until the marginal loss to each target from further adjustment of policy is equalized. This can be found by differentiating equation 7-9. It can be seen that the policymaker should set

(7-10) $$q(\partial q/\partial m) = -\mu p^c(\partial p^c/\partial m).$$

---

8. An alternative noncooperative equilibrium is a Stackelberg equilibrium, in which one country acts as a leader, setting policy given knowledge of the other country's reaction function. We do not explore this equilibrium here.

Substituting equations 7-5 and 7-8 into equation 7-10 gives

$$(\Omega_1 m - \Omega_2 m^* - (\Omega_1 - \Omega_2)p_0)\Omega_1$$
$$= -\mu[p_0 + \gamma(m - m^*)]\gamma,$$

which can be rewritten as

$$(7\text{-}11) \qquad\qquad m = \Gamma_1 m^* + \Gamma_2 p_0,$$

where

$$\Gamma_1 = \frac{\Omega_1\Omega_2 + \mu\gamma^2}{\Omega_1^2 + \mu\gamma^2} \text{ and } \Gamma_2 = \frac{\Omega_1(\Omega_1 - \Omega_2) - \mu\gamma}{\Omega_1^2 + \mu\gamma^2}.$$

Equation 7-11 is the reaction function for the home country. A similar reaction function exists for the foreign country. Note that $\Gamma_1 < 1$, since $\Omega_2 < \Omega_1$.

The reaction functions for policy in each country are plotted in figure 7-1. The Nash-Cournot equilibrium will be at the point where $m = m^*$ (that is, at the point where the two reaction functions intersect). To calculate this point, set $m = m^*$ in equation 7-11:

$$(7\text{-}12) \qquad\qquad m = \frac{\Omega_1(\Omega_1 - \Omega_2) - \mu\gamma}{\Omega_1(\Omega_1 - \Omega_2)} p_0;$$

therefore,

$$m < p_0$$
$$p^c = p_0$$
$$q = -(\mu\gamma/\Omega_1)p_0 < 0.$$

In response to an initial price shock ($p_0$), therefore, monetary policy is excessively contractionary, leading to lower output than desired in each country.

Now consider the outcome when policymakers cooperate. We assume that the cooperative outcome is equivalent to the case in which a global planner undertakes the optimization. Again, this assumption is quite arbitrary but is made to limit the range of alternative equilibrium solutions. The question of the actual bargaining process behind this final cooperative outcome is ignored here, as it is in the studies that this chapter surveys, but deserves greater attention.

Figure 7-1. *Equilibria of a Static Two-Country Game*

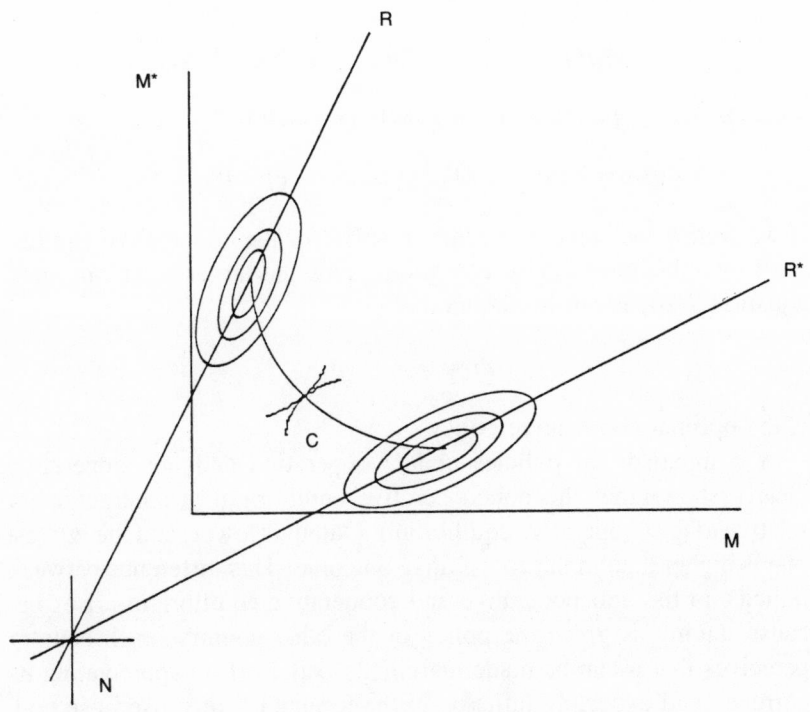

Intuitively, one can see from the symmetry of the model that $m = m^*$ and $e = 0$ in the equilibrium. Given that $m = m^*$, equation 7-8 implies that $p_c = p_0$. The global planner understands that $p^c$ cannot be affected by policy, and therefore the optimal policy is to set $q = 0$. From equation 7-1, this implies setting $m = p_0$.

Consider this from a different perspective. Recall that in the non-cooperative outcome it was shown that the policymakers individually should set

$$(7\text{-}10) \qquad q(\partial q/\partial m) = -\mu p^c(\partial p^c/\partial m).$$

The individual policymakers assumed $\partial m^*/\partial m = 0$ in the Nash-Cournot equilibrium, whereas the global planner incorporates the externality in policy interactions into the optimization problem. The noncooperative policymakers perceive that

$$\partial q / \partial m = \Omega_1 \quad \text{and} \quad \partial p^c / \partial m = \gamma,$$

whereas the cooperative policymakers perceive that

$$\partial q / \partial m = \Omega_1 - \Omega_2 \quad \text{and} \quad \partial p^c / \partial m = 0.$$

If we follow the same procedure to solve for the cooperative equilibrium by substituting these conditions, plus the target equations, into equation 7-10, it can be shown that

$$m = m^* = p_0$$

is the optimal cooperative policy.

A comparison of policies under cooperation and noncooperation clearly shows that the noncooperative equilibrium is contractionary relative to the cooperative equilibrium. Output is lower, and the interest rate is higher than in the cooperative outcome. This difference between policies in the noncooperative and cooperative equilibrium arises because, taking as given the policy of the other country, each country perceives that it can be made marginally better off by appreciating its currency and exporting inflation to the foreign country. Because both countries pursue this strategy in the symmetric case, the exchange rate does not change, but policies are overcontractionary. In figure 7-1 this is shown by the location of the Nash equilibrium $(N)$, which is located to the southwest of the cooperative equilibrium $(C)$. Adding various shocks to the model will not change the result that cooperation is welfare improving.

## Implications of Adding Dynamics

Incorporating dynamics into the above model changes the nature of the game being played. For example, the question of time consistency can become important.[9] To draw out some important issues raised by adding dynamics, we will first consider a closed economy in which wage setters are forward looking and have complete knowledge of the

---

9. See the survey by Blackburn and Christensen (1989).

government's policy optimization problem. The issue of time-consistent versus optimal control policies will be explored in this closed-economy framework. The implications of time-consistent policies for policy coordination are then investigated in our two-country model.

### Closed Economy

This section will demonstrate the results presented in Barro and Gordon (1983a; 1983b) although the model is very different from the Barro-Gordon model. In Barro and Gordon, the policymaker loses from inflation variability but gains from higher output. Higher output can be achieved by generating unexpected inflation through a Lucas supply function. Here the policy problem is written differently. The policymaker is assumed to minimize a quadratic loss function of output and inflation. The time-consistency problem arises from the policymaker's and the wage setters' having a different desired real wage and, therefore, different desired levels of output. The assumption of objective functions is again quite arbitrary, but the assumption used here is not unrealistic. There is a large literature that argues that union leadership may have the incentive to maintain a high real wage for its membership at the expense of unemployment because it maximizes its chance of remaining in power.[10] This would imply that the union real wage would be above the full-employment real wage desired by the policymaker.

The policymaker is assumed to select a rule for the policy variable ($m$) to minimize a quadratic loss function consisting of deviations in output and inflation from desired levels. Future deviations are given a lower weight in evaluating loss. This is reflected in the use of a discount rate ($\eta$). More formally, the problem facing the policymaker is

$$(7\text{-}13) \quad \min \sum_{s=0}^{\infty} (1 + \eta)^{-s} \{(q_{t+s} - q_0)^2 + \mu\pi_{t+s}^2\},$$

subject to

$$(7\text{-}14) \quad p_t = w_t + \Theta q_t$$

$$(7\text{-}15) \quad q_t = m_t - p_t$$

10. See the surveys by Oswald (1985) and Burda (1987) for a discussion of these issues.

(7-16) $$\pi_t = p_t - p_{t-1}$$

(7-17) $$w_{t+1} = {_t}p_{t+1}.$$

The notation is the same as earlier, with the addition that $\eta$ is the discount rate for the policymaker, $w$ is the nominal wage, and $\pi$ is the rate of inflation. Note that interest rates are temporarily dropped to simplify the analysis. They will be included in the open-economy model below. Equation 7-17 contains the assumption that wage setters have rational expectations; in period $t$, wage setters choose the wage to be effective in period $t + 1$, based on the expectation of the price in period $t + 1$ conditional on all the information available in period $t$. In this problem wage setters implicitly have a desired level of output (given the desired real wage) that is different from that of the policymaker. Desired output for the policymaker is $q_0$; for the wage setters it is equal to 0.

The timing of the game between the policymaker and the wage setters is crucial. In this particular model, if policy is implemented before the wage is chosen, the issue of time consistency is no longer relevant. The solution in this case will be equivalent to the optimal control solution of the original problem. Consider this case first.

To solve this problem, note that equation 7-17 is rewritten as $w_t = p_t$. Wages are set each period on the basis of observed prices. From equation 7-14 it can be seen that this implies $q_t = 0$. Rewriting the constraints 7-14 through 7-17 with the targets $(q, \pi)$ as functions of the state variables $(p_{t-1})$ and the control variables $(m)$ gives

(7-18) $$q_t = 0$$

(7-19) $$\pi_t = m_t - p_{t-1}.$$

The particular structure of the model implies that equation 7-13 can be differentiated for any period to find the optimal policy for each period. The dynamic game can be reviewed as a sequence of one-period static games. The policymaker should set

(7-20) $$(q_t - q_0)(\partial q/\partial m) = -\mu\pi_t(\partial\pi/\partial m).$$

Differentiating equations 7-18 and 7-19 and substituting them into equation 7-20 allows us to see that the optimal policy is

$$m_t = p_{t-1}.$$

This equation implies that $q_t = \pi_t = 0$. The policymaker cannot affect output by monetary policy alone when the wage setters are given the second move. In this case the optimal policy is time consistent because the policymaker never has an incentive to cheat on the wage setter when the wage setter has the second move. The time consistency of the optimal control solution is a problem when the wage setters choose a wage *before* policy is set.

To illustrate that the optimal policy is time inconsistent, suppose now that wage setters choose a nominal wage before the policymaker implements policy, on the basis of the announced optimal control policy $m_t = p_{t-1}$. To solve this, it is convenient to write the model with target variables as a function of state variables $(w, p_{t-1})$ and control variables $(m)$:

(7-21) $$q_t = (m_t - w_t)/(1 + \theta)$$

(7-22) $$\pi_t = \theta m_t/(1 + \theta) + w_t/(1 + \theta) - p_{t-1}.$$

Now we assume that $w_t = p_{t-1}$. Differentiating equations 7-21 and 7-22 and substituting into the policymaker's first-order condition given in equation 7-20, we now find a reaction function:

(7-23) $$m_t = p_{t-1} + [(1 + \theta)/(1 + \theta^2\mu)]q_0.$$

Substituting equation 7-23 into equations 7-21 and 7-22 and assuming that $w_t = p_{t-1}$ gives the results for the target variables:

(7-24) $$q_t [1/(1 + \theta^2\mu)]q_0$$

(7-25) $$\pi_t = [\theta/(1 + \theta^2\mu)]q_0.$$

Notice that, once the wage setters have precommitted their wage based on the announced policy, the policymaker has the incentive to renege on the announced policy of zero inflation and to follow an expansionary monetary policy. This is shown in equation 7-25. Once the wage is fixed, the policymaker can expand monetary policy until the benefit from an extra unit of output is offset by the cost of an additional unit of inflation. The optimal policy is therefore shown to be time inconsistent: once the policy is announced, the policymaker has an incentive to change the policy. The optimal policy will not be observed if the wage setters are forward looking (unless some reputational mechanism can be established) because the wage setters fully understand the policymaker's incentives.

We now want to find a time-consistent policy. To aid in solving for the time-consistent equilibrium, the model can again be rewritten with the target variables $(q, \pi)$ as functions of the control variable $(m)$ and state variables $(w, p_{t-1})$. Define the value function $(V)$ as

$$(7\text{-}26) \quad V_t = \min_{\{m_t,\ m_{t+1},\ \ldots\}} \{(q_t - q_0)^2 + \mu\pi_t^2\} + (1+\eta)^{-1}V_{t+1},$$

subject to

$$(7\text{-}27) \qquad\qquad q_t = [(1/1 + \theta)](m_t - w_t)$$

$$(7\text{-}28) \quad \pi_t = [\theta/(1 + \theta)]\,m_t + [1/(1 + \theta)]w_t - p_{t-1}.$$

Note that the wage in period $t$ is now a state variable (that is, it is fixed in period $t$) to the policymaker. To find the time-consistent solution to this problem, we will use a dynamic programming technique of backward recursion. First we find the solution to the finite-horizon problem, and then we take the limit of this problem for the infinite-horizon case.

Suppose period $T$ is the final period and, by concentrating only on stationary solutions, assume that $V_{T+1} = 0$. The optimization of equation 7-26 requires that the policymaker should set

$$(7\text{-}29) \qquad (q_T - q_0)\,(\partial q/\partial m) = -\mu\pi_T\,(\partial\pi/\partial m).$$

Differentiating equations 7-27 and 7-28 and substituting them into equation 7-29 gives a rule for the control variable in period $T$:

$$(7\text{-}30) \quad m_T = \frac{1}{1+\mu\theta^2}\{(1-\theta\mu)w_T + (1+\theta)q_0 + \theta(1+\theta)\mu p_{T-1}\}.$$

This is the time-consistent, closed-loop[11] rule for the control variable $(m_T)$ expressed as a function of the state variables $(w_T$ and $p_{t-1})$ and the exogenous variable $(q_0)$.

The assumption of rational expectations in equation 7-17 implies

---

11. A closed-loop policy is a feedback policy rule that links policy instruments to developments in the evolution of the economy, whereas an open-loop policy is a specified sequence of policy settings with the sequence independent of the future evolution of the economy.

that $p_T = w_T$ in equilibrium. Given this, equation 7-14 implies that $q_T = 0$. That is, under rational expectations the government is unable to affect output in a systematic way, and therefore output is $q_0$ less than desired by the policymaker. Substituting $w_T = p_T$ together with the rule for $m$ into equations 7-27 and 7-18 allows us to show that, in period $T$,

$$(7\text{-}31) \qquad\qquad q_T = 0$$

and

$$(7\text{-}32) \qquad\qquad \pi_T = \frac{1}{\mu\theta}q_0.$$

The value function in period $T$ is a function of $q_0$ and is independent of variables inherited from earlier periods. Each period can therefore be solved independently, taking as given that future governments will be following the policy rule in equation 7-30. In each period the solution will be of the form given in equations 7-31 and 7-32. Taking the limit for large $T$ does not change the result.

The above example has shown that when wage setters have rational expectations and a desired level of output different from that of the policymaker, the time-consistent equilibrium will have an inflationary bias, and output will be less than what is desired by the policymaker. This is the Barro-Gordon result. Private agents know that once they choose a nominal wage, the policymaker has an incentive to inflate away the real wage for some output gain. Given that the wage setters know the trade-off between inflation and output in the policymaker's objective function, they have an incentive to set nominal wages at the point where they know the policymaker is unwilling to trade off an extra unit's loss on inflation for a unit's gain on output. Recall that in the time-inconsistent case, we calculated the optimal policy by assuming that the wage setters believe the policy announcement and that future policymakers would not renege on the announced policy even though they have the incentive to do so as time passes. If some reputational mechanism could be introduced whereby credible commitment was possible, then the optimal policy could be implemented. Unfortunately, if this is not found and the wage setters are rational, then the time-consistent policy we have calculated is the best policy that is credible to all agents.

Suppose that, instead of rational expectations, we assume that the wage setters choose a wage for period $t + 1$ on the basis of the price observed in period $t$. The assumption that $w_{t+1} = p_t$ is the same assumption we used to solve for the case in which the policymaker announced a policy of zero inflation and then optimized given that wage setters believe the announced policy. These results were given in equations 7-24 and 7-25. In this case, the economy still has an inflationary bias if wage setters desire a lower output level than the policymaker. However, the bias is much less.

### Two-Country Model

Now consider the implications of the above analysis for the two-country model of chapter 2. We add to that basic model some aspects of forward-looking behavior. First, we add wage setters who determine wages on the basis of expected price changes. We also introduce forward-looking behavior in the domestic bond markets and foreign exchange markets. The foreign exchange market and domestic bond markets are assumed to consist of many small agents who individually perceive that their actions have little impact and therefore do not act strategically. We can therefore take their actions as conditioned on the policy settings. Wage setters, in contrast, are assumed to be members of a union that is large enough to act strategically with the government. This significantly complicates the analysis, but the insights from adding this intertemporal aspect make it worth pursuing.

The equations for the home country are repeated here for convenience, together with any added assumptions:

$$(7\text{-}33) \qquad m_t - p_t = \phi q_t - \beta i_t$$

$$(7\text{-}34) \qquad q_t = \delta(e_t + p_t^* - p_t) - \sigma r_t$$

$$(7\text{-}35) \qquad p_t^c = \alpha p_t + (1 - \alpha)(p_t^* + e_t)$$

$$(7\text{-}36) \qquad i_t^* = i_t + {}_t e_{t+1} - e_t$$

$$(7\text{-}37) \qquad r_t = i_t - {}_t p_{t+1} + p_t$$

$$(7\text{-}38) \qquad p_t = w_t + \theta q_t$$

$$(7\text{-}39) \qquad w_{t+1} = \zeta \, {}_t p_{t+1}^c + (1 - \zeta) p_t^c$$

$$(7\text{-}40) \qquad \pi_t^c = p_t^c - p_{t-1}^c.$$

There is a similar set of equations for the foreign country. The main differences between this two-country model and the static two-country model analyzed above are reintroduction of the supply curve given in equation 7-38, the difference between real and nominal interest rates because of expected changes in domestic prices, and the allowance for expected changes in the exchange rate given in the interest parity condition in equation 7-36. Equation 7-39 incorporates the two assumptions about wage-setting behavior: $\zeta = 1$ is the case of forward-looking wage setters, and $\zeta = 0$ is the case of backward-looking wage setters.

Noncooperation is defined as the Nash-Cournot equilibrium in which each country chooses a path for its policy instruments $(m_{t+s})$ to minimize a loss function consisting of deviations in domestic output and inflation from a desired level. Formally, each country undertakes the following optimization:

$$\min_{\{m_{t+s}\}} \sum_{s=0}^{\infty} (1+\eta)^{-s}\{(q_{t+s} - q_0)^2 + \mu\pi_{t+s}^{c2}\},$$

subject to the global economy portrayed in equations 7-33 through 7-40 and taking as given the policies of the other countries. Cooperation is defined as the case in which a global planner maximizes a weighted average of the objective function of each country, where countries receive equal weighting.

Define the value function as

$$(7\text{-}41) \quad V_t = \min \{(q_t - q_0)^2 + \mu\pi_t^{c2}\} + (1+\eta)^{-1}V_{t+1},$$

subject to equations 7-33 through 7-40.

To solve this problem, we first solve the problem in an arbitrary terminal period $T$. We restrict the analysis to stationary solutions and therefore assume that in the last period $(T)$ $e_{T+1} = e_T$, $p_{T+1} = p_T$, and $V_{T+1} = 0$. This implies that $i = i^* = r$.

Consider the problem faced by the policymaker in the home country when wages are set before policy is implemented. The target variables are again written as a function of the state variables, the control variables, and the exogenous variables. Recall that the policymaker treats the wage set in period $T$ as a state variable because the wage setters choose their wage before policy is implemented.

It is shown in the appendix to this chapter that the model can be rewritten for period $T$ as equations 7-42 and 7-43:

(7-42)     $q = \beta_1(m - w) + \beta_2(m^* - w^*)$

(7-43)     $\pi^c = w + \gamma_1(m - w) + \gamma_2(m^* - w^*) - p^c_{T-1}.$

Equations 7-42 and 7-43 give the targets $q$ and $\pi^c$ as functions of the control variables $(m, m^*)$ and the state variables $(w, w^*, p^c_{T-1})$. In the noncooperative case, we find the policy rule of the home country by differentiating the objective function in equation 7-41 for period $T$ to find

(7-44)          $(q_T - q_0)\,(\partial q/\partial m) = -\mu\pi_T\,(\partial\pi/\partial m).$

Differentiating equations 7-42 and 7-43, substituting into equation 7-44, and then using the useful trick that we know the equilibrium will be symmetric ($m = m^*$ and $w = w^*$), we find the following rule:

$$m_T = \frac{\beta_1 + \theta\mu\gamma_1}{\beta_1 + \theta\mu\gamma_1} - \mu\gamma_1\theta w_T + \frac{\theta\,\beta_1}{\beta_1 + \theta\mu\gamma_1}q_0 + \frac{\mu\gamma_1\theta}{\beta_1 + \theta\mu\gamma_1}p^c_{T-1}.$$

Now consider the case in which wage setters are forward looking (that is, $\zeta = 1$). We have, from the assumption of rational expectations, that $w = p^c$ in the equilibrium. It can be seen from equation 7-43 that $m = w = p^c$. Substituting these relations into the rule for money gives

(7-45)                    $\pi^c_T = \dfrac{\beta_1}{\mu\gamma_1}q_0.$

It is clear from equation 7-42 that, with $m = w$,

(7-46)                              $q_T = 0.$

This is the solution in period $T$. We have shown that the target variables are only a function of $q_0$. Substituting these results into the value function given in equation 7-41, we see that the value function is only a function of $q_0$ given our assumption of stationarity of the solution. Each period, the problem is a repetition of the problem we solved for period $T$. The results in equations 7-45 and 7-46 will be unchanged as we solve the problem in each period, taking as given the policy rules followed by future governments.

The cooperative equilibrium can be found in a similar way. First, we solve the problem of a global planner choosing both $m$ and $m^*$ in an arbitrary terminal period $T$. In the noncooperative case, the policymakers individually perceived that

$$\partial q/\partial m = \beta_1 \quad \text{and} \quad \partial \pi/\partial m = \gamma_1.$$

In the cooperative case, we have that

$$\partial q/\partial m = \beta_1 + \beta_2 = 1/\theta \quad \text{and} \quad \partial \pi/\partial m = \gamma_1 + \gamma_2 = \theta/\Theta.$$

Substituting these results into the first-order conditions given in equation 7-44 gives a new rule for domestic monetary policy:

$$m_T = \frac{1 - \mu\Theta\theta + \theta^2\mu}{1 + \theta^2\mu}w_T + \frac{\Theta}{1 + \theta^2\mu}q_0 + \frac{\mu\Theta\theta}{1 + \theta^2\mu}p^c_{T-1}.$$

Again, by using the equilibrium property that $w = p^c$ we can see from the inflation equation 7-43 that $m = w = p^c$. Substituting into the new rule for money gives the cooperative equilibrium in period $T$:

$$(7\text{-}47) \qquad\qquad \pi^c_T = q_0/\phi\theta.$$

We can see directly from equation 7-42 that, with $m = w$,

$$(7\text{-}48) \qquad\qquad q_T = 0.$$

As in the noncooperative case, we find that the targets are independent of the state variables. The backward recursion will therefore lead to the same solution in each period.

In both the cooperative and noncooperative equilibria, the assumption of rational wage setters gives the same result for output ($q = 0$) as we found in the closed-economy example. The realized rates of inflation given in equations 7-45 and 7-47 respectively are the only difference between the two equilibria. In evaluating which inflation rate is higher, we need to compare $\mu\gamma_1/\beta_1$ with $\phi\theta$. We have that $\gamma_1/\beta_1 > \theta + (1-\alpha)(\beta_1-\beta_2)/(2\beta_1\delta)$. Given that $\beta_1>\beta_2$, we have that $\gamma_1/\beta_1>\theta$, which implies that inflation under cooperation is higher than inflation under noncooperation if $\mu > \phi$. Recall that $\mu$ is the weight on inflation in the objective function and that $\phi$ is the income elasticity of money demand. Therefore, it is more likely to be the case that inflation under cooperation is higher than under noncooperation, the higher is the weight on inflation in the objective function. Cooperation can therefore lead to a larger welfare loss than noncooperation.

This curious result can be better understood for considering the results of the closed-economy model above. The interaction of a wage setter and a government with different objectives implied an inflationary bias in the economy. In the open economy, the trade-off between output and inflation facing the government is changed by the effect a floating exchange rate has on inflation. This additional constraint on government policy acts to reduce the inflationary bias in the economy. With two such economies agreeing to cooperate and fixing the exchange rate between them, the wage setters in each country understand that the trade-off between output and inflation facing the policymakers is affected by this agreement, which effectively removes a constraint facing each government. The wage setters revert to more inflationary wage demands in order to preserve their real wages in the face of a coordinated monetary expansion. The final equilibrium is therefore more inflationary under cooperation than under noncooperation, as shown by Rogoff (1983).

In the particular example chosen, the Nash-Cournot and cooperative equilibria will be a sequence of repeated static games in which cooperation leads to a larger welfare loss than noncooperation. Note that this is different from the example in Oudiz and Sachs (1985). The models are identical except for the assumption of the wage-setting process. In Oudiz and Sachs the wage is set according to a Phillips curve relation. That feature adds persistence through lagged output, which disappears in the example here.

To explore the result in Oudiz and Sachs (1985), now assume that wage setters are backward looking (that is, $\zeta = 0$). Following the same procedures to solve the model, we find for noncooperation that

$$(7\text{-}49) \qquad \pi_c = \frac{\theta}{1 + \theta\mu\gamma_1/\beta_1}\, q_0$$

$$(7\text{-}50) \qquad q = \frac{1}{1 + \theta\mu\gamma_1/\beta_1}\, q_0.$$

Note that output given in equation 7-50 is now greater than 0 but less than desired output $q_0$. Solving for the cooperative equilibrium, we have

$$(7\text{-}51) \qquad \pi^c = \frac{\theta}{1 + \theta^2 \mu} \, q_0$$

$$(7\text{-}52) \qquad q = \frac{1}{1 + \theta^2 \mu} \, q_0.$$

Comparing cooperation with noncooperation, we see that noncooperation is more inflationary than cooperation if $\gamma_1/\beta_1 > \theta$. From our results above for the case of forward-looking wage setters, we have shown that this condition holds. Noncooperation is therefore more inflationary and leads to a larger output loss than cooperation when wage setters are backward looking. This is a case in which cooperation is welfare improving.

## On the Role of Uncertainty

The literature surveyed above has concentrated on the problem of inefficient equilibria in the case of perfect knowledge of the model and of the policymaker's reaction function. Uncertainty, it has been argued by many commentators, is the circumstance in which gains to coordination, through information sharing, are potentially large.[12] Papers by Roubini (1986b), Ghosh (1986), Frankel (1986), Holtham and Hughes-Hallett (1987), and Blackburn (1987) have introduced model uncertainty into the problem studied. The results from these studies illustrate that uncertainty can increase or decrease the gains or losses from coordination, depending on assumptions about the source of the uncertainty. Blackburn (1987) also addressed the problem of reputation in international policy coordination, extending the work of Barro and Gordon (1983a; 1983b) to a game between policymakers.

The results on uncertainty, although preliminary, do show that the results from studies assuming perfect foresight can be significantly changed. This area is fertile ground for further research.

## Summary

This chapter has used a relatively simple framework to illustrate the major results from the game-theoretic literature on policy interde-

---

12. See McKibbin (1985) for a discussion of this view.

pendence. We have shown that the nature of the gains or losses from coordinating policies across national borders depends on the structure of the economies, how shocks are transmitted between countries, the assumptions about government and private sector interactions within each economy, and the objectives of the governments and wage setters.

Whether there are potential gains to coordinating macroeconomic policies is ultimately an empirical issue. In the next chapter we use the concepts introduced here, together with the global simulation model, in an attempt to quantify the issues.

## Appendix: Solution of the Two-Country Dynamic Model

In this appendix we provide the solution to the two-country model in the text of chapter 7.

Denoting foreign equations with an asterisk, we add equation 7-33 to equation 7-33*, 7-34 to 7-34*, and 7-38 to 7-38*. This gives

$$(7\text{-A1}) \qquad\qquad q + q^* = -2\sigma r$$

$$(7\text{-A2}) \qquad m + m^* = p + p^* + \phi(q + q^*) = 2\beta r$$

$$(7\text{-A3}) \qquad\qquad p + p^* = w + w^* + \theta(q + q^*).$$

Substituting equations 7-A1 and 7-A3 into equation 7-A2 gives

$$(7\text{-A4}) \qquad q = -q^* + [(m + m^*) - (w + w^*)]/\Theta,$$

where $\Theta = \theta + \phi + \beta/\sigma$.

We can also difference equations 7-33 and 7-33* and substitute them into equations 7-38 and 7-38* to find

$$(7\text{-A5}) \qquad q^* = q - [m - m^* - (w - w^*)]/(\theta + \phi).$$

Using equations 7-A4 and 7-A5, we can write the target ($q$) as a function of the control variables ($m$ and $m^*$) and the state variables ($w$ and $w^*$):

$$(7\text{-A6}) \qquad\qquad q = \beta_1(m - w) + \beta_2(m^* - w^*),$$

where

$$\beta_1 = \frac{1}{2\Theta}\left(1 + \frac{\Theta}{\theta + \phi}\right) \quad \text{and} \quad \beta_2 = \frac{1}{2\Theta}\left(1 - \frac{\Theta}{\theta + \phi}\right).$$

Note that $\beta_1 + \beta_2 = 1/\Theta$.

To solve for $\pi$, we difference equations 7-34 and 7-34*, solve for $e$, and substitute this, together with equation 7-35, into equation 7-40 to find

$$(7\text{-A7}) \quad \pi^c = w + [\theta + (1 - \alpha)/2\delta]q - (\alpha/2\delta)q^* - p^c_{T-1}.$$

Substituting the equation for $q$ given in equation 7-A6 and the corresponding equation for $q^*$ from equation 7-A6 into equation 7-A7 gives

$$(7\text{-A8}) \quad \pi^c = w + \gamma_1(m - w) + \gamma_2(m^* - w^*) - p^c_{T-1},$$

where

$$\gamma_1 = \theta\beta_1 + (\beta_1 - \beta_2)(1 - \alpha)/2\delta$$
$$\gamma_2 = \theta\beta_2 + (\beta_2 - \beta_1)(1 - \alpha)/2\delta$$
$$\gamma_1 + \gamma_2 = \theta/\Theta.$$

Equations 7-A6 and 7-A8 give the targets $q$ and $\pi^c$ as functions of the control variables $(m, m^*)$ and the state variables $(w, w^*, p^c_{T-1})$.

CHAPTER EIGHT

# Empirical Analysis of Macroeconomic Policy Coordination

IN THIS CHAPTER we provide a quantitative perspective on the size and nature of gains from coordinating policies in the industrial economies. We first survey other studies that have attempted to quantify the payoff to coordinating global macroeconomic policies. We then outline our approach, which draws on the ideas from game theory developed in chapter 7.

The choice of national policies in an international setting is modeled as a game between the policymakers in each country. We specify an objective function for each policymaker, and, given the global model developed in earlier chapters, we measure and compare the outcomes of certain strategies pursued by different countries.

Two examples of cooperative versus noncooperative policy setting are presented. The first is a global disinflation similar in scale to the disinflation that occurred in the early 1980s. The second example is global adjustment to trade imbalances of the scale experienced in the late 1980s. In the first case, we assume that policymakers choose both fiscal and monetary policies, depending on national and international considerations. In the second case, we explore the payoff to choosing cooperative monetary policies, given a precommitted path of fiscal adjustment in the United States, Japan, and Germany.

The results suggest that there are potential gains to be realized from coordinating both monetary and fiscal policies, but smaller gains from monetary coordination only. In each case cooperation is not welfare worsening, despite the presence of substantial forward-looking behavior in the global model on which we base the analysis. Note that the entire analysis is undertaken on the assumption of complete information on the part of policymakers and private sector participants. Therefore, the analysis may ignore many other payoffs or costs to cooperation.

## Other Studies

As mentioned in chapter 7, where we surveyed the results of the theoretical literature on international policy coordination, whether there are gains to coordinating macroeconomic policies is theoretically ambiguous. What is crucial to measuring possible gains is the size of spillovers of policy changes among economies and the nature of reactions of policymakers within major economies.

The issues of macroeconomic interdependence have been studied in large-scale models such as project LINK[1] or the linked U.S.-Canadian model in Helliwell and McRae (1977). Recent model comparison exercises coordinated by The Brookings Institution (see Bryant and others 1988) have also contributed to this approach.[2] These studies attempt to measure the size and sign of the transmission of economic disturbances among countries. This is an important step toward understanding the empirical significance of economic spillovers, but there have been fewer attempts to implement empirically the game-theoretic approach.

The first attempt at an empirical implementation of the strategic game-theoretic approach was undertaken by Oudiz and Sachs (1984). In that study the authors used policy multipliers from several large-scale models of the world economy and applied static game theory to determine the gains from policy coordination. They assumed that the estimated results were generated from a Nash-Cournot equilibrium and then estimated the gains from coordination. The results showed a very small gain to be made through coordination.

Sachs and McKibbin (1985) applied the results from dynamic game theory to a four-region simulation model of the world economy to measure the gains from coordination.[3] The model was calibrated using 1983 data. In that paper, the authors found small gains to coordinating the macroeconomic policies of the major industrial regions in the face of an inflationary shock, such as the one that occurred in the late 1970s. They showed, however, that the gains for the developing countries are potentially large. In the face of a global inflationary shock,

---

1. See Fair (1979) for an early survey of the multipliers from the major models.

2. See also Frankel (1986) for an application of the results of this conference to policy coordination issues.

3. This model was an antecedent of the model developed in this book. The earlier model ignored the supply side and explicit modeling of forward-looking private sector decisions. The model also had only two industrial regions that were close to being symmetric.

a noncoordinated disinflation results in monetary contraction and fiscal expansion in the industrial regions. This leads to high world interest rates and a strong U.S. dollar. When the authors simulated the same shock while assuming a coordinated response, the policy mix was less extreme, and world interest rates were much lower. In the study, the comparison was the outcome of a Nash-Cournot game versus a co-operative equilibrium. In a further study, Ishii, McKibbin, and Sachs (1985) found that, if the model is used to generate a future baseline assuming projections from the Organization for Economic Cooperation and Development (OECD) for macroeconomic policies (rather than assuming optimization by policymakers) and then policymakers undertake the optimization in a cooperative manner, the result was a substantial gain from coordination.

Taylor (1985) examined the gains from coordination using an estimated reduced-form model consisting of the seven largest OECD countries. Comparing the outcome of Nash-Cournot equilibria and cooperative equilibria, he also found small gains from coordination that depended on the weights in the policymakers' objective function.

Hughes-Hallet (1987a) used dynamic game theory in a three-region empirical model (consisting of the United States, the European Community, and the rest of the world) to assess the difference between noncooperative and cooperative policy responses to the experience of the world economy since 1974. He found large gains for the United States from cooperation, but very little difference for the European Community.

Currie, Levine, and Vidalis (1987) also used the game-theoretic approach to measure the gains from cooperation in the MINILINK model (which is a stripped-down version of the OECD's INTERLINK model). They found that cooperation between the two blocs in the model (the United States and rest of the world) is significantly better than noncooperation if the issue of time inconsistency is ignored. If time-inconsistent equilibria are not ruled out, however, then cooperation is not necessarily better than noncooperation.

Canzoneri and Minford (1986) found small gains to cooperation in the LIVERPOOL model. Minford and Canzoneri (1987) used the LIVERPOOL model to compare observed policies in a historical period with optimal policies (whether cooperative or noncooperative). Similarly to Ishii, McKibbin, and Sachs (1985), they found that the gains from the optimization of policy are very large relative to the differences between cooperative and noncooperative policies.

The studies mentioned so far assumed that policymakers know the true model when calculating the gains to cooperation. Following on these studies, there have also been attempts to explore the implications of model uncertainty in assessing the empirical gains or losses from coordination. Frankel (1986) and Frankel and Rockett (1988) used the reduced-form multipliers from ten global models to calculate cooperative and noncooperative equilibria between a U.S. region and a non-U.S. aggregate region under different assumptions about the model held by policymakers in each region. They explored all combinations of possible beliefs for each region and the ten models and found that cooperation improved U.S. welfare relative to noncooperation in only a little more that half of the cases.

Holtham and Hughes-Hallett (1987), using the same data set as Frankel and Rockett (1988), found a higher proportion of gains to cooperation by ruling out cooperative agreements in which one policymaker expected the other policymaker to be worse off. They argued that some agreements such as these would not be observed.

Ghosh and Ghosh (1986) and Ghosh and Masson (1988) were more explicit in treating uncertainty about structural parameters in a given model. In contrast to the other studies on uncertainty, these authors assumed that policymakers explicitly take into account model uncertainty when entering international agreements. They found that the gains from coordinating policies can rise with the degree of uncertainty.

The remainder of this chapter will ignore the issue of uncertainty, focusing instead on the application of dynamic game theory to measuring outcomes under cooperative and noncooperative agreements in one "true" model.

## Measuring the Gains to Coordination

In this section we develop procedures presented in McKibbin and Sachs (1986b), where we studied the dynamic games involved in setting national policy. The full details of the technique are presented in appendix C to the book.

### Industrial Economies

We first specify a social welfare function for each of the major industrial economies and regions. Social welfare in each region is a function of a range of macroeconomic targets such as inflation, unemployment, the current account, and fiscal deficits, with different weights placed on each target in different countries.[4] In the example here, we assume that the weights applied to deviations of employment (in percent), inflation (in absolute levels), the fiscal deficit (as a proportion of GDP), and the current account (as a proportion of GDP) for the United States are, respectively, 0.4, 0.8, 0.3, 0.1; for Japan, 0.4, 0.8, 0.8, 0.4; for Germany, 0.3, 1.2, 0.2, 0.1; and for the ROECD region, 0.4, 0.8, 0.3, 0.1.[5] The intertemporal social loss function in each region is specified as an additively separable quadratic function of the targets in each period. Future periods are weighted by a social rate of time preference (assumed to be 10 percent in each country).

Following the approach taken in chapter 7, we define noncooperation as the case in which each industrial economy chooses the vector of its policy variables so as to maximize its intertemporal loss function, taking as given the behavior of the other economies and subject to the known global economy given by the MSG2 model. Cooperation is defined as the case in which a global planner chooses a vector of the same policy instruments, but with the objective of minimizing a weighted average of the individual loss functions of each country participating in the cooperative arrangement. The weights for the cooperative solution are arbitrary. Our approach initially is to weight the loss function of each country by each country's share in the total GDP of the coalitions in the base year. We then adjust weights until we find a case in which all participants gain by the cooperative arrangement relative to the outcome for noncooperation.

The problem facing the policymaker in each country is assumed to be the choice of a path for policy ($U$) that will minimize an expected loss function of a set of targets ($\tau$), given the world economy as represented by the MSG2 model. This can be written as

$$(8\text{-}1) \qquad \min_{\substack{t \\ U_s}} \left\{ \sum_{s=t}^{\infty} (1+\delta)^{t-s}\, \tau_s'\, \Omega \tau_s \right\},$$

4. We do not use welfare functions that are equivalent to the utility function of individuals in the model because we are attempting to measure what governments appear to do rather than what they should do. A similar study focusing on the case in which the objective function of the government reflects the objective functions of individual agents can be found in McKibbin (1986).

5. Abbreviations for the model's regions are as defined in chapter 3 (notes 3–6).

subject to

(8-2) $\quad X_{t+1} = \alpha_1 X_t + \alpha_2 e_t + \alpha_3 U_t + \alpha_4 E_t + \alpha_5 \epsilon_t$

(8-3) $\quad {}_t e_{t+1} = \beta_1 X_t + \beta_2 e_t + \beta_3 U_t + \beta_4 E_t + \beta_5 \epsilon_t$

(8-4) $\quad \tau_t = \gamma_1 X_t + \gamma_2 e_t + \gamma_3 U_t + \gamma_4 E_t + \gamma_5 \epsilon_t,$

where

$U$ = a vector of control variables

$\tau$ = a vector of target variables

$X$ = a vector of state variables (for example, asset stocks, wages)

$e$ = a vector of jumping variables (for example, asset prices), where ${}_t e_{t+1}$ is the rational expectation of $e_{t+1}$ conditional on information in period $t$

$E$ = a vector of exogenous variables

$\epsilon$ = a vector of stochastic shocks

$\delta$ = the social discount rate (assumed to be 10 percent).

As developed in appendix C of the book, the optimal time-consistent, closed-loop policy rules we calculate are written in the form

(8-5) $\quad U_t = \Gamma_1 X_t + \Gamma_2 E_t + \Gamma_3 \epsilon_t + \Gamma_{4t},$

where the vector $\Gamma_{4t}$ is a cumulation of all expected future values of exogenous variables and shocks.

Once we have the shocks to the model, we can use the policy rules, together with the dynamic system of equations, to solve for the loss incurred by each country for which we have specified a loss function.

### Developing Countries

We do not have explicit loss functions for the non-oil developing countries (LDCs). We can appeal, however, to standard trade theory for a relatively straightforward measure of the welfare effects of shocks that are external to the LDCs.

Consider an initial path of exports, imports, and foreign borrowing of the developing region. When interest rates and trade prices change, we can ask how large an *income transfer* the developing region would require to allow its countries to purchase the initial import basket, with unchanged levels of real exports and real foreign indebtedness. This income transfer measures the "compensating variation" that keeps the developing region as well off as it was before the external changes.

To illustrate the procedure, we assume that there are only two industrial regions (the United States and the ROECD, for notational convenience, with subscripts or superscripts $U$ and $O$) lending to the LDCs (subscript or superscript $L$). We have the following equations:

$$(8\text{-}6) \qquad DEBT_{t+1} = (1-n)DEBT_t - CA_t^L$$

$$(8\text{-}7) \qquad DEBT_t = A_{Lt}^U + \Lambda^o A_{Lt}^o$$

$$(8\text{-}8) \qquad CA_t^L = -r_t^U(A_{Lt}^U - r_t^O[\Lambda_t^O A_{Lt}^O])$$
$$+ \Lambda_t^L(N_{Lt}^U + N_{Lt}^O)$$
$$- (C_{Ut}^L + \Lambda_t^O C_{Ot}^L).$$

Note that we use the notation $\Lambda_t^i$ to indicate the real exchange rate of country $i$ relative to the United States (that is, $\Lambda^O = E^O P^O / P^U$). The term $\Lambda^{Lt}(N_{Lt}^U + N_{Lt}^O)$ is the value of developing country exports to the United States and the ROECD region, measured in real U.S. goods. The term $C_{Ut}^L + \Lambda_t^O C_{Ot}^L$ denotes LDC imports from the United States and the ROECD region in real U.S. goods. The underlying real growth rate of U.S. output is denoted $n$. All variables in equations 8-6 through 8-8 are deflated by U.S. prices.

Suppose the time path of $DEBT_t$ is unchanging, so that the path of $CA^L$ is fixed. Consider the increased cost of purchasing $C_U^L$ and $C_O^L$ for given real exports $N_L^U$ and $N_L^O$ when $r^U$, $r^O$, $\Lambda^O$, and $\Lambda^L$ change. By differentiating equation 8-8 we find

$$(8\text{-}9) \qquad dT^r = dr_t^U(A_{Lt}^U) + dr_t^O(\Lambda_t^O A_{Lt}^O)$$
$$+ d\Lambda_t^O(r_t^O A_{Lt}^O) - d\Lambda_t^L(N_{Lt}^U)$$
$$+ N_{Lt}^O + d\Lambda_t^O(C_{Ot}^L),$$

where $dT^r$ is the real transfer (in units of U.S. output) required to permit the LDCs to purchase the original consumption basket. Define $\gamma^i = (d\Lambda_t^i / \Lambda_t^i)$, which is the proportionate change in the price of country $i$'s good relative to the U.S. good. Rearranging equation 8-9, we have

$$(8\text{-}10) \qquad dT^r = dr_t^U(A_{Lt}^U) + dr_t^O(\Lambda_t^O A_{Lt}^O)$$
$$+ \ d\Lambda_t^O(r_t^O A_{Lt}^O) - \lambda_t^L[\Lambda_t^L N_{Lt}^U$$
$$+ \ \Lambda_t^L N_{Lt}^O] + \lambda_t^O[(A_t^O C_{Ot}^L)$$
$$\div \ (C_{Ut}^L + \Lambda_t^O C_{Ot}^L)]$$
$$\times \ (C_{Ut}^L + \Lambda^{Ot} C_{Ot}^L).$$

Define $s_O^L = [\Lambda_t^O C_{Ot}^L/(C_{Ut}^L + \Lambda_t^O C_{Ot}^L)]$, which is the share of ROECD goods in LDC imports. We can also define the percentage change in the real import price $(\Lambda^M)$ of the LDCs (that is, the relative price of LDC imports to the U.S. price) as

$$d\Lambda_t^M/\Lambda_t^M = \lambda_t^M = \lambda_t^O s_O^L.$$

We can rewrite equation 8-10 as

$$(8\text{-}11) \qquad dT^r = dr_t^U(A_{Lt}^U) + dr_t^O(\Lambda_t^O A_{Lt}^O)$$
$$+ \ d\Lambda_t^O(r_t^O A^O\text{Lt}) - \lambda_t^L TB_t^L$$
$$+ \ (\lambda_t^M - \lambda_t^L)(C_{Ut}^L + \Lambda_t^O C_{Ot}^L),$$

where $TB_t^L = \Lambda_t^L(N_{Lt}^U + N_{Lt}^O) - (C_{Ut}^L + \Lambda_t^O C_{Ot}^L)$.

From equation 8-11 we see that the required transfer (or compensating variation) has three components. First, when real interest rates rise, the transfers must increase by the change in real interest rates multiplied by the appropriate components of real debt. Second, when real export prices in terms of U.S. goods $(\Lambda^L)$ increase, the transfer is *reduced* if the debtor country is running a trade surplus ($TB^L >$ 0) and is *increased* if the debtor country is running a trade deficit. Third, when the terms of trade deteriorate (that is, $\lambda_t^M - \lambda_t^L > 0$), the transfer must be raised by the percentage of the terms of trade deterioration multiplied by the value of total imports. The total "loss" to the LDCs is measured by the sum of these three components.

## Two Examples of Cooperation versus Noncooperation

We consider only two examples of cooperation in this section. Chapter 9, where we explore the performance of alternative policy

Table 8-1. *Welfare Calculations for Disinflation by Model Region*[a]

| Model region | Noncooperation | Cooperation | Gain due to cooperation |
|---|---|---|---|
| United States | −3.08 | −2.33 | 0.75 |
| Japan | −0.67 | −0.60 | 0.07 |
| Germany | −1.26 | −0.88 | 0.38 |
| ROECD[b] | −3.69 | −3.53 | 0.16 |
| REMS[b] | −0.63 | −0.49 | 0.14 |
| LDCs[c] | | | |
| 1986 | −36.10 | −5.52 | 30.58 |
| 1987 | −23.35 | −8.80 | 14.55 |
| 1988 | −18.17 | −10.49 | 7.68 |
| 1989 | −9.15 | −11.71 | −2.56 |

a. The units for the welfare calculations for each region except the developing countries are arbitrary. The loss in individual targets whose squared deviation makes up these calculations can be found in table 8-2.

b. In this and subsequent tables of the chapter, abbreviations for model regions are as defined in chapter 3 (notes 3–6).

c. Amounts in billions of 1986 dollars. The results are calculated using the method outlined in the text. The data are based on the 1986 data for developing countries in the MSG2 model database. The U.S. dollar value of the three developing country variables used in these calculations are: net external debt ($663.3 billion); imports ($318 billion); trade balance ($9.7 billion). The values of these three variables for 1987 through 1989 are calculated assuming their 1986 ratios to GDP, projected to 1989 using actual GDP from 1987 to 1989.

rules, contains comparisons of cooperation and noncooperation over a range of alternative shocks.[6]

## Disinflation

The first case is a world economy that desires to disinflate from an initial state of excessive inflation. This situation is representative of the early 1980s. We assume that each country simultaneously desires a lower rate of inflation, with all other target variables in objective functions desired at their initial levels. This is equivalent to inheriting a high-inflation steady state of the model and a desire by all countries to move to a lower-inflation steady state, with costs placed on deviations of real variables from their long-run values. To achieve this disinflation, we assume that each country can adjust both monetary and fiscal policies.

We assume that the new desired rate of inflation is 8 percentage points lower for the United States and ROECD bloc and 4 percentage points lower for Japan and Germany. We calculate the optimal time-consistent policy rules that minimize the loss incurred in achieving the new, lower inflation rates by using the technique outlined above. Table 8-1 contains the welfare calculations under the noncooperative and

6. Although in that chapter we examine cooperation only among the United States, Japan, and Germany.

cooperative forms of disinflation. A negative sign indicates a loss for a country or region. Note that, for each region, cooperation leads to a smaller loss than noncooperation. Although the size of the differences is difficult to interpret without further information, the differences do appear to be potentially large when both Germany and the United States are approximately 30 percent better off under cooperation than under noncooperation. The gains to LDCs are also quite large because of lower real interest rates on their external debt. These gains to the LDCs, however, are not net efficiency gains for the world as a whole because the gains to the LDCs from reducing the transfer of real resource to the industrial regions is a loss to the industrial regions. This net effect is not directly captured because we use different measures of welfare for the industrial and the developing regions.

To get a better idea of the size of the differences between the cooperative and noncooperative outcomes, the paths of major variables are presented in tables 8-2 and 8-3.

In table 8-2 we present for each region the outcome for a number of key macroeconomic variables under noncooperative disinflation. As in McKibbin and Sachs (1986a), we find that the policy mix for each country and region is a monetary contraction and fiscal expansion. The reason for this particular policy mix can be understood by considering the policy multipliers in chapter 4. We saw in that chapter that a fiscal expansion in one country raises output and appreciates its exchange rate in the short run. This implies a small rise in inflation through higher domestic prices, but this rise is offset by lower imported prices, resulting in a smaller rise in the consumer price index than in domestic prices. A monetary expansion, in contrast, depreciates the exchange rate while increasing domestic demand, raising the price of both domestically produced and imported goods. The net effect is that a monetary expansion leads to a larger rise in the consumer price index per unit of output than does a fiscal expansion. Lower inflation can be achieved by tighter monetary policy. The output consequences of this can then be offset by looser fiscal policy, with only a small offset in the consumer price index. Each country acting alone can have this favorable outcome. The problem for the world economy comes because, as each country tries to pursue this policy mix, the exchange rate consequences do not emerge. Countries then become excessively contractionary. The result is high world interest rates (especially real interest rates, since inflation is falling) in the short run and excessive fiscal expansion and monetary contraction.

# Table 8-2. *Dynamic Adjustment to Global Noncooperative Disinflation*

| Model region | Year | | | | |
|---|---|---|---|---|---|
| | 1 | 2 | 3 | 4 | 5 |
| **United States** | | | | | |
| GDP[a] | −5.31 | −3.18 | −2.08 | −1.32 | −0.82 |
| Trade balance[a] | −0.88 | −0.98 | −1.08 | −1.17 | −1.23 |
| Budget deficit[a] | 3.64 | 2.91 | 2.62 | 2.43 | 2.33 |
| Inflation[b] | −3.72 | −5.28 | −6.08 | −6.60 | −6.93 |
| Nominal short-term interest rate[b] | 11.90 | 4.46 | 1.00 | −1.44 | −3.14 |
| Nominal long-term interest rate[b] | −1.61 | −3.37 | −4.46 | −5.23 | −5.77 |
| Money[c] | −16.16 | −14.38 | −17.08 | −21.30 | −26.60 |
| **Japan** | | | | | |
| GDP[a] | −3.19 | −0.11 | −0.11 | −0.15 | −0.19 |
| Trade balance[a] | −0.14 | 0.84 | 0.41 | 0.24 | 0.17 |
| Budget deficit[a] | 1.76 | 0.14 | 0.11 | 0.09 | 0.08 |
| Inflation[b] | −1.24 | −3.97 | −3.98 | −3.99 | −4.00 |
| Nominal short-term interest rate[b] | 17.98 | 2.29 | 1.77 | 0.55 | −0.57 |
| Nominal long-term interest rate[b] | 0.84 | −1.15 | −1.72 | −2.25 | −2.67 |
| Money[c] | −16.08 | −7.78 | −11.19 | −14.27 | −17.46 |
| Real exchange rate[c] | −11.80 | −16.96 | −12.68 | −10.81 | −9.86 |
| **Germany** | | | | | |
| GDP[a] | −4.05 | −3.28 | −3.13 | −2.93 | −2.69 |
| Real trade balance[a] | −1.57 | −0.31 | −0.06 | 0.22 | 0.48 |
| Budget deficit[a] | 2.41 | 1.22 | 0.81 | 0.43 | 0.08 |
| Inflation[b] | −2.47 | −2.87 | −3.00 | −3.13 | −3.24 |
| Nominal short-term interest rate[b] | 18.54 | 8.83 | 6.04 | 3.56 | 1.68 |
| Nominal long-term interest rate[b] | 3.09 | 1.08 | −0.07 | −0.98 | −1.66 |
| Money[c] | −17.90 | −14.19 | −15.41 | −16.90 | −18.83 |
| Real exchange rate[c] | −2.22 | −6.69 | −8.11 | −9.76 | −11.17 |
| **REMS** | | | | | |
| GDP[a] | −4.18 | −2.98 | −2.90 | −2.60 | −2.26 |
| Trade balance[a] | −0.88 | −0.29 | −0.24 | −0.11 | 0.01 |
| Budget deficit[a] | 1.42 | 1.05 | 1.02 | 0.94 | 0.84 |
| Inflation[b] | −2.32 | −2.73 | −3.05 | −3.21 | −3.29 |
| Nominal short-term interest rate[b] | 18.54 | 8.83 | 6.04 | 3.56 | 1.68 |
| Nominal long-term interest rate[b] | 3.09 | 1.08 | −0.07 | −0.98 | −1.66 |
| Money[c] | −18.48 | −14.00 | −15.13 | −16.51 | −18.31 |
| Real exchange rate[c] | −2.48 | −6.64 | −7.92 | −9.56 | −10.94 |
| **ROECD** | | | | | |
| GDP[a] | −5.92 | −4.76 | −3.95 | −3.26 | −2.66 |
| Trade balance[a] | −0.48 | 0.61 | 1.09 | 1.44 | 1.70 |
| Budget deficit[a] | 2.32 | 0.78 | −0.25 | −1.10 | −1.80 |
| Inflation[b] | −4.84 | −5.75 | −6.35 | −6.82 | −7.19 |
| Nominal short-term interest rate[b] | 16.52 | 6.47 | 2.87 | −0.09 | −2.28 |
| Nominal long-term interest rate[b] | −0.65 | −2.88 | −4.23 | −5.26 | −6.03 |
| Money[c] | −19.83 | −18.85 | −22.78 | −27.57 | −33.20 |
| Real exchange rate[c] | 2.22 | −3.48 | −6.29 | −8.79 | −10.74 |
| **LDCs** | | | | | |
| Trade balance[d] | 4.09 | 2.19 | 1.65 | 1.20 | 0.86 |
| Terms of trade[c] | −2.98 | −6.29 | −6.65 | −7.43 | −8.11 |
| **OPEC** | | | | | |
| Trade balance[d] | −1.96 | −1.27 | −0.80 | −0.48 | −0.28 |
| Terms of trade[c] | −9.15 | −10.09 | −9.55 | −9.66 | −9.89 |

a. Deviation from baseline as percent of real GDP.
b. Absolute deviation from baseline.
c. Percent deviation from baseline.
d. Deviation from baseline as percent of U.S. GDP.

# Table 8-3. *Dynamic Adjustment to Global Cooperative Disinflation*

| Model region | Year | | | | |
|---|---|---|---|---|---|
| | *1* | *2* | *3* | *4* | *5* |
| *United States* | | | | | |
| GDP[a] | −4.81 | −3.30 | −2.34 | −1.66 | −1.21 |
| Trade balance[a] | −0.73 | −0.57 | −0.51 | −0.50 | −0.49 |
| Budget deficit[a] | 1.06 | 1.52 | 1.45 | 1.41 | 1.40 |
| Inflation[b] | −4.01 | −5.34 | −6.04 | −6.50 | −6.80 |
| Nominal short-term interest rate[b] | −8.33 | −3.80 | −4.63 | −5.08 | −5.31 |
| Nominal long-term interest rate[b] | −5.45 | −5.15 | −5.31 | −5.38 | −5.40 |
| Money[c] | −3.29 | −9.61 | −14.20 | −19.82 | −26.09 |
| *Japan* | | | | | |
| GDP[a] | −2.86 | −0.09 | −0.05 | −0.06 | −0.09 |
| Trade balance[a] | 0.63 | 1.49 | 1.17 | 1.05 | 1.01 |
| Budget deficit[a] | 0.09 | −0.79 | −0.71 | −0.65 | −0.61 |
| Inflation[b] | −1.54 | −3.94 | −3.94 | −3.94 | −3.94 |
| Nominal short-term interest rate[b] | −0.68 | −5.32 | −3.48 | −2.86 | −2.62 |
| Nominal long-term interest rate[b] | −2.69 | −2.84 | −2.51 | −2.38 | −2.30 |
| Money[c] | −4.26 | −3.34 | −8.29 | −12.57 | −16.65 |
| Real exchange rate[c] | −10.57 | −17.31 | −13.64 | −12.15 | −11.46 |
| *Germany* | | | | | |
| GDP[a] | −4.17 | −2.42 | −2.16 | −1.93 | −1.73 |
| Real trade balance[a] | 0.42 | −0.04 | −0.09 | −0.07 | −0.05 |
| Budget deficit[a] | 0.85 | 0.84 | 0.92 | 0.94 | 0.93 |
| Inflation[b] | −2.28 | −3.04 | −3.18 | −3.31 | −3.41 |
| Nominal short-term interest rate[b] | −12.40 | −2.52 | −1.87 | −1.88 | −1.95 |
| Nominal long-term interest rate[b] | −3.11 | −2.01 | −1.95 | −1.95 | −1.96 |
| Money[c] | 0.68 | −6.21 | −9.43 | −12.46 | −15.61 |
| Real exchange rate[c] | −12.32 | −5.94 | −4.30 | −3.79 | −3.55 |
| *REMS* | | | | | |
| GDP[a] | −4.12 | −2.27 | −2.17 | −1.94 | −1.72 |
| Trade balance[a] | −0.14 | 0.05 | 0.17 | 0.29 | 0.37 |
| Budget deficit[a] | 1.45 | 0.81 | 0.75 | 0.67 | 0.59 |
| Inflation[b] | −2.52 | −2.93 | −3.21 | −3.34 | −3.43 |
| Nominal short-term interest rate[b] | −12.40 | −2.52 | −1.87 | −1.88 | −1.95 |
| Nominal long-term interest rate[b] | −3.11 | −2.01 | −1.95 | −1.95 | −1.96 |
| Money[c] | 0.51 | −6.46 | −9.80 | −12.87 | −16.04 |
| Real exchange rate[c] | −12.36 | −6.15 | −4.50 | −4.05 | −3.85 |
| *ROECD* | | | | | |
| GDP[a] | −6.30 | −3.06 | −1.91 | −1.21 | −0.78 |
| Trade balance[a] | 4.13 | 1.19 | 0.62 | 0.26 | 0.05 |
| Budget deficit[a] | −3.51 | −1.18 | −0.71 | −0.37 | −0.14 |
| Inflation[b] | −2.04 | −5.05 | −5.81 | −6.30 | −6.60 |
| Nominal short-term interest rate[b] | −17.10 | −5.16 | −5.02 | −5.19 | −5.33 |
| Nominal long-term interest rate[b] | −6.54 | −5.28 | −5.29 | −5.31 | −5.31 |
| Money[c] | 0.27 | −7.59 | −12.26 | −17.67 | −23.70 |
| Real exchange rate[c] | −15.80 | −6.10 | −4.45 | −3.76 | −3.35 |
| *LDCs* | | | | | |
| Trade balance[d] | −1.22 | 0.18 | 0.28 | 0.30 | 0.30 |
| Terms of trade[c] | −10.78 | −7.08 | −5.44 | −4.82 | −4.48 |
| *OPEC* | | | | | |
| Trade balance[d] | 0.05 | −0.42 | −0.28 | −0.18 | −0.13 |
| Terms of trade[c] | −10.17 | −8.09 | −6.36 | −5.65 | −5.27 |

a. Deviation from baseline as percent of real GDP.
b. Absolute deviation from baseline.
c. Percent deviation from baseline.
d. Deviation from baseline as percent of U.S. GDP.

The results in table 8-2 can be contrasted with those in table 8-3, where we assume that a global policymaker sets the monetary and fiscal policies for each region and allows for the spillover effects among countries that result from the policy actions. Over the first three years under this cooperative disinflation, each country achieves lower average inflation with a smaller output loss than under noncooperation. In each country or region, the fiscal expansion still occurs, but it is in smaller amounts. Monetary policy is also far less contractionary, and is initially expansionary in Germany, the REMS, and the ROECD. Nominal interest rates fall in each country in the cooperative scenario, rather than rise as in the noncooperative case. The real exchange rate paths vary. For the yen-dollar exchange rates, there is very little difference; but for the other cross-rates with the dollar, cooperation reduces the real appreciation of the dollar.

### Trade Balance Adjustment

In the second example of cooperation we consider the case in which the United States, Japan, and Germany adjust fiscal policy to correct the trade imbalances and then, either noncooperatively or cooperatively, adjust monetary policy to minimize the loss from the fiscal adjustment. Because in this example it is assumed that monetary policy is the only instrument available in each region, we modify the objective function to include only output and inflation, with the same weights as for the example of disinflation. It seems natural to drop the fiscal deficit and the current account from the objective function when dealing only with monetary policy.

We assume that the United States cuts government spending by 0.5 percent of GDP in the first year, then 1.0 percent, 1.5 percent, 2.0 percent, and 2.5 percent of GDP by the fifth year. Spending is then held at 2.5 percent of GDP below baseline indefinitely. Japan and Germany, in contrast, increase government spending by 0.5 percent, 1.0 percent, and 1.5 percent of GDP each year until the third year. Spending in Japan and Germany is then held at 1.5 percent of GDP above baseline indefinitely.

A comparison of welfare losses from these fiscal actions that are accompanied by either cooperative or noncooperative monetary policy actions is given in table 8-4. Each country or region is better off under cooperative adjustment, but the differences appear to be very small. Further results are given in tables 8-5 and 8-6.

Table 8-4. *Welfare Calculations for Each Region for Trade Balance Adjustment*[a]

| Model region | Noncooperation | Cooperation | Gain due to cooperation |
|---|---|---|---|
| United States | −4.541 | −4.537 | 0.004 |
| Japan | −0.295 | −0.292 | 0.003 |
| Germany | −2.180 | −2.175 | 0.005 |
| REMS | −0.202 | −0.123 | 0.079 |
| ROECD | −0.072 | −0.071 | 0.001 |
| LDCs[b] | | | |
| 1986 | 1.74 | 1.74 | 0.00 |
| 1987 | 2.89 | 3.14 | 0.25 |
| 1988 | 4.65 | 4.93 | 0.29 |
| 1989 | 9.14 | 9.31 | 0.17 |

a. The units for the welfare calculations for each region except the developing countries are arbitrary. The loss in individual targets whose squared deviation makes up these calculations can be found in table 8-2.

b. Amounts in billions of 1986 dollars. The results are calculated using the method outlined in the text. The data are based on the 1986 data for developing countries in the MSG2 model database. The U.S. dollar value of the three developing country variables used in these calculations are: net external debt ($663.3 billion); imports ($318 billion); trade balance ($9.7 billion). The values of these three variables for 1987 through 1989 are calculated assuming their 1986 ratios to GDP, projected to 1989 using actual GDP from 1987 to 1989.

The small differences apparent from the calculations of losses are clear in these tables. Given the fiscal adjustment, there seem to be small gains to be achieved by cooperatively setting monetary policy during the transition phase. These results also reinforce those from chapter 6 for policy adjustments to correct trade imbalances. The output loss is quite small especially when accompanied by monetary policy adjustment.

## Summary

We have attempted to provide some quantitative assessment of the potential size of the gains to be realized by coordinating macroeconomic policies. We must stress again that we have focused here only on those gains that might be achieved in a world of perfect information where losses are due to policymakers' ignoring the reactions of foreign economies to a change in policy. When both monetary and fiscal coordination are considered, we find potentially important gains to cooperation. When only monetary policy is considered, we find the gains are relatively small.

One implication of these results is that it is likely to be easier to achieve coordination of monetary policies rather than coordination of both fiscal and monetary policies. Apart from the obvious problem of setting domestic fiscal policy relative to monetary policy, we have also

# Table 8-5. *Dynamic Adjustment to Global Noncooperative Trade Balance Adjustment*

| Model region | Year | | | | |
|---|---|---|---|---|---|
| | *1* | *2* | *3* | *4* | *5* |
| *United States* | | | | | |
| GDP[a] | −0.59 | −0.78 | −0.87 | −0.74 | −0.58 |
| Trade balance[a] | 0.45 | 0.64 | 0.79 | 0.92 | 1.05 |
| Budget deficit[a] | −0.27 | −0.67 | −1.11 | −1.63 | −2.16 |
| Inflation[b] | 0.21 | 0.33 | 0.41 | 0.36 | 0.30 |
| Nominal short-term interest rate[b] | 2.55 | 3.08 | 3.34 | 1.87 | −1.72 |
| Nominal long-term interest rate[b] | −0.17 | −0.65 | −1.19 | −1.74 | −2.16 |
| Money[c] | −2.23 | −2.72 | −2.86 | −1.69 | 0.80 |
| *Japan* | | | | | |
| GDP[a] | 0.28 | 0.00 | −0.00 | −0.03 | −0.03 |
| Trade balance[a] | −0.81 | −1.29 | −1.80 | −1.77 | −1.70 |
| Budget deficit[a] | 0.35 | 0.89 | 1.35 | 1.34 | 1.33 |
| Inflation[b] | −0.18 | −0.00 | −0.00 | −0.00 | −0.00 |
| Nominal short-term interest rate[b] | −1.71 | −0.93 | 2.49 | 0.82 | −1.32 |
| Nominal long-term interest rate[b] | −1.01 | −1.04 | −1.15 | −1.59 | −1.86 |
| Money[c] | 1.49 | 1.02 | −0.76 | 0.30 | 1.68 |
| Real exchange rate[c] | 7.55 | 11.81 | 15.72 | 16.38 | 17.26 |
| *Germany* | | | | | |
| GDP[a] | 0.18 | 0.28 | 0.42 | 0.42 | 0.37 |
| Real trade balance[a] | −0.71 | −1.19 | −1.80 | −1.79 | −1.59 |
| Budget deficit[a] | 0.41 | 0.85 | 1.28 | 1.27 | 1.28 |
| Inflation[b] | −0.08 | −0.12 | −0.16 | −0.16 | −0.14 |
| Nominal short-term interest rate[b] | 0.05 | 0.32 | 2.18 | 1.37 | −1.68 |
| Nominal long-term interest rate[b] | −0.83 | −1.05 | −1.29 | −1.72 | −2.06 |
| Money[c] | 0.29 | 0.31 | −0.60 | −0.15 | 1.52 |
| Real exchange rate[c] | 5.32 | 7.67 | 10.18 | 11.02 | 11.18 |
| *REMS* | | | | | |
| GDP[a] | −0.22 | −0.30 | −0.30 | −0.01 | 0.02 |
| Trade balance[a] | −0.46 | −0.58 | −0.75 | −0.68 | −0.40 |
| Budget deficit[a] | 0.02 | 0.03 | 0.03 | −0.07 | −0.08 |
| Inflation[b] | −0.31 | −0.47 | −0.60 | −0.41 | −0.27 |
| Nominal short-term interest rate[b] | 0.05 | 0.32 | 2.18 | 1.37 | −1.68 |
| Nominal long-term interest rate[b] | −0.83 | −1.05 | −1.29 | −1.72 | −2.06 |
| Money[c] | −0.25 | −0.89 | −2.55 | −2.19 | −0.63 |
| Real exchange rate[c] | 5.14 | 7.05 | 9.01 | 9.50 | 9.49 |
| *ROECD* | | | | | |
| GDP[a] | 0.00 | −0.04 | −0.02 | 0.07 | 0.09 |
| Trade balance[a] | −0.18 | −0.26 | −0.41 | −0.51 | −0.52 |
| Budget deficit[a] | 0.00 | 0.02 | 0.01 | −0.02 | −0.03 |
| Inflation[b] | 0.01 | 0.02 | 0.02 | −0.02 | −0.03 |
| Nominal short-term interest rate[b] | 0.82 | 1.20 | 2.41 | 1.40 | −1.60 |
| Nominal long-term interest rate[b] | −0.61 | −0.90 | −1.22 | −1.67 | −2.02 |
| Money[c] | −0.51 | −0.79 | −1.51 | −0.78 | 1.05 |
| Real exchange rate[c] | 4.15 | 5.74 | 7.39 | 8.10 | 8.35 |
| *LDCs* | | | | | |
| Trade balance[d] | 0.25 | 0.36 | 0.63 | 0.37 | −0.29 |
| Terms of trade[c] | 4.05 | 5.82 | 7.60 | 8.02 | 8.02 |
| *OPEC* | | | | | |
| Trade balance[d] | −0.12 | −0.13 | −0.15 | −0.03 | 0.29 |
| Terms of trade[c] | 4.06 | 5.85 | 7.47 | 8.29 | 9.26 |

a. Deviation from baseline as percent of GDP.
b. Absolute deviation from baseline.
c. Percent deviation from baseline.
d. Deviation from baseline as percent of U.S. GDP.

## Table 8-6. *Dynamic Adjustment to Global Cooperative Trade Balance Adjustment*

| Model region | Year 1 | 2 | 3 | 4 | 5 |
|---|---|---|---|---|---|
| *United States* | | | | | |
| GDP[a] | −0.61 | −0.77 | −0.85 | −0.72 | −0.57 |
| Trade balance[a] | 0.44 | 0.63 | 0.79 | 0.91 | 1.05 |
| Budget deficit[a] | −0.27 | −0.68 | −1.12 | −1.63 | −2.17 |
| Inflation[b] | 0.21 | 0.33 | 0.41 | 0.37 | 0.31 |
| Nominal short-term interest rate[b] | 2.67 | 3.07 | 3.30 | 1.83 | −1.76 |
| Nominal long-term interest rate[b] | −0.17 | −0.67 | −1.20 | −1.75 | −2.16 |
| Money[c] | −2.33 | −2.70 | −2.82 | −1.63 | 0.86 |
| *Japan* | | | | | |
| GDP[a] | 0.27 | 0.00 | −0.00 | −0.03 | −0.03 |
| Trade balance[a] | −0.81 | −1.29 | −1.80 | −1.77 | −1.70 |
| Budget deficit[a] | 0.35 | 0.89 | 1.35 | 1.34 | 1.33 |
| Inflation[b] | −0.18 | 0.01 | 0.02 | 0.03 | 0.03 |
| Nominal short-term interest rate[b] | −1.65 | −0.93 | 2.49 | 0.79 | −1.33 |
| Nominal long-term interest rate[b] | −1.01 | −1.04 | −1.15 | −1.59 | −1.86 |
| Money[c] | 1.44 | 1.04 | −0.72 | 0.40 | 1.79 |
| Real exchange rate[c] | 7.50 | 11.83 | 15.76 | 16.39 | 17.27 |
| *Germany* | | | | | |
| GDP[a] | 0.11 | 0.36 | 0.53 | 0.51 | 0.45 |
| Real trade balance[a] | −0.76 | −1.18 | −1.77 | −1.77 | −1.56 |
| Budget deficit[a] | 0.43 | 0.83 | 1.25 | 1.24 | 1.25 |
| Inflation[b] | −0.14 | −0.04 | −0.01 | 0.00 | 0.03 |
| Nominal short-term interest rate[b] | 0.61 | 0.54 | 2.25 | 1.49 | −1.66 |
| Nominal long-term interest rate[b] | −0.69 | −0.95 | −1.20 | −1.62 | −1.97 |
| Money[c] | −0.15 | 0.27 | −0.37 | 0.20 | 2.11 |
| Real exchange rate[c] | 5.53 | 7.50 | 9.93 | 10.81 | 10.97 |
| *REMS* | | | | | |
| GDP[a] | −0.29 | −0.23 | −0.20 | 0.07 | 0.10 |
| Trade balance[a] | −0.50 | −0.56 | −0.72 | −0.66 | −0.38 |
| Budget deficit[a] | 0.04 | 0.01 | −0.01 | −0.09 | −0.10 |
| Inflation[b] | −0.37 | −0.39 | −0.44 | −0.24 | −0.09 |
| Nominal short-term interest rate[b] | 0.61 | 0.54 | 2.25 | 1.49 | −1.66 |
| Nominal long-term interest rate[b] | −0.69 | −0.95 | −1.20 | −1.62 | −1.97 |
| Money[c] | −0.70 | −0.93 | −2.32 | −1.84 | −0.04 |
| Real exchange rate[c] | 5.34 | 6.88 | 8.76 | 9.30 | 9.29 |
| *ROECD* | | | | | |
| GDP[a] | −0.02 | −0.02 | 0.00 | 0.09 | 0.10 |
| Trade balance[a] | −0.20 | −0.26 | −0.41 | −0.51 | −0.52 |
| Budget deficit[a] | 0.01 | 0.01 | 0.01 | −0.03 | −0.03 |
| Inflation[b] | −0.01 | 0.04 | 0.06 | 0.02 | 0.02 |
| Nominal short-term interest rate[b] | 1.17 | 1.25 | 2.36 | 1.39 | −1.66 |
| Nominal long-term interest rate[b] | −0.57 | −0.90 | −1.23 | −1.67 | −2.01 |
| Money[c] | −0.76 | −0.80 | −1.41 | −0.67 | 1.23 |
| Real exchange rate[c] | 4.27 | 5.64 | 7.26 | 8.01 | 8.27 |
| *LDCs* | | | | | |
| Trade balance[d] | 0.30 | 0.36 | 0.61 | 0.36 | −0.30 |
| Terms of trade[c] | 4.12 | 5.76 | 7.51 | 7.94 | 7.95 |
| *OPEC* | | | | | |
| Trade balance[d] | −0.13 | −0.13 | −0.15 | −0.02 | 0.30 |
| Terms of trade[c] | 4.07 | 5.79 | 7.39 | 8.23 | 9.21 |

a. Deviation from baseline as percent of GDP.
b. Absolute deviation from baseline.
c. Percent deviation from baseline.
d. Deviation from baseline as percent of U.S. GDP.

shown that monetary coordination alone implies policy settings that are close to ones that a government would follow in its own self-interest. Coordinating both fiscal and monetary policies, in contrast, implies policy adjustments that are quite different from ones that a country acting alone would pursue.

# CHAPTER NINE

# Implications of Macroeconomic Policy Rules for the World Economy

IN THE PRECEDING two chapters, policy in an individual country was described by an operating rule that was derived from optimizing a social loss function for the economy. These rules were calculated as complicated feedback rules over a whole range of perfectly observed economic variables. Although it is unlikely that optimal rules of this type would have much operational relevance for policy setting in real-life contexts, they do provide a benchmark for comparison with other, simpler policy rules.

It is worth considering whether simpler rules would, by precommitting policymakers, avoid the potentially undesirable outcomes of failures in policy coordination and yet lead the world reasonably close to an ideal outcome in the face of recurring shocks. Indeed, an increasing number of proposals have been made that presume that fixed rules for setting policy would benefit the global economy. Such policy rules, as usually specified, are relatively simple: targeting the domestic money stock in each region, as proposed by Milton Friedman (1959); targeting exchange rates, as advocated by Ronald McKinnon (1984, 1988); or global targeting of nominal income as proposed by Jeffrey Frankel (1989). Other rules are less rigid, such as the target zone proposal of John Williamson (1985), whereby exchange rates are managed within a band rather than pegged exactly. These rules have usually focused on monetary policy. Despite the inherent problem with adjusting domestic fiscal policies, however, some proponents have also advocated incorporating fiscal policy into the rules.[1]

The goal of this chapter is to examine the performance of eight alternative rules for policy in the economies of the United States, Japan,

---

1. The "blueprint" proposal of Williamson and Miller (1987) assigns rules for both monetary and fiscal policies. Weale and others (1989) have recently proposed using monetary and fiscal policy to target nominal income and total wealth. We do not examine that regime here.

and Germany (the Group of Three) in the face of seven shocks to the world economy. These disturbances include shocks to OPEC oil prices and to real demand and money demand in the Group of Three countries.

There are several possible ways to evaluate how the policy regimes perform. One approach is to estimate a variance-covariance matrix of historical shocks, given a model and a set of historical data, and to explore how different rules would have changed history in the face of shocks drawn from the historical experience. This is the approach followed by Taylor (1988b); Frankel, Goldstein, and Masson (1989); and McKibbin (1990b). A problem with this approach is that the historical shocks implied in the residuals from the model are not independent from specification errors in the model; nor are they independent of the formation of expectations under a given historical regime. We do not follow that approach here. The criterion we use in this chapter for evaluating how each rule performs is to calculate the variance of a range of variables, such as inflation and output, in response to independent shocks.

The first part of this chapter explicitly defines the policy regimes we investigate and outlines the technique we use in analyzing these regimes. The second section presents the results. We find the by now familiar result that the success of a particular regime depends on the type of shock hitting the world economy. Nominal income targeting dominates money targeting, especially in the face of money-velocity shocks. But no regime clearly dominates for all types of shocks. Thus, if any one of the regimes considered in this chapter were to be adopted in practice, it should be designed to be sufficiently flexible to permit modification in the face of shocks that it clearly does not handle well.

## Policy Regimes

A "regime" in this chapter is defined as a set of rules for monetary and fiscal policies in the Group of Three economies. The rules can be quite general, such as a feedback rule linking monetary and fiscal policies to all observed variables in the economy on the basis of the full optimization of a control problem. Alternatively, the rules may impose various specific restrictions on the fully general rule, such as targeting exchange rates or nominal income.[2]

2. Argy (1988) provides a useful survey of many of the regimes examined in this chapter.

Figure 9-1. *Alternative Policy Regimes Examined for Monetary and Fiscal Policies in the Group of Three Countries*[a]

---

*Floating exchange rates*

 1. Constant money growth rules in each country (Friedman 1959).
 2. Monetary policy chosen to target nominal income in each country (Taylor 1985).
 3. Monetary policy chosen noncooperatively on basis of ultimate targets in each country.
 4. Monetary policy chosen cooperatively on basis of ultimate targets in each country.

*Fixed nominal exchange rates*

 5. McKinnon (1984) rule I, by which $n - 1$ countries target nominal exchange rates and the $n$th country targets the money stock of the United States, Japan, and Germany (the Group of Three).
 6. McKinnon (1988) rule II, by which $n - 1$ countries target nominal exchange rates and the $n$th country targets the average price level of the Group of Three.
 7. McKinnon rule III, by which $n - 1$ countries target nominal exchange rates and the $n$th country targets the total nominal income of the Group of Three.
 8. Blueprint proposal, by which both monetary and fiscal policies are chosen to fix real exchange rates, target total nominal income, and target nominal income in the Group of Three (Williamson and Miller 1987).

---

a. In each regime where fiscal policy is not specified, we assume that it is unchanged given a shock and that it adjusts within the constraints imposed by the monetary regime to minimize the variance of a set of ultimate targets that we specify for each country.

The regimes we consider include closed-economy rules in a world of floating exchange rates, as well as rules that take into account interdependence in the world economy by requiring some form of policy coordination among countries. When rules specify restrictions only on the use of monetary policies, we make two alternative assumptions about fiscal policy: either it does not change (assumption A) or it is chosen by each country noncooperatively to reach objectives of inflation, unemployment, and fiscal deficits within the restriction imposed by the monetary regime (assumption B).

The policy regimes considered in this chapter are listed in figure 9-1. They are grouped according to those that allow exchange rates to fluctuate and those that impose a fixed exchange rate. In discussing these regimes, it is important to note that where both monetary and fiscal policies are specified, they are usually assigned by the proponents to particular targets. We do not deal with the assignment problem directly in this paper but merely specify the set of targets and the set of instruments and allow the algorithm used to solve the model to calculate the optimal assignment. In general, it is unlikely that in this assignment all the responsibility for one target would fall on one instrument.

The technicalities of our solution procedure have been summarized in chapter 8. It is worth briefly mentioning here the form the solution takes. The general problem facing policymakers is assumed to be the choice of policy instruments to minimize a loss function that is quadratic in the targets $(\tau)$, subject to the structure of the economy. When calculating the path for policy, we express it as a feedback rule on the observed state variables and exogenous variables in the economy.

The first regime we consider is a world of floating exchange rates with each country following the Friedman (1959) rule of targeting monetary aggregates (labeled "Friedman rule" in tables 9A-1–9A-7). In the second regime, we assume that each national government targets nominal GNP (see Taylor 1985), taking as given the policies of other countries (labeled "Nominal income" in the tables). In the third regime, we calculate the optimal time-consistent monetary policy rule for the Group of Three economies, assuming that each country targets a set of ultimate objectives, taking as given the policies of other countries. The result is the Nash equilibrium of a dynamic game among the three countries (which we label "noncooperative" in the tables). The ultimate objectives are assumed to vary among countries. In each country we arbitrarily assume that inflation and fiscal deficits are targets, but we also include unemployment in the United States. The relative weights are inflation, 0.6; fiscal deficit, 0.2; and unemployment, 0.4 in the United States and zero elsewhere.

The fourth regime is our way of formalizing a "cooperative" policy rule. As we described in chapter 8, in this case we set up the same problem as faced by the individual countries in the noncooperative regime but then assume that a global planner undertakes the optimization problem to find a monetary rule for each country. In case A, cooperation is confined to monetary policy; in case B, both monetary and fiscal policies are considered. The rule we find is an optimal, cooperative, time-consistent policy rule conditional on the objective functions we have specified for each country. Although these objective functions are arbitrarily chosen for illustration, this regime does give us a standard for comparing the other regimes.

The fifth regime is McKinnon's original (1984) proposal for $n - 1$ target countries to target nominal exchange rates and for the $n$th country to target the world money stock (labeled "McKinnon I" in the tables). This regime would be expected to work well for negatively correlated shifts in portfolio preferences, the case for which it was originally designed. The constraint on nominal exchange rates would force countries that experienced a shift away from their currencies to contract monetary policy and the countries with the increased demand to expand monetary policy. The result would be an automatic rebalancing of portfolios without any spillover into goods markets. McKinnon (1988) has subsequently revised this rule to accommodate shifts in global velocity by advocating a world traded-good price as the global target; this is called McKinnon rule II in this paper ("McKinnon II" in the tables). McKinnon rule III is a natural extension of this regime, with the global target defined as world nominal income.

The blueprint proposal put forward by Williamson and Miller (1987) uses monetary policy in $n - 1$ countries to target real effective exchange rates within a target zone, with the $n$th country then targeting world nominal demand.[3] Fiscal policies in each country are assigned to target their own nominal demand. The fiscal policy assignment is included in an attempt to tie down the steady-state price level. At first glance there appear to be more instruments than targets because world nominal demand is merely the sum of each individual country's nominal demand. In solving for the rule, we found this to be a problem only when world nominal demand was calculated using a base-period exchange rate. When world nominal demand was defined appropriately using current exchange rates, the use of the nominal exchange rate was sufficient to break down the linear dependence of targets. We also assumed that the targeting of nominal demand and real exchange rates was undertaken cooperatively and so avoided any asymmetries from allocating countries to particular targets.

---

3. We cannot at this stage incorporate the impact of a target zone on expectations in our modeling framework, although the approach of Krugman (1988) may be a future possibility.

## Results for Key Variables

The asymptotic operating characteristics of the eight regimes—including alternative assumptions about fiscal policy (when this is not specified by the regime)—are set out in a series of identically organized tables, tables 9A-1 through 9A-7. Each table refers to a different type of shock; for example, table 9A-1 contains the calculations for an oil price shock, and table 9A-4 for a shock to Japanese money demand. The results presented in each table are the asymptotic standard errors for a range of variables (arrayed across the rows of the tables) in response to a shock (specified in the table's title) drawn from a distribution with unit variance.[4] Each column in the tables pertains to one of the eight alternative regimes, with the monetary assumptions indicated above the rule and the fiscal assumptions below. Each entry in the table has been multiplied by a factor of 100 for convenience of presentation. For example, the interpretation of the upper left hand cell in table 9A-1 is that the steady-state standard deviation of U.S. output under an oil price shock of unit variance, when all countries float their currencies and target money, is 0.0305 (that is, 3.05 after adjusting by the scaling factor of 100).

Several points emerge from these tables and from the exercise in general. The first points concern stability of the regimes, and the second set concerns the relative strengths and weaknesses of the regimes in dealing with particular shocks.

First, each set of policy rules converged and was stable, except for the blueprint proposal. We were able to find a feedback representation of the blueprint regime that had stable parameter values, but the feedback rule we found was itself unstable. In the linearized version of the MSG2 model we can check for the stability of the model by calculating the eigenvalues of the system after substituting in the rules for the control variables. In the case of the blueprint regime, there were two unstable eigenvalues of exactly 1.02 detected. The 0.02 component is the difference between the real rate of interest and the steady-state growth rate in the model. This suggests that several of the equations for asset accumulation were gradually exploding at this constant rate. The interpretation of this problem is that the attempt to target real exchange rates leads to instrument instability; the specific problem

4. The technique for calculating these variances was described in McKibbin and Sachs (1986b). We will not elaborate on it further here.

is with the fiscal deficit. In a model such as the MSG2 model, where intertemporal budget constraints are carefully observed, any policy rule will imply a path for real asset prices as well as a long-run equilibrium solution. Targeting real exchange rates at an unchanging level along the solution path, as well as at an unchanged equilibrium value, is not consistent for some shocks.[5] Another way of looking at this problem is that fiscal policy can directly offset a real shock in the goods market through changes in aggregate demand. Over time, however, the changes in debt resulting from the spending changes will ultimately require a change in relative asset prices, including the real exchange rate.

These observations suggest that policymakers need to know the equilibrium real exchange rate if they are trying to target it. Does the wide band around the targeted real exchange rates explicit in the blueprint proposal (but which our analysis does not take explicitly into account) resolve this problem? Unfortunately, not necessarily. It depends very much on the relation between the equilibrium real exchange rate and the initial real exchange rate, as well as on the nature of the transition path between the two. If the target zone did not encompass the equilibrium exchange rate—or even if it encompassed it but the transition path led to a real exchange rate traversing the bands—the mandated policy responses at the band would be sufficient to cause instability similar to what we found with a rigid target for the real exchange rate. The information requirement of the blueprint in setting up the bands seems rather extreme. It appears to us that allowing the real exchange rate to adjust avoids the instability and long-run sustainability problems associated with this regime. This will be a focus of future work with the MSG2 model.

As regards the performance of alternative regimes in the face of different shocks, we can make several observations on the basis of the tabular comparison.

First, cooperation in monetary policy only and in both monetary and fiscal policy does not always lead to lower target variance than under simpler rules because we are imposing time consistency in the optimizing regimes. In other words, we only calculate optimal rules

5. This issue is examined in detail in McKibbin (1990c). Note that this instability is not the same as the assignment problem of targeting real exchange rates with monetary policy that was pointed out by Genberg and Swoboda (1988). In this chapter we do not assign particular instruments to targets.

that are completely credible to the private agents in the model, without imposing external commitments. Some of the simpler rules are not time consistent in the sense that if the policymakers were able to adjust policy they would find it desirable to do so. For the simple rules, therefore, we assume that the rules are binding even though there may be some gain to the policymakers from breaking the rules.

A second observation is that nominal-income rules tend to dominate comparable money-targeting rules (although this is ambiguous for the oil price shock). This is particularly the case for money-velocity shocks. A rise in the demand for money would tend to reduce output and prices and therefore reduces nominal income. The reaction of monetary authorities pursuing a nominal income target would be to raise nominal money balances. This response automatically supplies the additional money balances being demanded and prevents any spillovers from the money market into other markets. A similar automatic adjustment to velocity shocks applies in the McKinnon rule I, which targets nominal exchange rates. As the home currency appreciates in response to the higher home demand for money, the home monetary authority would increase money balances. With an increase in the global stock of money, the foreign monetary authority would need to reduce the foreign money supply to satisfy the McKinnon I constraint on global money balance. The decline in the foreign money supply would be neutral only if there was a corresponding fall in foreign money demand. The advantage of a more general form of the McKinnon proposal, represented by the McKinnon II and McKinnon III regimes, is that the global constraint is less severe. Under McKinnon rules II and III, the foreign monetary authority would not need to respond because the global target of a price level or global nominal income would presumably be unaffected by the home policy adjustment. In these modifications to the original McKinnon rule, the shocks are offset in the domestic and foreign economies.

Apart from long-run instability, which has already been discussed, the blueprint works very well for all country-specific shocks, but not for the oil price shock.[6] As can be seen, the instability takes a long

6. Note that we still calculate steady-state variances for variables under the blueprint proposal, even when some variables will have infinite variance, because we are interested in seeing where the instability manifests. The technique for calculating steady-state variance can be approximated by imposing a shock on the model and calculating the infinite sum of squared deviations of each variable. The results for the blueprint in the tables are calculated by using this approximation for twenty years after the shock so that we can explore the impact of the fundamental instability.

time to emerge for real shocks, but it eventually shows up in the deficit numbers. The blueprint regime is indeed capable of offsetting the country-specific real shocks, but it leads to instrument instability. In terms of monetary shocks, the blueprint regime also performs extremely well, and without the instability problems associated with the real shocks, because the shock in the money markets can be completely offset by monetary policy without any fiscal policy implications. Finally, note that for the oil price shock the instability of the blueprint shows most vividly. In this case the real exchange rates among the Group of Three need to adjust because of the asymmetry of the countries. The result of attempting to offset this is large fluctuations in fiscal deficits and in current account balances. The apparent contradiction of these results, compared with those of Currie and Wren-Lewis (1988) and Edison, Miller, and Williamson (1987), can possibly be attributed to the strict adherence to all intertemporal budget constraints in the MSG2 model. This adherence imposes certain paths for debt accumulation and relative price adjustment that are not considered in the models used in these other two studies.

## Summary

This chapter has examined the medium-term performance of alternative rules for the world economy. Not surprisingly, we find that no regime tends to dominate under all the shocks considered. Some regimes, such as the early McKinnon (1984) rule, can be unambiguously improved by relaxing constraints within the rule without losing the essential framework of the proposal. As a general proposition, some degree of flexibility in adjusting all regimes seems required to prevent them from collapsing in the face of certain shocks.

We also find some long-run stability problems with the Williamson and Miller (1987) "blueprint" proposal, at least in the way we implement it in the model. The problem is due to the targeting of real exchange rates at a fixed baseline level when underlying long-run fundamentals change.

Table 9A-1. *Asymptotic Standard Deviation of Variables in Response to an Oil Price Shock*
Standard deviation × 100

| | | | Monetary and fiscal regime[a] | | | | | | | | | | | |
| Variable | Friedman rule | Nominal income | Noncooperative | | Cooperative | | McKinnon I | | McKinnon II | | McKinnon III | | Blueprint |
| | A | A | A | B | A | B | A | B | A | B | A | B | |
|---|---|---|---|---|---|---|---|---|---|---|---|---|---|
| **United States** | | | | | | | | | | | | | |
| Output | 3.05 | 3.81 | 5.21 | 4.20 | 5.11 | 4.12 | 3.11 | 4.79 | 7.87 | 6.62 | 3.82 | 2.76 | 3.51 |
| Inflation | 4.55 | 3.89 | 2.53 | 2.01 | 2.57 | 1.93 | 4.54 | 2.63 | 0.50 | 0.37 | 3.79 | 4.20 | 2.05 |
| Current account | 0.27 | 0.45 | 0.83 | 1.58 | 0.81 | 1.21 | 0.29 | 0.95 | 1.31 | 3.46 | 0.46 | 0.87 | 34.41 |
| Budget deficit | 0.95 | 1.19 | 1.62 | 2.60 | 1.59 | 1.98 | 0.97 | 1.75 | 2.45 | 5.35 | 1.19 | 1.80 | 61.10 |
| **Japan** | | | | | | | | | | | | | |
| Output | 1.12 | 2.16 | 4.99 | 7.45 | 4.70 | 8.76 | 1.09 | 6.64 | 5.62 | 5.78 | 1.91 | 6.55 | 1.55 |
| Inflation | 3.64 | 2.93 | 0.20 | 0.00 | 0.41 | 0.00 | 3.49 | 0.08 | 1.13 | 0.58 | 3.12 | 0.10 | 2.19 |
| Current account | 0.23 | 0.22 | 0.19 | 0.75 | 0.18 | 0.87 | 0.23 | 0.23 | 0.26 | 0.85 | 0.23 | 0.53 | 9.37 |
| Budget deficit | 0.35 | 0.68 | 1.58 | 0.00 | 1.49 | 1.22 | 0.34 | 0.67 | 1.78 | 2.95 | 0.61 | 0.71 | 40.49 |
| Exchange rate | 2.45 | 2.78 | 10.37 | 10.77 | 10.70 | 16.72 | 0.00 | 0.00 | 0.00 | 0.00 | 0.00 | 0.00 | 3.82 |
| Real exchange rate | 4.67 | 4.82 | 4.94 | 10.90 | 4.38 | 17.63 | 4.85 | 6.09 | 3.99 | 1.51 | 4.81 | 4.51 | 0.00 |
| **Germany** | | | | | | | | | | | | | |
| Output | 3.63 | 2.86 | 3.12 | 3.52 | 2.95 | 3.59 | 3.72 | 5.38 | 2.91 | 3.22 | 3.16 | 4.76 | 21.76 |
| Inflation | 3.06 | 1.95 | 0.12 | 0.00 | 0.41 | 0.11 | 3.41 | 0.85 | 0.75 | 0.89 | 2.71 | 0.66 | 8.96 |
| Current account | 0.43 | 0.67 | 1.20 | 1.99 | 1.16 | 1.74 | 0.40 | 1.82 | 1.57 | 3.94 | 0.61 | 2.15 | 103.55 |
| Budget deficit | 1.14 | 0.90 | 0.98 | 0.00 | 0.93 | 0.48 | 1.17 | 2.04 | 0.92 | 1.89 | 0.99 | 1.57 | 138.37 |
| Exchange rate | 2.77 | 3.85 | 11.59 | 7.12 | 9.81 | 6.95 | 0.00 | 0.00 | 0.00 | 0.00 | 0.00 | 0.00 | 18.51 |
| Real exchange rate | 4.55 | 3.68 | 4.92 | 1.88 | 4.60 | 2.32 | 4.91 | 5.37 | 2.46 | 2.92 | 4.27 | 4.89 | 0.00 |
| **ROECD[b]** | | | | | | | | | | | | | |
| Output | 2.34 | 2.39 | 2.71 | 2.49 | 2.65 | 2.11 | 2.33 | 3.60 | 3.05 | 6.12 | 2.35 | 2.37 | 32.56 |
| Inflation | 4.20 | 5.16 | 7.09 | 6.97 | 6.93 | 5.37 | 4.10 | 1.79 | 8.16 | 13.54 | 4.86 | 4.71 | 47.68 |
| Current account | 0.27 | 0.55 | 1.08 | 1.33 | 1.04 | 0.78 | 0.26 | 1.04 | 1.55 | 3.53 | 0.46 | 0.66 | 46.99 |
| Budget deficit | 0.73 | 0.74 | 0.84 | 0.78 | 0.83 | 0.66 | 0.73 | 1.12 | 0.95 | 1.91 | 0.73 | 0.74 | 10.15 |
| Exchange rate | 2.87 | 1.45 | 11.02 | 12.31 | 11.25 | 10.27 | 2.83 | 4.13 | 13.44 | 25.97 | 2.06 | 3.98 | 244.03 |
| Real exchange rate | 2.72 | 2.67 | 5.78 | 8.70 | 5.68 | 6.47 | 2.44 | 4.96 | 10.09 | 20.79 | 2.73 | 3.37 | 188.40 |

a. Fiscal policy assumptions are that regime A is exogenous fiscal policy and regime B is noncooperative fiscal policy (except for the optimal cooperative regime, which assumes cooperative fiscal policy). Monetary assumptions, as described in the text and figure 9-1, are indicated just below the rule.

b. Here and in subsequent tables in the chapter, ROECD (rest of the OECD) is as defined in chapter 3 (note 4).

Table 9A-2. *Asymptotic Standard Deviation of Variables in Response to a U.S. Money Demand Shock*
Standard deviation × 100

| Variable | Friedman rule A | Nominal income A | Non-cooperative A | Non-cooperative B | Cooperative A | Cooperative B | McKinnon I A | McKinnon I B | McKinnon II A | McKinnon II B | McKinnon III A | McKinnon III B | Blueprint |
|---|---|---|---|---|---|---|---|---|---|---|---|---|---|
| **United States** | | | | | | | | | | | | | |
| Output | 25.13 | 0.20 | 0.23 | 0.19 | 0.23 | 0.19 | 16.31 | 1.90 | 0.41 | 0.17 | 0.24 | 0.10 | 0.00 |
| Inflation | 21.93 | 0.21 | 0.13 | 0.11 | 0.13 | 0.11 | 11.56 | 2.36 | 0.13 | 0.04 | 0.06 | 0.13 | 0.00 |
| Current account | 5.15 | 0.39 | 0.37 | 0.31 | 0.37 | 0.33 | 3.28 | 8.04 | 0.33 | 0.32 | 0.36 | 0.37 | 0.00 |
| Budget deficit | 7.83 | 0.06 | 0.07 | 0.14 | 0.07 | 0.11 | 5.08 | 11.33 | 0.13 | 0.14 | 0.07 | 0.07 | 0.60 |
| **Japan** | | | | | | | | | | | | | |
| Output | 2.35 | 0.04 | 0.09 | 0.11 | 0.10 | 0.04 | 12.99 | 2.16 | 0.38 | 0.05 | 0.52 | 0.09 | 0.00 |
| Inflation | 5.04 | 0.09 | 0.00 | 0.00 | 0.01 | 0.00 | 11.89 | 0.76 | 0.30 | 0.04 | 0.53 | 0.04 | 0.00 |
| Current account | 1.08 | 0.12 | 0.12 | 0.11 | 0.12 | 0.11 | 0.50 | 1.60 | 0.12 | 0.07 | 0.12 | 0.08 | 0.00 |
| Budget deficit | 0.74 | 0.01 | 0.03 | 0.00 | 0.03 | 0.07 | 4.11 | 5.83 | 0.12 | 0.21 | 0.17 | 0.27 | 0.00 |
| Exchange rate | 79.63 | 2.17 | 1.79 | 1.67 | 1.77 | 1.35 | 0.00 | 0.00 | 0.00 | 0.00 | 0.00 | 0.00 | 0.00 |
| Real exchange rate | 62.69 | 2.04 | 1.61 | 1.52 | 1.58 | 1.15 | 6.92 | 4.91 | 0.46 | 0.15 | 0.40 | 0.20 | 0.00 |
| **Germany** | | | | | | | | | | | | | |
| Output | 9.82 | 0.11 | 0.08 | 0.11 | 0.08 | 0.11 | 11.62 | 6.13 | 0.23 | 0.20 | 0.34 | 0.24 | 0.00 |
| Inflation | 6.53 | 0.11 | 0.00 | 0.00 | 0.01 | 0.01 | 8.44 | 2.45 | 0.21 | 0.09 | 0.32 | 0.11 | 0.00 |
| Current account | 3.12 | 0.32 | 0.28 | 0.23 | 0.28 | 0.24 | 3.56 | 6.13 | 0.27 | 0.24 | 0.32 | 0.29 | 0.00 |
| Budget deficit | 3.09 | 0.04 | 0.03 | 0.00 | 0.02 | 0.03 | 3.66 | 5.90 | 0.07 | 0.20 | 0.11 | 0.28 | 0.00 |
| Exchange rate | 69.97 | 1.01 | 1.37 | 1.11 | 1.32 | 1.06 | 0.00 | 0.00 | 0.00 | 0.00 | 0.00 | 0.00 | 0.00 |
| Real exchange rate | 53.62 | 0.94 | 1.05 | 0.83 | 1.03 | 0.79 | 13.46 | 3.31 | 0.63 | 0.25 | 0.71 | 0.28 | 0.00 |
| **ROECD** | | | | | | | | | | | | | |
| Output | 5.82 | 0.55 | 0.51 | 0.45 | 0.51 | 0.50 | 6.12 | 14.21 | 0.48 | 0.54 | 0.55 | 0.66 | 0.00 |
| Inflation | 7.91 | 0.73 | 0.65 | 0.56 | 0.65 | 0.66 | 11.91 | 20.77 | 0.67 | 0.77 | 0.81 | 0.96 | 0.00 |
| Current account | 4.16 | 0.34 | 0.31 | 0.26 | 0.31 | 0.30 | 4.17 | 8.34 | 0.29 | 0.32 | 0.34 | 0.38 | 0.00 |
| Budget deficit | 1.81 | 0.17 | 0.16 | 0.14 | 0.16 | 0.16 | 1.91 | 4.43 | 0.15 | 0.17 | 0.17 | 0.21 | 0.00 |
| Exchange rate | 73.45 | 2.67 | 2.56 | 2.17 | 2.57 | 2.33 | 41.37 | 53.95 | 1.80 | 1.99 | 2.28 | 2.49 | 0.00 |
| Real exchange rate | 57.11 | 2.29 | 2.14 | 1.80 | 2.14 | 1.93 | 30.38 | 45.57 | 1.64 | 1.71 | 1.97 | 2.09 | 0.00 |

a. Fiscal policy assumptions are that regime A is exogenous fiscal policy and regime B is noncooperative fiscal policy (except for the optimal cooperative regime, which assumes cooperative fiscal policy). Monetary assumptions, as described in the text and figure 9-1, are indicated just below the rule.

Table 9A-3. *Asymptotic Standard Deviation of Variables in Response to a U.S. Real Demand Shock*
Standard deviation × 100

| | Friedman rule | Nominal income | Noncooperative | | Cooperative | | McKinnon I | | McKinnon II | | McKinnon III | | Blueprint |
|---|---|---|---|---|---|---|---|---|---|---|---|---|---|
| | | | | | | | *Monetary and fiscal regime*[a] | | | | | | |
| *Variable* | A | A | A | B | A | B | A | B | A | B | A | B | ... |
| *United States* | | | | | | | | | | | | | |
| Output | 136.41 | 33.27 | 38.70 | 32.23 | 38.14 | 31.63 | 155.59 | 14.89 | 69.15 | 28.15 | 39.67 | 17.01 | 0.00 |
| Inflation | 57.94 | 35.18 | 21.74 | 18.92 | 22.14 | 18.18 | 81.42 | 7.53 | 21.03 | 5.98 | 9.71 | 20.93 | 0.00 |
| Current account | 42.85 | 64.42 | 60.91 | 51.57 | 61.01 | 55.53 | 39.11 | 4.12 | 54.42 | 53.16 | 60.76 | 61.93 | 0.00 |
| Budget deficit | 42.51 | 10.37 | 12.06 | 24.03 | 11.88 | 18.34 | 48.48 | 95.09 | 21.55 | 24.09 | 12.36 | 10.96 | 100.18 |
| *Japan* | | | | | | | | | | | | | |
| Output | 42.62 | 6.36 | 14.52 | 17.72 | 16.68 | 6.07 | 7.85 | 0.85 | 62.73 | 9.09 | 87.04 | 15.21 | 0.00 |
| Inflation | 39.08 | 15.46 | 0.57 | 0.00 | 1.16 | 0.01 | 10.48 | 0.28 | 49.58 | 6.76 | 88.53 | 6.45 | 0.00 |
| Current account | 18.37 | 19.84 | 20.51 | 18.35 | 20.48 | 17.68 | 17.57 | 1.91 | 19.52 | 12.36 | 19.93 | 13.19 | 0.00 |
| Budget deficit | 13.50 | 2.01 | 4.60 | 0.00 | 5.28 | 11.01 | 2.49 | 2.57 | 19.86 | 34.46 | 27.56 | 44.65 | 0.00 |
| Exchange rate | 186.90 | 361.66 | 297.62 | 277.94 | 295.32 | 224.43 | 0.00 | 0.00 | 0.00 | 0.00 | 0.01 | 0.00 | 0.00 |
| Real exchange rate | 214.09 | 340.08 | 267.96 | 253.96 | 262.69 | 191.72 | 99.36 | 15.83 | 76.28 | 24.69 | 66.89 | 33.23 | 0.00 |
| *Germany* | | | | | | | | | | | | | |
| Output | 72.75 | 18.80 | 13.85 | 18.01 | 12.51 | 19.12 | 30.22 | 4.79 | 38.08 | 33.05 | 57.38 | 39.89 | 0.00 |
| Inflation | 43.02 | 18.68 | 0.53 | 0.00 | 2.43 | 1.03 | 16.52 | 0.88 | 34.79 | 15.36 | 53.03 | 19.08 | 0.00 |
| Current account | 27.89 | 52.50 | 46.47 | 37.82 | 46.77 | 40.28 | 28.82 | 3.87 | 45.19 | 40.00 | 53.12 | 47.53 | 0.00 |
| Budget deficit | 22.91 | 5.92 | 4.36 | 0.00 | 3.94 | 4.46 | 9.52 | 2.33 | 12.00 | 33.12 | 18.07 | 46.16 | 0.00 |
| Exchange rate | 147.37 | 168.85 | 288.15 | 185.72 | 220.39 | 177.39 | 0.00 | 0.00 | 0.00 | 0.00 | 0.00 | 0.00 | 0.00 |
| Real exchange rate | 170.57 | 156.01 | 174.40 | 138.12 | 171.55 | 131.14 | 75.63 | 18.63 | 105.00 | 41.76 | 118.24 | 47.09 | 0.00 |
| *ROECD* | | | | | | | | | | | | | |
| Output | 53.26 | 91.51 | 84.54 | 74.20 | 84.94 | 83.78 | 52.38 | 5.07 | 80.52 | 90.14 | 91.79 | 110.29 | 0.00 |
| Inflation | 46.19 | 121.30 | 107.95 | 94.07 | 108.96 | 109.64 | 53.08 | 4.87 | 111.52 | 128.32 | 135.08 | 160.18 | 0.00 |
| Current account | 29.33 | 56.12 | 51.53 | 44.15 | 51.76 | 49.36 | 28.74 | 3.20 | 48.88 | 52.89 | 56.34 | 63.93 | 0.00 |
| Budget deficit | 16.59 | 28.51 | 26.34 | 23.12 | 26.47 | 26.10 | 16.32 | 1.58 | 25.09 | 28.09 | 28.60 | 34.36 | 0.00 |
| Exchange rate | 152.54 | 445.06 | 426.20 | 361.63 | 428.31 | 388.56 | 83.45 | 13.03 | 299.74 | 332.02 | 380.11 | 415.24 | 0.00 |
| Real exchange rate | 175.50 | 381.99 | 355.89 | 300.00 | 356.30 | 322.26 | 124.36 | 18.07 | 272.64 | 284.21 | 328.35 | 348.55 | 0.00 |

a. Fiscal policy assumptions are that regime A is exogenous fiscal policy and regime B is noncooperative fiscal policy (except for the optimal cooperative regime, which assumes cooperative fiscal policy). Monetary assumptions, as described in the text and figure 9-1, are indicated just below the rule.

Table 9A-4. *Asymptotic Standard Deviation of Variables in Response to a Japanese Money Demand Shock*
Standard deviation × 100

| | | | | | | | Monetary and fiscal regime[a] | | | | | | | |
|---|---|---|---|---|---|---|---|---|---|---|---|---|---|---|
| | Friedman rule | Nominal income | Non-cooperative | | Cooperative | | McKinnon I | | McKinnon II | | McKinnon III | | Blueprint |
| Variable | A | A | A | B | A | B | A | B | A | B | A | B | ... |
| **United States** | | | | | | | | | | | | | |
| Output | 1.02 | 0.09 | 0.10 | 0.10 | 0.10 | 0.10 | 8.21 | 0.90 | 0.42 | 0.08 | 0.26 | 0.04 | 0.00 |
| Inflation | 1.79 | 0.12 | 0.06 | 0.07 | 0.06 | 0.07 | 5.70 | 1.13 | 0.27 | 0.05 | 0.14 | 0.02 | 0.00 |
| Current account | 0.24 | 0.02 | 0.01 | 0.05 | 0.01 | 0.04 | 1.45 | 3.78 | 0.07 | 0.07 | 0.04 | 0.01 | 0.00 |
| Budget deficit | 0.32 | 0.03 | 0.03 | 0.09 | 0.03 | 0.07 | 2.56 | 5.61 | 0.13 | 0.12 | 0.08 | 0.01 | 0.00 |
| **Japan** | | | | | | | | | | | | | |
| Output | 22.18 | 0.19 | 0.52 | 0.75 | 0.52 | 0.70 | 4.87 | 1.15 | 1.05 | 0.24 | 1.16 | 0.17 | 0.00 |
| Inflation | 25.71 | 0.48 | 0.02 | 0.00 | 0.02 | 0.00 | 4.68 | 0.28 | 0.62 | 0.10 | 0.80 | 0.08 | 0.00 |
| Current account | 0.63 | 0.09 | 0.09 | 0.12 | 0.09 | 0.12 | 0.14 | 0.73 | 0.10 | 0.04 | 0.10 | 0.03 | 0.00 |
| Budget deficit | 7.02 | 0.06 | 0.16 | 0.00 | 0.17 | 0.04 | 1.54 | 2.17 | 0.33 | 0.51 | 0.37 | 0.57 | 0.60 |
| Exchange rate | 92.59 | 4.62 | 3.09 | 4.04 | 3.07 | 3.82 | 0.00 | 0.00 | 0.00 | 0.00 | 0.00 | 0.00 | 0.00 |
| Real exchange rate | 75.47 | 4.39 | 3.16 | 4.16 | 3.14 | 3.92 | 3.76 | 2.21 | 0.79 | 0.33 | 0.74 | 0.26 | 0.00 |
| **Germany** | | | | | | | | | | | | | |
| Output | 2.11 | 0.15 | 0.10 | 0.18 | 0.10 | 0.18 | 5.54 | 2.92 | 0.19 | 0.11 | 0.10 | 0.03 | 0.00 |
| Inflation | 1.82 | 0.13 | 0.00 | 0.00 | 0.01 | 0.00 | 4.00 | 1.15 | 0.16 | 0.03 | 0.08 | 0.01 | 0.00 |
| Current account | 0.54 | 0.02 | 0.04 | 0.10 | 0.04 | 0.10 | 1.65 | 2.89 | 0.13 | 0.07 | 0.09 | 0.02 | 0.00 |
| Budget deficit | 0.66 | 0.05 | 0.03 | 0.00 | 0.03 | 0.02 | 1.75 | 2.78 | 0.06 | 0.07 | 0.03 | 0.01 | 0.00 |
| Exchange rate | 1.84 | 0.13 | 0.30 | 0.20 | 0.26 | 0.19 | 0.00 | 0.00 | 0.00 | 0.00 | 0.00 | 0.00 | 0.00 |
| Real exchange rate | 2.81 | 0.20 | 0.18 | 0.07 | 0.18 | 0.06 | 6.37 | 1.56 | 0.26 | 0.08 | 0.15 | 0.03 | 0.00 |
| **ROECD** | | | | | | | | | | | | | |
| Output | 1.06 | 0.09 | 0.11 | 0.17 | 0.11 | 0.13 | 2.86 | 6.68 | 0.21 | 0.14 | 0.16 | 0.02 | 0.00 |
| Inflation | 1.87 | 0.19 | 0.23 | 0.34 | 0.23 | 0.29 | 5.63 | 9.77 | 0.38 | 0.21 | 0.27 | 0.03 | 0.00 |
| Current account | 0.06 | 0.04 | 0.06 | 0.10 | 0.06 | 0.08 | 1.95 | 3.93 | 0.13 | 0.09 | 0.09 | 0.01 | 0.00 |
| Budget deficit | 0.33 | 0.03 | 0.03 | 0.05 | 0.03 | 0.04 | 0.89 | 2.08 | 0.07 | 0.04 | 0.05 | 0.01 | 0.00 |
| Exchange rate | 0.95 | 0.14 | 0.31 | 0.58 | 0.31 | 0.49 | 19.56 | 25.40 | 1.05 | 0.60 | 0.67 | 0.09 | 0.00 |
| Real exchange rate | 0.90 | 0.12 | 0.17 | 0.42 | 0.17 | 0.34 | 14.22 | 21.44 | 0.78 | 0.47 | 0.49 | 0.06 | 0.00 |

a. Fiscal policy assumptions are that regime A is exogenous fiscal policy and regime B is noncooperative fiscal policy (except for the optimal cooperative regime, which assumes cooperative fiscal policy). Monetary assumptions, as described in the text and figure 9-1, are indicated just below the rule.

## Table 9A-5. Asymptotic Standard Deviation of Variables in Response to a Japanese Real Demand Shock

Standard deviation × 100

| Variable | Friedman rule A | Nominal income A | Monetary and fiscal regime[a] Noncooperative A | B | Cooperative A | B | McKinnon I A | B | McKinnon II A | B | McKinnon III A | B | Blueprint |
|---|---|---|---|---|---|---|---|---|---|---|---|---|---|
| **United States** | | | | | | | | | | | | | |
| Output | 10.86 | 15.72 | 16.30 | 17.03 | 16.25 | 16.67 | 20.19 | 2.53 | 70.40 | 13.06 | 42.66 | 6.70 | 0.00 |
| Inflation | 18.22 | 19.79 | 10.51 | 11.97 | 10.52 | 11.54 | 6.80 | 0.14 | 45.06 | 8.63 | 23.34 | 2.95 | 0.00 |
| Current account | 2.37 | 2.73 | 1.83 | 8.43 | 1.81 | 6.47 | 2.73 | 1.10 | 12.29 | 11.57 | 6.90 | 0.84 | 0.00 |
| Budget deficit | 3.39 | 4.90 | 5.08 | 15.39 | 5.06 | 11.78 | 6.29 | 3.52 | 21.94 | 19.56 | 13.29 | 1.87 | 0.00 |
| **Japan** | | | | | | | | | | | | | |
| Output | 155.34 | 31.50 | 85.90 | 125.15 | 86.90 | 117.39 | 210.94 | 25.99 | 175.09 | 40.01 | 194.13 | 28.78 | 0.00 |
| Inflation | 79.01 | 80.25 | 3.43 | 0.00 | 2.61 | 0.00 | 151.49 | 12.56 | 104.25 | 16.57 | 132.61 | 13.66 | 0.00 |
| Current account | 16.86 | 14.65 | 15.83 | 20.04 | 15.82 | 19.17 | 17.75 | 4.88 | 17.16 | 6.75 | 17.39 | 5.76 | 0.00 |
| Budget deficit | 49.19 | 9.98 | 27.20 | 0.00 | 27.52 | 7.27 | 66.80 | 95.75 | 55.44 | 84.41 | 61.47 | 94.88 | 100.18 |
| Exchange rate | 300.25 | 769.23 | 514.58 | 673.58 | 511.15 | 635.86 | 0.00 | 0.00 | 0.00 | 0.00 | 0.00 | 0.00 | 0.00 |
| Real exchange rate | 354.62 | 730.96 | 526.20 | 693.49 | 523.08 | 654.16 | 119.88 | 34.34 | 132.04 | 55.06 | 123.84 | 42.48 | 0.00 |
| **Germany** | | | | | | | | | | | | | |
| Output | 20.21 | 25.20 | 17.24 | 30.45 | 17.06 | 30.79 | 3.88 | 6.19 | 31.87 | 18.01 | 16.04 | 5.41 | 0.00 |
| Inflation | 16.89 | 22.44 | 0.66 | 0.00 | 1.34 | 0.65 | 2.33 | 0.81 | 26.08 | 5.60 | 12.68 | 0.87 | 0.00 |
| Current account | 3.29 | 3.35 | 7.02 | 17.25 | 6.96 | 15.85 | 10.16 | 4.22 | 21.33 | 12.27 | 14.89 | 3.46 | 0.00 |
| Budget deficit | 6.37 | 7.94 | 5.43 | 0.00 | 5.37 | 2.86 | 1.22 | 2.00 | 10.04 | 11.96 | 5.05 | 2.10 | 0.00 |
| Exchange rate | 11.33 | 22.47 | 49.62 | 32.84 | 43.21 | 31.86 | 0.00 | 0.00 | 0.00 | 0.00 | 0.00 | 0.00 | 0.00 |
| Real exchange rate | 22.89 | 32.58 | 29.25 | 11.50 | 29.40 | 10.31 | 10.98 | 3.03 | 42.62 | 13.28 | 24.48 | 5.55 | 0.00 |
| **ROECD** | | | | | | | | | | | | | |
| Output | 9.97 | 14.51 | 18.06 | 28.09 | 17.92 | 22.47 | 18.71 | 2.82 | 35.43 | 22.81 | 26.35 | 3.00 | 0.00 |
| Inflation | 16.85 | 31.79 | 38.13 | 57.11 | 37.90 | 47.99 | 28.62 | 4.16 | 63.41 | 34.98 | 44.18 | 5.17 | 0.00 |
| Current account | 4.29 | 6.09 | 9.34 | 16.37 | 9.32 | 13.14 | 10.20 | 2.84 | 21.67 | 14.82 | 15.40 | 2.45 | 0.00 |
| Budget deficit | 3.11 | 4.52 | 5.63 | 8.75 | 5.58 | 7.00 | 5.83 | 0.88 | 11.04 | 7.11 | 8.21 | 0.93 | 0.00 |
| Exchange rate | 11.90 | 23.29 | 51.07 | 96.35 | 51.95 | 81.76 | 57.83 | 13.57 | 174.38 | 99.64 | 111.31 | 15.45 | 0.00 |
| Real exchange rate | 10.72 | 20.26 | 27.76 | 69.84 | 27.65 | 56.23 | 41.98 | 9.27 | 129.90 | 77.05 | 81.46 | 10.53 | 0.00 |

a. Fiscal policy assumptions are that regime A is exogenous fiscal policy and regime B is noncooperative fiscal policy (except for the optimal cooperative regime, which assumes cooperative fiscal policy). Monetary assumptions, as described in the text and figure 9-1, are indicated just below the rule.

**Table 9A-6.** *Asymptotic Standard Deviation of Variables in Response to a German Money Demand Shock*

Standard deviation × 100

| | | | | | | | Monetary and fiscal regime[a] | | | | | | | |
| | Friedman rule | Nominal income | Noncooperative | | Cooperative | | McKinnon I | | McKinnon II | | McKinnon III | | Blueprint |
| Variable | A | A | A | B | A | B | A | B | A | B | A | B | ... |
|---|---|---|---|---|---|---|---|---|---|---|---|---|---|
| **United States** | | | | | | | | | | | | | |
| Output | 2.84 | 0.06 | 0.05 | 0.05 | 0.05 | 0.05 | 3.68 | 0.41 | 0.11 | 0.07 | 0.04 | 0.02 | 0.00 |
| Inflation | 2.50 | 0.08 | 0.03 | 0.03 | 0.03 | 0.03 | 2.56 | 0.51 | 0.06 | 0.05 | 0.01 | 0.00 | 0.00 |
| Current account | 0.88 | 0.03 | 0.02 | 0.03 | 0.02 | 0.02 | 0.65 | 1.71 | 0.02 | 0.06 | 0.01 | 0.00 | 0.00 |
| Budget deficit | 0.89 | 0.02 | 0.02 | 0.04 | 0.02 | 0.03 | 1.15 | 2.55 | 0.03 | 0.10 | 0.01 | 0.01 | 0.00 |
| **Japan** | | | | | | | | | | | | | |
| Output | 3.18 | 0.05 | 0.07 | 0.12 | 0.06 | 0.14 | 2.78 | 0.46 | 0.07 | 0.02 | 0.02 | 0.01 | 0.00 |
| Inflation | 1.34 | 0.10 | 0.00 | 0.00 | 0.00 | 0.00 | 2.53 | 0.16 | 0.06 | 0.01 | 0.01 | 0.00 | 0.00 |
| Current account | 1.38 | 0.03 | 0.01 | 0.02 | 0.01 | 0.03 | 0.10 | 0.35 | 0.02 | 0.03 | 0.02 | 0.02 | 0.00 |
| Budget deficit | 1.01 | 0.02 | 0.02 | 0.00 | 0.02 | 0.02 | 0.88 | 1.25 | 0.02 | 0.06 | 0.01 | 0.01 | 0.00 |
| Exchange rate | 4.31 | 0.23 | 0.07 | 0.24 | 0.07 | 0.33 | 0.00 | 0.00 | 0.00 | 0.00 | 0.00 | 0.00 | 0.00 |
| Real exchange rate | 5.53 | 0.23 | 0.02 | 0.26 | 0.03 | 0.35 | 1.55 | 1.07 | 0.06 | 0.06 | 0.05 | 0.01 | 0.00 |
| **Germany** | | | | | | | | | | | | | |
| Output | 36.73 | 0.47 | 0.40 | 0.54 | 0.40 | 0.53 | 1.79 | 1.31 | 0.76 | 0.49 | 0.81 | 0.47 | 0.00 |
| Inflation | 26.64 | 0.39 | 0.02 | 0.00 | 0.02 | 0.00 | 1.43 | 0.35 | 0.34 | 0.17 | 0.38 | 0.18 | 0.00 |
| Current account | 3.57 | 0.18 | 0.23 | 0.29 | 0.23 | 0.29 | 0.43 | 1.09 | 0.27 | 0.19 | 0.29 | 0.22 | 0.00 |
| Budget deficit | 11.57 | 0.15 | 0.13 | 0.00 | 0.13 | 0.01 | 0.56 | 0.86 | 0.24 | 0.36 | 0.25 | 0.43 | 0.60 |
| Exchange rate | 93.06 | 2.58 | 1.33 | 1.58 | 1.31 | 1.57 | 0.00 | 0.00 | 0.00 | 0.00 | 0.00 | 0.00 | 0.00 |
| Real exchange rate | 88.35 | 2.56 | 1.44 | 1.74 | 1.42 | 1.72 | 2.62 | 0.73 | 0.67 | 0.35 | 0.68 | 0.31 | 0.00 |
| **ROECD** | | | | | | | | | | | | | |
| Output | 5.51 | 0.23 | 0.17 | 0.22 | 0.17 | 0.21 | 1.33 | 3.07 | 0.13 | 0.16 | 0.10 | 0.04 | 0.00 |
| Inflation | 12.32 | 0.41 | 0.26 | 0.33 | 0.26 | 0.31 | 2.55 | 4.46 | 0.14 | 0.21 | 0.09 | 0.03 | 0.00 |
| Current account | 3.29 | 0.12 | 0.09 | 0.12 | 0.09 | 0.11 | 0.89 | 1.80 | 0.06 | 0.09 | 0.05 | 0.03 | 0.00 |
| Budget deficit | 1.72 | 0.07 | 0.05 | 0.07 | 0.05 | 0.07 | 0.41 | 0.96 | 0.04 | 0.05 | 0.03 | 0.01 | 0.00 |
| Exchange rate | 19.40 | 0.42 | 0.13 | 0.09 | 0.12 | 0.13 | 8.71 | 11.50 | 0.23 | 0.49 | 0.11 | 0.03 | 0.00 |
| Real exchange rate | 18.09 | 0.47 | 0.23 | 0.22 | 0.23 | 0.24 | 6.33 | 9.70 | 0.22 | 0.39 | 0.15 | 0.08 | 0.00 |

a. Fiscal policy assumptions are that regime A is exogenous fiscal policy and regime B is noncooperative fiscal policy (except for the optimal cooperative regime, which assumes cooperative fiscal policy). Monetary assumptions, as described in the text and figure 9-1, are indicated just below the rule.

Table 9A-7. *Asymptotic Standard Deviation of Variables in Response to a German Real Demand Shock*
Standard deviation × 100

| | | | | | | | Monetary and fiscal regime[a] | | | | | | | |
| Variable | Friedman rule | Nominal income | Noncooperative | | Cooperative | | McKinnon I | | McKinnon II | | McKinnon III | | Blueprint |
| | A | A | A | B | A | B | A | B | A | B | A | B | ... |
| **United States** | | | | | | | | | | | | | |
| Output | 4.52 | 10.23 | 8.73 | 8.38 | 8.43 | 8.22 | 5.61 | 2.29 | 18.33 | 10.97 | 7.42 | 3.87 | 0.00 |
| Inflation | 10.42 | 13.36 | 4.56 | 4.62 | 4.68 | 4.44 | 2.64 | 0.88 | 10.39 | 7.96 | 1.96 | 0.78 | 0.00 |
| Current account | 2.46 | 4.81 | 2.95 | 4.91 | 2.89 | 4.10 | 1.08 | 0.65 | 3.46 | 10.74 | 1.50 | 0.71 | 0.00 |
| Budget deficit | 1.41 | 3.19 | 2.72 | 6.11 | 2.63 | 4.50 | 1.75 | 1.75 | 5.71 | 17.08 | 2.31 | 1.17 | 0.00 |
| **Japan** | | | | | | | | | | | | | |
| Output | 1.01 | 8.71 | 10.98 | 20.31 | 10.64 | 23.39 | 2.40 | 2.24 | 11.80 | 2.50 | 2.98 | 2.07 | 0.00 |
| Inflation | 8.20 | 16.03 | 0.43 | 0.00 | 0.52 | 0.00 | 2.11 | 0.14 | 9.43 | 1.96 | 1.33 | 0.15 | 0.00 |
| Current account | 2.00 | 4.18 | 2.24 | 4.17 | 2.13 | 4.38 | 3.57 | 2.89 | 3.80 | 4.24 | 3.62 | 2.65 | 0.00 |
| Budget deficit | 0.32 | 2.76 | 3.48 | 0.00 | 3.37 | 2.88 | 0.76 | 1.12 | 3.74 | 9.97 | 0.94 | 1.02 | 0.00 |
| Exchange rate | 6.36 | 38.15 | 10.99 | 39.32 | 11.55 | 54.67 | 0.00 | 0.00 | 0.00 | 0.00 | 0.00 | 0.00 | 0.00 |
| Real exchange rate | 10.19 | 38.70 | 4.01 | 42.73 | 4.19 | 58.91 | 9.50 | 2.98 | 9.20 | 9.33 | 9.16 | 1.32 | 0.00 |
| **Germany** | | | | | | | | | | | | | |
| Output | 85.23 | 78.38 | 66.27 | 89.30 | 66.69 | 89.06 | 137.49 | 78.30 | 127.10 | 82.18 | 134.84 | 78.46 | 0.00 |
| Inflation | 18.87 | 65.09 | 2.53 | 0.00 | 3.00 | 0.24 | 65.95 | 29.95 | 57.39 | 28.14 | 64.00 | 29.93 | 0.00 |
| Current account | 43.34 | 30.02 | 39.00 | 48.43 | 39.00 | 49.00 | 48.86 | 36.87 | 45.71 | 31.02 | 48.15 | 37.24 | 0.00 |
| Budget deficit | 26.85 | 24.69 | 20.88 | 0.00 | 21.01 | 1.18 | 43.31 | 71.36 | 40.04 | 59.71 | 42.47 | 71.17 | 100.18 |
| Exchange rate | 164.74 | 430.19 | 221.96 | 263.41 | 217.82 | 261.14 | 0.00 | 0.00 | 0.00 | 0.00 | 0.00 | 0.00 | 0.00 |
| Real exchange rate | 191.83 | 425.94 | 240.52 | 289.64 | 237.42 | 287.17 | 115.39 | 49.74 | 110.92 | 58.18 | 113.98 | 51.66 | 0.00 |
| **ROECD** | | | | | | | | | | | | | |
| Output | 21.77 | 38.31 | 28.07 | 37.43 | 27.95 | 34.93 | 15.74 | 6.61 | 20.94 | 26.85 | 16.95 | 6.59 | 0.00 |
| Inflation | 28.86 | 68.41 | 43.38 | 55.78 | 42.99 | 51.78 | 12.89 | 5.36 | 23.43 | 35.29 | 15.32 | 5.49 | 0.00 |
| Current account | 10.20 | 20.59 | 14.45 | 19.31 | 14.32 | 17.91 | 6.69 | 4.88 | 10.21 | 15.41 | 7.51 | 4.74 | 0.00 |
| Budget deficit | 6.78 | 11.94 | 8.75 | 11.66 | 8.71 | 10.88 | 4.90 | 2.06 | 6.53 | 8.37 | 5.28 | 2.05 | 0.00 |
| Exchange rate | 37.19 | 70.03 | 21.49 | 15.81 | 20.83 | 20.90 | 18.81 | 5.77 | 38.55 | 81.16 | 18.04 | 5.73 | 0.00 |
| Real exchange rate | 42.34 | 78.20 | 38.84 | 37.13 | 38.11 | 40.60 | 26.08 | 12.71 | 36.24 | 64.21 | 25.58 | 14.05 | 0.00 |

a. Fiscal policy assumptions are that regime A is exogenous fiscal policy and regime B is noncooperative fiscal policy (except for the optimal cooperative regime, which assumes cooperative fiscal policy). Monetary assumptions, as described in the text and figure 9-1, are indicated just below the rule.

CHAPTER TEN

# Conclusions and Lessons for Policy

AT THE OUTSET of this book we presented a case for the importance of using a general equilibrium framework to understand the evolution of the world economy during the 1980s. From this perspective trade imbalances, fluctuations in asset prices, real activity, and inflation in different economies become part of a larger picture rather than being the result of individual "special factors" such as trade restrictions or sector-specific bubbles. We feel that, by attempting to present a general equilibrium framework, we have offered several useful insights into the world economy that have significant implications for the conduct of macroeconomic policies in an interdependent world.

### Lessons

Our theoretical analysis in chapter 2 showed that in the 1980s, with high capital mobility and extensive trade in goods and services, the institutional arrangements and policies of one country can have important consequences for the transmission of shocks to other countries. We found that a variety of direct channels exist for the transmission of shocks from one economy to another—directly through trade flows and changes in asset prices, and over time through changes in the composition of global wealth.

The empirical relevance of the spillovers between countries was illustrated in chapters 3 and 4. An important result from the global simulation model is that, in a global economy with freely floating exchange rates, the real consequences of monetary shocks are effectively insulated by changes in exchange rates. The net effects of monetary policy on current account balances, moreover, were shown to be negligible, even though monetary policy is effective in changing short-run output growth in each economy. Thus, attempts to coordinate only monetary policies, either directly or through targeting nominal exchange rates, are likely to have little success in changing world saving and investment balances but are likely to be more effective in controlling global inflation.

The usefulness of the simulation model was illustrated in chapter 5, where major swings in the global economy during the 1980s were shown to be explained reasonably well by the model. Much of our explanation for fluctuations in the world economy relies on the consequences of actual and expected changes in macroeconomic policy in the major economies over this period. One inference to draw from these results is that a substantial part of the macroeconomic instability observed during the 1980s was the result of swings in economic policy, or at least in policy responses to shocks, rather than the result of independent shocks. This suggests the need to pursue more stable macroeconomic policies with clearly focused goals.

The outbreak of political and economic reform in Eastern Europe suggests a new potential source of demand for global savings over the next several years. (See McKibbin 1990a for an analysis using the model in this book.) In chapter 6, our baseline projection for the global economy from 1986 (which ignores these recent developments), made under the assumption of little adjustment in U.S. fiscal policy, shows little change in the U.S. current account over a long period, with substantial diversion of world savings into the U.S. economy. Given the likely demand for global savings from other regions, it is timely for the United States to reduce its drain on world savings by undertaking appropriate fiscal adjustment. We showed in chapter 6 that it is possible for the United States to enter into a phase of fiscal contraction without necessarily plunging the world into global recession. Even with a substantial adjustment in U.S. fiscal policy, however, there is still likely to be insufficient U.S. private savings relative to investment to eliminate the U.S. trade deficit. This suggests that other policies, designed to stimulate savings rather than to reduce investment, would be desirable. We also showed in chapter 6 that U.S. bilateral trade policy directed toward Japan could have a perverse effect on the overall U.S. trade position, despite improving the bilateral trade position between the United States and Japan.

Our analysis of policy coordination suggests a potential dilemma for global macroeconomic policy. We showed that monetary coordination did little to improve trade balances. Coordination of fiscal policies, in contrast, was shown to be an area in which mutual gains could be realized. Unfortunately, the current institutional framework for setting fiscal policy in most countries does not lend itself to being part of international agreements. Indeed, fiscal policy in the United States is almost paralyzed to attain domestic goals, let alone international goals. In addition, the fiscal response in a coordinated agreement is quite different from that for noncoordinated fiscal policy in some of the cases we examined. Even if fiscal policy could be sufficiently flexible to form part of new set of international "rules of the game," it is likely to be difficult to convince sovereign policymakers to adjust policies significantly away from the policies they would otherwise follow in isolation.

## Further Work

The importance that structural and institutional arrangements have for the results in this book suggests that substantial gains in understanding could be achieved by further country disaggregation within the framework we have presented. Extensions to this model that disaggregate the EMS (European Monetary System) economies have already been undertaken by Roubini (1989). A detailed analysis of the Asian Pacific region has been started by Sundberg (1990; see also McKibbin and Sundberg 1990). In addition, considerable sectoral disaggregation within an economy has been shown to be feasible by Boone and others (1989).

It is inevitable that some building blocks will be empirically fragile in a global framework. Continuing empirical work is needed to help clarify several issues. Our reliance on rational expectations in asset markets is somewhat tenuous, given empirical evidence, although an alternative hypothesis is not well defined. The use of this assumption has proven extremely insightful, but is of fundamental importance for actual policy design. In our view it is far better at this stage to assume that asset prices adjust to news in an internally consistent way, rather than to assume no adjustment. In addition, the use of an annual time horizon suggests that the assumption may not be that unreasonable (as we showed in chapter 6 when examining uncovered interest parity).

We still have a long way to go before we can understand many of the short-term fluctuations we observe in markets. Yet it would seem to us that these fluctuations should not, in any case, be the sole focus of macroeconomic policy. The results of this book suggest that we can at least gain some understanding of medium-term fluctuations in the world economy by relying on economic theory as well as on a large body of applied research embedded in a general equilibrium framework.

# The MSG2 Model of the World Economy: Model Listing

THIS APPENDIX provides a detailed specification of the MSG2 model. The structure of each industrial economy is similar, and therefore only the equations for the U.S. economy are listed (except where major differences among countries exist).

Each variable is both time-dimensioned and country-dimensioned. Where no confusion will result, these two dimensions will not be shown explicitly; for example, $(C^j)_t$ (consumption of country $j$ in period $t$) is written $C$; $(C_i^j)_t$ (consumption by country $j$ of goods from country $i$ in period $t$) is written $C_i$.

Except where otherwise noted, a subscript or superscript $i$ refers to the set of countries or regions $i = \{J, G, E, R\}$. A subscript or superscript $k$ refers to the set $k = \{L, O\}$. Mnemonics for the model regions are as follows: $U$, United States; $J$, Japan; $G$, Germany; $E$, REMS (rest of the EMS, the European Monetary System); $R$, ROECD (rest of the OECD, the Organization for Economic Cooperation and Development); $L$, LDCs (non-oil developing countries); and $O$, OPEC (oil-exporting countries). Countries in the REMS, ROECD, LDC, and OPEC model regions are listed in chapter 3 (notes 3–6).

The remainder of this appendix lists the equations, definitions of variables, and parameter values of the model.

## Households

*Utility*

$$U_t = \int_t^\infty \log C_s e^{-(\beta 1 - n)s}\, ds$$

$$C = [\beta_2(C^d)^{\beta_3} + (1 - \beta_2)\,(C^m)^{\beta_3}]^{(1/\beta_3)}$$

$$C^m = [\Sigma_i \beta_{5i}(C_i)^{\beta_4}]^{(1/\beta_4)} \qquad \Sigma_i \beta_{5i} = 1.$$

*Demand Functions*

$$C = \beta_6\,(\beta_1 - n)\,(F + H)P/P^c$$
$$+ (1 - \beta_6)\,(Q - T + rF)$$
$$P/P^c$$
$$C^d = [\beta_2^{\sigma_1}(P^c/P)^{\sigma_1}]\,(C + G) \qquad \sigma_1 = 1/(1 - \beta_3)$$
$$C^m = [(1 - \beta_2)^{\sigma_1}(P^c/P^m)^{\sigma_1}]\,(C + G)$$
$$C_i = [\beta_{5i}^{\sigma_2}(P^m/E^{i*}P^i)^{\sigma_2}]C^m \qquad \sigma_2 = 1/(1 - \beta_4)$$
$$P^{c(1-\sigma_1)} = \beta_2^{\sigma_1}P^{(1-\sigma_1)} + (1-\beta_2)^{\sigma_1}P^{m(1-\sigma_1)}$$
$$P^{m(1-\sigma_2)} = \Sigma_i\,\beta_{5i}^{\sigma_2}(E^{i*}P^i)^{(1-\sigma_2)}$$
$$_tH_{t+1} = (1 + \beta_7 + r - n)H_t$$
$$- W(1 - \tau_1)L/P + TAX.$$

## Firms

*Production Function*

$$Q = \beta_{10}(V)^{\beta_{11}}\,(N)^{(1-\beta_{11})}$$
$$V = (K)^{\beta_{12}}(L)^{(1-\beta_{12})}$$
$$N = \beta_{13}\,\Pi_k\,(N_k)^{\beta_{14k}}.$$

*Factor Demands*

$$L = \beta_{11}(1 - \beta_{12})\,(PQ/W)$$
$$N = (1 - \beta_{11})\,(PQ/P^n)$$
$$N_L = \beta_{14L}P^nN/(E^LP^L)$$
$$N_O = \beta_{24}\beta_{14O}P^nN/(E^OP^O)$$
$$N_P = (1 - \beta_{24})\beta_{14O}P^nN/(E^OP^O)$$
$$K_{t+1} = (1 - \beta_{15} - n)K_t + J_t$$
$$I = [P^J + P^J(\beta_{17}/2)(J/K)]J/P$$
$$J = \beta_{16}[(q - 1)/\beta_{17}]K + (1 - \beta_{16})$$
$$[Q - (W/P)L - (P^n/P)N]$$

$$J_i = \beta_{18i}J/\Lambda_i \qquad \Sigma\beta_{18i} = 1$$

$$_tq_{t+1} = (1 + r + \beta_{15} + \beta_{19})q_t - (1 - \tau_2)\beta_{11}\beta_{12}(Q/K)$$
$$- (P^J/P)(0.5\beta_{17})(J/K)^2$$

$$P^n = \Lambda_k(E^kP^k)^{\beta_{14k}}$$

$$P^J = \Lambda_i(E^iP^i)^{\beta_{18i}}$$

$$_tVOIL_{t+1} = (1 + \beta_7 + r - n)VOIL_t - N_PP^OE^O/P$$

$$_tVPE_{t+1} = (1 + \beta_7 + r - n)VPE_t - \Sigma_i(C^i + I^i)(E^i/E^{i*}).$$

## Asset Markets

$$M/P = Q^{\beta_{20}}i^{\beta_{21}}$$

$$F = B + M/P + qK + A + VPE + VOIL$$

$$A = A_L^U - \Sigma_i A_U^i \qquad i = \{J, G, E, R, P\}$$

$$\Lambda^i = P^iE^i/P$$

$$\Lambda^{i*} = P^iE^{*i}/P$$

$$\Lambda^k = P^kE^k/P$$

$$i_t = r_t + {}_t\pi_t$$

$$r_t = R_t - ({}_tR_{t+1} - R_t)/R_t$$

$$r_t = r_t^i + ({}_t\Lambda_{t+1}^i - \Lambda_t^i)/\Lambda_t^i$$

$$_t\pi_t = ({}_tP_{t+1} - P_t)/P_t$$

$$_t\pi_t^c = ({}_tP_{t+1}^c - P_t^c)/P_t^c$$

$$E_t^{i*}/E_{t-1}^{i*} = (E_t^i/E_{t-1}^i)^{\beta_{23}}(E_{t-1}^{i*}/E_{t-2}^{i*})^{(1-\beta_{23})}$$
$$(E_{t-1}^i/E_{t-1}^{i*})^{.05}.$$

## Government Sector

$$DEF = g + rB - T$$

$$T = TAX + \tau_1(W/P)L + \tau_2[Q - (W/P)L - (P^n/P)N]$$

$$TAX = rB + TAX\,E$$
$$B_{t+1} = (1 - n)B_t + DEF_t.$$

## Wage Setting

*United States, ROECD*

$$w_t = (W_{t+1} - W_t)/W_t$$
$$w_t = \beta_{22}\ {}_t\pi_t^c + (1 - \beta_{22})\pi_{t-1}^c + 0.2(L/L^f - 1).$$

*Japan*

$$w_{t+1}^J = ({}_tw_{t+1}^J)^f.$$

*Germany, REMS*

$$w_t = \beta_{22}\ {}_t\pi_t^c + (1 - \beta_{22})\pi_{t-1}^c + 0.2(L/L^* - 1)$$
$$L^* = L^f + 0.2(L_{t-1}^* - L^f) + 0.7(L_{t-1} - L^f).$$

## Balance of Payments

$$X = \Sigma_i(C^i + I^i)$$
$$IM = \Sigma_i\Lambda^{i*}(C_i + I_i) + \Sigma_k\Lambda^k N_k$$
$$TB = EX - IM$$
$$CA = TB + rA$$
$$A_{t+1} = (1 - n)A_t + CA_t.$$

## Market Equilibruim

$$Q = (P^c/P)\,(C + G) + (P^J/P)I + TB + (P^n/P)N$$
$$M = M^s.$$

## LDC Equations

$$P^L = \Lambda_i(E^iP^i)^{\mu_{1i}}(X^L)^{\mu_2} \qquad \Sigma\mu 1i = 1$$

$$X^L = \Sigma_j N_L^j + C_L^O$$

$$IM^L = \Sigma_i C_i^L \Lambda^i$$

$$C_i^L \Lambda^i = \mu_{1i}(IM^L)$$

$$TB^L = X^L - IM^L$$

$$CAL = CAL_0$$

$$DEBT = \Sigma_i A_L^i \Lambda^i$$

$$DEBT_{t+1} = DEBT_t(1 - n) - CA^L$$

$$A_{Lt+1}^i(\Lambda_t^i) = (1 - n\Lambda_{Lt}^i)(A_t^i) + \mu_{3i}$$
$$(DEBT_{t+1} - (1 - n)DEBT_t).$$

Note that

$$i = \{U, J, G, E, R, O\}$$
$$j = \{U, J, G, E, R\}.$$

## OPEC Equations

$$P^o = \Lambda_i(E^iP^i)^{\phi_{1i}}(X^o)^{\phi_2} \qquad \Sigma\phi 1i = 1$$

$$X^o = \Sigma_j N_o^j + C_o^L$$

$$IM^o = \Sigma_i C_i^o \Lambda_i$$

$$C_i^o \Lambda^i = \phi_{1i}(IM^o)$$

$$TB^o = X^o - IM^O$$

$$CA^P = \phi_4\, 0.29X^P\Lambda^P - (0.29 - n)A^P$$

$$A^P = \Sigma_i A_i^P$$

$$A_{t+1}^P = (1 - n)(A_t^P) + CA_t^P$$

$$A_{it+1}^P = (1 - n)(A_{it}^P) + \theta_{3i}[A_{t+1}^P - (1 - n)A_t^P].$$

Note that

$$i = \{U, J, G, E, R, L, P\}$$
$$j = \{U, J, G, E, R\}.$$

## Variable Definitions

| | |
|---|---|
| $A_i^j$ | Real claims by country $j$ against country $i$ |
| $A^i$ | Total real claims held by country $i$ against other countries |
| $B$ | Real government debt |
| $C$ | Real consumption of total bundle of goods |
| $C^d$ | Real consumption of domestic bundle of goods |
| $C^m$ | Real consumption of imported bundle of goods |
| $C_i^j$ | Consumption by country $i$ of country $j$'s good |
| $CA$ | Real current account balance |
| $DEBT$ | LDC debt |
| $DEF$ | Real budget deficit |
| $E_j^i$ | Nominal exchange rate (units of currency $j$ per unit of currency $i$; for example, $E_u j$ is dollars per yen) |
| $E_j^{i*}$ | Nominal exchange rate that enters the price of home country exports in foreign markets |
| $F$ | Real financial wealth |
| $G$ | Real government expenditure on goods |
| $H$ | Real human wealth |
| $i$ | Short-term nominal interest rate |
| $I$ | Nominal investment expenditure inclusive of adjustment costs |
| $J$ | Gross fixed capital formation |
| $J_i^j$ | Imports by country $j$ of investment goods from country $i$ |
| $K$ | Capital stock |
| $L$ | Demand for labor |

| $L^f$ | Full employment labor demand |
| $M$ | Nominal money supply |
| $N$ | Basket of intermediate inputs used in production |
| $N_i^j$ | Import by country $j$ of intermediate inputs from country $i$ |
| $N_p$ | Domestic production of oil |
| $n$ | Growth rate of population plus labor-augmenting technical change |
| $P$ | Price of domestic goods |
| $P^m$ | Price of basket of imported goods |
| $P^c$ | Price of a basket of imported and domestic goods |
| $P^I$ | Price of basket of investment goods |
| $P^n$ | Price of basket of intermediate goods |
| $\pi$ | Product price inflation |
| $\pi^c$ | Consumer price inflation |
| $Q$ | Real gross output |
| $q$ | Tobin's $q$ |
| $R$ | Long-term real interest rate |
| $r$ | Short-term real interest rate |
| $T$ | Total nominal tax receipts |
| $TAX$ | Lump-sum tax on households |
| $TAXE$ | Exogenous tax |
| $TB$ | Trade balance in units of real domestic goods |
| $V$ | Intermediate good produced with domestic factors |
| $VOIL$ | Value of future stream of domestic oil production |
| $VPE$ | Value of net profit from slow pass-through of exchange rate changes into foreign prices of export goods |
| $W$ | Nominal wage |
| $w$ | Rate of change of nominal wage |
| $X$ | Real exports in units of domestic goods |
| $IM$ | Real imports in units of domestic goods |
| $\tau_1$ | Tax rate on household income |

$\tau_2$           Tax rate on corporate profits

$\sigma_1$           Elasticity of substitution between domestic and imported goods

$\sigma_3$           Elasticity of substitution between capital and labor

$\Lambda_j^i$           Relative price of country $i$'s good to country $j$'s good (real exchange rate)

$\Lambda_j^{i*}$           Relative price of country $i$'s good to country $j$'s good (real exchange rate), adjusted for short-term pricing behavior in foreign markets.


## Parameter Values

### United States

| | | | | | |
|---|---|---|---|---|---|
| $\beta 1$ | = | 0.050 | $\beta 2 =$ | 0.932 | $\beta 3 = 0.000$ |
| $\beta 4$ | = | 0.000 | $\beta 5j =$ | 0.344 | $\beta 5g = 0.106$ |
| $\beta 5r$ | = | 0.420 | $\beta 5e =$ | 0.130 | $\beta 6 = 0.300$ |
| $\beta 7$ | = | 0.100 | $\beta 8 =$ | 0.000 | $\beta 10 = 1.000$ |
| $\beta 11$ | = | 0.937 | $\beta 12 =$ | 0.350 | $\beta 13 = 1.000$ |
| $\beta 14l$ | = | 0.364 | $\beta 14o =$ | 0.636 | $\beta 15 = 0.100$ |
| $\beta 16$ | = | 0.300 | $\beta 17 =$ 20.000 | | $\beta 18u = 0.902$ |
| $\beta 18j$ | = | 0.034 | $\beta 18g =$ | 0.010 | $\beta 18e = 0.013$ |
| $\beta 18r$ | = | 0.041 | $\beta 19 =$ | 0.060 | $\beta 20 = 1.000$ |
| $\beta 21$ | = | $-0.600$ | $\beta 22 =$ | 0.400 | $\beta 23 = 0.500$ |
| $\beta 24$ | = | 0.118 | $\tau 1 =$ | 0.350 | $\tau 2 = 0.300$ |

### Japan

| | | | | | |
|---|---|---|---|---|---|
| $\beta 1$ | = | 0.050 | $\beta 2 =$ | 0.958 | $\beta 3 = 0.000$ |
| $\beta 4$ | = | 0.000 | $\beta 5u =$ | 0.502 | $\beta 5g = 0.075$ |
| $\beta 5r$ | = | 0.327 | $\beta 5e =$ | 0.097 | $\beta 6 = 0.300$ |
| $\beta 7$ | = | 0.100 | $\beta 8 =$ | 0.000 | $\beta 10 = 1.000$ |
| $\beta 11$ | = | 0.952 | $\beta 12 =$ | 0.350 | $\beta 13 = 1.000$ |
| $\beta 14l$ | = | 0.370 | $\beta 14o =$ | 0.630 | $\beta 15 = 0.100$ |
| $\beta 16$ | = | 0.300 | $\beta 17 =$ 20.000 | | $\beta 18j = 0.944$ |
| $\beta 18u$ | = | 0.028 | $\beta 18g =$ | 0.004 | $\beta 18e = 0.005$ |
| $\beta 18r$ | = | 0.018 | $\beta 19 =$ | 0.060 | $\beta 20 = 1.000$ |
| $\beta 21$ | = | $-0.600$ | $\beta 22 =$ | 0.200 | $\beta 23 = 0.750$ |
| $\beta 24$ | = | 0.434 | $\tau 1 =$ | 0.350 | $\tau 2 = 0.300$ |

## Germany

| | | |
|---|---|---|
| $\beta 1$ = 0.050 | $\beta 2$ = 0.783 | $\beta 3$ = 0.000 |
| $\beta 4$ = 0.000 | $\beta 5u$ = 0.079 | $\beta 5j$ = 0.075 |
| $\beta 5r$ = 0.302 | $\beta 5e$ = 0.545 | $\beta 6$ = 0.300 |
| $\beta 7$ = 0.100 | $\beta 8$ = 0.000 | $\beta 10$ = 1.000 |
| $\beta 11$ = 0.947 | $\beta 12$ = 0.350 | $\beta 13$ = 1.000 |
| $\beta 14l$ = 0.620 | $\beta 14o$ = 0.380 | $\beta 15$ = 0.100 |
| $\beta 16$ = 0.300 | $\beta 17$ = 20.000 | $\beta 18g$ = 0.615 |
| $\beta 18u$ = 0.166 | $\beta 18j$ = 0.029 | $\beta 18e$ = 0.210 |
| $\beta 18r$ = 0.030 | $\beta 19$ = 0.060 | $\beta 20$ = 1.000 |
| $\beta 21$ = −0.600 | $\beta 22$ = 0.300 | $\beta 23$ = 0.750 |
| $\beta 24$ = 0.334 | $\tau 1$ = 0.350 | $\tau 2$ = 0.300 |

## REMS

| | | |
|---|---|---|
| $\beta 1$ = 0.050 | $\beta 2$ = 0.743 | $\beta 3$ = 0.000 |
| $\beta 4$ = 0.000 | $\beta 5u$ = 0.085 | $\beta 5g$ = 0.278 |
| $\beta 5j$ = 0.038 | $\beta 5r$ = 0.599 | $\beta 6$ = 0.300 |
| $\beta 7$ = 0.100 | $\beta 8$ = 0.000 | $\beta 10$ = 1.000 |
| $\beta 11$ = 0.940 | $\beta 12$ = 0.350 | $\beta 13$ = 1.000 |
| $\beta 14l$ = 0.498 | $\beta 14o$ = 0.502 | $\beta 15$ = 0.100 |
| $\beta 16$ = 0.300 | $\beta 17$ = 20.000 | $\beta 18e$ = 0.637 |
| $\beta 18u$ = 0.218 | $\beta 18g$ = 0.101 | $\beta 18j$ = 0.014 |
| $\beta 18r$ = 0.031 | $\beta 19$ = 0.060 | $\beta 20$ = 1.000 |
| $\beta 21$ = −0.600 | $\beta 22$ = 0.300 | $\beta 23$ = 0.750 |
| $\beta 24$ = 0.464 | $\tau 1$ = 0.350 | $\tau 2$ = 0.300 |

## ROECD

| | | |
|---|---|---|
| $\beta 1$ = 0.050 | $\beta 2$ = 0.771 | $\beta 3$ = 0.000 |
| $\beta 4$ = 0.000 | $\beta 5u$ = 0.209 | $\beta 5g$ = 0.183 |
| $\beta 5j$ = 0.073 | $\beta 5e$ = 0.536 | $\beta 6$ = 1.000 |
| $\beta 7$ = 0.100 | $\beta 8$ = 0.000 | $\beta 10$ = 1.000 |
| $\beta 11$ = 0.937 | $\beta 12$ = 0.350 | $\beta 13$ = 1.000 |
| $\beta 14l$ = 0.364 | $\beta 14o$ = 0.636 | $\beta 15$ = 0.100 |
| $\beta 16$ = 0.300 | $\beta 17$ = 20.000 | $\beta 18r$ = 0.551 |
| $\beta 18j$ = 0.033 | $\beta 18g$ = 0.082 | $\beta 18e$ = 0.241 |
| $\beta 18u$ = 0.094 | $\beta 19$ = 0.060 | $\beta 20$ = 1.000 |
| $\beta 21$ = −0.600 | $\beta 22$ = 0.400 | $\beta 23$ = 0.750 |
| $\beta 24$ = 0.132 | $\tau 1$ = 0.350 | $\tau 2$ = 0.300 |

*LDCs*

| | | | | | |
|---|---|---|---|---|---|
| $\mu1u$ | = | 0.219 | $\mu1j$ = | 0.198 | $\mu1g$ = 0.116 |
| $\mu1e$ | = | 0.190 | $\mu1r$ = | 0.178 | $\mu1o$ = 0.099 |
| $\mu2$ | = | 0.500 | $\mu3u$ = | 0.364 | $\mu3j$ = 0.129 |
| $\mu3g$ | = | 0.124 | $\mu3e$ = | 0.134 | $\mu3r$ = 0.167 |
| $\mu3o$ | = | 0.081 | | | |

*OPEC*

| | | | | | |
|---|---|---|---|---|---|
| $\phi1u$ | = | 0.129 | $\phi1j$ = | 0.145 | $\phi1g$ = 0.102 |
| $\phi1e$ | = | 0.211 | $\phi1r$ = | 0.193 | $\phi1o$ = 0.220 |
| $\phi2$ | = | 0.500 | $\phi3u$ = | 0.714 | $\phi3j$ = 0.071 |
| $\phi3g$ | = | 0.071 | $\phi3e$ = | 0.071 | $\phi3r$ = 0.071 |
| $\phi3o$ | = | 0.000 | $\phi4$ = | 3.127 | |

# Detailed Simulation Results

THIS APPENDIX presents the simulation results for the effects of the various shocks considered in this book on key macroeconomic variables in the model regions. Tables B-1 through B-15 are arrayed in a uniform manner.

For example, table B-1 contains the results for the case of an increase, equivalent to 1 percent of GDP, in real government expenditure in the United States. The model was simulated for forty years. The time horizon presented in the table is five years, with the shock occurring in year 1. All variables are expressed as deviations from an initial baseline (unspecified in this case). GDP is recorded as a percentage deviation from the initial baseline (for example, 0.56 percent of GDP in year 1). Consumption, investment, exports, imports, the trade balance, and the budget deficit (all in real terms) are reported as deviations from baseline in percentage of baseline potential GDP. Thus, in year 1, private consumption rises relative to the baseline by 0.2 of 1 percent of U.S. potential GDP. Labor demand (that is, total man-hours in the economy) is reported as percentage deviation from baseline (for example, a rise of 0.7 percent in year 1). Inflation (defined as the percentage change in the consumer price index) and interest rates are reported as deviations in percentage points relative to the baseline (rather than as deviations in percentages of their baseline values). Thus, inflation in year 1 is seen to fall by 0.11 percentage points in year 1, and short-term interest rates increase by 1.17 percentage points (that is, 117 basis points). Long-term nominal interest rates (defined as ten-year bonds) rise by 1.27 percentage points. The four U.S. bilateral exchange rates are reported as percentage deviations from baseline. Note that positive (negative) values for changes in exchange rates indicate a depreciation (appreciation) of the U.S. dollar against the relevant foreign currency. The exchange rates presented for aggregated regimes such as REMS and ROECD should be interpreted as the average (weighted by GDP) of the currencies of the countries in the region.

Table B-1. *Sustained 1 Percent GDP U.S. Fiscal Expansion*
Deviation from baseline

| Model region and variable | Year | | | | |
|---|---|---|---|---|---|
| | *1* | *2* | *3* | *4* | *5* |
| *United States* | | | | | |
| GDP[a] | 0.56 | 0.43 | 0.30 | 0.17 | 0.06 |
| Private consumption[a] | 0.20 | 0.16 | 0.10 | 0.02 | −0.05 |
| Private investment[a] | −0.09 | −0.12 | −0.15 | −0.19 | −0.23 |
| Government consumption[a] | 1.00 | 1.00 | 1.00 | 1.00 | 1.00 |
| Exports[a] | −0.26 | −0.27 | −0.28 | −0.29 | −0.30 |
| Imports[a] | 0.29 | 0.35 | 0.36 | 0.36 | 0.36 |
| Trade balance[a] | −0.39 | −0.35 | −0.34 | −0.33 | −0.33 |
| Budget deficit[a] | 0.79 | 0.83 | 0.86 | 0.90 | 0.94 |
| Inflation[b] | −0.11 | 0.03 | 0.10 | 0.14 | 0.15 |
| Nominal short-term interest rate[b] | 1.17 | 1.11 | 1.10 | 1.14 | 1.21 |
| Nominal long-term interest rate[b] | 1.27 | 1.30 | 1.35 | 1.39 | 1.43 |
| Real short-term interest rate[b] | 1.11 | 0.99 | 0.96 | 0.99 | 1.06 |
| Real long-term interest rate[b] | 1.16 | 1.20 | 1.25 | 1.31 | 1.36 |
| Labor demand[c] | 0.70 | 0.61 | 0.46 | 0.30 | 0.15 |
| *Japan* | | | | | |
| GDP[a] | 0.18 | 0.01 | −0.01 | −0.03 | −0.05 |
| Private consumption[a] | −0.09 | −0.15 | −0.16 | −0.17 | −0.18 |
| Private investment[a] | −0.18 | −0.26 | −0.28 | −0.29 | −0.31 |
| Government consumption[a] | 0.00 | 0.00 | 0.00 | 0.00 | 0.00 |
| Exports[a] | 0.28 | 0.25 | 0.25 | 0.24 | 0.24 |
| Imports[a] | −0.16 | −0.16 | −0.18 | −0.19 | −0.20 |
| Trade balance[a] | 0.43 | 0.32 | 0.28 | 0.27 | 0.26 |
| Budget deficit[a] | −0.03 | 0.03 | 0.03 | 0.04 | 0.05 |
| Inflation[b] | 0.27 | 0.43 | 0.11 | 0.08 | 0.07 |
| Nominal short-term interest rate[b] | 0.44 | 0.89 | 1.02 | 1.10 | 1.16 |
| Nominal long-term interest rate[b] | 1.12 | 1.22 | 1.27 | 1.31 | 1.35 |
| Real short-term interest rate[b] | −0.00 | 0.79 | 0.94 | 1.03 | 1.10 |
| Real long-term interest rate[b] | 1.02 | 1.16 | 1.23 | 1.27 | 1.31 |
| Exchange rate (US$/¥)[c] | −4.99 | −4.26 | −4.05 | −3.96 | −3.92 |
| Real exchange rate (US$/¥)[c] | −4.85 | −3.75 | −3.55 | −3.54 | −3.58 |
| Labor demand[c] | 0.26 | −0.00 | −0.00 | −0.00 | −0.00 |
| *Germany* | | | | | |
| GDP[a] | 0.21 | 0.13 | 0.02 | −0.07 | −0.14 |
| Private consumption[a] | −0.00 | −0.04 | −0.08 | −0.11 | −0.13 |
| Private investment[a] | −0.16 | −0.20 | −0.25 | −0.28 | −0.31 |
| Government consumption[a] | 0.00 | 0.00 | 0.00 | 0.00 | 0.00 |
| Exports[a] | 0.21 | 0.16 | 0.11 | 0.07 | 0.03 |
| Imports[a] | −0.16 | −0.20 | −0.23 | −0.25 | −0.27 |
| Real trade balance[a] | 0.37 | 0.30 | 0.25 | 0.22 | 0.19 |
| Budget deficit[a] | −0.05 | −0.02 | 0.02 | 0.04 | 0.07 |
| Inflation[b] | 0.26 | 0.25 | 0.19 | 0.14 | 0.12 |
| Nominal short-term interest rate[b] | 0.56 | 0.81 | 0.94 | 1.02 | 1.10 |
| Nominal long-term interest rate[b] | 1.08 | 1.16 | 1.22 | 1.27 | 1.31 |
| Real short-term interest rate[b] | 0.32 | 0.62 | 0.79 | 0.90 | 0.99 |
| Real long-term interest rate[b] | 0.96 | 1.06 | 1.14 | 1.20 | 1.25 |
| Exchange rate (US$/DM)[c] | −4.45 | −3.83 | −3.54 | −3.37 | −3.25 |
| Real exchange rate (US$/DM)[c] | −4.29 | −3.51 | −3.15 | −2.98 | −2.90 |
| Labor demand[c] | 0.34 | 0.21 | 0.06 | −0.06 | −0.14 |

## Table B-1 *(continued)*

| Model region and variable | Year 1 | 2 | 3 | 4 | 5 |
|---|---|---|---|---|---|
| **REMS** | | | | | |
| GDP[a] | 0.29 | 0.18 | 0.06 | −0.03 | −0.10 |
| Private consumption[a] | 0.03 | −0.03 | −0.08 | −0.11 | −0.13 |
| Private investment[a] | −0.15 | −0.21 | −0.25 | −0.29 | −0.31 |
| Government consumption[a] | 0.00 | 0.00 | 0.00 | 0.00 | 0.00 |
| Exports[a] | 0.18 | 0.13 | 0.07 | 0.02 | −0.01 |
| Imports[a] | −0.24 | −0.29 | −0.32 | −0.35 | −0.36 |
| Trade balance[a] | 0.36 | 0.30 | 0.25 | 0.22 | 0.20 |
| Budget deficit[a] | −0.05 | −0.01 | 0.02 | 0.05 | 0.08 |
| Inflation[b] | 0.31 | 0.27 | 0.20 | 0.15 | 0.12 |
| Nominal short-term interest rate[b] | 0.56 | 0.81 | 0.94 | 1.02 | 1.10 |
| Nominal long-term interest rate[b] | 1.08 | 1.16 | 1.22 | 1.27 | 1.31 |
| Real short-term interest rate[b] | 0.30 | 0.61 | 0.79 | 0.90 | 0.99 |
| Real long-term interest rate[b] | 0.96 | 1.06 | 1.14 | 1.20 | 1.25 |
| Money[c] | 0.03 | 0.02 | 0.02 | 0.02 | 0.03 |
| Exchange rate (US$/ems)[c] | −4.45 | −3.83 | −3.54 | −3.37 | −3.25 |
| Real exchange rate (US$/ems)[c] | −4.28 | −3.47 | −3.10 | −2.93 | −2.84 |
| Labor demand[c] | 0.36 | 0.18 | 0.01 | −0.10 | −0.18 |
| **ROECD** | | | | | |
| GDP[a] | 0.17 | 0.09 | −0.01 | −0.09 | −0.15 |
| Private consumption[a] | −0.06 | −0.07 | −0.09 | −0.11 | −0.12 |
| Private investment[a] | −0.16 | −0.20 | −0.24 | −0.27 | −0.30 |
| Government consumption[a] | 0.00 | 0.00 | 0.00 | 0.00 | 0.00 |
| Exports[a] | 0.22 | 0.19 | 0.15 | 0.11 | 0.08 |
| Imports[a] | −0.16 | −0.17 | −0.18 | −0.19 | −0.20 |
| Trade balance[a] | 0.40 | 0.31 | 0.26 | 0.24 | 0.22 |
| Budget deficit[a] | −0.04 | −0.02 | 0.01 | 0.03 | 0.05 |
| Inflation[b] | 0.24 | 0.22 | 0.17 | 0.13 | 0.10 |
| Nominal short-term interest rate[b] | 0.50 | 0.78 | 0.92 | 1.01 | 1.09 |
| Nominal long-term interest rate[b] | 1.07 | 1.16 | 1.22 | 1.27 | 1.31 |
| Real short-term interest rate[b] | 0.26 | 0.59 | 0.78 | 0.91 | 1.01 |
| Real long-term interest rate[b] | 0.97 | 1.08 | 1.16 | 1.23 | 1.28 |
| Money[c] | 0.00 | 0.00 | 0.00 | 0.00 | 0.00 |
| Exchange rate (US$/roe)[c] | −4.03 | −3.35 | −3.03 | −2.84 | −2.71 |
| Real exchange rate (US$/roe)[c] | −3.91 | −3.06 | −2.67 | −2.50 | −2.42 |
| Labor demand[c] | 0.30 | 0.19 | 0.05 | −0.05 | −0.11 |
| **LDCs** | | | | | |
| Trade balance[d] | 0.10 | 0.15 | 0.17 | 0.18 | 0.20 |
| Terms of trade[c] | −2.83 | −2.26 | −2.10 | −2.06 | −2.06 |
| **OPEC** | | | | | |
| Trade balance[d] | −0.17 | −0.15 | −0.12 | −0.11 | −0.10 |
| Terms of trade[c] | −3.34 | −2.76 | −2.57 | −2.54 | −2.55 |

Source: Simulations of the MSG2 model. Here and in subsequent tables in this appendix, abbreviations for model regions are as defined in chapter 3 (notes 3–6).
a. As percent of real GDP.
b. Absolute deviation.
c. Percentage deviation.
d. As percent of U.S. GDP.

Table B-2. *Sustained 1 Percent GDP Japanese Fiscal Expansion*
Deviation from baseline

| Model region and variable | Year | | | | |
|---|---|---|---|---|---|
| | 1 | 2 | 3 | 4 | 5 |
| *United States* | | | | | |
| GDP[a] | −0.01 | −0.05 | −0.11 | −0.15 | −0.18 |
| Private consumption[a] | −0.10 | −0.16 | −0.21 | −0.24 | −0.26 |
| Private investment[a] | −0.09 | −0.13 | −0.16 | −0.18 | −0.19 |
| Government consumption[a] | 0.00 | 0.00 | 0.00 | 0.00 | 0.00 |
| Exports[a] | 0.06 | 0.05 | 0.04 | 0.04 | 0.04 |
| Imports[a] | −0.13 | −0.19 | −0.21 | −0.22 | −0.23 |
| Trade balance[a] | 0.09 | 0.08 | 0.07 | 0.07 | 0.07 |
| Budget deficit[a] | 0.02 | 0.04 | 0.06 | 0.07 | 0.08 |
| Inflation[b] | 0.19 | 0.20 | 0.16 | 0.11 | 0.07 |
| Nominal short-term interest rate[b] | 0.10 | 0.26 | 0.40 | 0.50 | 0.56 |
| Nominal long-term interest rate[b] | 0.49 | 0.55 | 0.58 | 0.61 | 0.62 |
| Real short-term interest rate[b] | −0.07 | 0.11 | 0.29 | 0.43 | 0.52 |
| Real long-term interest rate[b] | 0.44 | 0.51 | 0.56 | 0.60 | 0.62 |
| Labor demand[c] | 0.06 | −0.05 | −0.15 | −0.20 | −0.23 |
| *Japan* | | | | | |
| GDP[a] | 0.34 | −0.01 | −0.03 | −0.05 | −0.06 |
| Private consumption[a] | 0.30 | 0.15 | 0.11 | 0.09 | 0.06 |
| Private investment[a] | −0.00 | −0.09 | −0.09 | −0.10 | −0.11 |
| Government consumption[a] | 1.00 | 1.00 | 1.00 | 1.00 | 1.00 |
| Exports[a] | −0.54 | −0.64 | −0.64 | −0.64 | −0.63 |
| Imports[a] | 0.41 | 0.43 | 0.41 | 0.40 | 0.39 |
| Trade balance[a] | −0.84 | −0.77 | −0.70 | −0.66 | −0.64 |
| Budget deficit[a] | 0.82 | 0.93 | 0.94 | 0.94 | 0.95 |
| Inflation[b] | −0.28 | 0.27 | −0.02 | 0.03 | 0.04 |
| Nominal short-term interest rate[b] | 0.82 | 0.74 | 0.64 | 0.64 | 0.66 |
| Nominal long-term interest rate[b] | 0.70 | 0.69 | 0.69 | 0.70 | 0.70 |
| Real short-term interest rate[b] | 0.52 | 0.76 | 0.62 | 0.61 | 0.63 |
| Real long-term interest rate[b] | 0.66 | 0.68 | 0.67 | 0.68 | 0.69 |
| Exchange rate (US$/¥)[c] | 6.65 | 5.93 | 5.46 | 5.21 | 5.07 |
| Real exchange rate (US$/¥)[c] | 6.46 | 5.86 | 5.22 | 4.88 | 4.70 |
| Labor demand[c] | 0.49 | 0.00 | 0.00 | 0.00 | 0.00 |
| *Germany* | | | | | |
| GDP[a] | −0.01 | −0.06 | −0.10 | −0.13 | −0.16 |
| Private consumption[a] | −0.10 | −0.12 | −0.12 | −0.12 | −0.13 |
| Private investment[a] | −0.08 | −0.11 | −0.13 | −0.15 | −0.17 |
| Government consumption[a] | 0.00 | 0.00 | 0.00 | 0.00 | 0.00 |
| Exports[a] | 0.03 | 0.00 | −0.01 | −0.03 | −0.05 |
| Imports[a] | −0.14 | −0.17 | −0.17 | −0.18 | −0.18 |
| Real trade balance[a] | 0.09 | 0.06 | 0.05 | 0.04 | 0.03 |
| Budget deficit[a] | 0.01 | 0.03 | 0.04 | 0.05 | 0.06 |
| Inflation[b] | 0.18 | 0.14 | 0.11 | 0.09 | 0.07 |
| Nominal short-term interest rate[b] | 0.07 | 0.20 | 0.34 | 0.44 | 0.51 |
| Nominal long-term interest rate[b] | 0.45 | 0.51 | 0.55 | 0.57 | 0.59 |
| Real short-term interest rate[b] | −0.07 | 0.08 | 0.24 | 0.36 | 0.45 |
| Real long-term interest rate[b] | 0.39 | 0.46 | 0.51 | 0.55 | 0.57 |
| Exchange rate (US$/DM)[c] | 0.08 | 0.11 | 0.17 | 0.24 | 0.29 |
| Real exchange rate (US$/DM)[c] | 0.06 | 0.05 | 0.08 | 0.13 | 0.20 |
| Labor demand[c] | 0.04 | −0.05 | −0.10 | −0.13 | −0.17 |

## Table B-2 *(continued)*

| Model region and variable | Year | | | | |
|---|---|---|---|---|---|
| | *1* | *2* | *3* | *4* | *5* |
| *REMS* | | | | | |
| GDP[a] | −0.05 | −0.09 | −0.11 | −0.14 | −0.18 |
| Private consumption[a] | −0.12 | −0.13 | −0.12 | −0.12 | −0.12 |
| Private investment[a] | −0.09 | −0.12 | −0.14 | −0.15 | −0.17 |
| Government consumption[a] | 0.00 | 0.00 | 0.00 | 0.00 | 0.00 |
| Exports[a] | 0.03 | 0.00 | −0.01 | −0.03 | −0.04 |
| Imports[a] | −0.13 | −0.15 | −0.15 | −0.15 | −0.15 |
| Trade balance[a] | 0.09 | 0.07 | 0.05 | 0.04 | 0.03 |
| Budget deficit[a] | 0.02 | 0.04 | 0.04 | 0.05 | 0.06 |
| Inflation[b] | 0.16 | 0.14 | 0.11 | 0.09 | 0.07 |
| Nominal short-term interest rate[b] | 0.07 | 0.20 | 0.34 | 0.44 | 0.51 |
| Nominal long-term interest rate[b] | 0.45 | 0.51 | 0.55 | 0.57 | 0.59 |
| Real short-term interest rate[b] | −0.06 | 0.09 | 0.24 | 0.36 | 0.45 |
| Real long-term interest rate[b] | 0.39 | 0.46 | 0.51 | 0.55 | 0.57 |
| Money[c] | −0.02 | −0.02 | −0.01 | −0.01 | −0.00 |
| Exchange rate (US$/ems)[c] | 0.08 | 0.11 | 0.17 | 0.24 | 0.29 |
| Real exchange rate (US$/ems)[c] | 0.06 | 0.05 | 0.08 | 0.13 | 0.19 |
| Labor demand[c] | 0.02 | −0.05 | −0.09 | −0.12 | −0.16 |
| *ROECD* | | | | | |
| GDP[a] | −0.03 | −0.06 | −0.09 | −0.11 | −0.13 |
| Private consumption[a] | −0.07 | −0.09 | −0.10 | −0.11 | −0.11 |
| Private investment[a] | −0.08 | −0.11 | −0.13 | −0.14 | −0.16 |
| Government consumption[a] | 0.00 | 0.00 | 0.00 | 0.00 | 0.00 |
| Exports[a] | 0.04 | 0.02 | 0.01 | 0.00 | −0.01 |
| Imports[a] | −0.09 | −0.12 | −0.13 | −0.14 | −0.14 |
| Trade balance[a] | 0.09 | 0.08 | 0.09 | 0.08 | 0.08 |
| Budget deficit[a] | 0.01 | 0.02 | 0.03 | 0.04 | 0.05 |
| Inflation[b] | 0.13 | 0.12 | 0.10 | 0.08 | 0.06 |
| Nominal short-term interest rate[b] | 0.09 | 0.22 | 0.35 | 0.45 | 0.52 |
| Nominal long-term interest rate[b] | 0.46 | 0.51 | 0.55 | 0.58 | 0.60 |
| Real short-term interest rate[b] | −0.03 | 0.11 | 0.26 | 0.38 | 0.47 |
| Real long-term interest rate[b] | 0.41 | 0.48 | 0.53 | 0.57 | 0.59 |
| Exchange rate (US$/roe)[c] | 0.30 | 0.31 | 0.36 | 0.41 | 0.46 |
| Real exchange rate (US$/roe)[c] | 0.28 | 0.24 | 0.24 | 0.27 | 0.31 |
| Labor demand[c] | 0.05 | −0.01 | −0.04 | −0.07 | −0.09 |
| *LDCs* | | | | | |
| Trade balance[d] | 0.01 | 0.05 | 0.07 | 0.10 | 0.11 |
| Terms of trade[c] | 1.30 | 1.16 | 1.06 | 1.03 | 1.03 |
| *OPEC* | | | | | |
| Trade balance[d] | 0.05 | 0.02 | −0.01 | −0.04 | −0.05 |
| Terms of trade[c] | 1.46 | 1.24 | 1.08 | 1.00 | 0.97 |

Source: See table B-1.
a. As percent of real GDP.
b. Absolute deviation.
c. Percentage deviation.
d. As percent of U.S. GDP.

Table B-3. *Sustained 1 Percent GDP German Fiscal Expansion*
Deviation from baseline

| Model region and variable | Year | | | | |
|---|---|---|---|---|---|
| | 1 | 2 | 3 | 4 | 5 |
| *United States* | | | | | |
| GDP[a] | −0.00 | −0.03 | −0.05 | −0.07 | −0.08 |
| Private consumption[a] | −0.05 | −0.07 | −0.09 | −0.10 | −0.10 |
| Private investment[a] | −0.05 | −0.06 | −0.08 | −0.08 | −0.09 |
| Government consumption[a] | 0.00 | 0.00 | 0.00 | 0.00 | 0.00 |
| Exports[a] | 0.05 | 0.04 | 0.04 | 0.04 | 0.03 |
| Imports[a] | −0.05 | −0.07 | −0.07 | −0.07 | −0.07 |
| Trade balance[a] | 0.07 | 0.06 | 0.05 | 0.05 | 0.05 |
| Budget deficit[a] | 0.01 | 0.02 | 0.02 | 0.03 | 0.03 |
| Inflation[b] | 0.12 | 0.09 | 0.06 | 0.03 | 0.02 |
| Nominal short-term interest rate[b] | 0.11 | 0.19 | 0.24 | 0.26 | 0.28 |
| Nominal long-term interest rate[b] | 0.25 | 0.27 | 0.28 | 0.29 | 0.29 |
| Real short-term interest rate[b] | 0.04 | 0.13 | 0.20 | 0.24 | 0.27 |
| Real long-term interest rate[b] | 0.23 | 0.26 | 0.28 | 0.28 | 0.29 |
| Labor demand[c] | 0.07 | −0.00 | −0.05 | −0.07 | −0.08 |
| *Japan* | | | | | |
| GDP[a] | 0.01 | −0.02 | −0.02 | −0.02 | −0.03 |
| Private consumption[a] | −0.04 | −0.05 | −0.05 | −0.04 | −0.04 |
| Private investment[a] | −0.05 | −0.06 | −0.06 | −0.07 | −0.07 |
| Government consumption[a] | 0.00 | 0.00 | 0.00 | 0.00 | 0.00 |
| Exports[a] | 0.05 | 0.04 | 0.04 | 0.04 | 0.04 |
| Imports[a] | −0.05 | −0.05 | −0.05 | −0.05 | −0.05 |
| Trade balance[a] | 0.07 | 0.06 | 0.05 | 0.05 | 0.04 |
| Budget deficit[a] | 0.01 | 0.01 | 0.01 | 0.02 | 0.02 |
| Inflation[b] | 0.10 | 0.08 | 0.02 | 0.02 | 0.01 |
| Nominal short-term interest rate[b] | 0.10 | 0.18 | 0.22 | 0.25 | 0.27 |
| Nominal long-term interest rate[b] | 0.24 | 0.26 | 0.27 | 0.27 | 0.28 |
| Real short-term interest rate[b] | 0.02 | 0.16 | 0.20 | 0.24 | 0.26 |
| Real long-term interest rate[b] | 0.22 | 0.25 | 0.26 | 0.27 | 0.27 |
| Exchange rate (US$/¥)[c] | −0.11 | −0.09 | −0.08 | −0.07 | −0.06 |
| Real exchange rate (US$/¥)[c] | −0.12 | −0.10 | −0.13 | −0.13 | −0.12 |
| Labor demand[c] | 0.06 | −0.00 | −0.00 | −0.00 | −0.00 |
| *Germany* | | | | | |
| GDP[a] | 0.22 | 0.23 | 0.26 | 0.28 | 0.29 |
| Private consumption[a] | 0.26 | 0.24 | 0.22 | 0.20 | 0.18 |
| Private investment[a] | −0.00 | 0.01 | 0.03 | 0.03 | 0.03 |
| Government consumption[a] | 1.00 | 1.00 | 1.00 | 1.00 | 1.00 |
| Exports[a] | −0.50 | −0.48 | −0.45 | −0.43 | −0.41 |
| Imports[a] | 0.53 | 0.54 | 0.54 | 0.53 | 0.51 |
| Real trade balance[a] | −0.87 | −0.77 | −0.71 | −0.68 | −0.66 |
| Budget deficit[a] | 0.89 | 0.89 | 0.88 | 0.87 | 0.87 |
| Inflation[b] | −0.21 | −0.14 | −0.06 | −0.02 | 0.00 |
| Nominal short-term interest rate[b] | 0.60 | 0.41 | 0.35 | 0.32 | 0.32 |
| Nominal long-term interest rate[b] | 0.36 | 0.34 | 0.33 | 0.33 | 0.33 |
| Real short-term interest rate[b] | 0.73 | 0.48 | 0.37 | 0.33 | 0.31 |
| Real long-term interest rate[b] | 0.38 | 0.34 | 0.32 | 0.31 | 0.31 |
| Exchange rate (US$/DM)[c] | 3.00 | 2.52 | 2.29 | 2.19 | 2.13 |
| Real exchange rate (US$/DM)[c] | 2.93 | 2.24 | 1.89 | 1.72 | 1.64 |
| Labor demand[c] | 0.36 | 0.41 | 0.48 | 0.51 | 0.51 |

## Table B-3 *(continued)*

| Model region and variable | Year 1 | 2 | 3 | 4 | 5 |
|---|---|---|---|---|---|
| **REMS** | | | | | |
| GDP[a] | −0.63 | −0.33 | −0.23 | −0.20 | −0.20 |
| Private consumption[a] | −0.19 | −0.12 | −0.09 | −0.08 | −0.08 |
| Private investment[a] | −0.23 | −0.15 | −0.12 | −0.11 | −0.11 |
| Government consumption[a] | 0.00 | 0.00 | 0.00 | 0.00 | 0.00 |
| Exports[a] | −0.20 | −0.10 | −0.06 | −0.05 | −0.05 |
| Imports[a] | 0.01 | −0.04 | −0.05 | −0.05 | −0.04 |
| Trade balance[a] | −0.12 | 0.01 | 0.06 | 0.07 | 0.07 |
| Budget deficit[a] | 0.19 | 0.11 | 0.08 | 0.07 | 0.07 |
| Inflation[b] | −0.64 | −0.26 | −0.07 | 0.00 | 0.03 |
| Nominal short-term interest rate[b] | 0.60 | 0.41 | 0.35 | 0.32 | 0.32 |
| Nominal long-term interest rate[b] | 0.36 | 0.34 | 0.33 | 0.33 | 0.33 |
| Real short-term interest rate[b] | 0.95 | 0.51 | 0.35 | 0.30 | 0.28 |
| Real long-term interest rate[b] | 0.38 | 0.32 | 0.29 | 0.29 | 0.29 |
| Money[c] | −1.42 | −1.41 | −1.37 | −1.34 | −1.30 |
| Exchange rate (US$/ems)[c] | 3.00 | 2.52 | 2.29 | 2.19 | 2.13 |
| Real exchange rate (US$/ems)[c] | 2.45 | 1.53 | 1.16 | 1.01 | 0.96 |
| Labor demand[c] | −1.06 | −0.57 | −0.38 | −0.31 | −0.29 |
| **ROECD** | | | | | |
| GDP[a] | 0.15 | 0.03 | 0.00 | −0.00 | −0.00 |
| Private consumption[a] | −0.03 | −0.05 | −0.05 | −0.04 | −0.04 |
| Private investment[a] | −0.03 | −0.06 | −0.06 | −0.06 | −0.07 |
| Government consumption[a] | 0.00 | 0.00 | 0.00 | 0.00 | 0.00 |
| Exports[a] | 0.05 | 0.01 | 0.01 | 0.01 | 0.00 |
| Imports[a] | −0.16 | −0.12 | −0.11 | −0.10 | −0.10 |
| Trade balance[a] | 0.09 | 0.05 | 0.03 | 0.03 | 0.03 |
| Budget deficit[a] | −0.03 | 0.00 | 0.01 | 0.01 | 0.01 |
| Inflation[b] | 0.21 | 0.04 | 0.00 | 0.00 | 0.00 |
| Nominal short-term interest rate[b] | 0.28 | 0.26 | 0.26 | 0.27 | 0.28 |
| Nominal long-term interest rate[b] | 0.28 | 0.28 | 0.29 | 0.29 | 0.29 |
| Real short-term interest rate[b] | 0.18 | 0.24 | 0.26 | 0.27 | 0.27 |
| Real long-term interest rate[b] | 0.27 | 0.28 | 0.28 | 0.29 | 0.29 |
| Exchange rate (US$/roe)[c] | 0.94 | 0.77 | 0.70 | 0.67 | 0.66 |
| Real exchange rate (US$/roe)[c] | 0.91 | 0.76 | 0.65 | 0.60 | 0.58 |
| Labor demand[c] | 0.17 | −0.01 | −0.03 | −0.02 | −0.02 |
| **LDCs** | | | | | |
| Trade balance[d] | 0.06 | 0.06 | 0.06 | 0.06 | 0.06 |
| Terms of trade[c] | 0.97 | 0.70 | 0.57 | 0.51 | 0.49 |
| **OPEC** | | | | | |
| Trade balance[d] | 0.01 | −0.00 | −0.02 | −0.02 | −0.03 |
| Terms of trade[c] | 0.98 | 0.67 | 0.52 | 0.45 | 0.43 |

Source: See table B-1.
a. As percent of real GDP.
b. Absolute deviation.
c. Percentage deviation.
d. As percent of U.S. GDP.

Table B-4. *Sustained 1 Percent GDP REMS Fiscal Expansion*
Deviation from baseline

| *Model region and variable* | *Year* 1 | 2 | 3 | 4 | 5 |
|---|---|---|---|---|---|
| *United States* | | | | | |
| GDP[a] | 0.02 | −0.02 | −0.06 | −0.10 | −0.12 |
| Private consumption[a] | −0.05 | −0.08 | −0.11 | −0.13 | −0.14 |
| Private investment[a] | −0.07 | −0.09 | −0.11 | −0.12 | −0.13 |
| Government consumption[a] | 0.00 | 0.00 | 0.00 | 0.00 | 0.00 |
| Exports[a] | 0.08 | 0.08 | 0.07 | 0.07 | 0.06 |
| Imports[a] | −0.05 | −0.07 | −0.08 | −0.09 | −0.09 |
| Trade balance[a] | 0.10 | 0.09 | 0.09 | 0.09 | 0.08 |
| Budget deficit[a] | 0.00 | 0.01 | 0.03 | 0.04 | 0.05 |
| Inflation[b] | 0.11 | 0.11 | 0.10 | 0.07 | 0.05 |
| Nominal short-term interest rate[b] | 0.14 | 0.23 | 0.32 | 0.38 | 0.42 |
| Nominal long-term interest rate[b] | 0.39 | 0.42 | 0.45 | 0.47 | 0.48 |
| Real short-term interest rate[b] | 0.03 | 0.14 | 0.24 | 0.33 | 0.39 |
| Real long-term interest rate[b] | 0.35 | 0.39 | 0.43 | 0.46 | 0.47 |
| Labor demand[c] | 0.08 | 0.02 | −0.05 | −0.09 | −0.11 |
| *Japan* | | | | | |
| GDP[a] | 0.02 | −0.02 | −0.03 | −0.03 | −0.04 |
| Private consumption[a] | −0.05 | −0.07 | −0.07 | −0.07 | −0.07 |
| Private investment[a] | −0.07 | −0.09 | −0.10 | −0.11 | −0.11 |
| Government consumption[a] | 0.00 | 0.00 | 0.00 | 0.00 | 0.00 |
| Exports[a] | 0.08 | 0.07 | 0.07 | 0.07 | 0.07 |
| Imports[a] | −0.06 | −0.07 | −0.07 | −0.08 | −0.08 |
| Trade balance[a] | 0.11 | 0.09 | 0.09 | 0.08 | 0.08 |
| Budget deficit[a] | 0.00 | 0.02 | 0.02 | 0.02 | 0.03 |
| Inflation[b] | 0.11 | 0.12 | 0.06 | 0.04 | 0.03 |
| Nominal short-term interest rate[b] | 0.11 | 0.24 | 0.31 | 0.37 | 0.41 |
| Nominal long-term interest rate[b] | 0.37 | 0.41 | 0.43 | 0.45 | 0.46 |
| Real short-term interest rate[b] | −0.01 | 0.18 | 0.27 | 0.34 | 0.39 |
| Real long-term interest rate[b] | 0.34 | 0.39 | 0.42 | 0.44 | 0.45 |
| Exchange rate (US$/¥)[c] | −0.30 | −0.27 | −0.27 | −0.27 | −0.26 |
| Real exchange rate (US$/¥)[c] | −0.31 | −0.26 | −0.30 | −0.33 | −0.34 |
| Labor demand[c] | 0.07 | −0.00 | −0.00 | −0.00 | −0.00 |
| *Germany* | | | | | |
| GDP[a] | 0.12 | 0.10 | 0.08 | 0.06 | 0.03 |
| Private consumption[a] | 0.05 | 0.04 | 0.04 | 0.04 | 0.05 |
| Private investment[a] | −0.04 | −0.05 | −0.07 | −0.08 | −0.09 |
| Government consumption[a] | 0.00 | 0.00 | 0.00 | 0.00 | 0.00 |
| Exports[a] | 0.13 | 0.11 | 0.09 | 0.08 | 0.06 |
| Imports[a] | 0.02 | −0.00 | −0.01 | −0.01 | −0.01 |
| Real trade balance[a] | 0.09 | 0.09 | 0.09 | 0.08 | 0.07 |
| Budget deficit[a] | −0.04 | −0.04 | −0.03 | −0.02 | −0.01 |
| Inflation[b] | 0.01 | 0.05 | 0.05 | 0.05 | 0.04 |
| Nominal short-term interest rate[b] | 0.27 | 0.29 | 0.34 | 0.39 | 0.43 |
| Nominal long-term interest rate[b] | 0.41 | 0.43 | 0.46 | 0.47 | 0.48 |
| Real short-term interest rate[b] | 0.23 | 0.24 | 0.29 | 0.34 | 0.39 |
| Real long-term interest rate[b] | 0.38 | 0.40 | 0.43 | 0.45 | 0.47 |
| Exchange rate (US$/DM)[c] | 1.50 | 1.37 | 1.31 | 1.28 | 1.27 |
| Real exchange rate (US$/DM)[c] | 1.43 | 1.24 | 1.14 | 1.10 | 1.08 |
| Labor demand[c] | 0.16 | 0.14 | 0.11 | 0.09 | 0.07 |

## Table B-4 *(continued)*

| Model region and variable | Year 1 | 2 | 3 | 4 | 5 |
|---|---|---|---|---|---|
| **REMS** | | | | | |
| GDP[a] | 0.69 | 0.52 | 0.46 | 0.42 | 0.40 |
| Private consumption[a] | 0.41 | 0.34 | 0.29 | 0.25 | 0.21 |
| Private investment[a] | 0.13 | 0.08 | 0.06 | 0.04 | 0.03 |
| Government consumption[a] | 1.00 | 1.00 | 1.00 | 1.00 | 1.00 |
| Exports[a] | −0.20 | −0.25 | −0.27 | −0.27 | −0.27 |
| Imports[a] | 0.64 | 0.65 | 0.63 | 0.60 | 0.58 |
| Trade balance[a] | −0.70 | −0.70 | −0.68 | −0.66 | −0.65 |
| Budget deficit[a] | 0.74 | 0.78 | 0.80 | 0.82 | 0.83 |
| Inflation[b] | 0.22 | 0.13 | 0.07 | 0.04 | 0.03 |
| Nominal short-term interest rate[b] | 0.27 | 0.29 | 0.34 | 0.39 | 0.43 |
| Nominal long-term interest rate[b] | 0.41 | 0.43 | 0.46 | 0.47 | 0.48 |
| Real short-term interest rate[b] | 0.11 | 0.22 | 0.30 | 0.37 | 0.42 |
| Real long-term interest rate[b] | 0.38 | 0.42 | 0.45 | 0.47 | 0.49 |
| Money[c] | 1.04 | 1.03 | 1.01 | 0.98 | 0.94 |
| Exchange rate (US$/ems)[c] | 1.50 | 1.37 | 1.31 | 1.28 | 1.27 |
| Real exchange rate (US$/ems)[c] | 1.77 | 1.69 | 1.62 | 1.55 | 1.51 |
| Labor demand[c] | 1.20 | 0.95 | 0.84 | 0.77 | 0.72 |
| **ROECD** | | | | | |
| GDP[a] | 0.12 | 0.09 | 0.05 | 0.01 | −0.01 |
| Private consumption[a] | 0.03 | 0.01 | −0.00 | −0.01 | −0.01 |
| Private investment[a] | −0.04 | −0.06 | −0.08 | −0.09 | −0.10 |
| Government consumption[a] | 0.00 | 0.00 | 0.00 | 0.00 | 0.00 |
| Exports[a] | 0.13 | 0.10 | 0.09 | 0.07 | 0.06 |
| Imports[a] | −0.01 | −0.03 | −0.04 | −0.04 | −0.04 |
| Trade balance[a] | 0.09 | 0.11 | 0.11 | 0.11 | 0.11 |
| Budget deficit[a] | −0.04 | −0.03 | −0.01 | −0.00 | 0.00 |
| Inflation[b] | 0.02 | 0.07 | 0.07 | 0.06 | 0.05 |
| Nominal short-term interest rate[b] | 0.25 | 0.28 | 0.33 | 0.38 | 0.43 |
| Nominal long-term interest rate[b] | 0.41 | 0.43 | 0.46 | 0.47 | 0.49 |
| Real short-term interest rate[b] | 0.20 | 0.21 | 0.27 | 0.33 | 0.39 |
| Real long-term interest rate[b] | 0.37 | 0.40 | 0.43 | 0.46 | 0.47 |
| Exchange rate (US$/roe)[c] | 1.32 | 1.20 | 1.16 | 1.14 | 1.13 |
| Real exchange rate (US$/roe)[c] | 1.26 | 1.10 | 1.03 | 1.00 | 1.00 |
| Labor demand[c] | 0.15 | 0.10 | 0.05 | 0.01 | −0.02 |
| **LDCs** | | | | | |
| Trade balance[d] | 0.03 | 0.04 | 0.06 | 0.07 | 0.09 |
| Terms of trade[c] | 0.78 | 0.71 | 0.66 | 0.63 | 0.62 |
| **OPEC** | | | | | |
| Trade balance[d] | 0.02 | 0.00 | −0.02 | −0.03 | −0.04 |
| Terms of trade[c] | 0.85 | 0.74 | 0.66 | 0.60 | 0.57 |

Source: See table B-1.
a. As percent of real GDP.
b. Absolute deviation.
c. Percentage deviation.
d. As percent of U.S. GDP.

**Table B-5.** *Sustained 1 Percent GDP ROECD Fiscal Expansion*
Deviation from baseline

| Model region and variable | Year | | | | |
|---|---|---|---|---|---|
| | *1* | *2* | *3* | *4* | *5* |
| *United States* | | | | | |
| GDP[a] | 0.03 | −0.02 | −0.07 | −0.11 | −0.15 |
| Private consumption[a] | −0.07 | −0.11 | −0.15 | −0.17 | −0.19 |
| Private investment[a] | −0.09 | −0.12 | −0.14 | −0.16 | −0.18 |
| Government consumption[a] | 0.00 | 0.00 | 0.00 | 0.00 | 0.00 |
| Exports[a] | 0.11 | 0.10 | 0.09 | 0.08 | 0.08 |
| Imports[a] | −0.08 | −0.11 | −0.13 | −0.13 | −0.14 |
| Trade balance[a] | 0.14 | 0.12 | 0.11 | 0.11 | 0.11 |
| Budget deficit[a] | −0.00 | 0.02 | 0.04 | 0.05 | 0.06 |
| Inflation[b] | 0.16 | 0.15 | 0.12 | 0.09 | 0.07 |
| Nominal short-term interest rate[b] | 0.19 | 0.31 | 0.41 | 0.49 | 0.54 |
| Nominal long-term interest rate[b] | 0.51 | 0.56 | 0.59 | 0.62 | 0.64 |
| Real short-term interest rate[b] | 0.06 | 0.19 | 0.32 | 0.42 | 0.50 |
| Real long-term interest rate[b] | 0.46 | 0.52 | 0.57 | 0.60 | 0.63 |
| Labor demand[c] | 0.11 | 0.01 | −0.07 | −0.12 | −0.15 |
| *Japan* | | | | | |
| GDP[a] | 0.04 | −0.01 | −0.02 | −0.03 | −0.04 |
| Private consumption[a] | −0.07 | −0.09 | −0.09 | −0.09 | −0.09 |
| Private investment[a] | −0.09 | −0.12 | −0.13 | −0.14 | −0.15 |
| Government consumption[a] | 0.00 | 0.00 | 0.00 | 0.00 | 0.00 |
| Exports[a] | 0.11 | 0.10 | 0.10 | 0.10 | 0.09 |
| Imports[a] | −0.10 | −0.10 | −0.10 | −0.11 | −0.11 |
| Trade balance[a] | 0.15 | 0.12 | 0.11 | 0.11 | 0.10 |
| Budget deficit[a] | 0.00 | 0.02 | 0.02 | 0.03 | 0.03 |
| Inflation[b] | 0.16 | 0.15 | 0.07 | 0.06 | 0.05 |
| Nominal short-term interest rate[b] | 0.15 | 0.31 | 0.40 | 0.48 | 0.53 |
| Nominal long-term interest rate[b] | 0.49 | 0.54 | 0.57 | 0.60 | 0.62 |
| Real short-term interest rate[b] | 0.00 | 0.25 | 0.35 | 0.43 | 0.49 |
| Real long-term interest rate[b] | 0.45 | 0.51 | 0.55 | 0.58 | 0.60 |
| Exchange rate (US$/¥)[c] | −0.36 | −0.32 | −0.32 | −0.32 | −0.31 |
| Real exchange rate (US$/¥)[c] | −0.36 | −0.31 | −0.37 | −0.40 | −0.41 |
| Labor demand[c] | 0.09 | −0.00 | −0.00 | −0.00 | −0.00 |
| *Germany* | | | | | |
| GDP[a] | 0.14 | 0.08 | 0.04 | 0.02 | −0.01 |
| Private consumption[a] | 0.02 | 0.01 | 0.01 | 0.01 | 0.01 |
| Private investment[a] | −0.06 | −0.08 | −0.10 | −0.11 | −0.12 |
| Government consumption[a] | 0.00 | 0.00 | 0.00 | 0.00 | 0.00 |
| Exports[a] | 0.14 | 0.10 | 0.08 | 0.07 | 0.05 |
| Imports[a] | −0.03 | −0.05 | −0.05 | −0.06 | −0.06 |
| Real trade balance[a] | 0.13 | 0.10 | 0.08 | 0.07 | 0.06 |
| Budget deficit[a] | −0.05 | −0.03 | −0.02 | −0.01 | −0.00 |
| Inflation[b] | 0.10 | 0.08 | 0.06 | 0.06 | 0.06 |
| Nominal short-term interest rate[b] | 0.33 | 0.36 | 0.41 | 0.47 | 0.53 |
| Nominal long-term interest rate[b] | 0.52 | 0.56 | 0.59 | 0.62 | 0.64 |
| Real short-term interest rate[b] | 0.25 | 0.29 | 0.35 | 0.42 | 0.47 |
| Real long-term interest rate[b] | 0.47 | 0.51 | 0.55 | 0.58 | 0.61 |
| Exchange rate (US$/DM)[c] | 1.51 | 1.37 | 1.32 | 1.31 | 1.32 |
| Real exchange rate (US$/DM)[c] | 1.44 | 1.25 | 1.15 | 1.11 | 1.11 |
| Labor demand[c] | 0.20 | 0.11 | 0.08 | 0.05 | 0.02 |

## Table B-5 *(continued)*

| Model region and variable | Year 1 | 2 | 3 | 4 | 5 |
|---|---|---|---|---|---|
| **REMS** | | | | | |
| GDP[a] | 0.29 | 0.13 | 0.08 | 0.06 | 0.03 |
| Private consumption[a] | 0.05 | 0.03 | 0.02 | 0.02 | 0.01 |
| Private investment[a] | −0.01 | −0.06 | −0.08 | −0.09 | −0.11 |
| Government consumption[a] | 0.00 | 0.00 | 0.00 | 0.00 | 0.00 |
| Exports[a] | 0.23 | 0.16 | 0.14 | 0.12 | 0.10 |
| Imports[a] | −0.03 | 0.00 | −0.00 | −0.01 | −0.02 |
| Trade balance[a] | 0.14 | 0.08 | 0.06 | 0.04 | 0.03 |
| Budget deficit[a] | −0.10 | −0.06 | −0.05 | −0.04 | −0.03 |
| Inflation[b] | 0.26 | 0.11 | 0.07 | 0.06 | 0.06 |
| Nominal short-term interest rate[b] | 0.33 | 0.36 | 0.41 | 0.47 | 0.53 |
| Nominal long-term interest rate[b] | 0.52 | 0.56 | 0.59 | 0.62 | 0.64 |
| Real short-term interest rate[b] | 0.17 | 0.28 | 0.36 | 0.42 | 0.48 |
| Real long-term interest rate[b] | 0.47 | 0.52 | 0.56 | 0.59 | 0.52 |
| Money[c] | 0.26 | 0.27 | 0.27 | 0.26 | 0.26 |
| Exchange rate (US$/ems)[c] | 1.51 | 1.37 | 1.32 | 1.31 | 1.32 |
| Real exchange rate (US$/ems)[c] | 1.53 | 1.42 | 1.33 | 1.29 | 1.29 |
| Labor demand[c] | 0.46 | 0.24 | 0.18 | 0.15 | 0.11 |
| **ROECD** | | | | | |
| GDP[a] | 0.26 | 0.29 | 0.24 | 0.17 | 0.09 |
| Private consumption[a] | 0.29 | 0.23 | 0.18 | 0.12 | 0.07 |
| Private investment[a] | −0.03 | −0.02 | −0.03 | −0.06 | −0.08 |
| Government consumption[a] | 1.00 | 1.00 | 1.00 | 1.00 | 1.00 |
| Exports[a] | −0.37 | −0.35 | −0.36 | −0.37 | −0.39 |
| Imports[a] | 0.63 | 0.57 | 0.55 | 0.53 | 0.51 |
| Trade balance[a] | −0.78 | −0.64 | −0.57 | −0.54 | −0.53 |
| Budget deficit[a] | 0.88 | 0.88 | 0.89 | 0.92 | 0.94 |
| Inflation[b] | −0.34 | −0.05 | 0.05 | 0.09 | 0.09 |
| Nominal short-term interest rate[b] | 0.64 | 0.48 | 0.47 | 0.51 | 0.55 |
| Nominal long-term interest rate[b] | 0.59 | 0.60 | 0.62 | 0.65 | 0.67 |
| Real short-term interest rate[b] | 0.75 | 0.44 | 0.38 | 0.40 | 0.46 |
| Real long-term interest rate[b] | 0.54 | 0.54 | 0.56 | 0.60 | 0.63 |
| Exchange rate (US$/roe)[c] | 3.18 | 2.73 | 2.56 | 2.49 | 2.47 |
| Real exchange rate (US$/roe)[c] | 3.07 | 2.38 | 2.13 | 2.07 | 2.09 |
| Labor demand[c] | 0.39 | 0.46 | 0.39 | 0.29 | 0.18 |
| **LDCs** | | | | | |
| Trade balance[d] | 0.05 | 0.06 | 0.08 | 0.09 | 0.11 |
| Terms of trade[c] | 1.04 | 0.87 | 0.78 | 0.75 | 0.75 |
| **OPEC** | | | | | |
| Trade balance[d] | 0.01 | −0.00 | −0.02 | −0.04 | −0.05 |
| Terms of trade[c] | 1.07 | 0.86 | 0.74 | 0.68 | 0.66 |

Source: See table B-1.
a. As percent of real GDP.
b. Absolute deviation.
c. Percentage deviation.
d. As percent of U.S. GDP.

Table B-6. *Announced Gradual U.S. Fiscal Expansion of 3 Percent of GDP over Three Years*
Deviation from baseline

| Model region and variable | Year | | | | |
|---|---|---|---|---|---|
| | 1 | 2 | 3 | 4 | 5 |
| *United States* | | | | | |
| GDP[a] | −0.53 | 0.66 | 1.66 | 1.06 | 0.54 |
| Private consumption[a] | −0.22 | 0.33 | 0.68 | 0.37 | 0.08 |
| Private investment[a] | −0.46 | −0.31 | −0.22 | −0.41 | −0.59 |
| Government consumption[a] | 1.00 | 2.00 | 3.00 | 3.00 | 3.00 |
| Exports[a] | −0.49 | −0.61 | −0.75 | −0.82 | −0.87 |
| Imports[a] | 0.36 | 0.75 | 1.05 | 1.09 | 1.08 |
| Trade balance[a] | −0.58 | −0.79 | −1.03 | −1.00 | −0.98 |
| Budget deficit[a] | 1.12 | 1.71 | 2.36 | 2.54 | 2.70 |
| Inflation[b] | −1.11 | −0.43 | 0.59 | 0.69 | 0.68 |
| Nominal short-term interest rate[b] | −2.05 | −0.28 | 2.74 | 3.03 | 3.36 |
| Nominal long-term interest rate[b] | 2.74 | 3.42 | 3.92 | 4.12 | 4.30 |
| Real short-term interest rate[b] | −1.79 | −0.99 | 1.99 | 2.31 | 2.73 |
| Real long-term interest rate[b] | 2.31 | 2.95 | 3.52 | 3.79 | 4.03 |
| Labor demand[c] | −1.23 | 0.85 | 2.56 | 1.71 | 0.97 |
| *Japan* | | | | | |
| GDP[a] | −0.23 | −0.00 | −0.04 | −0.08 | −0.14 |
| Private consumption[a] | −0.56 | −0.52 | −0.48 | −0.52 | −0.55 |
| Private investment[a] | −0.51 | −0.61 | −0.77 | −0.85 | −0.91 |
| Government consumption[a] | 0.00 | 0.00 | 0.00 | 0.00 | 0.00 |
| Exports[a] | 0.48 | 0.71 | 0.75 | 0.76 | 0.75 |
| Imports[a] | −0.35 | −0.42 | −0.46 | −0.52 | −0.58 |
| Trade balance[a] | 0.82 | 0.93 | 0.91 | 0.85 | 0.81 |
| Budget deficit[a] | 0.13 | 0.07 | 0.09 | 0.12 | 0.14 |
| Inflation[b] | 0.18 | 0.55 | 1.24 | 0.41 | 0.33 |
| Nominal short-term interest rate[b] | −0.69 | 0.48 | 2.42 | 2.92 | 3.28 |
| Nominal long-term interest rate[b] | 2.81 | 3.32 | 3.71 | 3.91 | 4.06 |
| Real short-term interest rate[b] | −1.19 | −0.74 | 2.04 | 2.62 | 3.03 |
| Real long-term interest rate[b] | 2.46 | 3.01 | 3.53 | 3.76 | 3.94 |
| Exchange rate (US$/¥)[c] | −10.24 | −11.61 | −12.37 | −12.05 | −11.94 |
| Real exchange rate (US$/¥)[c] | −9.38 | −9.98 | −10.23 | −10.27 | −10.57 |
| Labor demand[c] | −0.41 | −0.00 | −0.00 | −0.00 | −0.00 |
| *Germany* | | | | | |
| GDP[a] | −0.27 | −0.03 | 0.20 | −0.14 | −0.43 |
| Private consumption[a] | −0.58 | −0.49 | −0.26 | −0.38 | −0.47 |
| Private investment[a] | −0.47 | −0.55 | −0.63 | −0.78 | −0.91 |
| Government consumption[a] | 0.00 | 0.00 | 0.00 | 0.00 | 0.00 |
| Exports[a] | 0.23 | 0.40 | 0.45 | 0.28 | 0.13 |
| Imports[a] | −0.54 | −0.61 | −0.63 | −0.73 | −0.81 |
| Real trade balance[a] | 0.78 | 0.88 | 0.85 | 0.73 | 0.64 |
| Budget deficit[a] | 0.13 | 0.07 | 0.00 | 0.11 | 0.21 |
| Inflation[b] | 0.11 | 0.46 | 0.86 | 0.70 | 0.55 |
| Nominal short-term interest rate[b] | −0.75 | 0.29 | 2.00 | 2.57 | 3.00 |
| Nominal long-term interest rate[b] | 2.60 | 3.10 | 3.51 | 3.74 | 3.92 |
| Real short-term interest rate[b] | −1.17 | −0.53 | 1.30 | 2.02 | 2.55 |
| Real long-term interest rate[b] | 2.16 | 2.69 | 3.17 | 3.46 | 3.69 |
| Exchange rate (US$/DM)[c] | −9.32 | −10.62 | −11.19 | −10.45 | −9.99 |

## Table B-6 *(continued)*

| Model region and variable | Year | | | | |
|---|---|---|---|---|---|
| | 1 | 2 | 3 | 4 | 5 |
| Real exchange rate (US$/DM)[c] | −8.51 | −9.12 | −9.58 | −8.89 | −8.60 |
| Labor demand[c] | −0.45 | −0.02 | 0.41 | −0.09 | −0.46 |
| *REMS* | | | | | |
| GDP[a] | −0.18 | 0.02 | 0.30 | −0.05 | −0.33 |
| Private consumption[a] | −0.75 | −0.67 | −0.30 | −0.42 | −0.50 |
| Private investment[a] | −0.48 | −0.57 | −0.64 | −0.80 | −0.93 |
| Government consumption[a] | 0.00 | 0.00 | 0.00 | 0.00 | 0.00 |
| Exports[a] | 0.22 | 0.34 | 0.34 | 0.16 | 0.01 |
| Imports[a] | −0.82 | −0.92 | −0.91 | −1.01 | −1.08 |
| Trade balance[a] | 0.89 | 0.98 | 0.88 | 0.76 | 0.66 |
| Budget deficit[a] | 0.15 | 0.11 | 0.03 | 0.14 | 0.23 |
| Inflation[b] | 0.21 | 0.52 | 0.92 | 0.74 | 0.58 |
| Nominal short-term interest rate[b] | −0.75 | 0.29 | 2.00 | 2.57 | 3.00 |
| Nominal long-term interest rate[b] | 2.60 | 3.10 | 3.51 | 3.74 | 3.92 |
| Real short-term interest rate[b] | −1.22 | −0.60 | 1.26 | 1.99 | 2.53 |
| Real long-term interest rate[b] | 2.14 | 2.67 | 3.16 | 3.46 | 3.69 |
| Money[c] | −0.08 | −0.09 | 0.01 | 0.04 | 0.07 |
| Exchange rate (US$/ems)[c] | −9.32 | −10.62 | −11.19 | −10.45 | −9.99 |
| Real exchange rate (US$/ems)[c] | −8.52 | −9.09 | −9.48 | −8.75 | −8.43 |
| Labor demand[c] | −0.53 | −0.19 | 0.29 | −0.23 | −0.60 |
| *ROECD* | | | | | |
| GDP[a] | −0.38 | −0.06 | 0.19 | −0.12 | −0.36 |
| Private consumption[a] | −0.48 | −0.37 | −0.24 | −0.33 | −0.39 |
| Private investment[a] | −0.46 | −0.52 | −0.60 | −0.74 | −0.86 |
| Government consumption[a] | 0.00 | 0.00 | 0.00 | 0.00 | 0.00 |
| Exports[a] | 0.14 | 0.38 | 0.54 | 0.41 | 0.29 |
| Imports[a] | −0.42 | −0.45 | −0.49 | −0.55 | −0.60 |
| Trade balance[a] | 0.66 | 0.80 | 0.88 | 0.77 | 0.71 |
| Budget deficit[a] | 0.13 | 0.03 | −0.04 | 0.05 | 0.13 |
| Inflation[b] | −0.02 | 0.37 | 0.81 | 0.64 | 0.50 |
| Nominal short-term interest rate[b] | −0.89 | 0.19 | 1.89 | 2.51 | 2.97 |
| Nominal long-term interest rate[b] | 2.56 | 3.08 | 3.50 | 3.75 | 3.94 |
| Real short-term interest rate[b] | −1.22 | −0.59 | 1.21 | 1.99 | 2.57 |
| Real long-term interest rate[b] | 2.19 | 2.74 | 3.24 | 3.55 | 3.80 |
| Exchange rate (US$/roe)[c] | −8.12 | −9.28 | −9.75 | −8.90 | −8.38 |
| Real exchange rate (US$/roe)[c] | −7.38 | −7.95 | −8.35 | −7.57 | −7.24 |
| Labor demand[c] | −0.53 | 0.06 | 0.52 | 0.08 | −0.25 |
| *LDCs* | | | | | |
| Trade balance[d] | −0.35 | −0.21 | 0.30 | 0.42 | 0.52 |
| Terms of trade[c] | −6.21 | −6.35 | −6.23 | −6.02 | −6.05 |
| *OPEC* | | | | | |
| Trade balance[d] | 0.02 | −0.05 | −0.30 | −0.29 | −0.30 |
| Terms of trade[c] | −6.33 | −6.74 | −7.41 | −7.29 | −7.41 |

Source: See table B-1.
a. As percent of real GDP.
b. Absolute deviation.
c. Percentage deviation.
d. As percent of U.S. GDP.

Table B-7. *Announced Gradual Japanese Fiscal Expansion of 3 Percent of GDP over Three Years*
Deviation from baseline

| Model region and variable | Year | | | | |
|---|---|---|---|---|---|
| | 1 | 2 | 3 | 4 | 5 |
| *United States* | | | | | |
| GDP[a] | −0.19 | −0.18 | −0.23 | −0.44 | −0.58 |
| Private consumption[a] | −0.27 | −0.36 | −0.54 | −0.69 | −0.78 |
| Private investment[a] | −0.25 | −0.32 | −0.42 | −0.52 | −0.58 |
| Government consumption[a] | 0.00 | 0.00 | 0.00 | 0.00 | 0.00 |
| Exports[a] | 0.10 | 0.14 | 0.15 | 0.12 | 0.11 |
| Imports[a] | −0.23 | −0.37 | −0.58 | −0.65 | −0.68 |
| Trade balance[a] | 0.17 | 0.22 | 0.23 | 0.21 | 0.21 |
| Budget deficit[a] | 0.09 | 0.10 | 0.14 | 0.21 | 0.26 |
| Inflation[b] | 0.22 | 0.43 | 0.69 | 0.51 | 0.34 |
| Nominal short-term interest rate[b] | −0.30 | 0.21 | 0.90 | 1.33 | 1.62 |
| Nominal long-term interest rate[b] | 1.34 | 1.56 | 1.74 | 1.84 | 1.90 |
| Real short-term interest rate[b] | −0.65 | −0.34 | 0.42 | 1.00 | 1.43 |
| Real long-term interest rate[b] | 1.14 | 1.41 | 1.65 | 1.80 | 1.90 |
| Labor demand[c] | −0.18 | −0.15 | −0.25 | −0.58 | −0.75 |
| *Japan* | | | | | |
| GDP[a] | −0.96 | −0.01 | −0.06 | −0.14 | −0.18 |
| Private consumption[a] | −0.26 | 0.08 | 0.39 | 0.29 | 0.21 |
| Private investment[a] | −0.23 | −0.07 | −0.29 | −0.31 | −0.33 |
| Government consumption[a] | 1.00 | 2.00 | 3.00 | 3.00 | 3.00 |
| Exports[a] | −0.89 | −1.18 | −1.91 | −1.91 | −1.89 |
| Imports[a] | 0.58 | 0.84 | 1.26 | 1.21 | 1.17 |
| Trade balance[a] | −1.30 | −1.54 | −2.24 | −2.05 | −1.96 |
| Budget deficit[a] | 1.20 | 1.85 | 2.80 | 2.83 | 2.85 |
| Inflation[b] | −1.36 | −0.91 | 2.29 | −0.00 | 0.10 |
| Nominal short-term interest rate[b] | −2.74 | −2.28 | 2.20 | 1.99 | 2.02 |
| Nominal long-term interest rate[b] | 1.18 | 1.68 | 2.14 | 2.14 | 2.16 |
| Real short-term interest rate[b] | −1.92 | −4.79 | 2.22 | 1.91 | 1.93 |
| Real long-term interest rate[b] | 0.97 | 1.38 | 2.10 | 2.09 | 2.12 |
| Exchange rate (US$/¥)[c] | 12.41 | 14.84 | 17.33 | 16.04 | 15.37 |
| Real exchange rate (US$/¥)[c] | 11.29 | 12.56 | 17.01 | 15.21 | 14.29 |
| Labor demand[c] | −1.64 | 0.00 | 0.00 | 0.00 | 0.00 |
| *Germany* | | | | | |
| GDP[a] | −0.22 | −0.17 | −0.24 | −0.40 | −0.53 |
| Private consumption[a] | −0.36 | −0.34 | −0.39 | −0.41 | −0.43 |
| Private investment[a] | −0.22 | −0.28 | −0.37 | −0.45 | −0.51 |
| Government consumption[a] | 0.00 | 0.00 | 0.00 | 0.00 | 0.00 |
| Exports[a] | 0.03 | 0.07 | −0.01 | −0.09 | −0.16 |
| Imports[a] | −0.33 | −0.38 | −0.52 | −0.55 | −0.56 |
| Real trade balance[a] | 0.21 | 0.25 | 0.20 | 0.15 | 0.10 |
| Budget deficit[a] | 0.09 | 0.08 | 0.12 | 0.17 | 0.21 |
| Inflation[b] | 0.19 | 0.33 | 0.53 | 0.41 | 0.31 |
| Nominal short-term interest rate[b] | −0.43 | 0.13 | 0.67 | 1.12 | 1.45 |
| Nominal long-term interest rate[b] | 1.20 | 1.43 | 1.61 | 1.73 | 1.80 |
| Real short-term interest rate[b] | −0.74 | −0.32 | 0.25 | 0.79 | 1.20 |
| Real long-term interest rate[b] | 0.97 | 1.23 | 1.45 | 1.61 | 1.72 |
| Exchange rate (US$/DM)[c] | 0.15 | 0.28 | 0.37 | 0.60 | 0.80 |

## Table B-7 *(continued)*

| Model region and variable | | Year | | | |
|---|---|---|---|---|---|
| | *1* | *2* | *3* | *4* | *5* |
| Real exchange rate (US$/DM)[c] | 0.08 | 0.17 | 0.14 | 0.31 | 0.52 |
| Labor demand[c] | −0.26 | −0.14 | −0.21 | −0.43 | −0.60 |
| *REMS* | | | | | |
| GDP[a] | −0.28 | −0.25 | −0.31 | −0.44 | −0.56 |
| Private consumption[a] | −0.40 | −0.39 | −0.41 | −0.41 | −0.41 |
| Private investment[a] | −0.23 | −0.29 | −0.37 | −0.45 | −0.51 |
| Government consumption[a] | 0.00 | 0.00 | 0.00 | 0.00 | 0.00 |
| Exports[a] | 0.03 | 0.07 | 0.00 | −0.08 | −0.13 |
| Imports[a] | −0.32 | −0.37 | −0.47 | −0.48 | −0.49 |
| Trade balance[a] | 0.23 | 0.26 | 0.21 | 0.16 | 0.11 |
| Budget deficit[a] | 0.11 | 0.10 | 0.13 | 0.16 | 0.20 |
| Inflation[b] | 0.17 | 0.31 | 0.50 | 0.40 | 0.31 |
| Nominal short-term interest rate[b] | −0.43 | 0.13 | 0.67 | 1.12 | 1.45 |
| Nominal long-term interest rate[b] | 1.20 | 1.43 | 1.61 | 1.73 | 1.80 |
| Real short-term interest rate[b] | −0.72 | −0.31 | 0.26 | 0.79 | 1.20 |
| Real long-term interest rate[b] | 0.98 | 1.24 | 1.46 | 1.62 | 1.73 |
| Money[c] | −0.04 | −0.07 | −0.05 | −0.03 | −0.01 |
| Exchange rate (US$/ems)[c] | 0.15 | 0.28 | 0.37 | 0.60 | 0.80 |
| Real exchange rate (US$/ems)[c] | 0.09 | 0.16 | 0.12 | 0.28 | 0.49 |
| Labor demand[c] | −0.30 | −0.19 | −0.21 | −0.39 | −0.54 |
| *ROECD* | | | | | |
| GDP[a] | −0.27 | −0.20 | −0.21 | −0.33 | −0.42 |
| Private consumption[a] | −0.27 | −0.26 | −0.30 | −0.34 | −0.36 |
| Private investment[a] | −0.23 | −0.28 | −0.35 | −0.42 | −0.48 |
| Government consumption[a] | 0.00 | 0.00 | 0.00 | 0.00 | 0.00 |
| Exports[a] | 0.01 | 0.08 | 0.06 | 0.02 | −0.02 |
| Imports[a] | −0.22 | −0.27 | −0.38 | −0.41 | −0.44 |
| Trade balance[a] | 0.17 | 0.25 | 0.27 | 0.26 | 0.25 |
| Budget deficit[a] | 0.09 | 0.07 | 0.08 | 0.12 | 0.15 |
| Inflation[b] | 0.08 | 0.26 | 0.50 | 0.37 | 0.28 |
| Nominal short-term interest rate[b] | −0.44 | 0.05 | 0.70 | 1.14 | 1.47 |
| Nominal long-term interest rate[b] | 1.21 | 1.45 | 1.63 | 1.75 | 1.83 |
| Real short-term interest rate[b] | −0.66 | −0.39 | 0.32 | 0.86 | 1.27 |
| Real long-term interest rate[b] | 1.04 | 1.30 | 1.53 | 1.69 | 1.80 |
| Exchange rate (US$/roe)[c] | 0.66 | 0.79 | 0.96 | 1.15 | 1.33 |
| Real exchange rate (US$/roe)[c] | 0.59 | 0.60 | 0.64 | 0.74 | 0.88 |
| Labor demand[c] | −0.26 | −0.08 | −0.03 | −0.21 | −0.32 |
| *LDCs* | | | | | |
| Trade balance[d] | −0.16 | −0.17 | 0.15 | 0.24 | 0.31 |
| Terms of trade[c] | 2.11 | 2.48 | 3.37 | 3.12 | 3.06 |
| *OPEC* | | | | | |
| Trade balance[d] | 0.13 | 0.12 | 0.03 | −0.06 | −0.13 |
| Terms of trade[c] | 2.56 | 3.00 | 3.56 | 3.12 | 2.92 |

Source: See table B-1.
a. As percent of real GDP.
b. Absolute deviation.
c. Percentage deviation.
d. As percent of U.S. GDP.

Table B-8. *Sustained 1 Percent U.S. Monetary Expansion*
Deviation from baseline

| Model region and variable | Year | | | | |
|---|---|---|---|---|---|
| | 1 | 2 | 3 | 4 | 5 |
| *United States* | | | | | |
| GDP[a] | 0.42 | 0.27 | 0.15 | 0.07 | 0.02 |
| Private consumption[a] | 0.22 | 0.14 | 0.08 | 0.04 | 0.01 |
| Private investment[a] | 0.15 | 0.09 | 0.05 | 0.02 | 0.00 |
| Government consumption[a] | 0.00 | 0.00 | 0.00 | 0.00 | 0.00 |
| Exports[a] | 0.06 | 0.03 | 0.02 | 0.01 | 0.00 |
| Imports[a] | 0.01 | −0.00 | −0.00 | −0.00 | −0.00 |
| Trade balance[a] | 0.03 | 0.01 | 0.00 | 0.00 | −0.00 |
| Budget deficit[a] | −0.13 | −0.08 | −0.05 | −0.02 | −0.01 |
| Inflation[b] | 0.33 | 0.25 | 0.18 | 0.13 | 0.08 |
| Nominal short-term interest rate[b] | −0.46 | −0.29 | −0.17 | −0.08 | −0.02 |
| Nominal long-term interest rate[b] | −0.09 | −0.04 | −0.01 | 0.01 | −0.02 |
| Real short-term interest rate[b] | −0.72 | −0.48 | −0.30 | −0.16 | −0.07 |
| Real long-term interest rate[b] | −0.16 | −0.08 | −0.03 | 0.00 | 0.02 |
| Labor demand[c] | 0.72 | 0.41 | 0.20 | 0.07 | −0.02 |
| *Japan* | | | | | |
| GDP[a] | −0.05 | −0.00 | −0.00 | −0.00 | 0.00 |
| Private consumption[a] | −0.01 | 0.00 | −0.00 | −0.00 | −0.00 |
| Private investment[a] | 0.00 | 0.01 | 0.01 | 0.00 | −0.00 |
| Government consumption[a] | 0.00 | 0.00 | 0.00 | 0.00 | 0.00 |
| Exports[a] | −0.02 | −0.00 | 0.00 | 0.00 | 0.01 |
| Imports[a] | 0.03 | 0.02 | 0.01 | 0.01 | 0.00 |
| Trade balance[a] | −0.05 | −0.01 | 0.00 | 0.01 | 0.01 |
| Budget deficit[a] | 0.01 | −0.00 | −0.00 | −0.00 | −0.00 |
| Inflation[b] | −0.06 | −0.05 | 0.04 | 0.04 | 0.03 |
| Nominal short-term interest rate[b] | −0.12 | −0.16 | −0.10 | −0.05 | −0.01 |
| Nominal long-term interest rate[b] | −0.03 | −0.02 | 0.00 | 0.01 | 0.02 |
| Real short-term interest rate[b] | −0.06 | −0.20 | −0.14 | −0.07 | −0.02 |
| Real long-term interest rate[b] | −0.14 | −0.03 | −0.01 | 0.01 | 0.02 |
| Exchange rate (US$/¥)[c] | 1.50 | 1.16 | 1.03 | 0.96 | 0.93 |
| Real exchange rate (US$/¥)[c] | 1.15 | 0.49 | 0.21 | 0.05 | −0.04 |
| Labor demand[c] | −0.07 | 0.00 | 0.00 | 0.00 | 0.00 |
| *Germany* | | | | | |
| GDP[a] | −0.08 | −0.04 | −0.00 | 0.01 | 0.01 |
| Private consumption[a] | −0.05 | −0.03 | −0.02 | −0.01 | −0.00 |
| Private investment[a] | 0.00 | 0.01 | 0.01 | 0.00 | 0.00 |
| Government consumption[a] | 0.00 | 0.00 | 0.00 | 0.00 | 0.00 |
| Exports[a] | −0.02 | −0.01 | 0.01 | 0.01 | 0.01 |
| Imports[a] | 0.01 | 0.01 | 0.01 | 0.00 | −0.00 |
| Real trade balance[a] | −0.04 | −0.01 | 0.01 | 0.01 | 0.01 |
| Budget deficit[a] | 0.02 | 0.01 | 0.00 | −0.00 | −0.00 |
| Inflation[b] | −0.06 | −0.03 | 0.01 | 0.03 | 0.03 |
| Nominal short-term interest rate[b] | −0.20 | −0.19 | −0.13 | −0.07 | −0.02 |
| Nominal long-term interest rate[b] | −0.05 | −0.03 | −0.00 | 0.01 | 0.02 |
| Real short-term interest rate[b] | −0.17 | −0.19 | −0.15 | −0.10 | −0.05 |
| Real long-term interest rate[b] | −0.06 | −0.04 | −0.02 | 0.00 | 0.01 |
| Exchange rate (US$/DM)[c] | 1.35 | 1.09 | 0.98 | 0.94 | 0.93 |
| Real exchange rate (US$/DM)[c] | 0.99 | 0.44 | 0.15 | 0.01 | −0.06 |
| Labor demand[c] | −0.12 | −0.05 | −0.00 | 0.01 | 0.01 |

## Table B-8 *(continued)*

| Model region and variable | Year | | | | |
| --- | --- | --- | --- | --- | --- |
| | *1* | *2* | *3* | *4* | *5* |
| *REMS* | | | | | |
| GDP[a] | −0.11 | −0.05 | −0.01 | 0.00 | 0.00 |
| Private consumption[a] | −0.10 | −0.06 | −0.04 | −0.02 | −0.01 |
| Private investment[a] | −0.00 | 0.00 | 0.01 | 0.00 | −0.00 |
| Government consumption[a] | 0.00 | 0.00 | 0.00 | 0.00 | 0.00 |
| Exports[a] | −0.02 | 0.00 | 0.01 | 0.02 | 0.01 |
| Imports[a] | −0.00 | −0.00 | −0.00 | −0.00 | −0.01 |
| Trade balance[a] | −0.02 | 0.00 | 0.02 | 0.02 | 0.02 |
| Budget deficit[a] | 0.03 | 0.01 | 0.00 | −0.00 | −0.00 |
| Inflation[b] | −0.07 | −0.03 | 0.01 | 0.03 | 0.03 |
| Nominal short-term interest rate[b] | −0.20 | −0.19 | −0.13 | −0.07 | −0.02 |
| Nominal long-term interest rate[b] | −0.05 | −0.03 | −0.00 | 0.01 | 0.02 |
| Real short-term interest rate[b] | −0.17 | −0.20 | −0.16 | −0.10 | −0.05 |
| Real long-term interest rate[b] | −0.06 | −0.04 | −0.02 | 0.00 | 0.01 |
| Money[c] | −0.04 | −0.03 | −0.02 | −0.01 | −0.01 |
| Exchange rate (US$/ems)[c] | 1.35 | 1.09 | 0.98 | 0.94 | 0.93 |
| Real exchange rate (US$/ems)[c] | 0.97 | 0.43 | 0.14 | 0.00 | −0.06 |
| Labor demand[c] | −0.16 | −0.07 | −0.01 | 0.01 | 0.01 |
| *ROECD* | | | | | |
| GDP[a] | −0.06 | −0.02 | 0.00 | 0.01 | 0.01 |
| Private consumption[a] | 0.00 | −0.00 | 0.00 | −0.00 | −0.00 |
| Private investment[a] | 0.00 | 0.01 | 0.01 | 0.01 | −0.00 |
| Government consumption[a] | 0.00 | 0.00 | 0.00 | 0.00 | 0.00 |
| Exports[a] | −0.03 | −0.01 | 0.00 | 0.01 | 0.01 |
| Imports[a] | 0.04 | 0.02 | 0.01 | 0.00 | −0.00 |
| Trade balance[a] | −0.07 | −0.02 | 0.00 | 0.01 | 0.01 |
| Budget deficit[a] | 0.02 | 0.01 | −0.00 | −0.00 | −0.00 |
| Inflation[b] | −0.09 | −0.02 | 0.02 | 0.03 | 0.03 |
| Nominal short-term interest rate[b] | −0.17 | −0.18 | −0.13 | −0.07 | −0.03 |
| Nominal long-term interest rate[b] | −0.04 | −0.03 | −0.00 | 0.01 | 0.02 |
| Real short-term interest rate[b] | −0.13 | −0.19 | −0.16 | −0.11 | −0.05 |
| Real long-term interest rate[b] | −0.05 | −0.04 | −0.02 | 0.00 | 0.02 |
| Exchange rate (US$/roe)[c] | 1.38 | 1.09 | 0.98 | 0.94 | 0.93 |
| Real exchange rate (US$/roe)[c] | 1.02 | 0.43 | 0.14 | 0.00 | −0.06 |
| Labor demand[c] | −0.10 | −0.03 | 0.01 | 0.02 | 0.01 |
| *LDCs* | | | | | |
| Trade balance[d] | −0.08 | −0.06 | −0.04 | −0.03 | −0.01 |
| Terms of trade[c] | 0.70 | 0.30 | 0.12 | 0.02 | −0.03 |
| *OPEC* | | | | | |
| Trade balance[d] | 0.09 | 0.05 | 0.02 | 0.00 | −0.01 |
| Terms of trade[c] | 0.90 | 0.43 | 0.19 | 0.05 | −0.02 |

Source: See table B-1.
a. As percent of real GDP.
b. Absolute deviation.
c. Percentage deviation.
d. As percent of U.S. GDP.

Table B-9. *Sustained 1 Percent Japanese Monetary Expansion*
Deviation from baseline

| Model region and variable | Year | | | | |
|---|---|---|---|---|---|
| | 1 | 2 | 3 | 4 | 5 |
| *United States* | | | | | |
| GDP[a] | −0.00 | 0.01 | −0.00 | −0.01 | −0.01 |
| Private consumption[a] | 0.01 | 0.00 | −0.00 | −0.00 | −0.00 |
| Private investment[a] | 0.00 | 0.00 | −0.00 | −0.00 | −0.00 |
| Government consumption[a] | 0.00 | 0.00 | 0.00 | 0.00 | 0.00 |
| Exports[a] | 0.00 | 0.00 | −0.00 | −0.00 | −0.00 |
| Imports[a] | 0.02 | −0.00 | 0.00 | 0.00 | 0.00 |
| Trade balance[a] | −0.00 | −0.00 | 0.00 | 0.00 | 0.00 |
| Budget deficit[a] | −0.00 | −0.00 | 0.00 | 0.00 | 0.00 |
| Inflation[b] | −0.03 | 0.02 | 0.01 | 0.01 | 0.00 |
| Nominal short-term interest rate[b] | −0.02 | −0.01 | −0.00 | 0.00 | 0.00 |
| Nominal long-term interest rate[b] | −0.00 | 0.00 | 0.00 | 0.00 | 0.00 |
| Real short-term interest rate[b] | −0.03 | −0.02 | −0.01 | −0.00 | 0.00 |
| Real long-term interest rate[b] | −0.00 | 0.00 | 0.00 | 0.00 | 0.00 |
| Labor demand[c] | −0.01 | 0.01 | −0.01 | −0.01 | −0.01 |
| *Japan* | | | | | |
| GDP[a] | 0.42 | 0.01 | 0.01 | 0.01 | 0.01 |
| Private consumption[a] | 0.13 | 0.00 | 0.00 | 0.00 | 0.00 |
| Private investment[a] | 0.14 | 0.01 | 0.00 | 0.00 | 0.00 |
| Government consumption[a] | 0.00 | 0.00 | 0.00 | 0.00 | 0.00 |
| Exports[a] | 0.11 | 0.00 | 0.00 | 0.01 | 0.01 |
| Imports[a] | −0.04 | −0.00 | −0.00 | −0.00 | −0.00 |
| Trade balance[a] | 0.13 | 0.01 | 0.00 | 0.00 | −0.00 |
| Budget deficit[a] | −0.12 | −0.00 | −0.00 | −0.00 | −0.00 |
| Inflation[b] | 0.33 | 0.63 | 0.02 | 0.01 | 0.00 |
| Nominal short-term interest rate[b] | −0.53 | −0.04 | −0.02 | −0.00 | 0.00 |
| Nominal long-term interest rate[b] | −0.06 | −0.00 | −0.00 | −0.00 | −0.00 |
| Real short-term interest rate[b] | −1.20 | −0.06 | −0.03 | −0.01 | −0.00 |
| Real long-term interest rate[b] | −0.13 | −0.01 | 0.00 | 0.00 | 0.00 |
| Exchange rate (US$/¥)[c] | −1.55 | −1.04 | −1.01 | −0.99 | −0.99 |
| Real exchange rate (US$/¥)[c] | −1.24 | −0.07 | −0.03 | −0.02 | −0.01 |
| Labor demand[c] | 0.68 | 0.00 | 0.00 | 0.00 | 0.00 |
| *Germany* | | | | | |
| GDP[a] | 0.00 | 0.00 | −0.00 | −0.00 | −0.01 |
| Private consumption[a] | 0.01 | 0.00 | −0.00 | −0.00 | −0.00 |
| Private investment[a] | 0.00 | 0.00 | 0.00 | −0.00 | −0.00 |
| Government consumption[a] | 0.00 | 0.00 | 0.00 | 0.00 | 0.00 |
| Exports[a] | 0.01 | 0.00 | 0.00 | −0.00 | −0.00 |
| Imports[a] | 0.02 | 0.00 | −0.00 | −0.00 | −0.00 |
| Real trade balance[a] | 0.00 | 0.00 | 0.00 | 0.00 | −0.00 |
| Budget deficit[a] | −0.00 | −0.00 | 0.00 | 0.00 | 0.00 |
| Inflation[b] | −0.03 | 0.01 | 0.01 | 0.01 | 0.00 |
| Nominal short-term interest rate[b] | −0.00 | −0.01 | −0.01 | −0.00 | 0.00 |
| Nominal long-term interest rate[b] | 0.00 | 0.00 | 0.00 | 0.00 | 0.00 |
| Real short-term interest rate[b] | −0.00 | −0.02 | −0.01 | −0.01 | −0.00 |
| Real long-term interest rate[b] | −0.00 | −0.00 | 0.00 | 0.00 | 0.00 |
| Exchange rate (US$/DM)[c] | 0.01 | −0.01 | −0.00 | 0.00 | 0.00 |
| Real exchange rate (US$/DM)[c] | 0.02 | −0.01 | −0.01 | −0.00 | 0.00 |
| Labor demand[c] | −0.00 | 0.01 | −0.00 | −0.01 | −0.01 |

## Table B-9 *(continued)*

| Model region and variable | Year 1 | 2 | 3 | 4 | 5 |
|---|---|---|---|---|---|
| **REMS** | | | | | |
| GDP[a] | 0.01 | 0.00 | −0.00 | −0.00 | −0.01 |
| Private consumption[a] | 0.01 | −0.00 | −0.00 | −0.00 | −0.00 |
| Private investment[a] | 0.00 | 0.00 | 0.00 | −0.00 | −0.00 |
| Government consumption[a] | 0.00 | 0.00 | 0.00 | 0.00 | 0.00 |
| Exports[a] | 0.01 | 0.00 | 0.00 | −0.00 | −0.00 |
| Imports[a] | 0.01 | 0.00 | −0.00 | −0.00 | −0.00 |
| Trade balance[a] | 0.00 | 0.00 | 0.00 | 0.00 | −0.00 |
| Budget deficit[a] | −0.00 | −0.00 | 0.00 | 0.00 | 0.00 |
| Inflation[b] | −0.03 | 0.01 | 0.01 | 0.01 | 0.00 |
| Nominal short-term interest rate[b] | −0.00 | −0.01 | −0.01 | −0.00 | 0.00 |
| Nominal long-term interest rate[b] | 0.00 | 0.00 | 0.00 | 0.00 | 0.00 |
| Real short-term interest rate[b] | −0.00 | −0.02 | −0.01 | −0.01 | −0.00 |
| Real long-term interest rate[b] | −0.00 | −0.00 | 0.00 | 0.00 | 0.00 |
| Money[c] | −0.00 | −0.00 | −0.00 | 0.00 | 0.00 |
| Exchange rate (US$/ems)[c] | 0.01 | −0.01 | −0.00 | 0.00 | 0.00 |
| Real exchange rate (US$/ems)[c] | 0.02 | −0.01 | −0.01 | −0.00 | 0.00 |
| Labor demand[c] | −0.00 | 0.00 | −0.00 | −0.01 | −0.01 |
| **ROECD** | | | | | |
| GDP[a] | 0.00 | 0.00 | −0.00 | −0.01 | −0.01 |
| Private consumption[a] | 0.01 | 0.00 | −0.00 | −0.00 | −0.00 |
| Private investment[a] | 0.00 | 0.00 | −0.00 | −0.00 | −0.00 |
| Government consumption[a] | 0.00 | 0.00 | 0.00 | 0.00 | 0.00 |
| Exports[a] | 0.01 | 0.00 | −0.00 | −0.00 | −0.00 |
| Imports[a] | 0.01 | 0.00 | 0.00 | −0.00 | −0.00 |
| Trade balance[a] | 0.00 | −0.00 | 0.00 | 0.00 | 0.00 |
| Budget deficit[a] | −0.00 | −0.00 | 0.00 | 0.00 | 0.00 |
| Inflation[b] | −0.03 | 0.02 | 0.01 | 0.01 | 0.00 |
| Nominal short-term interest rate[b] | −0.02 | −0.01 | −0.01 | −0.00 | 0.00 |
| Nominal long-term interest rate[b] | −0.00 | 0.00 | 0.00 | 0.00 | 0.00 |
| Real short-term interest rate[b] | −0.03 | −0.03 | −0.01 | −0.00 | 0.00 |
| Real long-term interest rate[b] | −0.00 | 0.00 | 0.00 | 0.00 | 0.00 |
| Exchange rate (US$/roe)[c] | −0.00 | −0.01 | −0.00 | 0.00 | 0.01 |
| Real exchange rate (US$/roe)[c] | −0.00 | −0.01 | −0.00 | 0.00 | 0.00 |
| Labor demand[c] | −0.01 | 0.00 | −0.01 | −0.01 | −0.01 |
| **LDCs** | | | | | |
| Trade balance[d] | −0.04 | −0.01 | −0.00 | −0.00 | 0.00 |
| Terms of trade[c] | −0.21 | −0.02 | −0.01 | −0.00 | −0.00 |
| **OPEC** | | | | | |
| Trade balance[d] | 0.00 | 0.00 | 0.00 | 0.00 | 0.00 |
| Terms of trade[c] | −0.17 | −0.01 | −0.01 | −0.00 | −0.00 |

Source: See table B-1.
a. As percent of real GDP.
b. Absolute deviation.
c. Percentage deviation.
d. As percent of U.S. GDP.

Table B-10. *Sustained 1 Percent German Monetary Expansion*
Deviation from baseline

| Model region and variable | Year | | | | |
|---|---|---|---|---|---|
| | 1 | 2 | 3 | 4 | 5 |
| *United States* | | | | | |
| GDP[a] | 0.01 | 0.01 | 0.01 | 0.01 | 0.01 |
| Private consumption[a] | 0.02 | 0.02 | 0.02 | 0.02 | 0.02 |
| Private investment[a] | 0.01 | 0.01 | 0.01 | 0.01 | 0.01 |
| Government consumption[a] | 0.00 | 0.00 | 0.00 | 0.00 | 0.00 |
| Exports[a] | −0.00 | −0.00 | −0.00 | −0.00 | −0.00 |
| Imports[a] | 0.02 | 0.02 | 0.02 | 0.02 | 0.02 |
| Trade balance[a] | −0.01 | −0.01 | −0.00 | −0.00 | −0.00 |
| Budget deficit[a] | −0.00 | −0.01 | −0.01 | −0.01 | −0.01 |
| Inflation[b] | −0.04 | −0.02 | −0.00 | 0.00 | 0.01 |
| Nominal short-term interest rate[b] | −0.03 | −0.05 | −0.05 | −0.05 | −0.04 |
| Nominal long-term interest rate[b] | −0.04 | −0.04 | −0.04 | −0.04 | −0.04 |
| Real short-term interest rate[b] | −0.02 | −0.05 | −0.05 | −0.05 | −0.05 |
| Real long-term interest rate[b] | −0.04 | −0.04 | −0.04 | −0.04 | −0.04 |
| Labor demand[c] | −0.02 | 0.01 | 0.01 | 0.01 | 0.01 |
| *Japan* | | | | | |
| GDP[a] | 0.00 | 0.00 | 0.00 | 0.00 | 0.00 |
| Private consumption[a] | 0.01 | 0.01 | 0.01 | 0.01 | 0.01 |
| Private investment[a] | 0.01 | 0.01 | 0.01 | 0.01 | 0.01 |
| Government consumption[a] | 0.00 | 0.00 | 0.00 | 0.00 | 0.00 |
| Exports[a] | −0.00 | −0.00 | −0.00 | −0.00 | −0.00 |
| Imports[a] | 0.02 | 0.02 | 0.01 | 0.01 | 0.01 |
| Trade balance[a] | −0.01 | −0.01 | −0.01 | −0.00 | −0.00 |
| Budget deficit[a] | −0.00 | −0.00 | −0.00 | −0.00 | −0.00 |
| Inflation[b] | −0.04 | −0.01 | 0.00 | 0.00 | 0.00 |
| Nominal short-term interest rate[b] | −0.02 | −0.04 | −0.05 | −0.04 | −0.04 |
| Nominal long-term interest rate[b] | −0.04 | −0.04 | −0.04 | −0.04 | −0.03 |
| Real short-term interest rate[b] | −0.01 | −0.04 | −0.05 | −0.05 | −0.04 |
| Real long-term interest rate[b] | −0.04 | −0.04 | −0.04 | −0.04 | −0.03 |
| Exchange rate (US$/¥)[c] | 0.04 | 0.03 | 0.02 | 0.02 | 0.01 |
| Real exchange rate (US$/¥)[c] | 0.05 | 0.04 | 0.04 | 0.03 | 0.02 |
| Labor demand[c] | −0.01 | 0.00 | 0.00 | 0.00 | 0.00 |
| *Germany* | | | | | |
| GDP[a] | 0.49 | 0.33 | 0.25 | 0.22 | 0.20 |
| Private consumption[a] | 0.16 | 0.12 | 0.09 | 0.08 | 0.08 |
| Private investment[a] | 0.15 | 0.10 | 0.07 | 0.06 | 0.06 |
| Government consumption[a] | 0.00 | 0.00 | 0.00 | 0.00 | 0.00 |
| Exports[a] | 0.21 | 0.14 | 0.10 | 0.09 | 0.08 |
| Imports[a] | 0.04 | 0.02 | 0.02 | 0.02 | 0.02 |
| Real trade balance[a] | 0.15 | 0.08 | 0.04 | 0.03 | 0.03 |
| Budget deficit[a] | −0.15 | −0.10 | −0.08 | −0.07 | −0.06 |
| Inflation[b] | 0.40 | 0.23 | 0.11 | 0.05 | 0.02 |
| Nominal short-term interest rate[b] | −0.33 | −0.17 | −0.10 | −0.06 | −0.05 |
| Nominal long-term interest rate[b] | −0.09 | −0.06 | −0.05 | −0.04 | −0.04 |
| Real short-term interest rate[b] | −0.58 | −0.29 | −0.15 | −0.09 | −0.06 |
| Real long-term interest rate[b] | −0.14 | −0.08 | −0.06 | −0.04 | −0.04 |
| Exchange rate (US$/DM)[c] | −1.59 | −1.29 | −1.17 | −1.13 | −1.11 |
| Real exchange rate (US$/DM)[c] | −1.23 | −0.66 | −0.42 | −0.33 | −0.29 |
| Labor demand[c] | 0.80 | 0.50 | 0.36 | 0.29 | 0.27 |

## Table B-10 *(continued)*

| Model region and variable | Year 1 | 2 | 3 | 4 | 5 |
|---|---|---|---|---|---|
| **REMS** | | | | | |
| GDP[a] | 0.52 | 0.32 | 0.24 | 0.22 | 0.21 |
| Private consumption[a] | 0.16 | 0.11 | 0.09 | 0.08 | 0.08 |
| Private investment[a] | 0.16 | 0.09 | 0.07 | 0.06 | 0.05 |
| Government consumption[a] | 0.00 | 0.00 | 0.00 | 0.00 | 0.00 |
| Exports[a] | 0.20 | 0.12 | 0.09 | 0.08 | 0.07 |
| Imports[a] | −0.01 | 0.01 | 0.00 | 0.00 | 0.00 |
| Trade balance[a] | 0.14 | 0.06 | 0.03 | 0.02 | 0.01 |
| Budget deficit[a] | −0.15 | −0.09 | −0.07 | −0.06 | −0.06 |
| Inflation[b] | 0.46 | 0.22 | 0.09 | 0.04 | 0.02 |
| Nominal short-term interest rate[b] | −0.33 | −0.17 | −0.10 | −0.06 | −0.05 |
| Nominal long-term interest rate[b] | −0.09 | −0.06 | −0.05 | −0.04 | −0.04 |
| Real short-term interest rate[b] | −0.60 | −0.28 | −0.14 | −0.08 | −0.06 |
| Real long-term interest rate[b] | −0.14 | −0.08 | −0.05 | −0.04 | −0.04 |
| Money[c] | 1.03 | 1.02 | 1.01 | 1.01 | 1.01 |
| Exchange rate (US$/ems)[c] | −1.59 | −1.29 | −1.17 | −1.13 | −1.11 |
| Real exchange rate (US$/ems)[c] | −1.22 | −0.63 | −0.40 | −0.31 | −0.28 |
| Labor demand[c] | 0.83 | 0.48 | 0.34 | 0.29 | 0.27 |
| **ROECD** | | | | | |
| GDP[a] | −0.07 | 0.00 | 0.00 | −0.01 | −0.01 |
| Private consumption[a] | 0.02 | 0.02 | 0.02 | 0.01 | 0.01 |
| Private investment[a] | 0.00 | 0.02 | 0.01 | 0.01 | 0.01 |
| Government consumption[a] | 0.00 | 0.00 | 0.00 | 0.00 | 0.00 |
| Exports[a] | −0.00 | 0.02 | 0.01 | 0.01 | 0.01 |
| Imports[a] | 0.09 | 0.06 | 0.04 | 0.04 | 0.04 |
| Trade balance[a] | −0.03 | −0.00 | 0.00 | 0.01 | 0.01 |
| Budget deficit[a] | 0.01 | −0.00 | −0.00 | −0.00 | 0.00 |
| Inflation[b] | −0.12 | 0.01 | 0.03 | 0.02 | 0.01 |
| Nominal short-term interest rate[b] | −0.13 | −0.10 | −0.07 | −0.06 | −0.05 |
| Nominal long-term interest rate[b] | −0.06 | −0.05 | −0.04 | −0.04 | −0.04 |
| Real short-term interest rate[b] | −0.09 | −0.11 | −0.09 | −0.07 | −0.05 |
| Real long-term interest rate[b] | −0.06 | −0.05 | −0.05 | −0.04 | −0.04 |
| Exchange rate (US$/roe)[c] | −0.28 | −0.18 | −0.14 | −0.12 | −0.11 |
| Real exchange rate (US$/roe)[c] | −0.28 | −0.21 | −0.14 | −0.11 | −0.09 |
| Labor demand[c] | −0.08 | 0.02 | 0.02 | 0.00 | −0.01 |
| **LDCs** | | | | | |
| Trade balance[d] | −0.04 | −0.03 | −0.02 | −0.01 | −0.01 |
| Terms of trade[c] | −0.39 | −0.21 | −0.13 | −0.10 | −0.09 |
| **OPEC** | | | | | |
| Trade balance[d] | −0.00 | 0.00 | 0.01 | 0.01 | 0.00 |
| Terms of trade[c] | −0.38 | −0.19 | −0.12 | −0.09 | −0.08 |

Source: See table B-1.
a. As percent of real GDP.
b. Absolute deviation.
c. Percentage deviation.
d. As percent of U.S. GDP.

**Table B-11.** *Sustained 1 Percent ROECD Monetary Expansion*
Deviation from baseline

| Model region and variable | Year | | | | |
|---|---|---|---|---|---|
| | 1 | 2 | 3 | 4 | 5 |
| *United States* | | | | | |
| GDP[a] | −0.01 | 0.00 | 0.01 | 0.00 | 0.00 |
| Private consumption[a] | 0.01 | 0.01 | 0.01 | 0.01 | 0.00 |
| Private investment[a] | 0.00 | 0.01 | 0.01 | 0.00 | 0.00 |
| Government consumption[a] | 0.00 | 0.00 | 0.00 | 0.00 | 0.00 |
| Exports[a] | −0.01 | −0.00 | 0.00 | 0.00 | 0.00 |
| Imports[a] | 0.02 | 0.02 | 0.01 | 0.01 | 0.01 |
| Trade balance[a] | −0.02 | −0.00 | −0.00 | 0.00 | 0.00 |
| Budget deficit[a] | 0.00 | −0.00 | −0.00 | −0.00 | −0.00 |
| Inflation[b] | −0.04 | −0.01 | 0.00 | 0.01 | 0.01 |
| Nominal short-term interest rate[b] | −0.05 | −0.05 | −0.04 | −0.03 | −0.02 |
| Nominal long-term interest rate[b] | −0.02 | −0.01 | −0.01 | 0.00 | 0.00 |
| Real short-term interest rate[b] | −0.03 | −0.05 | −0.05 | −0.04 | −0.03 |
| Real long-term interest rate[b] | −0.02 | −0.02 | −0.01 | −0.01 | 0.00 |
| Labor demand[c] | −0.03 | 0.00 | 0.01 | 0.01 | 0.00 |
| *Japan* | | | | | |
| GDP[a] | −0.01 | −0.00 | −0.00 | −0.00 | 0.00 |
| Private consumption[a] | 0.01 | 0.01 | 0.00 | 0.00 | −0.00 |
| Private investment[a] | 0.00 | 0.01 | 0.00 | 0.00 | 0.00 |
| Government consumption[a] | 0.00 | 0.00 | 0.00 | 0.00 | 0.00 |
| Exports[a] | −0.00 | 0.00 | 0.00 | 0.00 | 0.00 |
| Imports[a] | 0.02 | 0.01 | 0.01 | 0.00 | 0.00 |
| Trade balance[a] | −0.01 | −0.00 | 0.00 | 0.00 | 0.00 |
| Budget deficit[a] | −0.00 | −0.00 | −0.00 | −0.00 | −0.00 |
| Inflation[b] | −0.03 | −0.01 | 0.01 | 0.01 | 0.01 |
| Nominal short-term interest rate[b] | −0.03 | −0.04 | −0.04 | −0.03 | −0.02 |
| Nominal long-term interest rate[b] | −0.01 | −0.01 | −0.01 | 0.00 | 0.00 |
| Real short-term interest rate[b] | −0.02 | −0.05 | −0.04 | −0.03 | −0.02 |
| Real long-term interest rate[b] | −0.02 | −0.01 | −0.01 | 0.00 | 0.00 |
| Exchange rate (US$/¥)[c] | 0.04 | 0.02 | 0.01 | 0.00 | −0.00 |
| Real exchange rate (US$/¥)[c] | 0.04 | 0.02 | 0.02 | 0.01 | 0.00 |
| Labor demand[c] | −0.02 | 0.00 | 0.00 | 0.00 | 0.00 |
| *Germany* | | | | | |
| GDP[a] | −0.04 | −0.00 | 0.01 | 0.00 | −0.00 |
| Private consumption[a] | 0.00 | 0.00 | 0.00 | −0.00 | −0.01 |
| Private investment[a] | 0.00 | 0.01 | 0.01 | 0.00 | 0.00 |
| Government consumption[a] | 0.00 | 0.00 | 0.00 | 0.00 | 0.00 |
| Exports[a] | −0.01 | 0.01 | 0.01 | 0.01 | 0.00 |
| Imports[a] | 0.03 | 0.02 | 0.01 | 0.00 | 0.00 |
| Real trade balance[a] | −0.02 | 0.00 | 0.01 | 0.01 | 0.01 |
| Budget deficit[a] | 0.01 | −0.00 | −0.00 | −0.00 | 0.00 |
| Inflation[b] | −0.07 | −0.01 | 0.02 | 0.02 | 0.02 |
| Nominal short-term interest rate[b] | −0.09 | −0.09 | −0.07 | −0.05 | −0.03 |
| Nominal long-term interest rate[b] | −0.03 | −0.02 | −0.01 | −0.01 | 0.00 |
| Real short-term interest rate[b] | −0.07 | −0.09 | −0.08 | −0.06 | −0.04 |
| Real long-term interest rate[b] | −0.04 | −0.03 | −0.02 | −0.01 | −0.01 |
| Exchange rate (US$/DM)[c] | −0.12 | −0.07 | −0.04 | −0.02 | −0.00 |
| Real exchange rate (US$/DM)[c] | −0.12 | −0.09 | −0.05 | −0.02 | −0.00 |
| Labor demand[c] | −0.06 | 0.00 | 0.01 | 0.00 | −0.01 |

## Table B-11 *(continued)*

| Model region and variable | Year | | | | |
|---|---|---|---|---|---|
| | *1* | *2* | *3* | *4* | *5* |
| *REMS* | | | | | |
| GDP[a] | −0.07 | 0.01 | 0.01 | −0.00 | −0.01 |
| Private consumption[a] | 0.02 | 0.02 | 0.01 | 0.00 | −0.00 |
| Private investment[a] | −0.00 | 0.01 | 0.01 | 0.00 | −0.00 |
| Government consumption[a] | 0.00 | 0.00 | 0.00 | 0.00 | 0.00 |
| Exports[a] | −0.01 | 0.01 | 0.01 | 0.01 | −0.00 |
| Imports[a] | 0.08 | 0.03 | 0.02 | 0.01 | 0.01 |
| Trade balance[a] | −0.02 | 0.01 | 0.02 | 0.01 | 0.01 |
| Budget deficit[a] | 0.02 | −0.00 | −0.00 | −0.00 | 0.00 |
| Inflation[b] | −0.14 | 0.01 | 0.04 | 0.04 | 0.03 |
| Nominal short-term interest rate[b] | −0.09 | −0.09 | −0.07 | −0.05 | −0.03 |
| Nominal long-term interest rate[b] | −0.03 | −0.02 | −0.01 | −0.01 | 0.00 |
| Real short-term interest rate[b] | −0.04 | −0.11 | −0.10 | −0.07 | −0.05 |
| Real long-term interest rate[b] | −0.04 | −0.04 | −0.03 | −0.01 | −0.01 |
| Money[c] | −0.03 | −0.02 | −0.01 | −0.00 | 0.00 |
| Exchange rate (US$/ems)[c] | −0.12 | −0.07 | −0.04 | −0.02 | −0.00 |
| Real exchange rate (US$/ems)[c] | −0.13 | −0.12 | −0.07 | −0.02 | 0.01 |
| Labor demand[c] | −0.09 | 0.03 | 0.02 | −0.00 | −0.02 |
| *ROECD* | | | | | |
| GDP[a] | 0.48 | 0.25 | 0.14 | 0.08 | 0.05 |
| Private consumption[a] | 0.11 | 0.07 | 0.04 | 0.03 | 0.01 |
| Private investment[a] | 0.15 | 0.08 | 0.04 | 0.02 | 0.01 |
| Government consumption[a] | 0.00 | 0.00 | 0.00 | 0.00 | 0.00 |
| Exports[a] | 0.16 | 0.09 | 0.05 | 0.03 | 0.02 |
| Imports[a] | −0.06 | −0.02 | −0.01 | −0.01 | −0.00 |
| Trade balance[a] | 0.14 | 0.04 | 0.01 | −0.00 | −0.01 |
| Budget deficit[a] | −0.14 | −0.07 | −0.04 | −0.02 | −0.01 |
| Inflation[b] | 0.50 | 0.23 | 0.12 | 0.07 | 0.04 |
| Nominal short-term interest rate[b] | −0.37 | −0.19 | −0.10 | −0.06 | −0.03 |
| Nominal long-term interest rate[b] | −0.07 | −0.04 | −0.02 | −0.00 | −0.00 |
| Real short-term interest rate[b] | −0.69 | −0.34 | −0.19 | −0.10 | −0.06 |
| Real long-term interest rate[b] | −0.14 | −0.07 | −0.04 | −0.02 | −0.01 |
| Exchange rate (US$/roe)[c] | −1.52 | −1.19 | −1.06 | −1.00 | −0.97 |
| Real exchange rate (US$/roe)[c] | −1.16 | −0.51 | −0.21 | −0.08 | −0.02 |
| Labor demand[c] | 0.78 | 0.38 | 0.19 | 0.09 | 0.04 |
| *LDCs* | | | | | |
| Trade balance[d] | −0.03 | −0.02 | −0.02 | −0.01 | −0.01 |
| Terms of trade[c] | −0.23 | −0.11 | −0.05 | −0.02 | −0.00 |
| *OPEC* | | | | | |
| Trade balance[d] | 0.00 | 0.01 | 0.01 | 0.00 | 0.00 |
| Terms of trade[c] | −0.21 | −0.09 | −0.03 | −0.00 | 0.01 |

Source: See table B-1.
a. As percent of real GDP.
b. Absolute deviation.
c. Percentage deviation.
d. As percent of U.S. GDP.

Table B-12. *Sustained 1 Percent Increase in U.S. Money Growth*
Deviation from baseline

| Model region and variable | Year | | | | |
|---|---|---|---|---|---|
| | 1 | 2 | 3 | 4 | 5 |
| *United States* | | | | | |
| GDP[a] | 0.75 | 0.80 | 0.73 | 0.62 | 0.49 |
| Private consumption[a] | 0.36 | 0.39 | 0.36 | 0.31 | 0.26 |
| Private investment[a] | 0.26 | 0.27 | 0.25 | 0.21 | 0.16 |
| Government consumption[a] | 0.00 | 0.00 | 0.00 | 0.00 | 0.00 |
| Exports[a] | 0.12 | 0.12 | 0.11 | 0.09 | 0.08 |
| Imports[a] | −0.01 | −0.02 | −0.01 | −0.00 | 0.00 |
| Trade balance[a] | 0.08 | 0.07 | 0.06 | 0.05 | 0.04 |
| Budget deficit[a] | −0.23 | −0.24 | −0.22 | −0.19 | −0.15 |
| Inflation[b] | 0.64 | 0.91 | 1.06 | 1.14 | 1.17 |
| Nominal short-term interest rate[b] | 0.53 | 0.44 | 0.45 | 0.52 | 0.62 |
| Nominal long-term interest rate[b] | 0.68 | 0.73 | 0.79 | 0.85 | 0.90 |
| Real short-term interest rate[b] | −0.37 | −0.64 | −0.70 | −0.66 | −0.56 |
| Real long-term interest rate[b] | −0.42 | −0.38 | −0.32 | −0.25 | −0.18 |
| Labor demand[c] | 1.32 | 1.32 | 1.15 | 0.93 | 0.69 |
| *Japan* | | | | | |
| GDP[a] | −0.07 | −0.01 | −0.01 | −0.00 | 0.00 |
| Private consumption[a] | 0.03 | 0.04 | 0.03 | 0.03 | 0.03 |
| Private investment[a] | 0.03 | 0.05 | 0.05 | 0.04 | 0.03 |
| Government consumption[a] | 0.00 | 0.00 | 0.00 | 0.00 | 0.00 |
| Exports[a] | −0.06 | −0.03 | −0.02 | −0.01 | −0.00 |
| Imports[a] | 0.07 | 0.07 | 0.06 | 0.06 | 0.05 |
| Trade balance[a] | −0.14 | −0.09 | −0.07 | −0.05 | −0.03 |
| Budget deficit[a] | 0.01 | −0.01 | −0.01 | −0.01 | −0.01 |
| Inflation[b] | −0.11 | −0.17 | −0.01 | 0.03 | 0.05 |
| Nominal short-term interest rate[b] | −0.16 | −0.36 | −0.37 | −0.32 | −0.25 |
| Nominal long-term interest rate[b] | −0.18 | −0.16 | −0.12 | −0.08 | −0.04 |
| Real short-term interest rate[b] | 0.02 | −0.35 | −0.40 | −0.37 | −0.30 |
| Real long-term interest rate[b] | −0.19 | −0.19 | −0.15 | −0.10 | −0.06 |
| Exchange rate (US$/¥)[c] | 3.09 | 3.78 | 4.58 | 5.40 | 6.24 |
| Real exchange rate (US$/¥)[c] | 2.45 | 2.06 | 1.77 | 1.47 | 1.18 |
| Labor demand[c] | −0.09 | 0.00 | 0.00 | 0.00 | 0.00 |
| *Germany* | | | | | |
| GDP[a] | −0.07 | −0.07 | −0.02 | 0.02 | 0.05 |
| Private consumption[a] | −0.01 | −0.02 | −0.01 | 0.00 | 0.01 |
| Private investment[a] | 0.03 | 0.04 | 0.04 | 0.04 | 0.04 |
| Government consumption[a] | 0.00 | 0.00 | 0.00 | 0.00 | 0.00 |
| Exports[a] | −0.05 | −0.03 | −0.00 | 0.02 | 0.04 |
| Imports[a] | 0.05 | 0.05 | 0.05 | 0.05 | 0.04 |
| Real trade balance[a] | −0.12 | −0.09 | −0.05 | −0.03 | −0.01 |
| Budget deficit[a] | 0.01 | 0.01 | −0.00 | −0.01 | −0.02 |
| Inflation[b] | −0.09 | −0.10 | −0.06 | −0.01 | 0.02 |
| Nominal short-term interest rate[b] | −0.19 | −0.35 | −0.38 | −0.35 | −0.29 |
| Nominal long-term interest rate[b] | −0.20 | −0.18 | −0.14 | −0.10 | −0.06 |
| Real short-term interest rate[b] | −0.09 | −0.28 | −0.36 | −0.36 | −0.32 |
| Real long-term interest rate[b] | −0.21 | −0.20 | −0.17 | −0.13 | −0.09 |
| Exchange rate (US$/DM)[c] | 2.84 | 3.57 | 4.35 | 5.18 | 6.05 |
| Real exchange rate (US$/DM)[c] | 2.20 | 1.92 | 1.57 | 1.23 | 0.93 |
| Labor demand[c] | −0.11 | −0.11 | −0.04 | 0.03 | 0.06 |

## Table B-12  *(continued)*

| Model region and variable | Year 1 | 2 | 3 | 4 | 5 |
|---|---|---|---|---|---|
| **REMS** | | | | | |
| GDP[a] | −0.12 | −0.11 | −0.06 | −0.01 | 0.02 |
| Private consumption[a] | −0.03 | −0.06 | −0.05 | −0.04 | −0.03 |
| Private investment[a] | 0.03 | 0.03 | 0.04 | 0.04 | 0.04 |
| Government consumption[a] | 0.00 | 0.00 | 0.00 | 0.00 | 0.00 |
| Exports[a] | −0.04 | −0.02 | 0.01 | 0.04 | 0.05 |
| Imports[a] | 0.08 | 0.07 | 0.06 | 0.05 | 0.03 |
| Trade balance[a] | −0.12 | −0.08 | −0.04 | −0.01 | 0.01 |
| Budget deficit[a] | 0.02 | 0.02 | 0.01 | −0.01 | −0.01 |
| Inflation[b] | −0.10 | −0.11 | −0.07 | −0.01 | 0.02 |
| Nominal short-term interest rate[b] | −0.19 | −0.35 | −0.38 | −0.35 | −0.29 |
| Nominal long-term interest rate[b] | −0.20 | −0.18 | −0.14 | −0.10 | −0.06 |
| Real short-term interest rate[b] | −0.08 | −0.27 | −0.36 | −0.37 | −0.33 |
| Real long-term interest rate[b] | −0.21 | −0.20 | −0.17 | −0.13 | −0.09 |
| Money[c] | −0.02 | −0.04 | −0.05 | −0.05 | −0.05 |
| Exchange rate (US$/ems)[c] | 2.84 | 3.57 | 4.35 | 5.18 | 6.05 |
| Real exchange rate (US$/ems)[c] | 2.19 | 1.90 | 1.54 | 1.20 | 0.90 |
| Labor demand[c] | −0.14 | −0.13 | −0.06 | 0.00 | 0.04 |
| **ROECD** | | | | | |
| GDP[a] | −0.06 | −0.04 | 0.01 | 0.05 | 0.06 |
| Private consumption[a] | 0.05 | 0.04 | 0.05 | 0.05 | 0.04 |
| Private investment[a] | 0.03 | 0.04 | 0.05 | 0.05 | 0.04 |
| Government consumption[a] | 0.00 | 0.00 | 0.00 | 0.00 | 0.00 |
| Exports[a] | −0.05 | −0.03 | −0.01 | 0.02 | 0.03 |
| Imports[a] | 0.09 | 0.09 | 0.08 | 0.07 | 0.05 |
| Trade balance[a] | −0.15 | −0.11 | −0.08 | −0.05 | −0.04 |
| Budget deficit[a] | 0.01 | 0.01 | −0.01 | −0.02 | −0.02 |
| Inflation[b] | −0.13 | −0.11 | −0.06 | −0.00 | 0.04 |
| Nominal short-term interest rate[b] | −0.17 | −0.34 | −0.39 | −0.36 | −0.30 |
| Nominal long-term interest rate[b] | −0.21 | −0.19 | −0.15 | −0.10 | −0.06 |
| Real short-term interest rate[b] | −0.05 | −0.27 | −0.37 | −0.38 | −0.35 |
| Real long-term interest rate[b] | −0.22 | −0.21 | −0.18 | −0.14 | −0.19 |
| Exchange rate (US$/roe)[c] | 2.84 | 3.55 | 4.32 | 5.16 | 6.04 |
| Real exchange rate (US$/roe)[c] | 2.19 | 1.88 | 1.51 | 1.18 | 0.91 |
| Labor demand[c] | −0.10 | −0.06 | 0.01 | 0.06 | 0.07 |
| **LDCs** | | | | | |
| Trade balance[d] | −0.03 | −0.08 | −0.10 | −0.10 | −0.09 |
| Terms of trade[c] | 1.64 | 1.40 | 1.17 | 0.95 | 0.76 |
| **OPEC** | | | | | |
| Trade balance[d] | 0.08 | 0.10 | 0.08 | 0.06 | 0.04 |
| Terms of trade[c] | 1.84 | 1.66 | 1.42 | 1.17 | 0.93 |

Source: See table B-1.
a. As percent of real GDP.
b. Absolute deviation.
c. Percentage deviation.
d. As percent of U.S. GDP.

Table B-13. *Sustained 1 Percent Increase in Japanese Money Growth*
Deviation from baseline

| Model region and variable | Year | | | | |
|---|---|---|---|---|---|
| | 1 | 2 | 3 | 4 | 5 |
| *United States* | | | | | |
| GDP[a] | −0.01 | 0.02 | 0.01 | −0.00 | −0.00 |
| Private consumption[a] | 0.01 | 0.01 | −0.00 | −0.00 | −0.01 |
| Private investment[a] | 0.00 | 0.01 | 0.00 | −0.00 | −0.00 |
| Government consumption[a] | 0.00 | 0.00 | 0.00 | 0.00 | 0.00 |
| Exports[a] | 0.00 | −0.00 | −0.00 | −0.00 | −0.00 |
| Imports[a] | 0.03 | −0.01 | −0.01 | −0.01 | −0.01 |
| Trade balance[a] | −0.01 | −0.01 | −0.01 | −0.01 | −0.01 |
| Budget deficit[a] | −0.00 | −0.00 | −0.00 | 0.00 | 0.00 |
| Inflation[b] | −0.05 | 0.03 | 0.02 | 0.01 | 0.00 |
| Nominal short-term interest rate[b] | −0.06 | −0.02 | −0.01 | −0.00 | 0.00 |
| Nominal long-term interest rate[b] | −0.01 | −0.00 | −0.00 | −0.00 | −0.00 |
| Real short-term interest rate[b] | −0.06 | −0.04 | −0.02 | −0.01 | 0.00 |
| Real long-term interest rate[b] | −0.01 | −0.00 | −0.00 | −0.00 | −0.00 |
| Labor demand[c] | −0.03 | 0.01 | −0.01 | −0.02 | −0.02 |
| *Japan* | | | | | |
| GDP[a] | 0.71 | 0.01 | 0.01 | 0.01 | 0.01 |
| Private consumption[a] | 0.22 | −0.00 | −0.00 | −0.01 | −0.01 |
| Private investment[a] | 0.23 | 0.01 | 0.01 | 0.01 | 0.01 |
| Government consumption[a] | 0.00 | 0.00 | 0.00 | 0.00 | 0.00 |
| Exports[a] | 0.19 | 0.00 | 0.00 | 0.00 | 0.00 |
| Imports[a] | −0.07 | −0.00 | −0.00 | −0.00 | −0.00 |
| Trade balance[a] | 0.24 | 0.05 | 0.05 | 0.05 | 0.04 |
| Budget deficit[a] | −0.21 | −0.00 | −0.00 | −0.00 | −0.00 |
| Inflation[b] | 0.56 | 2.01 | 1.00 | 1.00 | 1.00 |
| Nominal short-term interest rate[b] | 0.26 | 0.96 | 0.96 | 0.96 | 0.96 |
| Nominal long-term interest rate[b] | 0.90 | 0.97 | 0.97 | 0.97 | 0.97 |
| Real short-term interest rate[b] | −1.81 | −0.04 | −0.04 | −0.04 | −0.04 |
| Real long-term interest rate[b] | −0.21 | −0.03 | −0.03 | −0.03 | −0.03 |
| Exchange rate (US$/¥)[c] | −2.74 | −3.06 | −4.05 | −5.01 | −5.98 |
| Real exchange rate (US$/¥)[c] | −2.21 | −0.46 | −0.47 | −0.45 | −0.41 |
| Labor demand[c] | 1.16 | 0.00 | 0.00 | 0.00 | 0.00 |
| *Germany* | | | | | |
| GDP[a] | 0.00 | 0.01 | 0.01 | 0.00 | −0.00 |
| Private consumption[a] | 0.02 | 0.00 | 0.00 | −0.00 | −0.00 |
| Private investment[a] | 0.01 | 0.01 | 0.00 | 0.00 | 0.00 |
| Government consumption[a] | 0.00 | 0.00 | 0.00 | 0.00 | 0.00 |
| Exports[a] | 0.01 | 0.01 | 0.00 | 0.00 | −0.00 |
| Imports[a] | 0.03 | 0.00 | 0.00 | −0.00 | −0.00 |
| Real trade balance[a] | 0.01 | 0.00 | −0.00 | −0.00 | −0.00 |
| Budget deficit[a] | −0.00 | −0.00 | −0.00 | −0.00 | 0.00 |
| Inflation[b] | −0.05 | 0.02 | 0.02 | 0.01 | 0.01 |
| Nominal short-term interest rate[b] | −0.02 | −0.03 | −0.02 | −0.01 | −0.00 |
| Nominal long-term interest rate[b] | −0.01 | −0.01 | −0.00 | −0.00 | −0.00 |
| Real short-term interest rate[b] | −0.01 | −0.05 | −0.03 | −0.01 | −0.01 |
| Real long-term interest rate[b] | −0.01 | −0.01 | −0.01 | −0.01 | −0.01 |
| Exchange rate (US$/DM)[c] | −0.00 | −0.04 | −0.03 | −0.03 | −0.02 |
| Real exchange rate (US$/DM)[c] | 0.01 | −0.04 | −0.04 | −0.03 | −0.03 |
| Labor demand[c] | −0.01 | 0.01 | 0.00 | −0.01 | −0.01 |

## Table B-13 *(continued)*

| Model region and variable | Year | | | | |
|---|---|---|---|---|---|
| | 1 | 2 | 3 | 4 | 5 |
| *REMS* | | | | | |
| GDP[a] | 0.01 | 0.01 | 0.01 | 0.00 | 0.00 |
| Private consumption[a] | 0.01 | 0.00 | −0.00 | −0.00 | −0.00 |
| Private investment[a] | 0.01 | 0.01 | 0.00 | 0.00 | 0.00 |
| Government consumption[a] | 0.00 | 0.00 | 0.00 | 0.00 | 0.00 |
| Exports[a] | 0.01 | 0.01 | 0.00 | 0.00 | −0.00 |
| Imports[a] | 0.02 | 0.00 | −0.00 | −0.00 | −0.00 |
| Trade balance[a] | 0.01 | 0.00 | 0.00 | −0.00 | −0.00 |
| Budget deficit[a] | −0.00 | −0.00 | −0.00 | −0.00 | 0.00 |
| Inflation[b] | −0.05 | 0.02 | 0.01 | 0.01 | 0.01 |
| Nominal short-term interest rate[b] | −0.02 | −0.03 | −0.02 | −0.01 | −0.00 |
| Nominal long-term interest rate[b] | −0.01 | −0.01 | −0.00 | −0.00 | −0.00 |
| Real short-term interest rate[b] | −0.02 | −0.05 | −0.03 | −0.01 | −0.01 |
| Real long-term interest rate[b] | −0.01 | −0.01 | −0.00 | −0.00 | −0.00 |
| Money[c] | −0.00 | −0.00 | −0.00 | 0.00 | 0.00 |
| Exchange rate (US$/ems)[c] | −0.00 | −0.04 | −0.03 | −0.03 | −0.02 |
| Real exchange rate (US$/ems)[c] | 0.00 | −0.04 | −0.04 | −0.04 | −0.03 |
| Labor demand[c] | −0.01 | 0.01 | 0.00 | −0.01 | −0.01 |
| *ROECD* | | | | | |
| GDP[a] | −0.00 | 0.01 | 0.00 | −0.00 | −0.00 |
| Private consumption[a] | 0.01 | 0.00 | 0.00 | −0.00 | −0.00 |
| Private investment[a] | 0.01 | 0.01 | 0.00 | 0.00 | −0.00 |
| Government consumption[a] | 0.00 | 0.00 | 0.00 | 0.00 | 0.00 |
| Exports[a] | 0.01 | 0.00 | 0.00 | −0.00 | −0.00 |
| Imports[a] | 0.03 | 0.00 | 0.00 | 0.00 | −0.00 |
| Trade balance[a] | −0.00 | −0.00 | −0.01 | −0.01 | −0.01 |
| Budget deficit[a] | −0.00 | −0.00 | −0.00 | 0.00 | 0.00 |
| Inflation[b] | −0.05 | 0.02 | 0.02 | 0.01 | 0.01 |
| Nominal short-term interest rate[b] | −0.05 | −0.03 | −0.02 | −0.01 | −0.00 |
| Nominal long-term interest rate[b] | −0.01 | −0.01 | −0.00 | −0.00 | −0.00 |
| Real short-term interest rate[b] | −0.05 | −0.05 | −0.03 | −0.01 | −0.00 |
| Real long-term interest rate[b] | −0.01 | −0.00 | −0.00 | −0.00 | −0.00 |
| Exchange rate (US$/roe)[c] | −0.03 | −0.04 | −0.03 | −0.02 | −0.02 |
| Real exchange rate (US$/roe)[c] | −0.02 | −0.04 | −0.03 | −0.03 | −0.02 |
| Labor demand[c] | −0.03 | 0.01 | −0.01 | −0.01 | −0.01 |
| *LDCs* | | | | | |
| Trade balance[d] | −0.06 | −0.01 | −0.01 | −0.00 | −0.00 |
| Terms of trade[c] | −0.39 | −0.11 | −0.11 | −0.10 | −0.10 |
| *OPEC* | | | | | |
| Trade balance[d] | 0.00 | 0.00 | 0.00 | −0.00 | −0.00 |
| Terms of trade[c] | −0.33 | −0.11 | −0.11 | −0.11 | −0.10 |

Source: See table B-1.
a. As percent of real GDP.
b. Absolute deviation.
c. Percentage deviation.
d. As percent of U.S. GDP.

Table B-14. *OPEC Oil Price Rise of 100 Percent*
Deviation from baseline

| Model region and variable | Year | | | | |
|---|---|---|---|---|---|
| | *1* | *2* | *3* | *4* | *5* |
| *United States* | | | | | |
| GDP[a] | −2.68 | −3.87 | −4.61 | −5.02 | −5.19 |
| Private consumption[a] | −1.48 | −2.15 | −2.57 | −2.83 | −2.96 |
| Private investment[a] | −1.12 | −1.57 | −1.85 | −2.00 | −2.07 |
| Government consumption[a] | 0.00 | 0.00 | 0.00 | 0.00 | 0.00 |
| Exports[a] | −0.27 | −0.42 | −0.51 | −0.56 | −0.58 |
| Imports[a] | −0.19 | −0.26 | −0.32 | −0.38 | −0.42 |
| Trade balance[a] | 0.01 | −0.00 | −0.01 | −0.02 | −0.02 |
| Budget deficit[a] | 0.85 | 1.22 | 1.45 | 1.59 | 1.65 |
| Inflation[b] | 2.87 | 2.03 | 1.34 | 0.80 | 0.42 |
| Nominal short-term interest rate[b] | 0.35 | 1.81 | 2.80 | 3.42 | 3.77 |
| Nominal long-term interest rate[b] | 3.16 | 3.50 | 3.69 | 3.78 | 3.80 |
| Real short-term interest rate[b] | −1.71 | 0.46 | 2.01 | 3.02 | 3.64 |
| Real long-term interest rate[b] | 2.73 | 3.30 | 3.64 | 3.81 | 3.88 |
| Labor demand[c] | 0.21 | −1.48 | −2.41 | −2.79 | −2.81 |
| *Japan* | | | | | |
| GDP[a] | −1.91 | −2.17 | −2.26 | −2.36 | −2.47 |
| Private consumption[a] | −1.37 | −1.53 | −1.60 | −1.66 | −1.70 |
| Private investment[a] | −1.01 | −1.22 | −1.33 | −1.40 | −1.45 |
| Government consumption[a] | 0.00 | 0.00 | 0.00 | 0.00 | 0.00 |
| Exports[a] | 0.08 | 0.04 | 0.03 | −0.01 | −0.04 |
| Imports[a] | −0.39 | −0.53 | −0.63 | −0.70 | −0.73 |
| Trade balance[a] | 0.38 | 0.32 | 0.28 | 0.24 | 0.19 |
| Budget deficit[a] | 0.67 | 0.77 | 0.82 | 0.87 | 0.90 |
| Inflation[b] | 2.53 | 1.26 | 0.71 | 0.48 | 0.31 |
| Nominal short-term interest rate[b] | 0.51 | 1.93 | 2.77 | 3.29 | 3.58 |
| Nominal long-term interest rate[b] | 3.05 | 3.37 | 3.53 | 3.61 | 3.64 |
| Real short-term interest rate[b] | −0.68 | 1.27 | 2.32 | 3.00 | 3.40 |
| Real long-term interest rate[b] | 2.74 | 3.18 | 3.41 | 3.53 | 3.58 |
| Exchange rate (US$/¥)[c] | −3.32 | −3.48 | −3.59 | −3.56 | −3.43 |
| Real exchange rate (US$/¥)[c] | −3.84 | −4.88 | −5.68 | −5.99 | −5.96 |
| Labor demand[c] | 0.31 | −0.00 | −0.00 | −0.00 | −0.00 |
| *Germany* | | | | | |
| GDP[a] | −1.53 | −2.05 | −2.61 | −3.13 | −3.58 |
| Private consumption[a] | −1.36 | −1.52 | −1.69 | −1.85 | −1.99 |
| Private investment[a] | −0.79 | −1.08 | −1.33 | −1.51 | −1.66 |
| Government consumption[a] | 0.00 | 0.00 | 0.00 | 0.00 | 0.00 |
| Exports[a] | −0.33 | −0.62 | −0.92 | −1.19 | −1.41 |
| Imports[a] | −0.95 | −1.18 | −1.32 | −1.42 | −1.47 |
| Real trade balance[a] | 0.34 | 0.17 | 0.00 | −0.14 | −0.26 |
| Budget deficit[a] | 0.54 | 0.72 | 0.90 | 1.06 | 1.21 |
| Inflation[b] | 1.80 | 1.58 | 1.24 | 0.91 | 0.65 |
| Nominal short-term interest rate[b] | −0.33 | 1.26 | 2.36 | 3.06 | 3.47 |
| Nominal long-term interest rate[b] | 2.83 | 3.24 | 3.48 | 3.60 | 3.65 |
| Real short-term interest rate[b] | −1.84 | 0.02 | 1.42 | 2.37 | 2.97 |
| Real long-term interest rate[b] | 2.23 | 2.78 | 3.14 | 3.35 | 3.46 |
| Exchange rate (US$/DM)[c] | −0.78 | −0.10 | 0.45 | 0.89 | 1.25 |
| Real exchange rate (US$/DM)[c] | −2.19 | −2.06 | −1.62 | −1.03 | −0.38 |
| Labor demand[c] | −0.20 | −0.97 | −1.73 | −2.38 | −2.91 |

## Table B-14 *(continued)*

| Model region and variable | Year 1 | 2 | 3 | 4 | 5 |
|---|---|---|---|---|---|
| *REMS* | | | | | |
| GDP[a] | −2.10 | −2.94 | −3.63 | −4.22 | −4.71 |
| Private consumption[a] | −1.67 | −1.84 | −1.99 | −2.14 | −2.28 |
| Private investment[a] | −0.89 | −1.26 | −1.53 | −1.73 | −1.87 |
| Government consumption[a] | 0.00 | 0.00 | 0.00 | 0.00 | 0.00 |
| Exports[a] | −0.55 | −0.97 | −1.31 | −1.59 | −1.81 |
| Imports[a] | −1.01 | −1.13 | −1.20 | −1.24 | −1.26 |
| Trade balance[a] | 0.25 | −0.04 | −0.26 | −0.42 | −0.54 |
| Budget deficit[a] | 0.69 | 0.95 | 1.16 | 1.33 | 1.48 |
| Inflation[b] | 2.52 | 1.91 | 1.37 | 0.95 | 0.64 |
| Nominal short-term interest rate[b] | −0.33 | 1.26 | 2.36 | 3.06 | 3.47 |
| Nominal long-term interest rate[b] | 2.83 | 3.24 | 3.48 | 3.60 | 3.65 |
| Real short-term interest rate[b] | −2.29 | −0.18 | 1.33 | 2.34 | 2.98 |
| Real long-term interest rate[b] | 2.18 | 2.77 | 3.15 | 3.38 | 3.50 |
| Money[c] | 0.26 | 0.46 | 0.57 | 0.61 | 0.62 |
| Exchange rate (US$/ems)[c] | −0.78 | −0.10 | 0.45 | 0.89 | 1.25 |
| Real exchange rate (US$/ems)[c] | −1.43 | −0.86 | −0.22 | 0.46 | 1.14 |
| Labor demand[c] | 0.06 | −1.12 | −2.03 | −2.73 | −3.27 |
| *ROECD* | | | | | |
| GDP[a] | −2.97 | −3.74 | −4.24 | −4.55 | −4.71 |
| Private consumption[a] | −1.52 | −1.83 | −2.03 | −2.15 | −2.23 |
| Private investment[a] | −1.11 | −1.46 | −1.68 | −1.82 | −1.90 |
| Government consumption[a] | 0.00 | 0.00 | 0.00 | 0.00 | 0.00 |
| Exports[a] | −0.85 | −1.15 | −1.36 | −1.51 | −1.61 |
| Imports[a] | −0.51 | −0.69 | −0.83 | −0.94 | −1.02 |
| Trade balance[a] | 0.03 | 0.05 | 0.03 | 0.01 | −0.03 |
| Budget deficit[a] | 0.91 | 1.15 | 1.30 | 1.40 | 1.46 |
| Inflation[b] | 2.31 | 1.67 | 1.15 | 0.75 | 0.45 |
| Nominal short-term interest rate[b] | −0.30 | 1.31 | 2.42 | 3.13 | 3.54 |
| Nominal long-term interest rate[b] | 2.89 | 3.29 | 3.53 | 3.65 | 3.70 |
| Real short-term interest rate[b] | −2.03 | 0.14 | 1.68 | 2.70 | 3.33 |
| Real long-term interest rate[b] | 2.48 | 3.07 | 3.43 | 3.63 | 3.73 |
| Exchange rate (US$/roe)[c] | 1.06 | 1.71 | 2.21 | 2.60 | 2.89 |
| Real exchange rate (US$/roe)[c] | 0.86 | 1.18 | 1.50 | 1.84 | 2.16 |
| Labor demand[c] | −0.18 | −1.24 | −1.85 | −2.13 | −2.19 |
| *LDCs* | | | | | |
| Trade balance[d] | −0.37 | 0.07 | 0.38 | 0.58 | 0.70 |
| Terms of trade[c] | 2.36 | 2.24 | 2.23 | 2.34 | 2.54 |
| *OPEC* | | | | | |
| Trade balance[d] | 0.08 | −0.15 | −0.30 | −0.37 | −0.39 |
| Terms of trade[c] | 65.58 | 64.83 | 64.40 | 64.26 | 64.33 |

Source: See table B-1.
a. As percent of real GDP.
b. Absolute deviation.
c. Percentage deviation.
d. As percent of U.S. GDP.

Table B-15. *Cessation of Loans to LDCs in the Amount
of 1 Percent of U.S. GNP*
Deviation from baseline

| Model region and variable | Year | | | | |
|---|---|---|---|---|---|
| | 1 | 2 | 3 | 4 | 5 |
| *United States* | | | | | |
| GDP[a] | −0.09 | 0.03 | 0.15 | 0.24 | 0.31 |
| Private consumption[a] | 0.11 | 0.19 | 0.26 | 0.31 | 0.34 |
| Private investment[a] | 0.18 | 0.24 | 0.29 | 0.33 | 0.36 |
| Government consumption[a] | 0.00 | 0.00 | 0.00 | 0.00 | 0.00 |
| Exports[a] | −0.28 | −0.25 | −0.23 | −0.22 | −0.20 |
| Imports[a] | 0.09 | 0.14 | 0.16 | 0.18 | 0.19 |
| Trade balance[a] | −0.32 | −0.29 | −0.28 | −0.27 | −0.26 |
| Budget deficit[a] | 0.02 | −0.03 | −0.06 | −0.09 | −0.12 |
| Inflation[b] | −0.30 | −0.29 | −0.24 | −0.20 | −0.15 |
| Nominal short-term interest rate[b] | −0.51 | −0.72 | −0.92 | −1.08 | −1.20 |
| Nominal long-term interest rate[b] | −1.12 | −1.20 | −1.27 | −1.31 | −1.33 |
| Real short-term interest rate[b] | −0.25 | −0.48 | −0.72 | −0.93 | −1.10 |
| Real long-term interest rate[b] | −1.02 | −1.13 | −1.22 | −1.28 | −1.32 |
| Labor demand[c] | −0.31 | −0.09 | 0.08 | 0.19 | 0.27 |
| *Japan* | | | | | |
| GDP[a] | −0.18 | 0.07 | 0.09 | 0.11 | 0.13 |
| Private consumption[a] | −0.01 | 0.08 | 0.08 | 0.08 | 0.07 |
| Private investment[a] | 0.15 | 0.24 | 0.27 | 0.28 | 0.30 |
| Government consumption[a] | 0.00 | 0.00 | 0.00 | 0.00 | 0.00 |
| Exports[a] | −0.35 | −0.27 | −0.26 | −0.24 | −0.23 |
| Imports[a] | −0.02 | −0.02 | −0.00 | 0.01 | 0.02 |
| Trade balance[a] | −0.32 | −0.28 | −0.28 | −0.27 | −0.26 |
| Budget deficit[a] | 0.06 | −0.01 | −0.02 | −0.03 | −0.04 |
| Inflation[b] | −0.16 | −0.37 | −0.11 | −0.11 | −0.09 |
| Nominal short-term interest rate[b] | −0.63 | −0.85 | −0.98 | −1.11 | −1.22 |
| Nominal long-term interest rate[b] | −1.15 | −1.22 | −1.27 | −1.31 | −1.33 |
| Real short-term interest rate[b] | −0.24 | −0.75 | −0.87 | −1.02 | −1.15 |
| Real long-term interest rate[b] | −1.06 | −1.17 | −1.23 | −1.28 | −1.31 |
| Exchange rate (US$/¥)[c] | −1.31 | −1.20 | −1.07 | −1.01 | −0.98 |
| Real exchange rate (US$/¥)[c] | −1.24 | −1.24 | −0.98 | −0.83 | −0.75 |
| Labor demand[c] | −0.38 | 0.00 | 0.00 | 0.00 | 0.00 |
| *Germany* | | | | | |
| GDP[a] | −0.25 | −0.16 | −0.12 | −0.08 | −0.03 |
| Private consumption[a] | −0.12 | −0.09 | −0.10 | −0.11 | −0.11 |
| Private investment[a] | 0.13 | 0.17 | 0.20 | 0.22 | 0.25 |
| Government consumption[a] | 0.00 | 0.00 | 0.00 | 0.00 | 0.00 |
| Exports[a] | −0.32 | −0.27 | −0.24 | −0.21 | −0.16 |
| Imports[a] | −0.06 | −0.03 | −0.02 | −0.01 | −0.00 |
| Real trade balance[a] | −0.28 | −0.28 | −0.28 | −0.26 | −0.23 |
| Budget deficit[a] | 0.10 | 0.07 | 0.05 | 0.04 | 0.02 |
| Inflation[b] | −0.09 | −0.11 | −0.13 | −0.13 | −0.13 |
| Nominal short-term interest rate[b] | −0.75 | −0.76 | −0.90 | −1.05 | −1.17 |
| Nominal long-term interest rate[b] | −1.13 | −1.20 | −1.26 | −1.30 | −1.33 |
| Real short-term interest rate[b] | −0.65 | −0.64 | −0.77 | −0.92 | −1.06 |
| Real long-term interest rate[b] | −1.04 | −1.11 | −1.18 | −1.24 | −1.28 |
| Exchange rate (US$/DM)[c] | −2.13 | −1.90 | −1.86 | −1.88 | −1.91 |
| Real exchange rate (US$/DM)[c] | −2.03 | −1.63 | −1.48 | −1.43 | −1.44 |
| Labor demand[c] | −0.45 | −0.33 | −0.30 | −0.26 | −0.21 |

## Table B-15 *(continued)*

| Model region and variable | Year 1 | 2 | 3 | 4 | 5 |
|---|---|---|---|---|---|
| **REMS** | | | | | |
| GDP[a] | −0.13 | −0.08 | −0.06 | −0.02 | 0.04 |
| Private consumption[a] | −0.07 | −0.05 | −0.06 | −0.06 | −0.06 |
| Private investment[a] | 0.16 | 0.18 | 0.21 | 0.23 | 0.26 |
| Government consumption[a] | 0.00 | 0.00 | 0.00 | 0.00 | 0.00 |
| Exports[a] | −0.30 | −0.26 | −0.23 | −0.21 | −0.17 |
| Imports[a] | −0.08 | −0.05 | −0.03 | −0.02 | −0.01 |
| Trade balance[a] | −0.26 | −0.26 | −0.26 | −0.24 | −0.22 |
| Budget deficit[a] | 0.07 | 0.05 | 0.04 | 0.02 | 0.01 |
| Inflation[b] | −0.04 | −0.10 | −0.13 | −0.14 | −0.13 |
| Nominal short-term interest rate[b] | −0.75 | −0.76 | −0.90 | −1.05 | −1.17 |
| Nominal long-term interest rate[b] | −1.13 | −1.20 | −1.26 | −1.30 | −1.33 |
| Real short-term interest rate[b] | −0.67 | −0.63 | −0.76 | −0.92 | −1.06 |
| Real long-term interest rate[b] | −1.05 | −1.12 | −1.19 | −1.25 | −1.29 |
| Money[c] | 0.13 | 0.12 | 0.10 | 0.10 | 0.09 |
| Exchange rate (US$/ems)[c] | −2.13 | −1.90 | −1.86 | −1.88 | −1.91 |
| Real exchange rate (US$/ems)[c] | −1.99 | −1.57 | −1.42 | −1.38 | −1.40 |
| Labor demand[c] | −0.32 | −0.27 | −0.25 | −0.21 | −0.15 |
| **ROECD** | | | | | |
| GDP[a] | −0.22 | −0.09 | −0.01 | 0.06 | 0.12 |
| Private consumption[a] | −0.04 | 0.01 | 0.03 | 0.04 | 0.05 |
| Private investment[a] | 0.14 | 0.19 | 0.23 | 0.26 | 0.29 |
| Government consumption[a] | 0.00 | 0.00 | 0.00 | 0.00 | 0.00 |
| Exports[a] | −0.29 | −0.23 | −0.20 | −0.17 | −0.13 |
| Imports[a] | 0.03 | 0.06 | 0.07 | 0.08 | 0.08 |
| Trade balance[a] | −0.30 | −0.30 | −0.31 | −0.30 | −0.29 |
| Budget deficit[a] | 0.07 | 0.03 | 0.01 | −0.01 | −0.03 |
| Inflation[b] | −0.15 | −0.15 | −0.16 | −0.15 | −0.13 |
| Nominal short-term interest rate[b] | −0.67 | −0.73 | −0.88 | −1.03 | −1.16 |
| Nominal long-term interest rate[b] | −1.11 | −1.19 | −1.25 | −1.30 | −1.33 |
| Real short-term interest rate[b] | −0.51 | −0.56 | −0.72 | −0.89 | −1.05 |
| Real long-term interest rate[b] | −1.02 | −1.11 | −1.19 | −1.25 | −1.30 |
| Exchange rate (US$/roe)[c] | −1.71 | −1.55 | −1.55 | −1.59 | −1.64 |
| Real exchange rate (US$/roe)[c] | −1.63 | −1.38 | −1.30 | −1.31 | −1.35 |
| Labor demand[c] | −0.40 | −0.22 | −0.12 | −0.04 | 0.03 |
| **LDCs** | | | | | |
| Trade balance[d] | 0.91 | 0.82 | 0.74 | 0.65 | 0.58 |
| Terms of trade[c] | −1.36 | −1.15 | −1.07 | −1.05 | −1.06 |
| **OPEC** | | | | | |
| Trade balance[d] | −0.09 | −0.05 | 0.01 | 0.07 | 0.10 |
| Terms of trade[c] | −2.52 | −2.17 | −1.94 | −1.79 | −1.68 |

Source: See table B-1.
a. As percent of real GDP.
b. Absolute deviation.
c. Percentage deviation.
d. As percent of U.S. GDP.

# Numerical Solution of Models with and without Strategic Behavior

THE ASSUMPTION of rational expectations, first implemented by John Muth (1961), has important implications for the solution of macro-economic models. In models with rational agents,[1] current variables depend on the path of future variables.[2] In this appendix, our method for solving these models is developed. The first part of the appendix gives an intuitive explanation of other techniques that are available for solving large rational expectations models. The second part develops our technique, which also allows for strategic policymakers.

## Solution of Rational Expectations Models

A model written in minimal state-space representation is in the form

$$Z_{t+1} = a_1 Z_t + a_2 E_t,$$

where $Z$ is an $m \times 1$ vector of evolving variables, and $E$ is an $s \times 1$ vector of exogenous variables.

We can partition the $Z$ vector so that the first $n$ variables are state or predetermined variables in period $t$, and the remaining $m - n$ variables are "jumping variables" (that is, variables that change instantaneously in response to revisions in expectations about future variables):

$$X_{t+1} = \alpha_1 X_t + \alpha_2 e_t + \alpha_3 E_t$$
$$_t e_{t+1} = \beta_1 X_t + \beta_2 e_t + \beta_3 E_t,$$

---

1. That is, agents who use all information available in deciding their actions and do not make any systematic errors.

2. See Begg (1982), Sheffrin (1983), and Taylor (1985) for surveys of the use and relevance of the rational expectations assumptions.

where $X$ is a vector of state variables whose value is inherited from the past evolution of the system; $e$ is a vector of jumping variables, determined within the current period by the structure of the model and by information about current and all future variables.

This model could easily be solved given $X_0$, $e_0$, and a path for $E$. Unfortunately, we only have initial values for the set of state variables $X_0$. To solve the model in period 0, and for every period until $T$, requires knowledge of $e_0$, which in turn requires knowledge of the solution in period 1 and so forth. To solve the model requires use of restrictions provided by initial values of state variables and some terminal conditions on jumping variables. The terminal values can be given as a fixed value in some finite terminal period or, in an infinite-horizon problem, by a tranversality condition that imposes that in the infinite limit a variable is bounded. Once we have imposed a terminal solution, we have a "two-point boundary-value problem." Two points on the equilibrium path of the economy are known, and these are both needed to define the path between them.

Analytical solutions to models containing rational expectations can be found in simple cases by using techniques that solve these types of two-point boundary-value problems. Numerical solutions to more complex systems have been slower to emerge, although there are now several techniques in common use. For a linear system, an analytical solution is provided by Blanchard and Kahn (1980). In the case of nonlinear systems, the technique of multiple shooting has been applied to the economics literature by Lipton and others (1982). The multiple-shooting technique can be described intuitively as follows. In "shooting," initial values are assumed for the jumping variables $e_0$. The model is then solved forward until the terminal period (or some finite period that is considered a good approximation to the infinite horizon) is reached. The terminal conditions on the jumping variables $e_T$ are then compared with the solution values for the jumping variables $e_T$. If these are not equal, the initial guesses are optimally updated. In the case of multiple shooting, the solution interval is divided into subintervals. With the aid of auxiliary variables, the model is then solved, shooting within each subinterval until convergence of the model solution to the terminal conditions is reached.

A problem with this algorithm is that each subinterval increases the dimensionality of the system to be solved. The algorithm can also very quickly become computationally expensive to solve.

Fair and Taylor (1983) have also produced a technique that has become popular because it tends to find a solution to models at a much lower cost than that for the multiple-shooting algorithm. In the Fair-Taylor technique, an arbitrary terminal period is chosen. The paths of expected variables $\{e_1, \ldots, e_T\}$ are guessed, and the model is solved by assuming these expectations. The solution path for the expected variables is then compared with the guess, and the guess is updated. This iterative procedure is repeated until the expected path equals the actual path. The terminal period is then extended, and the procedure repeated until the terminal period choice has no effect on the solution path.

## An Alternative Numerical Technique

In the remainder of this appendix, an alternative technique is developed. It is based on the solution to dynamic games developed in Oudiz and Sachs (1985). Put simply, the idea is to search numerically for a coefficient matrix linking the vector of jumping variables at a point in time to the vector of state variables, such that the model remains on the stable manifold. Once we find a stable coefficient matrix, then, given $X_0$, we can determine $e_0$. Therefore, we have converted the model into a standard-difference-equation model that can easily be solved. This is discussed more rigorously below.

Consider a general system of equations summarized by

(C-1) $\qquad X_{t+1} = \phi_1 (X_t, e_t, U_t, E_t, Z_t, X_{t+1}, {}_t e_{t+1})$

(C-2) $\qquad Z_t = \phi_2 (X_t, e_t, U_t, E_t, Z_t, X_{t+1}, {}_t e_{t+1})$

(C-3) $\qquad {}_t e_{t+1} = \phi_3 (X_t, e_t, U_t, E_t, Z_t, X_{t+1}, {}_t e_{t+1})$

(C-4) $\qquad \tau_t = \phi_4 (X_t, e_t, U_t, E_t, Z_t, X_{t+1}, {}_t e_{t+1}),$

where

$\qquad X_t =$ a vector of state variables given at time $t$

$\qquad e_t =$ a vector of jumping variables (such as forward-looking asset prices)

$\qquad {}_t e_{t+1} =$ the expected value of $e_{t+1}$ conditional on information in period $t$

$U_t$ = a vector of control variables (such as monetary and fiscal policies)

$\tau_t$ = a vector of target variables

$E_t$ = a vector of exogenous variables

$Z_t$ = a vector of endogenous variables that enter contemporaneously.

The initial step of the solution technique is to linearize this system around some point, usually either the steady state or a point on the transition path, using a first-order Taylor approximation. Finding numerical derivatives and solving for the endogenous variables $Z$ as a function of the other variables in the system, the model can be rewritten as

(C-5) $$\overline{X}_{t+1} = \alpha_1\overline{X}_t + \alpha_2\overline{e}_t + \alpha_3\overline{U}_t + \alpha_4\overline{E}_t$$

(C-6) $$_t\overline{e}_{t+1} = \beta_1\overline{X}_t + \beta_2\overline{e}_t + \beta_3\overline{U}_t + \beta_4\overline{E}_t$$

(C-7) $$\overline{\tau}_t = \gamma_1\overline{X}_t + \gamma_2\overline{e}_t + \gamma_3\overline{U}_t + \gamma_4\overline{E}_t,$$

where each of the coefficient matrices ($\alpha_1$, $\beta_2$, $\gamma_3$, and so on) are numerical derivatives evaluated at the point of linearization,[3] and a bar over a variable indicates the deviation of a variable from the point of linearization. To avoid excessive notation, the bars over variables will be dropped in what follows, with the understanding that all future references will be to variables as deviations from some level.

The final assumption added to the system above is that agents take into account all available information in forming expectations about future variables. Agents have rational or model-consistent expectations; therefore their expectations of future variables are taken to be correct on average. The assumption is that

(C-8) $$_t e_{t+1} = E\{e_{t+1} \mid \Omega_t\} = e_{t+1} - \zeta_{t+1}$$

where $\zeta$ is a white noise disturbance, and, as earlier, a subscript $t$ before a variable indicates the expectation of that variable made in period $t$ on the basis of the information available in that period.

The solution of this simultaneous system is complicated because the solution for current variables depends on the infinite future. The al-

---

3. For example, $\alpha_1 = dX_{t+1} / dX_t$ evaluated at $X_0$.

gorithm developed here can solve this problem as well as a more complex problem involving optimizing policymakers. The more general problem involving policy optimization will be developed first, and the solution for the standard problem will then be seen as a particular case.

Now introduce optimizing policymakers. For country $i$, the problem is to choose a vector of control variables $U_{it}$ to minimize

(C-9) $$W_{it} = \sum_{s=t}^{\infty} (1 + \delta)^{t-s} \{\tau_{is}' \Omega_i \tau_{is}\},$$

subject to

(C-10) $$X_{t+1} = \alpha_1 X_t + \alpha_2 e_t + \alpha_3 U_t + \alpha_4 E_t$$

(C-11) $$e_{t+1} = \beta_1 X_t + \beta_2 e_t + \beta_3 U_t + \beta_4 E_t$$

(C-12) $$\tau_{it} = \gamma_{1i} X_t + \gamma_{2i} e_t + \gamma_{3i} U_t + \gamma_{4i} E_t,$$

where matrices related to control variables are stacked in the following way:

$$\alpha_3 = [\alpha_{31'} \ \alpha_{32'} \ . \ . \ . \ , \alpha_{3j}] \qquad \text{for } j \text{ countries}$$

$$U_t = \begin{bmatrix} U_{1t} \\ U_{2t} \\ \vdots \\ U_{jt} \end{bmatrix}.$$

When the optimization is undertaken by more than one country, each policymaker is assumed to undertake the optimization taking as given the policies of other governments. This is the Nash-Cournot equilibrium of the dynamic game that is the equilibrium used here to represent noncooperative behavior between governments. An alternative is to assume that a central planner undertakes the optimization of some weighted combination of the two countries' welfare functions. This alternative can then be considered the case of cooperation. Other assumptions are possible, such as one country or group of countries acting as Stackelberg leaders in formulating policy. These other equilibrium concepts are not explored further here.

Within the class of equilibria considered here, there are various possible solutions that depend on the constraints placed on policymakers by such issues as time consistency and credibility. Kydland and Prescott (1977) point out that, in a model with forward-looking agents, the government finding an optimal control solution to a problem in period $t$ will usually find it optimal in period $t + 1$ to deviate from the preannounced path. The optimal control solution does not satisfy Bellman's criterion for optimality.[4] Once private agents have made decisions on the basis of the announced policy, the problem changes. In a repeated game, the preannounced rule is no longer credible unless the present government can make some form of binding commitment to follow the chosen path of time.

In addition to the issue of the time consistency of policies, there is the issue of the form of the rule being followed. The government can choose the entire path of policy settings (open-loop policy), or it can choose a rule for the control variables that depends on the realizations of future state and exogenous variables (closed-loop policy). Here we focus on time-consistent, closed-loop policies.

Our solution uses a technique of dynamic programming based on Oudiz and Sachs (1985). The technique proposed here is to first solve a finite-period optimization problem in which the terminal period is arbitrarily chosen to be some period $T$. The problem is solved in period $T$, giving a solution for the jumping and control variables in period $T$. The problem is then solved in period $T - 1$, taking as given the policy rules being followed in the next period and the state variables inherited. The forward-looking variables are then conditioned on the known future rules. The rules that are found for the finite-period problem will be time dimensioned. The second step of the procedure is to find the limit of the finite-period problem as $T$ approaches infinity. The limit is found by repeating the backward recursion procedure until rules are found, for the control variables and the jumping variables, that do not change as the terminal period is arbitrarily extended. The case in which policymakers are not optimizing is found by setting the rules that link the control variables to the state and exogenous variables to zero during the backward recursion. The rule for the jumping variables is therefore the unique stable manifold of the system. The uniqueness derives from the linearity of the system. This is formally derived as follows.

Define the value function for any country $i$ as

4. See footnote 7 of chapter 7.

$$V_{it} = \min_{U_{it}} \tau'_{it}\Omega_i\tau_{it} + (1+\delta)^{-1}V_{it+1}(X_{t+1'}\, C_{3t+1}),$$

subject to equations C-10 through C-12, where $C_{3t+1}$ is a constant containing the accumulated values of future exogenous variables. In solving this problem we are trying to find matrices $\Gamma_1$ and $\Gamma_2$, of a linear policy rule

$$U_t = \Gamma_1 X_t + \Gamma_2 E_t + C_{4t},$$

and matrices $S_1, S_2, S_3, S_4$ and $S_5$, such that

$$V(X_t, C_{3t}) = S_{1i} X_t + S_{2i}E_t + X'_t S_{3i}X_t + 2X'_t S_{4i}E_t + E'_t S_{5i}E_t,$$

where

$$V_{it} = \min_{U_{it}} \tau'_{it}\Omega_i\tau_{it} + (1+\delta)^{-1}V_{it+1}(X_{t+1'}\, C_{3t+1}),$$

subject to equations C-10 through C-12. We also need to find matrices $H_1$ and $H_2$ that ensure that the jumping variables adjust to keep the model on the stable manifold, where

$$e_t = H_1 X_t + H_2 E_t + C_{5t}.$$

The iterative technique that solves this problem begins by converting the infinite-period problem into a finite-period problem in which the terminal period is some arbitrary period $T$. Assume that in period $T + 1$ the jumping variables have stabilized and $V_{T+1}(X_{T+1}, C_{3T+1}) = 0$. Thus,

(C-13) $$_Te_{T+1} = e_T.$$

Substituting equation C-13 into equation C-11 gives

(C-14) $$e_T = \theta_1 X_T + \theta_{2i}U_{iT} + \theta_3 E_T.$$

The target variables can now be written as a function of state, control, and exogenous variables by substituting equation C-14 into equation C-12 to find

(C-15) $$\tau_{iT} = \mu_{1i}X_T + \mu_{2i}U_{iT} + \mu_{3i}E_T.$$

This equation can be substituted into the loss function C-9 for period $T$, and the problem can be written as

$$\min_{U_{iT}} (\mu_{1i}X_T + \mu_{2i}U_{iT} + \mu_{3i}E_T)\,'\Omega_i(\mu_{1i}X_T + \mu_{2i}U_{iT} + \mu_{3i}E_T).$$

Solving this single-period problem, we find that the first-order condition for country 1 is

$$\mu_{21}'\Omega_1\mu_{1i}X_T + \mu_{21}'\Omega_1\mu_{2i}U_{1T} + \mu_{21}'\Omega_1\mu_{3i}E_T + C_1 = 0.$$

This equation can be stacked for each country and rewritten as

$$MM_T U_T = -NN_T X_T - PP_T E_T + C_{1T},$$

or

(C-16) $$U_T = \Gamma_{1T} X_T + \Gamma_{2T} E_T + C_{4T}.$$

Equation C-16 gives a rule for the control variables as a function of the state and exogenous variables in period $T$, conditional on the known future. This can be substituted into equation C-14 to give a rule for the jumping variables, conditional on the known government policy rule:

(C-17) $$e_T = H_{1T}X_T + H_{2T}E_T + C_{5T},$$

where

$$H_{1T} = \theta_1 + \theta_2\Gamma_{1T}, \qquad H_{2T} = \theta_3 + \theta_2\Gamma_{2T},$$

and $\theta_2$ a stacked matrix $[\theta_{2i} \mid \theta_{2j}]$ for each country $i, j$.

The rules for control variables and jumping variables given in equations C-16 and C-17 can be substituted into equation C-12 for the target variables. This can then be substituted into the welfare function to find the value function in period $T$ as a function of the state and exogenous variables in $T$ as well as the constants:

(C-18) $$V_{iT} = f(X_T, E_T, C_{2T}).$$

Given the value function in each period and accumulating all future exogenous variables and constants into a constant $C_3$, we can solve the problem in any period $t$ in which the policymaker is to select the vector of control variables, $U_{it}$, to minimize

(C-19) $$\{\tau_{it}'\Omega_i\tau_{it}\} + (1+\delta)^{-1} V_{it+1}\{X_{t+1'} C_{3t+1}\},$$

subject to equations C-10 through C-12.

To solve this problem, note that we have $V_{it+1}$ as a function of $X_{t+1}$. Using the equation of motion of the state variables given in equation C-10, we can therefore write $V_{it+1}$ as a function of variables in period $t$.

Consider the specific steps in solving this problem. We have, from the solution of the problem in period $t + 1$,

(C-20) $$e_{t+1} = H_{1t+1}X_{t+1} + C_{3t+1},$$

where

$$C_{3t+1} = C_{5t+1} + H_{2t+1}E_{t+1}.$$

We can substitute the equation for the jumping variables $e_{t+1}$ from equation C-11 and the equation of motion for the state variables $X_{t+1}$ given in equation C-10 into equation C-20. Simplifying gives

(C-21) $$e_t = \theta_1 X_t + \theta_{2i} U_{it} + \theta_3 E_t + \theta_{4t}.$$

Equation C-21 can again be substituted into equation C-12 for the target variables given to find

(C-22) $$\tau_{it} = \mu_{1i} X_t + \mu_{2i} U_{it} + \mu_{3i} E_t + \mu_{4it}.$$

The optimization problem can now be written with the current target variables as a function of the state, control, and exogenous variables; similarly, the value function $V_{t+1}$ can be written as a function of the current state, control, and future exogenous variables:

$$\min_{U_{it}} \tau_{it}' \Omega_i \tau_{it} + (1+\delta)^{-1} V_{it+1}(X_{t+1}, C_{3t+1}),$$

subject to

$$\tau_{it} = \mu_{1i} X_t + \mu_{2i} U_{it} + \mu_{3i} E_t + \mu_{4it}$$

and

$$X_{t+1} = \alpha_1 X_t + \alpha_2(\theta_1 X_t + \theta_{2i} U_{it} + \theta_3 E_t + \theta_{4t}) + \alpha_{3i} U_{it} + \alpha_4 E_t.$$

The rewritten problem can now be solved in period $t$ to find

(C-23) $$U_t = \Gamma_{1t} X_t + \Gamma_{2t} E_t + C_{4t}$$

and

(C-24)             $e_t = H_{1t} X_t + H_{2t} E_t + C_{5t}.$

The method described above solves the finite-period problem in which period $T$ is an arbitrary terminal period. Note that the rule matrices are time subscripted because, in general, the rule in any period will be influenced by the terminal period. To find the solution to the infinite-period problem, we search for the limit to the backward-recursion procedure where the rule matrices become independent of period $T$. The backward-recursion procedure is repeated until the rule matrices converge to a stable value. The convergence is governed by the same conditions required to solve any set of differential equations. A necessary condition is that the number of eigenvalues outside the unit circle must be equal to the number of jumping variables.

Once we have found the feedback rules for the control variables and the jumping variables, in any period we can then find the solution to the model by knowing the state variables that have been inherited and the values of the constants that are derived by using rules to accumulate all future exogenous variables, as well as future constant policy responses. In this procedure, it is a simple matter to set the policy rules to equal zero at each step of the iteration. The rules for jumping variables summarized in the $H$ matrices ensure that the solution is on the unique stable manifold of the model, given the cumulated future values of the constants derived from the future path of all exogenous variables.

The procedure developed in this appendix is substantially faster than the other algorithms discussed earlier, and it has the added advantage of allowing various simulation exercises to be performed without requiring the recalculation of the rule matrices. Once these rule matrices have been calculated, they can be used to simulate any shocks to exogenous variables or initial conditions.

# Data Sources and Assumptions

SOURCES FOR, and assumptions about, the data for industrial, non-oil developing (LDC), and oil-exporting developing (OPEC) countries are given in this appendix.

## Industrial Countries

National accounts data and data for inflation, interest rates, and exchange rates for each industrial country or region used in calibrating the model are the 1986 values from the Organization for Economic Cooperation and Development's *Economic Outlook* (December 1989). Sources of other data used in the text are so indicated.

Bilateral trade data are based on the 1986 values of trade in the International Monetary Fund's *Direction of Trade Statistics* (annual; 1989). To capture the fact that trade in services is included in the national accounts data for each country, the bilateral trade data are scaled up by the ratio of exports of goods to exports of goods and services found in the national accounts data for each country.

Government debt values for 1986 are based on calculations of the ratio of net stock of government debt to GDP held by domestic residents, as found in Chouraqui, Jones, and Montador (1986). For bilateral asset holding between industrial countries, we assume that all bilateral debt is denominated in U.S. dollars and that net bilateral holdings of each country are only with the United States, LDCs, and OPEC. To calculate the net holding of assets with the United States, we use the data for the net international investment position of the United States less net direct investment, as provided in Scholl (1988, especially table 1).

## Developing Countries

Bilateral trade flows are also based on the IMF's *Direction of Trade Statistics* (annual; 1989). For debt to LDCs we have used data from the World Bank on debt by currency of denomination for 1983. We assume that these data represent holdings by residents of the country of denomination. We apply these proportions of total debt to apportion the data for total net debt in 1986 that are given in the 1988 edition of the IMF's *World Economic Outlook* (annual; table A46).

## OPEC Asset Holdings

To calculate the allocation of OPEC asset holdings, we use the data in Mattione (1985, Tables 2-5, 2-9) and data from the Japanese Ministry of Finance (detailed in Ishii, McKibbin, and Sachs 1985). We also assume that U.S. dollar claims in Europe are essentially Eurodollar deposits that are claims against U.S. residents. The data in Mattione (1985) are only for 1983. To construct data for 1986, we first cumulate the OPEC assets for 1983 with OPEC current accounts for 1984, 1985, and 1986 (as given in the IMF's *World Economic Outlook*) to calculate a new total of assets for 1986. The 1983 proportions are then applied to the new 1986 total.

# References

Alesina, A. 1987. "Macroeconomic Policy in a Two-Party System as a Repeated Game." *Quarterly Journal of Economics* 102:651–78.

Alesina, A., and G. Tabellini. 1987. "Rules and Discretion with Noncoordinated Monetary and Fiscal Policies." *Economic Inquiry* 25:619–30.

Allen, P. R., and P. B. Kenen. 1980. *Asset Markets, Exchange Rates and Economic Integration.* Cambridge University Press.

Argy, V. 1988. "Monetary-Fiscal, Exchange Rate Policy Rules: A Survey." Working Paper 8854B. Macquarie University Centre for Studies in Money, Banking and Finance, Sydney, Australia.

Argy, V., W. McKibbin, and E. Siegloff. 1989. "Exchange Rate Regimes for a Small Economy in a Multi-country World." *Princeton Studies in International Finance* 67:December.

Argy, V., and J. Salop. 1979. "Price and Output Effects of Monetary and Fiscal Policy under Flexible Exchange Rates." *International Monetary Fund Staff Papers* 26:224–56.

Baldwin, R. E., and P. R. Krugman. 1987. "The Persistence of the U.S. Trade Deficit." *Brookings Papers on Economic Activity* 1:1–43.

Barro, R. J. 1974. "Are Government Bonds Net Wealth? *Journal of Political Economy* 827:1095–1117.

Barro, R. J., ed. 1989. *Modern Business Cycle Theory.* Harvard University Press.

Barro, R. J., and D. B. Gordon. 1983a. "Rules, Discretion and Reputation in a Model of Monetary Policy." *Journal of Monetary Economics* 12:101–21.

———.1983b. "A Positive Theory of Monetary Policy in a Natural Rate Model." *Journal of Political Economy* 91:589–610.

Begg, J. 1982. *The Rational Expectation Revolution in Macroeconomics: Theories and Evidence.* Johns Hopkins University Press.

Bernheim, B. D. 1987. "Ricardian Equivalence: An Evaluation of Theory and Evidence." *NBER Macroeconomics Annual* 2:263–304.

Blackburn, K. 1989. "Credibility and Reputation in International Macroeconomic Policy Games." In *The International Transmission Mechanism, Exchange Rates, and Policy Coordination,* edited by P. Artus, Y. Barroux, and G. McKenzie. London: Macmillan.

Blackburn, K., and M. Christensen. 1989. "Monetary Policy and Policy Credibility: Theories and Evidence." *Journal of Economic Literature* 27:1–45.

Blanchard, O. J. 1981. "Output, the Stock Market, and Interest Rates." *American Economic Review* 71:132–43.

———. 1985. "Debt, Deficits and Finite Horizons." *Journal of Political Economy* 93:223–47.

Blanchard, O. J., and C. M. Kahn. 1980. "The Solution of Linear Difference Models under Rational Expectations." *Econometrica* 48:1305–11.

Blanchard, O. J., and L. H. Summers. 1986. "Hysteresis and the European Unemployment Problem." *NBER Macroeconomics Annual* 1:15–78.

Boone, P., J. W. Lee, and J. Sachs. 1989. "Structural Adjustment and International Linkages in the Korean Economy." Harvard University.

Branson, W. H., A. A. Fraga, and R. A. Johnson. 1986. "Expected Fiscal Policy and the Recession of 1982." In *Prices, Competition and Equilibrium*, edited by M. H. Peston and R. E. Quandt, 109–28. London: Philip Allan.

Branson, W. H., and D. Henderson. 1985. "The Specification and Influence of Asset Markets." In Jones and Kenen (1985), 749–805.

Bruno, M., and J. D. Sachs. 1985. *Economics of Worldwide Stagflation*. Harvard University Press.

Bryant, R. C. 1980. *Money and Monetary Policy in Interdependent Nations*. Brookings Institution.

Bryant, R., J. F. Helliwell, and P. Hooper. 1989. "Domestic and Cross-Border Consequences of U.S. Macroeconomic Policies." In Bryant and others (1989), 59–115.

Bryant, R. C., and others, eds. 1988. *Empirical Macroeconomics for Interdependent Economies*. Brookings Institution.

Bryant, R. C., and others, eds. 1989. *Macroeconomic Policies in an Interdependent World*. Brookings Institution, Center for Economic Policy Research (London), International Monetary Fund.

Bryant, R. C., and R. Portes, eds. 1987. *Global Macroeconomics: Policy Conflict and Cooperation*. London: Macmillan.

Buffie, E. F. 1989. "Economic Policy and Foreign Debt in Mexico." In *Developing Country Debt and Economic Performance: Country Studies*, edited by J. D. Sachs. University of Chicago Press.

Buiter, W. H., and R. C. Marston. 1985. *International Economic Policy Coordination*. Cambridge University Press.

Burda, M. 1987. "Essays on the Rise of Unemployment in Europe." Ph.D. dissertation, Harvard University.

Campbell, J. Y., and N. G. Mankiw. 1987. "Permanent Income, Current Income and Consumption." National Bureau of Economic Research Working Paper 2436. Cambridge, Mass.

Canzoneri, M. B., and J. Gray. 1985. "Monetary Policy Games and the Consequences of Non-Cooperative Behavior." *International Economic Review* 26: 547–64.

Canzoneri, M. B., and D. W. Henderson. 1991. *A Game Theoretic Approach*. MIT Press.

Canzoneri, M. B., and P. Minford. 1986. "When International Policy Coordination Matters: An Empirical Analysis." Centre for Economic Policy Research Discussion Paper 119. London.

Carlozzi, N., and J. B. Taylor. 1985. "International Capital Mobility and the Coordination of Monetary Rules." In *Exchange Rate Management under Uncertainty*, edited by J. Bhandari, 186–211.

Carmichael, J. 1982. "On Barro's Theorem of Debt Neutrality: The Irrelevance of Net Wealth." *American Economic Review* 72:202–13.

Chouraqui, J.-C., B. Jones, and R. B. Monrador. 1986. "Public Debt in a Medium-Term Context and Its Implications for Fiscal Policy." OECD Department of Economics and Statistics Working Paper 30, Paris, May.

Congressional Budget Office. 1990. *The Economic and Budget Outlook: Fiscal Years 1991–1999*. Government Printing Office, January.

Cooper, R. N. 1968. *The Economics of Interdependence*. McGraw-Hill.

———. 1969. "Macroeconomic Policy Adjustment in Interdependent Economies." *Quarterly Journal of Economics* 83:1–24.

———. 1985. "Economic Interdependence and Coordination of Economic Policies." In Jones and Kenen (1985), 1195–1233.

Corden, W. M. 1960. "The Geometric Representation of Policies to Attain Internal and External Balance." *Review of Economic Studies* 28:1–22.

———. 1981. *Inflation, Exchange Rates and the World Economy: Lectures on International Monetary Economics*. University of Chicago Press.

———. 1985. "On Transmission and Coordination under Flexible Exchange Rates." In Buiter and Marston (1985), 8–36.

Currie, D. A., and P. Levine. 1985. "Macroeconomic Policy Design in an Interdependent World." In Buiter and Marston (1985), 228–73.

Currie, D. A., P. Levine, and N. Vidalis. 1987. "International Cooperation and Reputation in an Empirical Two-Bloc Model." In Bryant and Portes (1987), 75–121.

Currie, D. A., and S. Wren-Lewis. 1988. "Evaluating the Extended Target Zone Proposal for the G3." Centre for Economic Policy Research Discussion Paper 221. London.

Deardorff, A. V., and R. M. Stern. 1986. *The Michigan Model of World Production and Trade: Theory and Applications*. MIT Press.

Dellas, H. 1986. "A Real Model of the World Business Cycle." *Journal of International Money and Finance* 5:381–94.

Dirk, M. 1988. *Government Debt in International Financial Markets*. London: Pinter.

Dixon, P. B. and others. 1982. *ORANI: A Multisectoral Model of the Australian Economy*. North-Holland.

Dornbusch, R. 1976. "Expectations and Exchange Rate Dynamics." *Journal of Political Economy* 84:1161–76.

———. 1987. "Exchange Rates and Prices." *American Economic Review* 77:93–106.

Dornbusch, R., and J. A. Frenkel, eds. 1979. *International Economic Policy: Theory and Evidence*. Johns Hopkins University Press.

*Economic Report of the President, 1990*.

Edison, H., M. Miller, and J. Williamson. 1987. "On Evaluating and Extending the Target Zone Proposal." *Journal of Policy Modeling*, Spring.

Eichengreen, B. 1985. "International Policy Coordination in Historical Perspective: A View From the Interwar Years." In Buiter and Marston (1985), 139–83.

Fair, R. C. 1979. "On Modeling the Economic Linkages among Countries." In Dornbusch and Frenkel (1979), 209–45.

Fair, R. C., and J. B. Taylor. 1983. "Solution and Maximum Likelihood Estimation of Dynamic Non-Linear Rational Expectations Models." *Econometrica* 51:1169–85.

Feldstein, M. 1987. "The Stock Market Decline and Economic Policy." Testimony to the House Banking Committee, October 29.

Fitoussi, J. P., and E. S. Phelps. 1986. "Causes of the 1980s Slump in Europe." *Brookings Papers on Economic Activity* 2:487–513.

Fleming, J. M. 1962. "Domestic Financial Policies under Fixed and Floating Exchange Rates." *International Monetary Fund Staff Papers* 9:369–80.

Frankel, J. A. 1986. "The Sources of Disagreement among International Macro Models and Implications for Policy Coordination." National Bureau of Economic Research Working Paper 1925. Cambridge, Mass.

———. 1989. "International Nominal Targetting (INT): A Proposal for Overcoming Obstacles to Policy Coordination." Paper prepared for a Conference on Global Disequilibrium, May.

Frankel, J. A., and K. E. Rockett. 1988. "International Macroeconomic Policy Coordination When Policymakers Do Not Agree on the True Model." *American Economic Review* 78:318–40.

Frenkel, J. A., M. Goldstein, and P. R. Masson. 1989. "Simulating the Effects of Some Simple Coordinated versus Uncoordinated Policy Rules." In Bryant and others (1989), 203–39.

Frenkel, J. A., and A. Razin. 1988. *Fiscal Policies and the World Economy*. MIT Press.

Friedman, M. 1959. *A Program for Monetary Stability*. Fordham University Press.

Genberg, H., and A. Swoboda. 1989. "Policy and Current Account Determination under Floating Exchange Rates." *IMF Staff Papers* 36:1–30.

Ghosh, A. 1986. "International Policy Coordination in an Uncertain World." *Economic Letters* 21:271–76.

Ghosh, S., and A. Ghosh. 1986. "International Policy Coordination When the Model Is Unknown." Geneva, Switzerland.

Ghosh, A. R., and P. R. Masson. 1988. "International Policy Coordination in a World with Model Uncertainty." *International Monetary Fund Staff Papers* 35:230–58.

Hamada, K. 1974. "Alternative Exchange Rate Systems and the Interdependence of Monetary Policies." In *National Monetary Policies and the International System*, edited by R. Z. Aliber, 13–33. University of Chicago Press.

———. 1976. "A Strategic Analysis of Monetary Interdependence." *Journal of Political Economy* 84:677–700.

———. 1979. "Macroeconomic Strategy and Coordination under Alternative Exchange Rates." In Dornbusch and Frenkel (1979), 292–324.

Hayashi, F. 1982a. "Tobin's Marginal q and Average q: A Neoclassical Interpretation." *Econometrica* 50:213–24.

———. 1982b. "The Permanent Income Hypothesis: Estimation and Testing by Instrumental Variables." *Journal of Political Economy* 90:895–916.

Helliwell, J., and R. McRae. 1977. "The Interdependence of Monetary, Debt and Fiscal Policies in an International Setting." In *The Political Economy of Monetary Reform*, edited by R. Z. Aliber. London: Macmillan.

Holtham, G., and A. Hughes Hallet. 1987. "International Policy Cooperation and Model Uncertainty." In Bryant and Portes (1987), 128–77.

Hooper, P., and C. L. Mann. 1989. "The U.S. External Deficit: Its Causes and Persistence." In *The U.S. External Deficit: Causes, Consequences and Cures*, Proceedings of the Twelfth Annual Economic Policy Conference, Federal Reserve Bank of St. Louis, 3–105. Boston: Kluwer Academic Publishing.

Hughes Hallet, A. 1987. "Optimal Policy Design in Interdependent Economies." In *Developments of Control Theory For Economic Analysis*, edited by C. Carraro and D. Saktore. Netherlands: Kluwer Academic Publishers.

International Monetary Fund. 1987. *World Economic Outlook*. Washington, April.

———. Annual. *Direction of Trade Statistics*. Washington.

Ishii, N., W. J. McKibbin, and J. Sachs. 1985. "The Economic Policy Mix, Policy Cooperation and Protectionism: Some Aspects of Macroeconomic Interdependence among the United States, Japan and Other OECD Countries." *Journal of Policy Modelling* 7:533–72.

Jones, R. W., and P. B. Kenen, eds. 1985. *Handbook of International Economics*. Amsterdam: North-Holland.

Kamien, M. I., and N. L. Schwartz. 1983. *Dynamic Optimization: The Calculus of Variations and Optimal Control in Economics and Management*. Amsterdam: North-Holland.

Krugman, P. R. 1986. "Pricing to Market When the Exchange Rate Changes." National Bureau of Economic Research Working Paper 1926. Cambridge, Mass.

———. 1988. "Target Zones and Exchange Rate Dynamics." National Bureau of Economic Research Working Paper 2481. Cambridge, Mass.

———. 1989. "Differences in Income Elasticities and Trends in Real Exchange Rates." *European Economic Review* 33.

Kydland, F. E., and E. C. Prescott. 1977. "Rules Rather Than Discretion: The Inconsistency of Optimal Plans." *Journal of Political Economy* 77:473–91.

Lipton, D., and others. 1982. "Multiple Shooting in Rational Expectations Models." *Econometrica* 50:1329–33.

Lipton, D., and J. D. Sachs. 1983. "Accumulation and Growth in a Two-Country Model: A Simulation Approach." *Journal of International Economics* 15:135–59.

Lucas, R. E., Jr. 1967. "Adjustment Costs and the Theory of Supply." *Journal of Political Economy* 75:321–34.

McKibbin, W. J. 1985. "Summary of Papers and Proceedings of the Brookings Workshop on Intergovernmental Consultations and Cooperation about Macroeconomic Policies." Brookings Discussion Papers in International Economics 36.

———. 1986. "The International Coordination of Macroeconomic Policies." Ph.D. dissertation, Harvard University.

———. 1989. "Time-Consistent Policy: A Survey of the Issues." *Australian Economic Papers*, Dec.:167–80.

————. 1990a. "Some Global Macroeconomic Implications of German Unification."
Brookings Discussion Paper in International Economics 81.

————. 1990b. "Stochastic Simulations of Alternative Monetary Regimes in the MSG2
Multi-Country Model." Background paper for the Brookings Conference on Empirical Evaluation of Alternative Policy Regimes. Washington, March 8–9.

————. 1990c. "On Fundamental Equilibrium Exchange Rates." Paper presented at
the Institute for International Economics Conference on Equilibrium Exchange
Rates: An Update. May.

McKibbin, W. J., N. Roubini, and J. D. Sachs. 1989. "Resolving Global Imbalances:
A Simulation Approach." In *Trade and Investment Relations among the United
States, Canada, and Japan*, edited by R. M. Stern. University of Chicago Press.

McKibbin, W. J., and J. D. Sachs. 1986a. "Coordination of Monetary and Fiscal
Policies in the OECD." National Bureau of Economic Research Working Paper
1800. Revised in *International Aspects of Fiscal Policy*, edited by J. A. Frenkel.
University of Chicago Press (1988).

————. 1986b. "Comparing the Global Performance of Alternative Exchange Arrangements." National Bureau of Economic Research Working Paper 2000.
Revised in *Journal of International Money and Finance* 7:387–410 (1988).

————. 1989. "Implications of Policy Rules for the World Economy." In Bryant
and others (1989), 151–94.

McKibbin, W. J., and M. Sundberg. 1990. "Macroeconomic Linkages between the
OECD and the Asian Pacific Region." Brookings Discussion Paper in International Economics 80.

McKinnon, R. I. 1984. *An International Standard for Monetary Stabilization*. Washington: Institute for International Economics.

————. 1988. "Monetary and Exchange Rate Policies for International Financial
Stability: A Proposal." *Journal of Economic Perspectives* 2:83–103.

Mann, C. 1987. "After the Fall: The Declining Dollar and Import Prices." Federal
Reserve Board.

Marris, S. 1985. *Deficits and the Dollar: The World Economy at Risk*. Policy Analyses
in International Economics 14. Washington: Institute for International Economics.

Marston, R. C. 1985. "Stabilization Policies in Open Economies." In Jones and
Kenen (1985).

Masson, P. R., and others. 1988. "*MULTIMOD*—Multi-region Econometric Model,"
pt. 2. *IMF Staff Studies for the World Economic Outlook*, July. Washington.

Mattione, R. P. 1985. *OPEC's Investments and the International Financial System*.
Brookings Institution.

Meade, J. E. 1951. *The Theory of International Economic Policy*, vol. 1: *The Balance
of Payments*. Oxford University Press.

Meese, R. A., and K. Rogoff. 1983. "Empirical Exchange Rate Models of the
Seventies: Do They Fit Out Of Sample?" *Journal of International Economics*
14:3–24.

Miller, M., and M. Salmon. 1985. "Policy Coordination and Dynamic Games." In
Buiter and Marston (1985), 184–227.

Minford, P., P. R. Agenor, and E. Nowell. 1986. "A New Classical Econometric
Model of the World Economy." *Economic Modeling* 3 (London): 154–74.

Minford, P., and M. B. Canzoneri. 1987. "Policy Interdependence: Does Strategic Behavior Pay? An Empirical Investigation Using the Liverpool World Model." Centre for Economic Policy Research Discussion Paper 201. London.

Mundell, R. A. 1963. "Capital Mobility and Stabilization Policy under Fixed and Flexible Exchange Rates." *Canadian Journal of Economic and Political Science* 29:475–85.

―――. 1968. *International Economics*. Macmillan.

Mussa, M. 1979. "Macroeconomic Interdependence and the Exchange Rate Regime." In Dornbusch and Frenkel (1979), 160–208.

Muth, J. 1961. "Rational Expectations and the Theory of Price Movements." *Econometrica* 29:315–35.

Niehans, J. 1968. "Monetary and Fiscal Policies in Open Economies under Fixed Exchange Rates: An Optimizing Approach." *Journal of Political Economy* 68: 893–920.

Obstfeld, M., and A. Stockman. 1985. "Exchange Rate Dynamics." In Jones and Kenen (1985).

Okun, A. 1965. "The Gap between Actual and Potential Output." In *The Battle against Unemployment*, edited by A. Okun, 13–22. Norton.

Organization for Economic Cooperation and Development (OECD). Annual. *Economic Outlook*. Paris.

Oswald, A. J. 1985. "The Economic Theory of Trade Unions: An Introductory Survey." *Scandinavian Journal of Economics* 87:160–97.

Oudiz, G., and J. D. Sachs. 1984. "Macroeconomic Policy Coordination among the Industrial Economies." *Brookings Papers on Economic Activity* 1:1–75.

―――. 1985. "International Policy Coordination in Dynamic Macroeconomic Models." In Buiter and Marston (1985), 274–330.

Persson, T. 1988. "Credibility of Macroeconomic Policy: An Introduction and Broad Survey." *European Economic Review* 32:519–32.

Persson, T., and L. E. O. Svensson. 1989. "Why a Stubborn Conservative Would Run a Deficit: Policy with Time-Inconsistent Preferences." *Quarterly Journal of Economics* 104:325–45.

Rogoff, K. S. 1983. "Productive and Counter-productive Cooperative Monetary Policies." International Finance Discussion Paper 233. Board of Governors of the Federal Reserve System.

Roubini, N. 1986a. "Strategic Interactions between Europe and the US: A Three-Country Model." Harvard University.

―――. 1986b. "International Policy Coordination and Model Uncertainty." Harvard University.

―――. 1989. "Leadership and Cooperation in the European Monetary System: A Simulation Approach." National Bureau of Economic Research Working Paper 3044. Cambridge, Mass.

Sachs, J. D. 1980. "Wages, Flexible Exchange Rates and Macroeconomic Policy." *Quarterly Journal of Economics* 94:731–47.

―――. 1982. "Energy and Growth under Flexible Exchange Rates: A Simulation Study." In *International Transmission of Economic Disturbances under Flexible Rates*, edited by J. Bhandari and B. Putnam. MIT Press.

————. 1985. "The Dollar and The Policy Mix: 1985." *Brookings Papers on Economic Activity* 1:117–85.

————. 1986. "High Unemployment in Europe: Diagnosis and Policy Implications." National Bureau of Economic Research Working Paper 1850. Cambridge, Mass.

————. 1988. "Global Adjustments to a Shrinking U.S. Trade Deficit." *Brookings Papers on Economic Activity* 2:639–74.

Sachs, J. D., and W. J. McKibbin. 1985. "Macroeconomic Policies in the OECD and LDC External Adjustment." National Bureau of Economic Research Working Paper 1534. Cambridge, Mass.

Sachs, J. D., and C. Wyplosz. 1984. "Real Exchange Rate Effects of Fiscal Policy." National Bureau of Economic Research Working Paper 1255. Cambridge, Mass.

Scholl, R. B. 1988. "The International Investment Position of the United States in 1987." *Survey of Current Business*, June: 76–84.

Sheffrin, S. 1983. *Rational Expectations*. Cambridge University Press.

Sundberg, M. 1990. "The International Transmission of Macroeconomic Policy Disturbances among Countries of the Pacific Basin." Ph.D. dissertation, Harvard University.

Taylor, J. B. 1980. "Aggregate Dynamics and Staggered Contracts." *Journal of Political Economy* 80:1–23.

————. 1985a. "International Coordination in the Design of Macroeconomic Policy Rules." *European Economic Review* 28:53–81.

————. 1985b. "What Would Nominal GNP Targeting Do to the Business Cycle." In *Understanding Business Cycles*, edited by Karl Brunner, 61–84. Carnegie-Rochester Conference Series on Public Policy. Amsterdam: North-Holland.

————. 1988a. "The Treatment of Expectations in Large Multicountry Econometric Models." In Bryant and others (1988), 161–82.

————. 1988b. "Should the International Monetary System Be Based on Fixed or Flexible Exchange Rates?" *International Monetary Policy Rules: An Econometric Evaluation* (forthcoming), chap. 7.

Tesar, L. 1990. "Non-traded Goods, Risk Sharing and Trade in Capital." University of Rochester.

Treadway, A. B. 1969. "On Rational Entrepreneurial Behavior and the Demand for Investment." *Review of Economic Studies* 36:227–39.

Turnovsky, S. 1982. *Macroeconomic Analysis and Stabilization Policy*. Cambridge University Press.

Van der Ploeg, R. 1987. "International Policy Coordination in Interdependent Economies." Centre for Economic Policy Research Discussion Paper 169. London.

Weale, M., and others. 1989. *Macroeconomic Policy: Inflation, Wealth and the Exchange Rate*. London: Unwin Hyman.

Whalley, J. 1985. *Trade Liberalization among the Major World Trading Areas*. MIT Press.

Williamson, J. 1985. *The Exchange Rate System*. Washington: Institute for International Economics.

Williamson, J., and M. H. Miller. 1987. *Targets and Indicators: A Blueprint for the International Co-ordination of Economic Policy*. Washington: Institute of International Economics.

# Index